APOSTLE ON THE EDGE

Also by Michael R. Cosby

Portraits of Jesus: An Inductive Approach to the Gospels

APOSTLE ON THE EDGE

An Inductive Approach to Paul

Michael R. Cosby

WESTMINSTER
JOHN KNOX PRESS
LOUISVILLE · KENTUCKY

First edition
Published by Westminster John Knox Press
Louisville, Kentucky

09 10 11 12 13 14 15 16 17 18—10 9 8 7 6 5 4 3 2 1

Scripture quotations, unless otherwise identified, are from the New Revised Standard Version of the Bible and copyright © 1989 by the Division of Christian Education of the National Council of the Churches of Christ in the U.S.A. and are used by permission.

Photographs by David Pettegrew are used with the permission of David Pettegrew. Photographs by Lynne Cosby are used with the permission of Lynne Cosby. Photographs taken by Michael Cosby are used with the permission of Michael Cosby. Photographs taken by Gordon Brubacher are used with the permission of Gordon Brubacher. Photographs taken by Rhonda Brubacher are used with the permission of Rhonda Brubacher. The photographs of Papyrus 46—Romans 11:3–12:8 and Romans 16:14–23—are copyright © the Regents of the University of Michigan and used with the permission of Traianos Gagos. Photographs from The Schøyen Collection are used with the permission of Martin Schøyen. The photograph of Codex Sinaiticus is used by permission of the British Library. The photograph of the altar relief depicting a sacrifice of a bull on page 49 and the photograph of the *Suovetaurila* on page 204 were taken by Barbara F. McManus and are used with the permission of Barbara F. McManus, courtesy of The VRoma Project, www.vroma.org. All maps were created by Alex Getty and are used by permission.

Book design by Sharon Adams
Cover design by designpointinc.com

Library of Congress Cataloging-in-Publication Data

Cosby, Michael R.
 Apostle on the edge : an inductive approach to Paul / Michael R. Cosby.
  p. cm.
 Includes indexes.
 ISBN 978-0-664-23308-2 (alk. paper)
 1. Bible. N.T. Epistles of Paul—Criticism, interpretation, etc.   I. Title.
 BS2650.52.C67   2009
 227'.06—dc22

2009006570

Contents

To the students of my "Apostle to the Gentiles: Paul in Acts and His Letters" classes
for their valuable feedback on earlier, photocopied versions of this book.
Most admitted at the end of the semester that they were very glad that they did all
of the work that this textbook requires.

Abbreviations

*	work especially recommended
AB	Anchor Bible
ANF	*Ante-Nicene Fathers*
Ant.	*Antiquities of the Jews,* by Josephus
AT	author's translation
BCE	before Common Era
c.	century
ca.	*circa,* around
CE	Common Era
cf.	*confer,* compare
DSS	Dead Sea Scrolls
e.g.	*exempli gratia* (Latin, "for example")
ET	English translation
ff.	following
ICC	International Critical Commentary
IDB	*Interpreter's Dictionary of the Bible*
i.e.	*id est* (Latin, "that is")
KJV	King James Version
LCL	Loeb Classical Library
LXX	Septuagint
NASB	New American Standard Bible
NEB	New English Bible
NIBCNT	New International Biblical Commentary on the New Testament
NICNT	New International Commentary on the New Testament
NIGTC	New International Greek Testament Commentary
NIV	New International Version
NRSV	New Revised Standard Version
NT	New Testament
OT	Old Testament
TAPA	*Transactions of the American Philological Association*
War	*Jewish War* (or *Wars of the Jews*), by Josephus

Translations of Ancient Works

Apuleius, Lucius. *The Golden Ass.* Translated by W. Adlington. LCL. Cambridge, MA: Harvard University Press, 1915.

Asclepius: Collection and Interpretation of the Testimonies. Edited by Emma J. and Ludwig Edelstein. Baltimore: Johns Hopkins University Press, 1945. English translation also in *Hellenistic Religions: The Age of Syncreticism,* edited by F. C. Grant (New York: Bobbs-Merrill, 1953).

Athenaeus. *The Deipnosophists.* Translated by Charles B. Gulick. LCL. 7 vols. Cambridge, MA: Harvard University Press, 1927–41.

Complete Dead Sea Scrolls in English, rev. ed. Translated by Geza Vermes. New York: Penguin Books, 2004.

Dead Sea Scrolls: A New Translation. Translation and commentary by Michael Wise, Martin Abegg Jr., and Edward Cook. New York: HarperCollins, 1996.

Eusebius. *The History of the Church from Christ to Constantine.* Translated by G. A. Williamson. Minneapolis: Augsburg, 1965.

Hellenistic Religions: The Age of Syncreticism. Edited by F. C. Grant. New York: Bobbs-Merrill, 1953.

Josephus. Translated by H. St. J. Thackeray et al. 10 vols. LCL. Cambridge, MA: Harvard University Press, 1926–65.

Josephus, Flavius. *The Works of Josephus.* Translated by Joseph Whiston. Updated version. Peabody, MA: Hendrickson Publishers, 1987.

Juvenal. *The Sixteen Satires.* Translated by Peter Green. Penguin Classics. New York: Penguin Books, 1967.

Lucian. Translated by A. M. Harmon. 8 vols. LCL. Cambridge, MA: Harvard University Press, 1913–67.

Mishnah. Translated by Herbert Danby. Oxford: Oxford University Press, 1933.

New Testament Apocrypha. Vol. 1, *Gospels and Related Writings.* Edited by E. Hennecke and W. Schneemelcher. Philadelphia: Westminster Press, 1963.

New Testament Apocrypha. Vol. 2, *Writings Relating to the Apostles; Apocalypses and Related Subjects.* Edited by E. Hennecke and W. Schneemelcher. Philadelphia: Westminster Press, 1965.

The Old Testament Pseudepigrapha. Vol. 1, *Apocalyptic Literature and Testaments.* Edited by James H. Charlesworth. Garden City, NY: Doubleday, 1983.

The Old Testament Pseudepigrapha. Vol. 2, *Expansions of the "Old Testament" and Legends, Wisdom and Philosophical Literature, Prayers, Psalms, and Odes, Fragments of Lost Judeo-Hellinistic Works.* Edited by James H. Charlesworth. Garden City, NY: Doubleday, 1985.

Pausanias. *Description of Greece.* Translated by W. H. S. Jones. 5 vols. LCL. Cambridge, MA: Harvard University Press, 1918–35.

Philo. Translation by F. H. Colson and G. H. Whitaker. 10 vols. Cambridge, MA: Harvard University Press, 1929–62.

Plato. *Collected Dialogues of Plato.* Edited by E. Hamilton and H. Cairns. Princeton, NJ: Princeton University Press, 1961.

Prudentius. Translated by H. J. Thomson. 2 vols. LCL. Cambridge, MA: Harvard University Press, 1949–53.

Strabo. *Geography of Strabo.* Translated by Horace L. Jones. LCL. 8 vols. Cambridge, MA: Harvard University Press, 1917–32.

Thucydides. *History of the Peloponnesian War.* Translated by Charles F. Smith. 4 vols. LCL. Cambridge, MA: Harvard University Press, 1919–23.

Acknowledgments

I thank Traianos Gagos for granting permission to use pictures of Papyrus 46 from the collection of papyri posted by the Advanced Papyrological Information System (APIS) at the University of Michigan (http://www.lib.umich.edu/papyrus-collection). Thanks also to Martin Schøyen for allowing me to use pictures from his extensive, private collection (http://www.schoyencollection.com).

Thanks to Reta Finger for using in her classes on Paul the photocopied chapters of this book in its earlier stages. I appreciate her insights. Thanks to Messiah College for a scholar chair that provided some class-release time for research and writing. Thanks to Jon Berquist, Daniel Braden, and the others at Westminster John Knox for their work on editing and producing *Apostle on the Edge*.

Thanks most of all to my wife, Lynne, for the many hours she spent editing book chapters and offering suggestions for improvement. I am blessed to have such a great partner and coworker.

Introduction

CROSSING THE CHASM OF CULTURE AND TIME

One of the most important things to realize about Paul's Epistles is that he did not write them to us. When we read Paul's Letters, we are reading someone else's mail. He wrote, or more correctly dictated, them for people who lived in ancient Mediterranean locations—people who understood his words in ways that we are incapable of doing today. For us, interpreting Paul's Letters can be almost as frustrating as it is intriguing.

Most of Paul's intended readers were in ongoing dialogue with him, and when he wrote to them, he addressed familiar circumstances. Because Paul's audiences shared experiences with him, they had the necessary context for interpreting his messages. And because they shared with Paul views of everyday life that often seem strange to us, his original readers understood his words as cultural insiders, whereas we are outsiders. We simply miss part of his meaning because we live in a different time, speak a different language, and have different cultural norms. We need ways to bridge the historical and cultural divide if we are to understand what he wrote.

However, most people do not have the time to study ancient Mediterranean cultures. The number of documents written by ancient authors is intimidating enough. When we add to this sizeable collection the other resources helpful for understanding Paul's world—archaeological discoveries such as inscriptions, papyrus scraps, tombstones, and the remains of ancient houses and temples and other public buildings—the task can seem overwhelming. Yet Paul's Epistles have such importance for Christian faith that those who are serious about understanding his words must make the attempt to cross the chasm of culture and time. This book provides the resources to begin to build a bridge from our time to his.

OUR SIDE OF THE CHASM: EVERYTHING ELECTRONIC

When I receive letters from friends, I usually open them with great anticipation. Unlike the junk mail that fills my post office box, personal letters create curiosity. I am interested in them because I know the ones who wrote them. Sometimes the messages bring laughter, sometimes tears. However, many details in letters from my friends—information that makes perfectly good sense to me—are confusing to those who are outsiders to these events. Letters continue conversations, and conversations are based on shared experiences.

Let's say, for example, that I receive the following e-mail from a college friend whom I have not seen in years:

> Go Grizzlies!
> Hello! This is your conscience speaking. Thought you had gotten rid of me, didn't you? Well, I'm back. Your eyes are probably as wide as Strick's were when he and Ed paddled over to check out "the animal" swimming across the Blackfoot that time. . . .

As I read through the message, memories flood into my mind. Some of what he says is sarcastic, and I laugh out loud. It is "insider" humor. If a colleague hears me laughing and asks, "What's so funny?" I cannot simply read the e-mail without explanation. The colleague would say, "I don't get it."

Where do I begin? I have to explain that at the University of Montana, where I did my undergraduate work, the athletic teams are called the Grizzlies. Then I need to recount

a particular rafting trip down the Blackfoot River in western Montana. I was part of a group of students who floated the river in rubber rafts during the high water of spring runoff. Some of the rapids were rough. Several times our rafts flipped, dumping us into the frigid water. One part of the river was smooth, however, and we started to get bored. The two guys in the lead raft saw an animal swimming across the river, so they paddled over to get a closer look. I recognized that it was a rather large black bear, and I shouted a warning. But they could not hear me due to the roaring river. They reached the bear just as it emerged from the water and turned to face them. One of the guys, whom we called Strick, looked at us in terror and screamed, "It's a bear!" I have never seen a rubber raft move so quickly. The front rose into the air like a speedboat as the two paddled frantically away from the imposing animal. No one was hurt, and what had been a scary situation a few seconds earlier became hilariously funny.

After hearing these details, my colleague understands my old friend's cryptic remarks but does not laugh as I do. Humor thrives on immediacy of recognition—in this case, a shared experience. The impact diminishes if you need an explanation to get the point. My relationship with the writer provides a context for interpretation.

GLIMPSING THE OTHER SIDE THROUGH INDUCTIVE STUDY

While an undergraduate, I first experienced studying the Bible inductively in a student-led, small group. At first I hesitated to join, because Sunday school bored me; and I worried that this study would be more of the same. But our freewheeling discussions of 1 Corinthians challenged me to examine the text carefully. If I simply spouted whatever my theological heritage taught me to say about a passage, the other students in the group wanted to know where I saw that in the text. They would not let me get away with lazy answers. I could not merely force our study passage from 1 Corinthians to conform to my own theological position. Growth resulted.

Excitement replaced boredom, and I found new vitality in the words of an ancient letter. But I faced a new danger. Questioning what the text actually said led me to question what I learned in church. I realized that some of my beliefs seemed to have little basis in Scripture. This realization created insecurity, but curiosity prevailed. I switched from thinking, "Yawn, this religious stuff is boring," to, "Wow, the New Testament is radical!" I was shocked at some of what I saw in the Gospels and realized that my view of Jesus had been far too tame. And I was astounded when I observed Paul's brooding anger and sarcasm in his Letters.

While growing up I had felt rather distant from leaders like Paul. I assumed that apostles lived on a different plane of existence. Paul was more of an icon than a person. So I was stunned to discover that he felt and expressed the same emotions that I do.

To say that Paul got angry and forcefully expressed his displeasure with his readers seemed irreverent. But I began to wonder if my definition of saint was too otherworldly and out of touch with the flesh-and-blood Paul. Slowly I realized that my view of Paul needed to be shaped by what his Letters revealed about him. Asking inductive questions became the source for exciting discoveries and troubling dilemmas. Faith became more a journey of discovery and less an affirmation of tired truisms. I replaced "Obviously what Paul means in this passage is . . ." with "Paul, Paul, what in the world do you mean by that?" When I tried to understand Paul's intended meaning, I realized how little I knew.

My curiosity about the Bible became so intense that I ended up becoming a professor, and one of my favorite classes is a study of Paul's Letters. My students are often captivated and unsettled by what they see of Paul in his Letters, and they want to know what relevance his words have for life today. Some of our most stimulating discussions in class deal with such issues as what he says in 1 Corinthians about divorce, sexual ethics, spiritual gifts, and female leadership.

To provide academic rigor and to promote personal relevance, this book facilitates study of Paul's Letters in their Mediterranean context. Throughout you will find quotations from ancient authors that illuminate beliefs commonly held by various people during that time period.

The inductive questions in each chapter push you to read carefully. Other questions challenge you to draw details together into larger conceptual frameworks. And interspersed with these are questions that promote pondering how Paul's teachings relate to contemporary life. Important vocabulary words are boldfaced, and each chapter contains a glossary with definitions of these terms. Following each glossary are suggestions for further reading, in which starred (*) works are especially recommended.

CHAPTER 1

Piecing the Fragments Together

Paul was one of the most dynamic figures of early Christianity. Seemingly a man of tireless energy, he spread the good news of salvation through faith in Jesus Christ over a substantial portion of the Roman Empire. After his death the forcefulness of his missionary thrust lived on through the influence of his Letters, and his writings continue to play a major role in shaping Christian theology. Paul stands among the most significant figures in the history of the church.

Unfortunately, over the centuries Christians have revered the apostle to such an extent that his dynamic and volatile personality has been obscured behind the mists of sainthood. Many do not encounter Paul when reading his Letters in the New Testament. They focus so much on the theological and devotional content of his words

that they miss the man. Failure to recognize his angry outbursts and sarcastic put-downs limits our ability to understand him.

Paul's Epistles come to life when we realize that he was embroiled in a raging controversy in the early church. His Letters reveal the sometimes-discouraged attempts of a pioneer who was often misunderstood and criticized for what he taught his Gentile converts. Paul's vigorous efforts to proclaim salvation by faith alone brought him under intense opposition from other missionaries, who sometimes visited his churches and sought to convince his converts that he was misinformed. When attacked, Paul defended his credentials and integrity, sometimes with anger (Gal. 1:6–2:21; 5:11–12), sometimes with biting sarcasm (2 Cor. 10:1, 9–18; 11:5–6, 16–21). To miss these aspects of his Letters is a tragic loss.

1

Paul did not write theoretical, scholarly books while sitting in a comfortable office. He did not pen his theology with philosophical precision. He wrote in the midst of sometimes trying conditions, and his words reflect the strain under which he dictated his correspondence. Paul's Letters respond to news he received via messengers from various churches. They represent the attempts of a seasoned missionary to address pressing issues that he would much rather have answered in person than by correspondence. He produced what is called **mission theology**: explanations about God, salvation, and holy living addressed to specific Christians facing particular problems—not generalized teaching designed to be published and distributed around the Mediterranean world. He answered concrete questions that his new converts asked about the situations they faced; he corrected mistaken notions that were confusing Christians; and he exhorted individuals to behave in certain ways.

However, we have only Paul's responses to these questions. If we had the other half of the conversation, we could do a better job of interpreting Paul's Epistles. Reading his correspondence is somewhat like listening to a friend or relative talk to someone on the telephone. We hear only half of the conversation. We cannot ask Paul what the other people said to him. We are forced to rely only on his Letters as our basis for piecing together the other half of the conversation.

DEALING WITH
PRIMARY SOURCES

Imagine that in the future you become a religious leader who is so influential that a Christian denomination is named after you. After your death, stories about you abound among members of your denomination, and separating fact from fiction starts to be a problem. Several centuries from now Maria, a member of your church who lives in Brazil, decides to write her doctoral dissertation on your life. She must learn the English spoken in your area during the twenty-first century so that she can read your writings in their original language. She also needs to journey to North America and visit the places that were significant in your life.

She succeeds in locating some of your descendants, who agree to help her search for old memorabilia. While looking through photos and other family mementos, she discovers ten letters bound together by an old rotting string. Carefully she removes the string and finds that these brittle, faded letters were written by you. What a find! Unfortunately, the letters are not dated; they are addressed to different people and obviously written under a variety of circumstances at different times during your life. How will she determine when you wrote them? They contribute a great deal to her study, but she must use other information to figure out the probable circumstances surrounding your writing these particular letters.

To piece together the fragments of your life into a coherent presentation, Maria does a lot of background work. In addition to overcoming the language barrier, she studies the history of your time period for clues that might be helpful. She becomes familiar with your culture so as not to interpret what you wrote from her own twenty-third-century, South American perspectives. But unless some calamity obliterates most records of your time period,

MS 113 Bible: Romans. Egypt, 3rd c.

This fragment of a copy of Paul's Letter to the Romans, written in all capitals with no spaces between letters, was discovered in Egypt and dates to the third century CE. It contains Romans 4:24–5:3; 5:8–13. (Courtesy of Schøyen Collection, MS 113)

Maria will have far more information about you than New Testament scholars have about Paul. She will most likely have pictures of you. In addition to the ten original letters she discovered, she will have copies of other documents you wrote. And she will have stories written by some of your close friends and associates, providing anecdotal material to round out her biography. New Testament scholars, however, must work in the absence of most of the records that Maria would be able to access.

For example, the only early physical description of Paul is found in a second-century document entitled *The Acts of Paul.* In this story, Paul baptizes a lion, and later on his life is miraculously spared in an arena because the lion released to devour him turns out to be none other than this Christian lion. The author of this legend describes Paul as "a man small of stature, with a bald head and crooked legs, in a good state of body, with eyebrows meeting and nose somewhat hooked, full of friend-liness; for now he appeared like a man, and now he had the face of an angel."[1] This fabricated description and its accompanying narrative resulted in the author, a presbyter from Asia, being severely censured and removed from his office (Tertullian, *On Baptism* 17). He said he wrote the document out of love for Paul, but his superiors determined the effort to be misleading. Ironically, down through the centuries, Christian artists typically depict Paul as a bald man who looks much like the description given in *The Acts of Paul.* Indeed, in some books written even today, this description of Paul surfaces. Separating fact from fiction about Paul continues to be a problem.

Unlike our imaginary Maria, with her discovery of letters written by you, we have none of Paul's original manuscripts. We have only copies of copies of the originals.

1. *New Testament Apocrypha*, vol. 2, *Writings Relating to the Apostles; Apocalypses and Related Subjects*, ed. E. Hennecke and W. Schneemelcher, rev. ed. (Louisville, KY: Westminster John Knox Press, 2003), 354.

BCE and CE in Modern Usage

To facilitate working with those from other religious traditions, scholars increasingly use the abbreviations BCE (Before the Common Era) and CE (Common Era) instead of BC (before Christ) and AD (*Anno Domini*, Latin for "in the year of the Lord"). This change avoids conflicts over time designations with those who do not confess that Jesus is Lord/Messiah and do not set their calendars by him. CE designates the same year as AD (e.g., 66 CE = AD 66), and BCE designates the same year as BC (e.g., 164 BCE = 164 BC). The years are the same; only the abbreviations have changed.

No two of these copies are identically the same: all contain minor differences from each other. Scholars who engage in **textual criticism** seek to determine as nearly as possible the original wording of Paul's Letters. They cannot guarantee complete accuracy. We deal with probabilities, not certainties.

In our efforts to write Paul's biography, our primary sources are the careful reconstructions of his letters compiled by textual critics. Paul's Epistles are the earliest extant documents of Christianity, written from approximately 50 to 65 **CE**. By comparison, the earliest Gospel is Mark, probably written between 65 and 70 CE. Yet even Paul's earliest extant letter, probably 1 Thessalonians, was penned after he had been a Christian for about fifteen years. We do not have any of his earlier writings. All of his Epistles come from his later years as a mature Christian missionary. On a few occasions he does speak of his earlier years in these Letters, but he does so

only in attempts to defend himself against accusations from opponents (see 2 Cor. 11:21–12:13; Gal. 1:11–2:14; Phil. 3:2–11). So although we can chronicle some developments in his thinking as we study his correspondence, we do not have manuscripts from his pre-Christian days as a Pharisee to see what he believed then. Nor do we have documents from his early Christian experience that reveal what he believed shortly after his encounter with Christ.

So how do we go about writing Paul's biography? If we use only his Letters, we face insurmountable difficulties. They represent sporadic correspondence, bits and pieces of Paul's life. And how do we go about determining the order in which they were written? In the New Testament his letters are arranged primarily according to length, with the longest and most theological letter, Romans, placed first in the collection, and the brief letter to Philemon placed last. To arrange his Epistles in their actual historical sequence, we must rely on the narrative framework given in Acts. There are certain problems with reconciling events in Acts with what Paul says in his Letters, and we will study these. But regardless of the difficulties involved, Acts provides our earliest coherent description of Paul's activities. Without its account of Paul's missionary endeavors, we simply cannot determine any coherent outline of his life (although a few scholars have tried).

Consequently, in our study we will first read the account of Paul in Acts, and then we will analyze each letter, from the earliest to the latest. Because the Letters were written by the apostle himself, they deserve dominant importance when studying Paul

—although their content is admittedly limited. Acts presents an even more limited portrait of Paul, reporting selected events from his conversion through three missionary journeys and finally to a house arrest in Rome. However partial these glimpses of Paul may be, they are nevertheless powerful. We can reconstruct enough of the apostle's life and beliefs to occupy many fascinating and rewarding hours of study. Overall, his life was not boring!

In 2 Corinthians 11:23–28, for example, Paul lists hardships he endured during his missionary journeys. He is responding to criticism, and he feels self-conscious about giving his autobiographical sketch; but it reveals something about his adventurous career.

> Are they ministers of Christ? I am talking like a madman—I am a better one: with far greater labors, far more imprisonments, with countless floggings, and often near death. Five times I have received from the Jews the forty lashes minus one. Three times I was beaten with rods. Once I received a stoning. Three times I was shipwrecked; for a night and a day I was adrift at sea; on frequent journeys, in danger from rivers, danger from bandits, danger from my own people, danger from Gentiles, danger in the city, danger in the wilderness, danger at sea, danger from false brothers and sisters; in toil and hardship, through many a sleepless night, hungry and thirsty, often without food, cold and naked. And, besides other things, I am under daily pressure because of my anxiety for all the churches.

When Paul specifies thirty-nine lashes, he refers to synagogue discipline. Synagogue elders ordered this punishment to turn wayward people back to the Jewish faith, away from heretical beliefs. Acts mentions none of these five floggings, but they report that Paul experienced such abuse in his efforts to reach the Jewish people with the gospel

of Christ. Being beaten with rods, however, was a Roman punishment. From Acts we know of Paul receiving such a beating only once—at Philippi: "The magistrates had them stripped of their clothing and ordered them to be beaten with rods. After they had given them a severe flogging, they threw them into prison" (16:22–23). The stoning probably matches that which he suffered at Lystra (14:19). Acts gives no record of the three shipwrecks; it records one shipwreck that Paul experienced on the way to Rome (27:39–44), but that occurred *after* 2 Corinthians was written. The other hardships— danger from rivers, bandits, and so on—are not reported in Acts, and we can only speculate on them. Substantial mystery surrounds our best attempts to tell the story of Paul.

DETERMINING PAUL'S CULTURAL BACKGROUND

Nowhere do we find in either Acts or Paul's Letters any mention of his age or date of birth. Paul never states his place of birth, either, although Acts 22:3 reports that he was born in Tarsus, a major city in Cilicia (also Acts 9:11; 21:39; 23:34), and Acts 7:58 calls him a young man at the time Stephen was stoned (early 30s CE). Most likely he was born around 5 CE and became a Christian about 32. Information on the events of his youth and early manhood is limited, but there are indications that he was raised in a strict Jewish home in which his parents carefully trained him in the tenets of their faith.

In Philippians 3:5–6 Paul says that he was "circumcised on the eighth day, a member of the people of Israel, of the tribe of

Benjamin, a Hebrew born of Hebrews; as to the law a Pharisee; . . . as to righteousness under the law, blameless." His family traced their lineage to the tribe of Benjamin and ordered their home life according to the teachings of the Pharisees. They followed the Scriptures diligently, and Paul was most likely a zealously religious youth.

Paul's self-designation "Hebrew born of Hebrews" (Phil. 3:5) suggests that he learned to speak **Aramaic** in his home and local synagogue. Aramaic, the language spoken in Babylon (area of modern-day Iraq), became the main language used by his ancestors after Nebuchadnezzar destroyed Jerusalem and exiled them to Babylon in 586 **BCE** (see 2 Kgs. 25:1–26). In 538 BCE, Cyrus, king of Persia (area of modern-day Iran) and conqueror of Babylon, allowed a group of these exiles to return and rebuild the temple in Jerusalem (Ezra 1:2–4 records the edict of Cyrus). After nearly fifty years in Babylonian exile, however, most of them no longer spoke **Hebrew**. Bilingual teachers (scribes) had to translate the Hebrew Scriptures into Aramaic so the people could understand (Neh. 8:7–8). This practice continued to be true in Paul's day; and when New Testament passages mention someone speaking Hebrew, they mean Aramaic (as in Acts 22:2).

The majority of Jews in the first century, however, spoke Greek, the common language throughout the Mediterranean world. This linguistic shift primarily resulted from **Alexander the Great**'s conquest of all the countries from Greece to India between 333 and 323 BCE. Alexander was the son of Philip II of Macedonia. His private tutor was the excellent philosopher Aristotle. Although Alexander was a brilliant military leader, his agenda involved much more than conquest. He sought to establish a vast Greek civilization. Along with his army he brought architects, artists, doctors, and other specialists who estab-

A depiction of Alexander the Great, modeled after an ancient statue and sold by vendors in Greece. Alexander's influence on the Mediterranean world into which Paul was born is hard to overstate. He brought Greek language and culture to a vast area. (Courtesy of Michael Cosby)

lished cities modeled on the Greek *polis*. Many cities he named Alexandria, and the most famous of these was Alexandria, Egypt, an important center for learning in the ancient world. Greek culture had a pervasive and lasting impact on most of the civilizations that came under Alexander's control. The process whereby people began to adopt Greek language and lifestyle came to be called *hellenization*, a term derived from *Hellas*, the Greek word for Greece. *Hellenism* is the adoption of Greek language and culture.

By the first century CE most Jews who lived outside of Judea spoke Greek and could not understand Aramaic. During this time, "Hebrew" came to have a more narrowly defined meaning than "Jewish." For example, Acts 6:1 describes a conflict in the early church in Jerusalem by saying that "the Hellenists complained against the Hebrews because their widows were being neglected in the daily distribution of food." Here the text distinguishes between Jewish Christians from Judea, who spoke Aramaic, and Hellenistic Jewish Christians from outside areas.

This distinction, however, did not run strictly along geographical borders. So deeply had the hellenization process affected the heart of Judaism that some Jews living in Jerusalem could not understand Hebrew or Aramaic. Acts 6:9 indicates the existence of synagogues in Jerusalem in which services were conducted in Greek instead of Aramaic (also 9:28–29). Yet despite this trend, members of some synagogues outside of Judea carefully maintained their ethnic identity in spite of their surroundings, conducting services in Aramaic. Philo of Alexandria, a first-century Hellenistic Jew highly trained in the Greek thought of his day, used the term "Hebrew" to specify Jews who spoke Aramaic (*Dreams* 2.250; *Abraham* 28).[2]

The degree and nature of Paul's exposure to Greek and Roman culture is unclear. In his Epistles, he quotes not the Hebrew Bible but a Greek translation of the Scriptures called the **Septuagint** (abbreviated **LXX**). Long before his time, translating the Hebrew Scriptures into Greek became necessary as the process of assimilating to other cultures occurred among the Jewish people living outside of Judea. Already in the third century BCE many Judeans could not understand Hebrew, so around 250 BCE Jewish scholars in Alexandria, Egypt, translated the Hebrew **Torah** (Pentateuch) into Greek. Paul uses the Septuagint like a Hellenistic Jew, but it is not clear whether he grew up with this translation or later began using it during his missionary work among Gentiles.

If Paul grew up in **Tarsus**, from his youth he was exposed to Hellenistic thought in this major center of Greek thinking and culture.[3] The Syrian ruler Antiochus IV Epiphanes established a Jewish colony there approximately 171 BCE, and during his reign (175–164) he heavily hellenized the city. The Roman general Pompey made Tarsus the capital of the province of Cilicia in 66 BCE. Mark Antony and Augustus Caesar granted freedom and Roman citizenship to Tarsus, and the city became widely known for its cultural achievements and

2. Archaeologists also discovered an inscription at Corinth that reads "Synagogue of the Hebrews." See B. Powell, "Greek Inscriptions from Corinth," *American Journal of Archaeology*, 2nd series, 7 (1903): 60–61, #40.

3. Strabo, *Geography* 14.5.10–15; Dio Chrysostom 34. Also see A. N. Sherwin-White, *Roman Society and Roman Law in the New Testament* (Oxford: Oxford University Press, 1963), 180.

These two papyrus pages come from a codex of Leviticus that dates to about 200 CE. They represent the Septuagint, a Greek translation of the Hebrew Scriptures that was popular among many early Christians, including Paul. (Courtesy of Schøyen Collection, MS 2649)

famous philosophers (see Strabo, *Geography* 14.673). Understandably, therefore, Paul expresses pride in the reputation of his hometown when he says in Acts 21:39, "I am a Jew, from Tarsus in Cilicia, a citizen of an important city."

The sketchiness of the information on Paul's early life makes it quite probable that scholars will continue to debate the nature and extent of the cultural and religious influences on him. Yet in spite of the fact that many details of Paul's life remain hidden from us, we can still learn a great deal about him from Acts and from his Letters. And having a time line enriches our understanding of his Letters. The following chart provides a brief outline of Paul's life. You will have many occasions to refer back to

it. This overview sketches the *approximate* times of events in Paul's career and lists passages that mention them. The question marks after some entries indicate the tenuous nature of assigning dates to some of the letters.

LOOKING AHEAD

The next few chapters explore background information on Jewish sects of Paul's time and their beliefs about the coming Messiah, as well as the religious beliefs and practices of the Gentiles whom Paul evangelized. You will find some of the quotations of ancient sources to be rather peculiar by modern standards. But they open windows into

CHARTING THE APOSTLE'S LIFE

Approximate Date	Details of Paul's Life	Paul's Letters	Acts
5ff. CE	Tarsus (birth and early childhood in Judaism)	Phil. 3:3–6 2 Cor. 11:22 Rom. 9:3; 11:1, 14	9:11; 21:39; 22:3; 23:34; 26:4–5
	Roman Citizen by Birth		16:37–40; 22:25–29; 23:27
	Tentmaker		18:3
	Aramaic = first language	Phil. 3:5	21:40; 22:2; 26:14
??	Rabbinic training in Jerusalem under Gamaliel	cf. Gal. 1:13–14	22:3; cf. 23:6; 26:4–8
30–33	Persecution of Christians	Gal. 1:13–14, 23; Phil. 3:6; 1 Cor. 15:9	7:58–8:3; 9:1–2; 22:4–5; 26:11
33	Conversion on the way to Damascus	Gal. 1:15–16	9:3–19; 22:6–16; 26:12–18
33–35	In Damascus and Arabia	2 Cor. 11:32–33; Gal. 1:17	9:20–25
35	Return to Jerusalem	Gal. 1:18–19	9:26–29; 22:17–21
35	To Tarsus	Gal. 1:21	9:30
↓	In Antioch with Barnabas		11:22–26
	To Jerusalem for Famine Relief		11:27–30
48			
47–48	**1st Missionary Journey**		13–14
	Cyprus		13:4b–12
	South Galatia		13:13–14:25
	Antioch		14:26–28
49	**Jerusalem Council**	Gal. 2:1–10 (?)	15:1–35
49–50	**2nd Missionary Journey**		15:40–18:22
	Syria and Cilicia		15:40–41
	South Galatia		16:1–5
	Troas		16:8–10
	Philippi	1 Thess. 2:2	16:11–40
	Thessalonica	1 Thess. 2:2; Phil. 4:15–16	17:1–9
	Beroea		17:10–14
	Athens	1 Thess. 3:1	17:15–34
50	**1–2 Thessalonians**		
50–52	Corinth (for 18 months)	2 Cor. 11:7–9	18:1–18a
	Cenchreae		18:18b
	Ephesus		18:19–21
	Caesarea to Antioch		18:22
52–57	**3rd Missionary Journey**		18:23; 19:1–21:16
52	Across Asia		18:23
52–55	Ephesus (3 yrs.)		19:1–41; 20:31

(continued)

CHARTING THE APOSTLE'S LIFE (continued)

Approximate Date	Details of Paul's Life	Paul's Letters	Acts
55	**Corinthians A** (now lost)	1 Cor. 5:9; 7:1; 16:17	
55	**1 Corinthians (Corinthians B)**		
55 (Spr)	Painful visit to Corinth	2 Cor. 2:1, 5	
55 (Spr)	**Painful Letter (=Corinthians C)**	2 Cor. 2:3–4	
55	**(Philippians?)**		
55	Troas	2 Cor. 2:12	
56 (Win-Spr)	Macedonia	2 Cor. 2:13	20:1–4
56 (Win)	**2 Corinthians (Corinthians D)**		
57	Corinth (3 months—longer?)		20:3
57	**Galatians**		
57	**Romans**		
57	Troas		20:5–12
57	Miletus		20:17–38
57	To Tyre		21:1–6
57	Caesarea		21:7–14
57	Jerusalem	Rom. 15:25–32	21:15–23:30
57-??	To Rome		23:31–28:31
57–59	Caesarea		23:33–26:32
59	To Rome		27:1–28:14
60–62	Roman Imprisonment		28:15–31
60–62	**Colossians, Ephesians, Philemon (Philippians??)**		
64/65	Spain (?)	Rom. 15:24, 28 (*1 Clement 5.7*)	
??	**Pastoral Epistles (??)**		
65 ?	Paul's Death	(*1 Clement 5.7*)	

Paul's world that are valuable for analyzing his Letters. Some obscure comments in his Epistles become clear when you understand more about the Mediterranean world of his time.

GLOSSARY

Acts of Paul, The. Fanciful, second-century document that narrates imaginary events in the life of Paul. The author lost his position in the church as a result of writing the book. Yet Christians down through the centuries have relied on the description of Paul found in this text as their basis for depicting the apostle.

Alexander the Great. Greek ruler who in 333–323 BCE conquered many regions from Greece to India. As a result of his influence, Greek became the common language across a vast region in the ancient Mediterranean world.

Aramaic. Language spoken in ancient Babylon (area of modern Iraq). When Judeans were exiled in Babylon in the sixth century BCE, they learned to speak Aramaic; and when some returned to Judea from exile, they mostly spoke Aramaic instead of Hebrew. This practice remained true up through the time of Jesus and Paul.

BCE. "Before the Common Era." Historically speaking, this abbreviation designates the same time as BC (before Christ).

CE. "Common Era." Historically speaking, this abbreviation designates the same time as AD (*Anno Domini* = Latin for "in the year of the Lord"). It allows people from different faith traditions to speak of the same year without dealing with a Christian theological overlay.

Hebrew. Language spoken by the Hebrew people. Most of the Hebrew Scriptures (Old Testament) were written in Hebrew.

Hellenism. Adoption of Greek language and culture.

Hellenization. The process whereby people adopted Greek language and lifestyle. The word is derived from *Hellas*, the Greek term for Greece.

LXX. Abbreviation for "Septuagint" (the Roman numerals for 70).

Mission theology. Theology that Paul produced in the process of performing his missionary work while addressing pressing matters of concern among the Christians to whom he wrote. Unlike modern statements of beliefs about God, salvation, afterlife, and so forth that are written for general readership, mission theology is a nonsystematic explanation of whatever issue Paul needed to address at the time in order to accomplish the task at hand.

Polis. Greek and English word for "city-state."

Septuagint. The main Greek translation of the Hebrew Scriptures (abbreviated LXX = 70 because of a story about the number of scholars involved in its translation). Especially as the early Christian movement expanded into Gentile regions, the LXX was the Christian Bible, because most converts could not read Hebrew.

Tarsus. The city in which Paul (Roman name)/Saul (Jewish name) was born. Located in the region that today is southeastern Turkey.

Textual criticism. The attempt to reconstruct as closely as possible the original reading of a document. We do not possess any of the original New Testament documents—only a series of copies of copies, no two of which are identical. Before the invention of the printing press by Johannes Gutenberg around 1439, all biblical manuscripts were copied by hand, and this allowed many mistakes to be made in the transmission process. Textual critics trace manuscript changes backward through time from later copies to earlier copies in an effort to explain how the changes happened. Their goal is to produce a text that comes close to the original reading of each of the New Testament documents.

Torah. Typically a title for the Pentateuch, the first five books of the Hebrew Bible, although sometimes it was used to refer to the Scriptures as a whole.

FURTHER READING
ON PAUL THE APOSTLE

Barrett, C. K. *Paul: An Introduction to His Thought.* Louisville, KY: Westminster John Knox Press, 1994. Not an overly exciting read, but contains valuable information.

Bruce, F. F. *Paul: Apostle of the Heart Set Free.* Grand Rapids: Wm. B. Eerdmans Publishing Co., 1977. Accessible. Interesting perspectives.

Dunn, James D. G. *The Theology of Paul the Apostle.* Grand Rapids: Wm. B. Eerdmans Publishing Co., 1998. Long book based on Romans. Not for beginners. Good resource.

Elias, Jacob W. *Remember the Future: The Pastoral Theology of Paul the Apostle.* Scottdale, PA: Herald Press, 2006. Tries to recreate the circumstances of Paul and each of the churches that he founded. Focuses on conflict and resolution.

Fitzmyer, Joseph A. *Paul and His Theology: A Brief Sketch.* Englewood Cliffs, NJ: Prentice-Hall, 1989. Brief book packed with information. Not an easy read but a good resource.

*Hawthorne, Gerald F., and Ralph P. Martin, eds. *Dictionary of Paul and His Letters.* Downers Grove, IL: InterVarsity Press, 1993. Good collection of articles. As with any collection of essays, some are better than others. Written for general audience.

Hengel, Martin, and Anna Maria Schwemer. *Paul between Damascus and Antioch: The Unknown Years.* Louisville, KY: Westminster John Knox Press, 1997. Valuable information about the early church. Somewhat technical.

*Keck, Leander E. *Paul and His Letters.* Philadelphia: Fortress Press, 1979. Basic text, written for nontechnical readers.

Malina, Bruce J., and Jerome H. Neyrey. *Portraits of Paul: An Archaeology of Ancient Personality.* Louisville, KY: Westminster John Knox Press, 1996. Focuses on how ancient Mediterranean people thought about themselves. Tries to recreate sociological models of ancient life and then to apply these to understanding Paul.

Murphy-O'Connor, Jerome. *Paul: A Critical Life.* New York: Oxford University Press, 1996. Detailed, somewhat technical book. Good work to grow into.

Ridderbos, H. N. *Paul: An Outline of His Theology.* Grand Rapids: Wm. B. Eerdmans Publishing Co., 1975. Good collection of material. Dry presentation.

Riesner, Rainer. *Paul's Early Period: Chronology, Mission Strategy, Theology.* Grand Rapids: Wm. B. Eerdmans Publishing Co., 1998. Good background material, but a difficult read for students.

*Roetzel, Calvin. *The Letters of Paul: Conversations in Context.* 4th ed. Louisville, KY: Westminster John Knox Press, 1998. Updated version of a book of essays that tries to show Paul's personality. Fairly engaging. Nontechnical.

———. *Paul: The Man and the Myth.* Columbia: University of South Carolina Press, 1998. Focuses on Jewish backgrounds, arguing that Paul never abandoned first-century Judaism.

Sandmel, Samuel. *The Genius of Paul.* Philadelphia: Fortress Press, 1979. Interesting insights on Paul from a Jewish New Testament scholar.

Stendahl, Krister. *Paul among Jews and Gentiles, and Other Essays.* Philadelphia: Fortress Press, 1976. Challenges the view that Paul had an introspective conscience like some of his Western European interpreters. A bit dated, but provides insights into recent discussions on Paul's theology.

Wallace, Richard, and Wynne Williams. *The Three Worlds of Paul of Tarsus.* New York: Routledge, 1998. Valuable background information on Greek and Roman thought and culture. Weak on Jewish backgrounds.

Wiles, Virginia. *Making Sense of Paul: A Basic Introduction to Pauline Theology.* Peabody, MA: Hendrickson Publishers, 2000. Written for undergraduate students. Uses modern analogies to make Paul's thought world more understandable.

Witherington, Ben, III. *The Paul Quest: The Renewed Search for the Jew of Tarsus.* Downers Grove, IL: InterVarsity Press, 1998. Accessible. Easier to grasp than technical works on the search for the historical Paul.

Young, Brad H. *Paul, the Jewish Theologian: A Pharisee among Christians, Jews, and Gentiles.* Peabody, MA: Hendrickson Publishers, 1997. Emphasizes the Jewish roots of Paul's theology and argues that Paul did not distance himself from the laws of Moses.

CHAPTER 2

Zealous for the Law

Although Christians often equate being a Pharisee with being a hypocrite, Paul never makes such a connection. On the contrary, he saw his previous Pharisaic identity as respectable. Although as a Christian he vigorously rejected some of his former beliefs, he never indicates in his Letters that he remembered his life as a Pharisee with embarrassment. He was not a hypocrite like the Pharisaic adversaries whom Jesus attacks in passages such as Matthew 23. Paul was apparently content with his achievements under Mosaic law until his experience on the road to Damascus (Acts 9:3–7).

In Galatians 1:14 Paul states, "I advanced in Judaism beyond many among my people of the same age, for I was far more zealous for the traditions of my ancestors." This burning zeal caused him to persecute the followers of Jesus (Gal. 1:13), something

he later regretted deeply (1 Cor. 15:9). But while a Pharisee, he served God with a clear conscience. And as a Christian he could look back upon his achievements as something to boast about, except for the fact that he now believed that Christ's sacrificial death for salvation nullified all such trust in human achievement.

When defending his teaching that salvation comes only through faith in Jesus Christ, Paul contrasts himself with Jewish Christians who teach that in order to be a true follower of Christ one must be circumcised and follow Mosaic law.

> For it is we who are the circumcision, who worship in the Spirit of God and boast in Christ Jesus and have no confidence in the flesh— even though I, too, have reason for confidence in the flesh. If anyone else has reason to be confident in the flesh, I have more: circumcised on the eighth day, a member of the people of

Israel, of the tribe of Benjamin, a Hebrew born of Hebrews; as to the law, a Pharisee; as to zeal, a persecutor of the church; as to righteousness under the law, blameless. Yet whatever gains I had, these I have come to regard as loss because of Christ. (Phil. 3:3–7)

Paul believed that, as a Pharisee, he kept the law of Moses ("blameless"); and he

This page of Papyrus 46, a codex produced in Egypt around 200 CE, contains Romans 11:3–12:8. Because P46 is the oldest known copy of Paul's Letters, it is the closest we get to his original words. Of the 104 original leaves, 86 survive and are stored in the University of Michigan Papyrus Collection and in the Chester Beatty Collection in Dublin, Ireland. (Courtesy of APIS, University of Michigan [Inventory #6238, Processing #3553, Section 30])

viewed his righteousness as reason for human confidence, not as a source of shame. As a Christian he rejected placing confidence in human effort, but he saw his former life as an accomplishment, not an embarrassment.

Paul only mentions his Pharisaic background in his Letters when he feels the need to defend himself against the attacks of Christians who challenge his credibility. Yet he does not provide any specific information about his Pharisaic studies. Where Paul's Letters are silent, however, the book of Acts makes further claims about Paul's pre-Christian experiences. In a speech delivered to Jews in Jerusalem, Paul states in Acts 22:3 that he was educated "at the feet of Gamaliel." This teacher seems to be the same **Gamaliel** who, as a member of the Sanhedrin, argues for a hands-off policy toward the followers of Jesus in Acts 5:34–39. Historically, the famous Pharisaic teacher Gamaliel I flourished in Jerusalem from 20 to 50 CE.

Paul was not the only Pharisee to embrace Christian belief, although his understanding of salvation by faith alone differed from that held by some other converts from this group (Acts 15:5; cf. 11:2; 15:1). Many Pharisaic Christians insisted that Gentiles must be circumcised and obey the laws of Moses (15:5). They were not alone in this contention. Most Jewish Christians in Jerusalem held the law in high regard and doubted anything that challenged this belief. During Paul's final trip to Jerusalem, the apostles there warned him,

> You see, brother, how many thousands of believers there are among the Jews, and they are all zealous for the law. They have been told about you that you teach all the Jews living among the Gentiles to forsake Moses, and that you tell them not to circumcise their children or observe the customs. (21:20–21)

This radical reverence for the laws of Moses, which so characterized Pharisaic life, has a lengthy history. Understanding how their beliefs and practices developed provides deeper insight into Paul the Pharisee.

SOURCES FOR STUDYING THE PHARISEES

Although we cannot be certain, the name **Pharisees** apparently means "separated ones" (Aramaic *Peresh* means "separated"; the Hebrew form is *Perush*). Most likely the word originated as a term of contempt used by their opponents, who called them "separatists." By Jesus' time, however, the title had become official, and the Pharisees regarded it as an accurate description of themselves as those who remained loyal to the law, separated from others who were careless in this regard.

The origin and early development of the Pharisees remain somewhat obscure. Only a few ancient sources speak of the group, and each presents its own difficulties in interpretation. Josephus's writings, the New Testament, and the Mishnah are the main sources, and other information may be gleaned from the Dead Sea Scrolls, the *Psalms of Solomon*, and the Talmud.

Josephus: Pharisees as a Philosophical Sect

The Jewish historian **Josephus** describes the Pharisees in various books. His first and most accurate work is *Jewish War*. Completed about 75 CE, this history of the time from Antiochus Epiphanes (175 BCE) to the destruction of Jerusalem by Titus in 70 CE consists of seven scrolls. Josephus completed his *Antiquities of the Jews* in 93/94 CE (see *Ant.* 20.12.1 [§267]). This history of the Jewish people, from earliest times to the war with Rome that began in 66 CE, consists of twenty scrolls. In his autobiography (composition date unknown), Josephus claims that he was a Pharisee (*Life* 2 [§§10–12]).

Josephus's works are important for understanding the times about which he writes. But he was a vain man, and his descriptions of various events are uneven and at times distorted by careless use of sources or by deliberate manipulation. Thus, caution is needed when using his descriptions of the Pharisees.

Josephus first mentions the Pharisees during the time of John Hyrcanus, a brutal Jewish leader who ruled from 134 to 104 BCE. His account shows the Pharisees to be politically active during that time. Although initially friendly toward Hyrcanus, the Pharisees became embroiled in conflict with the leader. To emphasize their political influence, Josephus says that they "have so great a power over the multitude, that when they say anything against the king or against the high priest, they are presently believed" (*Antiquities* 13.10.5 [§§288–289 Whiston]).

Hyrcanus not only abandoned the Pharisees but also sought to "abolish the decrees they had imposed on the people, and punish those that observed them" (13.10.6 [§296]). Josephus elaborates on these Pharisaic laws by explaining:

> The Pharisees have delivered to the people a great many observances by succession from their fathers, which are not written in the law of Moses; and for that reason . . . the Sadducees reject them and say that we are to esteem those observances to be obligatory which are in the written word, but are not to observe what are derived from the tradition of our forefathers; and concerning these things it is that great disputes and differences have arisen among them, while the Sadducees are able to persuade none but the rich, and have not the populace obsequious to them, but the Pharisees have the multitude on their side. (*Ant.* 13.10.6 [§§297–298 Whiston])

The political involvement of the Pharisees resulted in disaster while Alexander Janneus ruled over Judea from 103 to 76 BCE. He brutally suppressed the Pharisees because they dared to oppose him.

> His rage was grown so extravagant, that his barbarity proceeded to a degree of impiety: for when he had ordered eight hundred to be hung upon crosses in the midst of the city, he had the throats of their wives and children cut before their eyes; and these executions he saw as he was drinking and lying down with his concubines. Upon which, so deep a surprise seized upon the people, that eight thousand of his opposers fled away the very next night, out of all Judea, whose flight was only terminated by Alexander's death. (*War* 1.4.6 [§§97–98 Whiston]; see also *Ant.* 13.15.1 [§§389–391])

This atrocity of executing the wives and children before the eyes of crucified Pharisees severely checked the political aspirations of the Pharisees. But their chance to exert national influence again arose after the death of Janneus, when his wife, Alexandra Salome, assumed his rule.

> Now the Pharisees joined themselves to her, to assist her in the government. These are a certain sect of the Jews that appear more religious than others, and seem to interpret the laws more accurately. Now, Alexandra hearkened to them to an extraordinary degree, as being herself a woman of great piety towards God. But these Pharisees artfully insinuated themselves into her favor by little and little, and became themselves the real administrators of the public affairs; they banished and reduced whom they pleased; they bound and loosed [men] at their pleasure; and, to say all at once, they had the enjoyment of the royal authority, whilst the expenses and the difficulties of it belonged to Alexandra. . . . Accordingly, they themselves slew Diogenes, a person of figure, and one that had been a friend to Alexander: and accused him as having assisted the king with his advice, for crucifying the eight hundred men [before mentioned]. They also prevailed with Alexandra to put to death the rest of those who had irritated him against them. (*War* 1.5.2–3 [§§110–113 Whiston])[1]

Thus, according to Josephus, the Pharisees exerted significant political influence on society during the decades following the Maccabean rebellion. But he does not provide any information on the origin of this Jewish sect. Many scholars believe that the Pharisees emerged from the ranks of the Hasidim, who joined the Maccabean rebellion in 167 BCE (*hasidim* in Hebrew means "faithful ones"). First Maccabees 2:42 states that a group of "mighty warriors of Israel, all who offered himself willingly for the law," joined forces to fight the Syrians who, under the brutal rule of **Antiochus IV**

---

1. Josephus gives a longer account of this event in *Antiquities* 13.15.5–16.5 (§§398–429), which makes the Pharisees seem slightly less brutal. Written about 94 CE, after the Pharisees had emerged as the dominant leaders in Judaism, this version differs somewhat from that of *War* 1.5.1–3, which was written in 75 CE, shortly after the Jewish War in 66–70. By this time Josephus claims to be a Pharisee (*Life* 9–12), and his modifications of the story of Salome might be politically motivated to increase their stature before the Romans. See Jacob Neusner, *From Politics to Piety: The Emergence of Pharisaic Judaism* (Englewood Cliffs, NJ: Prentice-Hall, 1973), 45–66.

Epiphanes (175–164 BCE), hunted down and slaughtered those who continued to keep the faith of their Hebrew heritage.

Jews who held differing theological views united in battle against a common enemy who threatened to annihilate their right to obey the laws of Moses. Once they succeeded in driving the Syrians out of their position of power over Judea, however, these competing sects began to oppose each other in an attempt to run the country according to their own religious beliefs. The Pharisees may well have been one of these factions. They tended to be more progressive than some of the others, such as the ultraconservative sectarians who later condemned society and established their headquarters in the desert near the Dead Sea (known as the Qumran Community).[2]

For his Roman readers, Josephus provides several brief descriptions of the beliefs of the main Jewish groups in Judea. In an attempt to explain these with words his readers understand, in *Antiquities* 18.1.2–6 he describes their beliefs in philosophical terms. A similar passage in *War* 2.8.2–14 (§§119–166) focuses primarily on the Essenes and provides only short comments on the Pharisees, Sadducees, and Zealots. In this earlier version, Josephus appears to have been most interested in the Essenes' beliefs and customs. By the time he writes *Antiquities*, however, Josephus seems more concerned with the Pharisees, omitting the lengthy account of the Essenes.

Because the New Testament does not mention the Essenes, and they are not as important as the Pharisees for our study of Paul, we will limit our study to his comments in *Antiquities*. However, if you want to read about the Essenes' quaint customs, including bathing and toilet rituals, you may want to read *War* 2.8.2–13 (§§119–161). In *Antiquities* Josephus seems more interested in the Pharisees, explaining that they live simply and follow the dictates of reason. He adds that they give great respect to the teaching of their elders and follow these instructions for how to live. He also explains that they affirm both God's sovereign control over the earth and the free will of humans.

When they determine that all things are done by fate, they do not take away the freedom from men of acting as they think fit; since their notion is, that it hath pleased God to make a temperament, whereby what he wills is done, but so that the will of men can act virtuously or viciously. They also believe that souls have an immortal vigor in them, and that under the earth there will be rewards or punishments, according as they have lived virtuously or viciously in this life; and the latter are to be detained in an everlasting prison, but that the former shall have power to revive and live again; on account of which doctrines, they are able greatly to persuade the body of the people; and whatsoever they do about divine worship, prayers, and sacrifices, they perform them according to their direction; insomuch that the cities gave great attestations to them on account of their entire virtuous conduct, both in the actions of their lives and their discourses also.

But the doctrine of the **Sadducees** is this: That souls die with the bodies; nor do they regard the observation of anything besides what the law enjoins them. . . . but this doctrine is received but by a few, yet by those still of the greatest dignity; but they are able to do almost nothing of themselves; for when they become magistrates, as they are unwillingly and by force sometimes obliged to be, they addict themselves to the notions of the Pharisees, because the multitude would not otherwise bear them.

---

2. Although some scholars do not believe that the Dead Sea Scrolls community was a group of Essenes, the majority remains convinced that the rigorous stipulations for conduct specified in the *Community Rule* (1QS), for example, were written by and for the DSS sectarians.

The doctrine of the **Essenes** is this: That all things are best ascribed to God. They teach the immortality of souls, and esteem that the rewards of righteousness are to be earnestly striven for; and when they send what they have dedicated to God into the temple, they do not offer sacrifices, because they have more pure lustrations of their own; on account of which they are excluded from the common court of the temple, but offer their sacrifices themselves. . . . They exceed all other men that addict themselves to virtue. . . . This is demonstrated by that institution of theirs which will not suffer anything to hinder them from having all things in common; so that a rich man enjoys no more of his own wealth than he who hath nothing at all. There are about four thousand men that live in this way, and neither marry wives, nor are desirous to keep servants; as thinking the latter tempts men to be unjust, and the former gives the handle to domestic quarrels.

But of the fourth sect of Jewish philosophy [**Zealots**], Judas the Galilean was the author. These men agree in all other things with the Pharisaic notions; but they have an inviolable attachment to liberty; and say that God is to be their only Ruler and Lord. They also do not value dying any kind of death, nor indeed do they heed the deaths of their relations and friends, nor can any such fear make them call any man Lord. (*Ant.* 18.1.2–6 [§§11–25 Whiston])

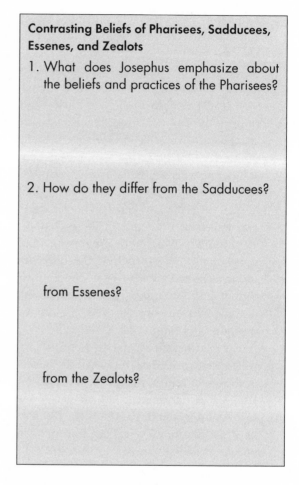

Contrasting Beliefs of Pharisees, Sadducees, Essenes, and Zealots

1. What does Josephus emphasize about the beliefs and practices of the Pharisees?

2. How do they differ from the Sadducees?

from Essenes?

from the Zealots?

New Testament Gospels: Pharisees as Snakes and Hypocrites

Most references to the Pharisees in the New Testament are found in the Gospels, where as a group they oppose Jesus. They reveal little interest in political matters, but show great concern over keeping the "traditions of the elders." Thus, in Mark 7:1–13 they criticize Jesus' followers for not obeying these traditions, and Jesus attacks them for disobeying the Scriptures because of their traditions. Such conflict stories in the Gospels indicate that the Pharisees carefully avoided eating with non-Pharisees, whom they considered sinful (2:15–17); they fasted as regular practice (2:18); they observed the Sabbath according to very strict rules (2:23–24; 3:1–6); and they ritually washed their dishes and hands before every meal (7:2–5). Matthew 23 indicates that they also focused on proper use of oaths (23:16–22), tithing of everything including table spices (23:23–24), ceremonial cleansing of dishes (23:25–26), and building and adorning tombs for the prophets as a means of honoring them and asserting obedience to their teachings (23:29–30).

By the first century CE, the Pharisees as a group primarily focused on implementing their oral traditions, which provided practical guidelines for how to obey the laws of Moses. They do not appear to have been active in politics at this time, although some of the more influential leaders were part of the **Sanhedrin**, the main ruling body of the Jews. Over time they moved away from radical political involvement to preoccupation with their purity laws. Nevertheless, they were quite capable of active social involvement. During the early days of the Christian movement, Saul/Paul obtained authority from the Sanhedrin to hunt down, beat, and imprison Christians in an effort to eradicate their "heresy."

Because Pharisaic leaders opposed Jesus and his followers, the Gospels depict them in a negative way. The Gospel authors do not attempt a balanced view of the Pharisees, showing that some were, like Paul, men of good conscience, serving God sincerely. They mostly portray the Pharisees as hypocritical, treacherously pursuing Jesus until they can seize an opportunity to murder him. Thus, in Matthew 23 Jesus delivers a stinging condemnation of the Pharisees for a number of abuses, most of which center on hypocrisy. He concludes his criticism by asserting, "You snakes, you brood of vipers! How can you escape being sentenced to hell?" (23:33).

Unfortunately, many Christians know only this negative portrait of Pharisees as enemies of Jesus who focus on laws and do not care about people. Although such behavior characterized a number of Pharisees, just as it sadly characterizes many Christians, not all of them were hypocritical legalists. Consequently, the negative portrait of the Pharisees in the Gospels needs to be balanced by documents written by the successors of the Pharisees.

Rabbinic Sources: Pharisees as True Servants of God

Although Pharisees are enemies in the Gospels, they are good guys in rabbinic writings. Following the destruction of Jerusalem in 70 CE, some Pharisees established an academy at Yavneh, northwest of Jerusalem. The scholarship conducted at Yavneh, and at other centers of Pharisaic education that developed later, finally culminated in the production of the **Mishnah** in approximately 200 CE. The Hebrew verb *shanah* means "to repeat," which reflects the mode of learning practiced by the students of the Rabbis. The rabbi taught his students orally, and they *repeated* back his instruction. This process continued until the students memorized the subject matter. Thus by the "repetition" (*mishnah* in Hebrew) of their oral traditions, the Pharisees' successors, the Rabbis, maintained their teachings orally until the circle of Rabbi Judah the Prince (*ha-Nasi*) codified them into written form around 200 CE.

Rabbi Judah seems to have been relatively unconcerned with historical developments. Enormously important historical events, such as the Maccabean Rebellion in 167–142 BCE, the revolt against Rome in 66–70 CE, the destruction of the temple in 70 CE, and the Bar Kokhba rebellion in 132–135 CE—none of these are mentioned in the Mishnah. Probably because messianic fervor nearly destroyed the Jewish people during the two rebellions against Rome in 66–70 and 132–135 CE, the Mishnah contains virtually nothing at all about Messiah. Indeed, a later rabbinic text reveals how insidious some of the rabbis believed messianic speculation to be. In *Midrash Eikhah* 2.9, the story says that Rabbi Akiba interpreted Numbers 24:17 as a messianic text referring to Bar Kokhba. Rabbi Johanan ben Torta retorted, "Akiba, grass will grow on your cheeks [i.e., from your skull] and the son of David will still not have come."

The Pharisees' preoccupation with purity laws, which the New Testament lampoons, finds full expression in the Mishnah. For example, in light of Mishnah *Shabbath*, their motivation for sharply criticizing Jesus' disciples' failure to keep the traditions of the elders pertaining to Sabbath observance becomes quite clear. This tractate lists pages of meticulous regulations of what one must not do on the Sabbath. A tailor must not carry a needle out of his shop if the time is near sundown on Friday, lest he forget that it is in his pocket and thus be guilty of carrying a burden on the Sabbath (*Shabbath* 1.2). One must not let clothes soak in dye over the Sabbath (1.5). "Camels may not be led along tied together, but a man may hold their ropes in his hand provided that he does not twist them together" (5.3).[3] One must not wear sandals "shod with nails" on the Sabbath, for that would be bearing a burden (6.2). An amputee may go out with a wooden stump on the Sabbath, but only if it does not have knee pads, which are susceptible to uncleanness (6.8). One is guilty of breaking the Sabbath if one takes "milk enough for a gulp,

or honey enough to put on a sore, or oil enough to anoint the smallest member [little toe of a one-day-old child], or water enough to rub off eye plaster" (8.1). "[He is culpable] that takes out [on the Sabbath] wood enough to cook the smallest egg, or spices enough to flavour a light egg" (9.5). These regulations extend through twenty-four sections, vividly illustrating the minutiae that the Rabbis sought to legislate. How many of these laws were taught by Pharisees during the first century is impossible to know, but the tendency toward amassing such regulations was evidently prevalent in Paul's time.

Care must be taken when reading accounts of pre-70 CE Pharisaism in the Mishnah, for the stories about Pharisaic leaders of Jesus' time are of questionable accuracy. Jacob Neusner led the way in analyzing these stories critically, demonstrating that a substantial amount of modification occurred during the years between 70 and 200 CE. Oral transmission tends to result in people telling stories so that they address the present concerns of the group that preserves them. Thus the recorded form of the stories in the Mishnah reveals at least as much about the concerns of the Rabbis in the late second century as about the activities of Pharisees in the first century.[4]

During the third and fourth centuries the Mishnah assumed central importance as a textbook for studying Jewish legal matters. As rabbis continued to interpret the various sections of the Mishnah, however, a growing body of written material was collected in the academies. Over time these

---

3. Translations by Herbert Danby, *The Mishnah* (London: Oxford University Press, 1933).

4. See, for example, J. Neusner, *The Rabbinic Traditions about the Pharisees before 70*, vols. 1–2 (Netherlands: E. J. Brill, 1971).

commentaries were recorded with the Mishnah passages they sought to explain, and the combined work became known as the **Jerusalem (or Palestinian) Talmud**, which was completed shortly after 400. *Talmud* means "teaching" or "doctrine," and the Talmud consists primarily of legal material (halakah) but also has a large number of edifying stories (haggadah). In form a page of the Talmud has a section of the Mishnah, plus a collection of interpretive comments in Aramaic by various rabbis (called Gemara = "interpretation"), plus haggadic materials (edifying stories).

Interpretive work on the Mishnah also took place in Babylon, where rabbis produced an even more important work called the **Babylonian Talmud** during the fifth and sixth centuries. This Talmud is approximately four times as long as the Palestinian Talmud, extending to around six thousand pages. It is also given a more authoritative place in the Jewish community, being studied more than the Palestinian Talmud. Yet both of these Talmuds were produced centuries after the time of Paul, and great caution should be used when seeking to explain first-century Pharisaic practices from their passages. Be cautious of books that explain Paul's teachings by uncritically providing frequent quotations from rabbinic sources.

Dead Sea Scrolls: Pharisees as Liberals

Although Christians today typically view Pharisees as uptight legalists and may even use rabbinic literature to provide evidence for this opinion, some Jews in the first century considered the Pharisees to be far too loose with the law. Among these were members of the Dead Sea Scrolls community.

In 1947 some Bedouins discovered ancient scrolls in caves in the Judean desert near Qumran, close to the northwest part of the Dead Sea. The scrolls were hidden in large clay jars and most likely represent the library of a sect of Jews who lived in that area from the middle of the second century BCE until a Roman army overran the region in 68 CE, during the war with the Jews. Members of the Dead Sea Scrolls community hid their scrolls in a number of caves in the surrounding area to protect them, and the discovery of these represents one of the great archaeological finds of the twentieth century.[5]

Most scholars believe that the sectarians at Qumran were Essenes, because the beliefs and practices revealed in the **Dead Sea Scrolls** are very similar to the descriptions of Essenes given by Josephus and others.[6] These sectarians made the Pharisees seem lax by comparison when it came to their zeal for obeying the laws of Moses. For example, Jesus says to the Pharisees, "If one of you has a child or an ox that has fallen into a well, will you not immediately pull it out on a sabbath day?" (Luke 14:5). A comment in the Mishnah expresses a similar sentiment and may reflect first-century Pharisaic beliefs: "If a man has a pain in his throat, they may drop medicine into his mouth on the Sabbath, since there is doubt whether life is in danger, and whenever there is doubt whether life is in danger, this

5. Edward M. Cook, *Solving the Mysteries of the Dead Sea Scrolls: New Light on the Bible* (Grand Rapids: Zondervan, 1994), gives an absorbing account of the discovery that reads like a detective novel.

6. See, for example, *War* 2.8.2–13 (§§119–161); and Philo of Alexandria, *Quod omnis prober liber sit* 75–91.

Cave 4 at Qumran is the most photographed of the Dead Sea Scroll caves. Archaeologists discovered in it a large number of scrolls. (Courtesy of Michael Cosby)

overrides the Sabbath" (*Yoma* 8.6). By contrast, the Dead Sea sectarians would let an animal die before they would break their Sabbath rest: "No man shall assist a beast to give birth on the Sabbath day. And if it should fall into a cistern or pit, he shall not lift it out on the Sabbath."[7]

On occasion the Dead Sea Scrolls speak harshly against the "seekers of smooth things," those who make obedience to the law too easy. These people may include the Pharisees, whom the sectarians at Qumran considered too lenient in their keeping of Mosaic laws. In the hymns of the Dead Sea Scrolls, the founder of the sect, the **Teacher of Righteousness**, asserts,

> To the interpreters of error I have been an
> opponent,
>   [but a man of peace] to all those who see
>   true things.
> To all those who seek smooth things
>   I have been a spirit of zeal;
> like the sound of the roaring of many waters
>   so have [all] the deceivers thundered
>   against me;
>   [all] their thoughts were devilish
>   [schemings].
>   (*Hymn* 10)[8]

> I thank Thee, O Lord,
>   for Thou has [fastened] Thine eye
>   upon me.
> Thou has saved me from the zeal
>   of lying interpreters,
> and from the congregation of those
>   who seek smooth things.
>   (*Hymn* 8)

> Teachers of lies [have smoothed] Thy people
>   [with words],
>   and [false prophets] have led them astray;
> . . . .
> And they, teachers of lies and seers of
>   falsehood,
>   have schemed against me a devilish
>   scheme,
> to exchange the Law engraved on my heart
>   by Thee
>   for the smooth things (which they speak)
>   to Thy people.
> And they withhold from the thirsty the drink
>   of Knowledge.
>   (*Hymn* 12)

7. *Damascus Document* 11, in *The Complete Dead Sea Scrolls in English,* trans. Geza Vermes, rev. ed. (New York: Penguin Books, 2004), 142.

8. Translations from Vermes, *Dead Sea Scrolls in English*, 262, 264, 269.

If these criticisms refer to Pharisees, they provide an interesting balance to the normal Christian viewpoint that Pharisees were far too austere in their practices of obeying Mosaic laws (tithing table spices [Matt. 23:23] etc.). In the eyes of the Dead Sea sectarians, the Pharisees were much too liberal.

Psalms of Solomon: **Pharisees as Righteous Disciples**

A radically different view emerges from the ***Psalms of Solomon,*** a collection of poems written between 60 and 30 BCE by one or more Judeans who were estranged from the high priest and his followers in Jerusalem. The theology expressed in these psalms makes it most likely that Pharisees wrote them. Since the publication in 1891 of a commentary by Ryle and James on the *Psalms of Solomon,*[9] few have contested the belief that they are Pharisaic in origin. Although we may not with complete certainty ascribe the poems to Pharisees, we can use them with relative confidence.

The *Psalms of Solomon* reveal a strong belief that God is the sovereign Ruler not just over Israel but also over all the nations (e.g., 2.7–8, 32–36; 5.3–4; 17.3–4, 30); and as we saw in Josephus's writings, the Sadducees rejected this viewpoint. These psalms also express belief that God is a righteous Judge (e.g., 2.3–10, 13, 15–18, 36; 8.7–8, 23–26; 9.2–5), and that sinners will not live on after death but will experience eternal destruction. The righteous, on the other hand, will be raised from the dead and live forever.

> The sinner stumbles. . . . He falls . . . and he
>   will not get up.
> The destruction of the sinner is forever,
>   and he will not be remembered when
>   [God] looks after the righteous.
> This is the share of sinners forever,
>   but those who fear the Lord shall rise up to
>   eternal life,
>   and their life shall be in the Lord's light,
>   and it shall never end.
>   (3.9–12)

> And sinners shall perish forever in the day of
>   the Lord's judgment,
>   when God oversees the earth at his
>   judgment.
> But those who fear the Lord shall find mercy
>   in it
>   and shall live by their God's mercy;
>   but sinners shall perish for all time.
>   (15.12–13; see also 13.11; 14.3–6)[10]

The righteous are those who have true piety, including a trust that welcomes the Lord's chastisement, because through it one becomes more pious.

> Happy is the man whom the Lord remembers
>   with rebuking,
>   and protects from the evil way with a whip
>   that he may be cleansed from sin that it
>   may not increase.
> The one who prepares his back for the whip
>   shall be purified,
>   for the Lord is good to those who endure
>   discipline.
> For he will straighten the ways of the
>   righteous,
>   and will not bend [them] by discipline;
>   and the mercy of the Lord [is] upon those
>   who truly love him.
>   (10.1–3)

Such piety, however, does not exclude vitriolic hatred for enemies.

---

9. H. E. Ryle and M. R. James, *Psalmoi Solōmontos: Psalms of the Pharisees, Commonly called the Psalms of Solomon* (Cambridge: Cambridge University Press, 1891).

10. Translations taken from *The Old Testament Pseudepigrapha,* vol. 2, ed. James H. Charlesworth (Garden City, NY: Doubleday, 1985).

Lord, let his part be in disgrace before you;
    may he go out groaning and return
       cursing.
Lord, may his life be in pain and poverty and
    anxiety;
    may his sleep be painful and his awakening
       be anxious.
. . . .
May the flesh of those who try to impress
    people be scattered by wild animals,
and the bones of the criminals [lie] dishon-
    ored out in the sun.
Let crows peck out the eyes of the hypocrites.
                    (4.14–16, 19–20)

May God remove the lips of the criminals in
    confusion far from the innocent,
and [may] the bones of the slanderers be
    scattered far from those who fear the
    Lord.
May he destroy the slanderous tongue in
    flaming fire far from the devout.
                    (12.4–5)

The righteous ask God to keep them from sin (16.7) and to help them speak only the truth (16.9–10). Thus piety involves more than mere outward observance of the law of Moses; it includes a deep longing to be completely righteous before God—a sentiment that stands in stark contrast with the Gospel depictions of Pharisaic hypocrisy.

The righteous do not entirely lose their tendency to sin, however, and the *Psalms of Solomon* place a major emphasis on confessing sin, repenting, and appealing to the covenant mercies of God (e.g., 9.8–11; 16.11). The pious are those who remove from their homes and themselves all iniquity.

The righteous does not lightly esteem disci-
    pline from the Lord;
    his desire is [to be] always in the Lord's
    presence.
The righteous stumbles and proves the Lord
    right;
    he falls and watches for what God will do
    about him;
    he looks to where his salvation comes from.

The confidence of the righteous [comes] from
    God their savior;
    sin after sin does not visit the house of the
    righteous.
The righteous constantly searches his house,
    to remove his unintentional sins.
                    (3.4–7)

Yet there is no mention of atonement by sacrifice in these psalms, except for condemnation of defiled offerings by sinful Jews (2.2–5; 8.11–13; cf. 1.8). The "firstfruits of the lips from a pious and righteous heart" are the firstfruits offered to God (15.5).

The *Psalms of Solomon* reveal a balance between the concepts of the sovereignty of God and human free will that is quite similar to Josephus's description of the Pharisees (*Ant.* 13.172). People are responsible for their sins and are judged by God for them: "He did [this] to them according to their sins" (*Pss. Sol.* 2.7). Yet God does not give people strictly what they deserve, especially showing mercy to Israel (cf. 9.6–7). God chooses to establish a future messianic rule in Jerusalem (17.21–46).

The author (or authors) of the *Psalms of Solomon* had been politically involved in Jerusalem. He was well aware of the activities of the religious leaders in Jerusalem; he speaks of an immoral man on the religious council who sought to destroy him by deceitful lies and slanderous remarks (4.9–13; 12.1–5). There are some indications that he was among those who were forced to flee from Jerusalem into the desert to save their lives (17.11–18). Yet the psalms do not promote the belief espoused by the Dead Sea Scrolls Community that those who truly serve God should stay in the desert, away from the defilements of Jerusalem. The psalmist sees his place in society, not separated from it.

IS "TRADITION"
A FOUR-LETTER WORD?

Paul grew up a Pharisee, and before he encountered Christ he diligently studied and promoted this theological perspective. After he became a Christian, he did not completely abandon his heritage. Indeed, some of what he says in his letters reflects acceptance of certain beliefs of the Pharisees, while other comments fundamentally challenge central Pharisaic convictions. Understanding Paul's background helps us to recognize these endorsements and challenges. For our own sake, we do well to realize that some of the theological changes involved with following Christ cost Paul dearly, bringing charges of apostasy from his former friends. We may also experience rejection if we challenge what we have been taught by our own religious leaders.

On the positive side, Christian traditions are sources of spiritual heritage and blessing. They give us a sense of place. And in spite of internal diversity, each tradition shapes its members in distinct ways, instilling in them certain beliefs and approaches to interpreting the Bible. Consequently, to question our traditions may pose threats to our personal securiy.

As we study and reflect, we may realize that many aspects of our traditions are good and need to be maintained, whereas others are weak and need to be corrected—and some might even be fallacious. We need honesty and courage to change our beliefs when evidence shows them to be deficient. Such decisions can cause tension with friends and family members who might think we are betraying them. Sometimes asking questions can produce guilt, even giving a feeling that we are betraying God, because God and tradition are so closely linked at the emotional level.

We need to learn to live in creative tension with our traditions, drawing spiritual nurture from them and at the same time seeking to be a catalyst for positive change. Traditions, like human beings, always are in need of improvement.

GLOSSARY

Antiochus IV Epiphanes. Despotic Syrian ruler who sought to force hellenization on the Jewish people. His brutal treatment of the Jews led to the Maccabean Rebellion.

Dead Sea Scrolls. Important collection of ancient manuscripts discovered in jars hidden in caves near Qumran, on the northwest shore of the Dead Sea. These texts were apparently hidden by members of the Dead Sea Scrolls Community to protect them from destruction. The first manuscripts were found in 1947 by Bedouins who had no idea of their immense value.

Essenes. Ultrastrict sect of Jews who placed immense value on rigid observance of the laws of Moses. They considered the Pharisees to be rather lax in keeping the commandments. They emphasized sharing of their goods with other Essenes, and some were celibate. Most biblical scholars believe that the Dead Sea Scrolls Community was composed of Essenes.

Gamaliel. Prominent Pharisaic scribe in Jerusalem whom Acts 22:3 claims was Paul's teacher.

Exercise on the Beliefs of the Pharisees

From the information provided by Josephus, the New Testament, the Mishnah, the Dead Sea Scrolls, and the *Psalms of Solomon*, summarize the beliefs of the Pharisees in the following areas:

1. What did they consider inspired by God and therefore authoritative for determining their beliefs and practice?

2. What did they believe about God's sovereignty and human choice? (Does God direct all, or do people decide freely?)

3. What did they believe about how God deals with sin?

4. What did they believe about the meaning of being truly devoted to God?

5. What did they believe about the resurrection of the dead and final judgment?

6. What did they believe about ritual purity (fasting, washing of dishes, Sabbath observance, and so forth)?

Hasidim. Jewish zealots for the laws of Moses (in Hebrew *Hasidim* means "faithful ones"). Called Hasideans in 1 Maccabees 2:42, they formed the backbone of the Maccabean army, which fought for Israelite independence in the second century BCE.

Josephus. Important Jewish historian who was a contemporary of Paul. His works, including *Jewish War* and *Antiquities of the Jews*, are valuable for reconstructing historical events that occurred during the centuries leading up to the Christian era.

Mishnah. Written version of the oral traditions of the Pharisees. This authoritative collection of law and edifying stories was compiled under the leadership of Rabbi Judah around 200 CE. The Hebrew word *shanah* means "to repeat," and this term reflects the mode of instruction and learning practiced by Pharisaic scribes and their students. "Mishnah" means "repetition."

Pharisees. The name apparently means "separated ones" (derived from the Aramaic *peresh*). An important Jewish sect of Paul's day that placed considerable emphasis on faithfulness to the laws of Moses as interpreted by their more prominent members (famous scribes like Hillel and Shammai). Jesus came into sharp conflict with them over their oral traditions, called the "traditions of the elders." Paul was raised and educated as a Pharisee.

Psalms of Solomon. Collection of poems apparently written by Pharisees between 60 and 30 BCE. Valuable source for understanding Pharisaic piety.

Sadducees. Prominent Jewish sect in the first century. They consisted of priests, and their members included prominent members of the priestly aristocracy. They believed that only the Pentateuch was inspired by God and authoritative for laws governing life. They placed primary emphasis on human choice in their theological views; they did not believe in angels and demons or in afterlife.

Sanhedrin. The main ruling body of the Jews, about seventy influential elders consisting of both Sadducees and Pharisees, who convened in Jerusalem.

Talmud. Collection of authoritative Jewish writings that consists of a large number of expansions to the Mishnah. "Talmud" means "teaching" or "doctrine." It consists primarily of legal material (halakah) but also has a large number of edifying stories (haggadah). In form a page of the Talmud has a section of the Mishnah, plus a collection of interpretive comments in Aramaic by various rabbis (called Gemara = "interpretation"), plus haggadic materials. The **Jerusalem Talmud** was completed shortly after 400 CE. The larger and more influential **Babylonian Talmud** (6,000 pages long) was written during the fifth and sixth centuries.

Teacher of Righteousness. Founder of the Dead Sea Scrolls Community.

Zealots. Jewish revolutionaries who waged war against occupying Roman troops (according to Josephus).

FURTHER READING ON THE PHARISEES

Cohen, Shaye J. D. *From the Maccabees to the Mishnah.* Philadelphia: Westminster Press, 1987. Fairly readable book by a Jewish author. Many valuable insights.

Kern, Kathleen. *We Are the Pharisees.* Scottdale, PA: Herald Press, 1995. Explores misconceptions Christians have about Pharisees.

*Lohse, Eduard. *The New Testament Environment.* Nashville: Abingdon Press, 1976. Clearly written. Good place to start. Overview of history, philosophies, religious beliefs, and so forth.

Neusner, Jacob. *From Politics to Piety: The Emergence of Pharisaic Judaism.* Englewood Cliffs, NJ: Prentice-Hall, 1973. Deals with the problems of using ancient sources of information about the Pharisees for historical reconstruction. Readable.

———. *The Rabbinic Traditions about the Pharisees before 70.* 3 vols. Leiden: E. J. Brill, 1971. Technical. For more advanced research.

Neusner, Jacob, and Bruce D. Chilton, eds. *In Quest of the Historical Pharisees.* Waco, TX: Baylor University Press, 2007. Has 548 pages of historical analysis by various authors. For research.

Rivkin, Ellis. *A Hidden Revolution: The Pharisees' Search for the Kingdom Within.* Nashville: Abingdon Press, 1978. No footnotes or interaction with other scholarly views. Easy to read, but one needs background in the subject matter to be able to assess his views.

*Roetzel, Calvin J. *The World That Shaped the New Testament.* Rev. ed. Louisville, KY: Westminster John Knox Press, 2002. Written for undergraduate readers. Not technical. Good place to start.

Saldarini, Anthony J. *Pharisees, Scribes and Sadducees in Palestinian Society: A Sociological Approach.* Wilmington, DE: Michael Glazier, 1988. Scholarly work. Good research tool, with 325 pages.

Sanders, E. P. *Jewish Law from Jesus to the Mishnah.* Philadelphia: Trinity Press International, 1990. Scholarly work with 400 pages.

Schürer, Emil. *The History of the Jewish People in the Age of Jesus Christ.* Revised and edited by Geza Vermes and Fergus Millar. 2 vols. Edinburgh: T&T Clark, 1973. Revised edition of a monumental work. A standard work on the time period. Packed with information derived from coins, inscriptions, archaeological finds, texts, and so forth.

Stemberger, Günter. *Jewish Contemporaries of Jesus: Pharisees, Sadducees, Essenes.* Minneapolis: Fortress Press, 1995. Technical. More advanced resource for research.

Young, Brad H. *Paul, the Jewish Theologian: A Pharisee among Christians, Jews, and Gentiles.* Peabody, MA: Hendrickson Publishers, 1997. Emphasizes the Jewish roots of Paul's theology and argues that Paul did not distance himself from the law of Moses.

CHAPTER 3

Messianic Expectations Turned Upside Down

Saul of Tarsus grew up in a zealously religious Pharisaic home. From an early age he heard about the Messiah, and his fervent expectations about this coming ruler formed an important part of his belief system. What did he anticipate would happen when the Messiah appeared? In this chapter you will discover what first-century Jews expected to occur when this long-awaited agent of God arrived. As you will see, nothing in these Jewish predictions predisposed Saul to believe that Jesus was God's chosen Messiah. The focus of Jesus' lifestyle and ministry turned Saul's messianic expectations upside down, and at first he zealously resisted the Christian proclamation about Jesus the Christ.

He participated in the murder of Stephen, a Christian convert (Acts 7:54–8:1), and then he launched an effort to purge the region of Christians. "Saul was ravaging the church by entering house after house; dragging off both men and women, he committed them to prison" (8:3). Jewish communities dealt harshly with those whom they considered theologically aberrant. When someone departed from acceptable belief and practice, the elders could order that person beaten with a whip at the door of the synagogue. This means of bringing the straying one back to the true faith of the covenant community was called **synagogue discipline**. When Paul declares in 2 Corinthians 11:24, "Five times I have received from the Jews the forty lashes minus one," he is referring to synagogue discipline. Rabbinic literature specifies this practice as "forty lashes minus one for the mercy of God."

Deuteronomy 25:3 limits the number of lashes to forty, and later Jewish writers sought to provide explanations of this law and its proper use. Josephus states in *Antiquities* 4.8.21 (§238), "But for him that acts contrary to this law, let him be beaten with forty stripes, save one, by the public executioner; let him undergo this punishment, which is a most ignominious one for a free man, and this because he was such a slave to gain as to lay a blot on his own dignity." At the end of the second century, Mishnah *Makkoth* 3.1–9 specifies a number of offenses that warrant lashes, including illegal sexual relations and even tattooing. Later records also indicate that a scholar who deserved a synagogue ban because of his false teachings might receive the lesser penalty of lashes. The fact that Paul says he received five such beatings indicates that he did not give up his position in the Jewish community easily but persistently tried to convince audiences in the synagogues that Jesus was the Messiah. He paid dearly for his persistence.

Those who came under a synagogue ban were completely excluded from the Jewish community, losing all religious, economic, and educational contact. Given the deep attachment felt toward the synagogue, such a ban was a powerful deterrent against aberrant behavior or beliefs. And followers of Jesus felt its sting, as a first-century Jewish prayer reveals. The earliest Palestinian version of the Eighteen Benedictions, which was discovered in the **genizah** (storage room for old manuscripts) of an old synagogue in Cairo, contains a curse against Christian Jews. Benediction 12 reads, "May the Nazareans [Christians] and heretics perish in a moment, be blotted out of the book of life, and not be written with the just." Thus, at the end of the first century, cursing Christians was a standard part of the daily prayers of many Jewish people.

Wolfgang Schrage points out the development of such hostility in later Jewish writings.

> According to a saying of R. Tarphon (c. 100), heretics are worse than Gentiles and idolaters. The latter deny God without knowing Him, the former know Him but deny Him all the same. T. Shab., 13,5 (129). "One should not sell to them nor buy from them; one should have no dealings with them; one should not teach their sons a trade; one should not be healed by them whether in respect of property (slaves and cattle) or of person," T. Chul., 2, 21 (503). It is even forbidden to help heretics and apostates in danger; one should not pull them out of a pit but thrust them into it, T.BM, 2, 33 (375). They were excluded from the saving benefits of Israel and condemned to eternal perdition. "Heretics and apostates and traitors and freethinkers and deniers of the Torah and those who leave the ways of the community, . . . hell is barred behind them and they are judged in it for all generations (for ever)," T. Sanh., 13, 5 (434).[1]

Although these mandates were composed considerably later than the first century, they show the direction that Jewish hostility would take toward Jewish Christians. The early followers of Jesus experienced the larger Jewish community's distaste for their messianic beliefs, and Saul the Pharisee considered himself to be an agent of God's judgment against these heretics. After his conversion, however, Saul the Christian received severe beatings because others viewed him as apostate. He later received back what earlier he meted out.

1. W. Schrage, Ἀποσυνάγωγος [*aposynagōgos*], in *Theological Dictionary of the New Testament*, vol. 7, ed. G. Kittel and G. Friedrich (Grand Rapids: Wm. B. Eerdmans Publishing Co., 1971), 849.

Acts 9:1–22 recounts Saul's dramatic encounter with Jesus while he journeyed from Jerusalem northeastward to the city of Damascus, to arrest followers of Jesus and drag them back to Jerusalem for punishment. He was temporarily blinded by the encounter and was led to Damascus, where the Christians were obviously fearful of him. But Saul was baptized by a Christian named Ananias, and much to the chagrin of local Jews, he almost immediately began to proclaim the very faith that he previously sought to eradicate.

When some of the Jews at Damascus plotted to kill Saul, he returned to Jerusalem and sought to meet the leaders of the Christian movement. They were obviously reluctant to meet him, fearing a trap. But a follower of Jesus named Barnabas brought Saul to the apostles, and the former persecutor recounted his encounter with the risen Jesus. Shortly thereafter, Saul got into serious trouble in Jerusalem for preaching salvation in Jesus. So the apostles sent Saul back to his hometown of Tarsus, and things settled down quite a bit in Jerusalem once he was gone (9:26–31).

WANTED! MACHO MESSIAH

One of the major stumbling blocks to Saul's becoming a follower of Jesus Christ was what he believed about the person and role of the **Messiah**. Although we cannot know for sure the exact list of expectations he had, we have enough information about messianic beliefs of the time to reconstruct a fair approximation of what Saul the Pharisee believed the Messiah would be like. One of the best sources of pre-Christian messianic beliefs is the *Psalms of Solomon*, a collection of poems written in the first century BCE.

Psalms of Solomon 17 provides a vivid description of what the author believed the Messiah would come to accomplish, and this poem provides further evidence for why Saul found believing in Jesus as Messiah to be so difficult. Some of the expectations expressed in this poem differ strikingly from the career of Jesus of Nazareth. *Psalms of Solomon* 17 forcefully asserts that the Messiah will be a powerful monarch who will rule righteously.

Not only will he be a king from the line of David who will rule over Israel, but he will also "destroy the unrighteous rulers" and "purge Jerusalem" from the Gentiles, "who trample her to destruction" (17.21–22).[2] This poem states that the Messiah will drive the Gentiles out of Israel and will "smash the arrogance of sinners like a potter's jar," shattering them with an iron rod (17.23–24). He will gather Jews who are faithful to the laws of Moses and establish them in the land of Israel (17.26–28). He will purge Jerusalem from sin and establish it as his capital city, from which location he will righteously judge the entire world (17.30). People from other countries will come to behold the splendor of this righteous ruler, who is completely obedient to God. "He himself (will be) free from sin, (in order) to rule a great people" (17.36). And those faithful Jews who are fortunate enough to live to see Messiah's reign will be delivered from profane enemies and live under God's promised king (17.44–46).

2. Translations from *The Old Testament Pseudepigrapha*, ed. James H. Charlesworth, vol. 2 (Garden City, NY: Doubleday, 1985), 667–69.

THE LION OF JUDAH ROARS

Another good source of information about pre-Christian messianic beliefs is *1 Enoch*, an apocalypse popular among Jews in Saul's day. Written as if by Enoch (see Gen. 5:18–24), this document provides a more heavenly view of the Messiah. *First Enoch* 46.1 describes the Messiah as appearing with God and having a "face . . . like that of a human being" and a "countenance . . . full of grace like that of one among the holy angels."[3] In the story, an angel tells Enoch:

> This is the Son of Man, to whom belongs righteousness, and with whom righteousness dwells. . . . The Lord of the Spirits has chosen him, and he is destined to be victorious before the Lord of the Spirits in eternal uprightness. This Son of Man whom you have seen is the One who will remove the kings and the mighty ones from their comfortable seats and the strong ones from their thrones. He shall loosen the reins of the strong and crush the teeth of the sinners. He shall depose the kings from their thrones and kingdoms. (46.3–5)

This image of a conquering king goes beyond *Psalms of Solomon* 17, adding an element of heavenly stature and preexistence. "Even before the creation of the sun and the moon, before the creation of the stars" the Son of Man "was given a name in the presence of the Lord of the Spirits" (*1 Enoch* 48.3).

This heavenly figure is said to be "the light for the Gentiles," and "all those who dwell upon the earth shall fall and wor-

ship before him; they shall glorify, bless, and sing the name of the Lord of the Spirits" (48.4–5). The account adds, "For this purpose he became the Chosen One; he was concealed in the presence of (the Lord of the Spirits) prior to the creation of the world, for all eternity" (48.6). This magnificent "Elect One" has eternal glory, and "his power is unto all generations" (49.2–3). He is amazingly wise and strong, and to him is given the power to "judge the secret things" of human beings (49.4). Such expectations would not predispose Jews to view a carpenter from Nazareth as the Messiah.

In addition to the material from *1 Enoch*, **2 Esdras**, an apocalyptic document written as if by Ezra, contains further messianic predictions. This text is found in the Old Testament Apocrypha/Deuterocanon, and its first-century author's own expectations are delivered as an angel's interpretation of a vision given to Ezra.

> And as for the lion whom you saw rousing up out of the forest and roaring and speaking to the eagle [the symbol of imperial Rome] and reproving him for his unrighteousness, and as for all his words that you have heard, this is the Messiah whom the Most High has kept until the end of day, who will arise from the offspring of David, and will come and speak with them. He will denounce them for their ungodliness and for their wickedness. . . . For first he will bring them alive before his judgment seat, and when he has reproved them, then he will destroy them. But in mercy he will set free the remnant of my people, those who have been saved throughout my borders, and he will make them joyful until the end comes, the day of judgment, of which I spoke to you at the beginning. (12:31–34)

Some of what 2 Esdras says about the Messiah and the end time are unique.

3. Translations of *1 Enoch* are from *The Old Testament Pseudepigrapha*, ed. James H. Charlesworth, vol. 1 (Garden City, NY: Doubleday, 1983).

Near the northwest shore of the Dead Sea, Bedouin accidentally made one of the most significant archaeological finds of the twentieth century. They discovered Hebrew manuscripts that were a thousand years older than the oldest Hebrew manuscripts known to exist at that time. This stone jar recovered at Qumran contained some of the Dead Sea Scrolls. (Courtesy of Schøyen Collection, MS 1655/1)

For my son the Messiah shall be revealed with those who are with him, and those who remain shall rejoice four hundred years. After those years my son the Messiah shall die, and all who draw human breath. Then the world shall be turned back to primeval silence for seven days, as it was at the first beginnings, so that no one shall be left. After seven days the world that is not yet awake shall be roused, and that which is corruptible shall perish. The earth shall give up those who are asleep in it, and the dust those who rest there in silence; and the chambers shall give up the souls that have been committed to them. The Most High shall be revealed on the seat of judgment, and compassion shall pass away, and patience shall be withdrawn. Only judgment shall remain, truth shall stand, and faithfulness shall grow strong. Recompense shall follow, and the reward shall be manifested; righteous deeds shall awake, and unrighteous deeds shall not sleep. The pit of torment shall appear, and opposite it shall be the place of rest; and the furnace of hell shall be disclosed, and opposite it the paradise of delight. (7:28–36)

Such expectations of an exalted, heavenly figure who plays a role in the final judgment of humans would make it very difficult for Jews like Saul to believe that Jesus was Messiah.

WAS THAT ONE MESSIAH OR TWO?

Another significant source of information about messianic expectations is the Dead Sea Scrolls (DSS). A separatist community produced these scrolls and hid them in the many caves located near their dwellings by the northwest shore of the Dead Sea. The members of this group were **eschatological** in their orientation toward time. They believed that they were living in the last years of human history before the cataclysmic final events of the age (*eschaton* in

This ancient inkwell, discovered at Qumran near the Dead Sea in Israel, still contains carbon ink residues. The ink, made of lampblack and gum, is of the same type that is found on the Dead Sea Scrolls. (Courtesy of Schøyen Collection, MS 1655/2)

Greek means "last," and *eschatology* is the study of last things).

The Qumran sectarians fiercely condemned the larger Jewish culture of their day, and they eagerly anticipated the violent dawn of a messianic age in which rule according to their strict observance of Mosaic law would be enforced. The eschatological sect who produced the DSS apparently expected two Messiahs, one a priestly figure and the other a kingly figure ("the Messiahs of

Aaron and Israel" [1QS 9]).[4] In the years leading up to the appearance of the Messiahs, the men at Qumran believed that they were to follow the instructions given to them by their founding leader, whom they called The Teacher of Righteousness.

> The men of holiness . . . shall depart from none of the counsels of the Law to walk in the stubbornness of their hearts, but shall be ruled by the primitive precepts in which the men of the Community were first instructed until there shall come the Prophet and the Messiahs of Aaron and Israel. (1QS 9)

Another DSS called the *Damascus Document* (CD) sets the time of the Messiah's arrival at forty years after the death of the Teacher of Righteousness—a time frame that caused difficulties for the group after the forty years were over. Christians later experienced similar struggles when Jesus did not return to earth soon, as they expected he would.

One of the fervent hopes of eschatologically oriented groups such as the DSS sect was their expectation of a great **messianic banquet**. *Messianic Rule* (1QSa) describes how the messianic meal shall be conducted. This text explains that all the faithful congregation of Israel will gather together at the command of the Priest-Messiah. And then the warrior Messiah, the descendant of David, will come, "and the chiefs of the [clans of Israel] shall sit before him, [each] in the order of his dignity, according to [his

---

4. Translations of Dead Sea Scrolls are by Geza Vermes, *The Complete Dead Sea Scrolls in English*, rev. ed. (New York: Penguin Books, 2004). The titles of the scrolls follow a certain format. The initial number indicates the cave in which the scroll was found. This number is followed by "Q," designating Qumran, and then an abbreviation for the title of the scroll, and finally a Latin numeral for the section of the scroll being cited. See a translation of the DSS for further details.

place] in their camps and marches. And before them shall sit all the heads of [family of the congreg]ation, and the wise men of [the holy congregation,] each in the order of his dignity" (1QSa 2).[5] The passage goes on to explain how the Priest-Messiah will pronounce a blessing over the food and begin the great banquet. Then he will pass the food to the Messiah of Israel, and then it will be distributed to the rest of the congregation, each "in the order of his dignity."

A DSS called the *Blessings* (1QSb) focuses on the conquering power of the Messiah.

> [May you (Messiah) smite the peoples] with the might of your hand and ravage the earth with your sceptre; may you bring death to the ungodly with the breath of your lips! . . . May He make your horns of iron and your hooves of bronze; may you toss like a young bull [and trample the peoples] like the mire of the streets! . . . The rulers . . . [and all the kings of the] nations shall serve you. He (God) shall strengthen you with His holy Name and you shall be as a [lion; and you shall not lie down until you have devoured the] prey which naught shall deliver. (1QSb 5)

And a commentary on Genesis called *The Blessings of Jacob* interprets Genesis 49:10, "The scepter shall not depart from Judah, nor the ruler's staff from between his feet," as a reference to Messiah.

> Whenever Israel rules there shall [not] fail to be a descendant of David upon the throne. For the *ruler's staff* is the Covenant of kingship, [and the clans] of Israel are the *feet*, until the Messiah of Righteousness comes, the Branch of David. For to him and to his seed was granted the Covenant of kingship over his people for everlasting generations. (4QPBless)

5. The brackets found in this translation designate missing letters or words that the translator has inserted into the text. The scrolls are ancient and brittle, and some have numerous pieces broken out of them.

Messianic Position Available

Pretend that you are placing an advertisement in the employment section of a national magazine or a local newspaper. Drawing from the descriptions above, formulate your job description for the Messiah.

Similarly, a DSS commentary on Isaiah gives a messianic explanation for the meaning of Isaiah 11:1–3: "A shoot shall come out from the stump of Jesse, and a branch shall grow out of his roots . . .": "[Interpreted, this concerns the Branch] of David who shall arise at the end [of days]. . . . God will uphold him with [the spirit of might, and will give him] a throne of glory and a crown of [holiness]. . . . [He will put a sceptre] in his hand and he shall rule over all the [nations], . . . and his sword shall judge [all] the peoples" (4Q161).

HOW COULD A PHARISEE BELIEVE IN A CRUCIFIED MESSIAH?

The Pharisees of Saul's day were looking for a religious and political deliverer, God's elect one who would liberate Israel from Roman oppression. The Messiah would not only obey the laws of Moses; he would also teach Jews how to keep them in the way that pleases God. Both a zealot for the law and a mighty warrior, the Messiah would be God's anointed leader to purge all the lawless people from Israel and establish Jerusalem as the center of world power. Saul longed for this great leader to come and worked hard to prepare for his arrival. From his reading of the Scriptures and from reflecting on Pharisaic oral traditions, he never would have imagined a suffering, crucified Messiah.

Deuteronomy 21:22–23 states, "When someone is convicted of a crime punishable by death and is executed, and you hang him on a tree, his corpse must not remain all night upon the tree; you shall bury him that same day, for anyone hung on a tree is under God's curse." Jewish people of the first century applied this law to crucifixion, and therefore the idea of a crucified Messiah was abhorrent to them. For Saul to get past his initial rejection of the Christian belief that Christ's death was a divinely ordained sacrifice for remission of sins required a major shift in his convictions.

Christians proclaimed that God's promised Messiah was Jesus, the Galilean prophet who turned expectations upside down. Instead of endorsing Pharisaic oral traditions, Jesus challenged them. Instead of working with the law-abiding Jewish leaders, he spoke against them and called them hypocrites. And instead of driving out foreign oppressors, he was crucified by the Romans. Saul considered the proclamation that Jesus was the Christ to be complete nonsense; and as a result of his passionate devotion to the laws of Moses, he set about to destroy this new movement of Jesus' followers.

> ### Change Comes Hard
> To imagine the transition that Saul went through, think of what it would be like if someone told you that some of your most fundamental beliefs about Christ are wrong. What would it take to convince you that your beliefs are mistaken?

Thus, for Saul to make Christ the center of his life required a major reorientation. This zealot for the traditions of the Pharisees formerly focused his entire existence on obeying the laws of Moses as interpreted by Pharisaic oral tradition. To go from fanatically trying to stomp out the sect of the Christians to becoming one of its foremost missionaries is nothing short of remarkable. It is stunning to think that Saul—or Paul, as he was later called—would not only abandon the law as the orientating center of life but also preach to Gentiles that God accepts them without regard to circumcision and other covenant requirements.

The passages we have studied in this chapter help us to understand the radical reversal of the apostle's messianic expectations. The next chapter will provide a deeper appreciation of Paul's missionary efforts among the Gentiles. A great many of the people who responded to his proclamation of the gospel grew up with some quite different ideas about gods and goddesses and how humans are supposed to serve these deities. Once we know more about their Greek and Roman religions, we can better understand the difficulties that Paul faced as a missionary. Helping converts face the problems of social ostracism for their new faith was difficult enough. But a sometimes harder task was to keep them from bringing their former religious practices with them into the church.

GLOSSARY

1 Enoch. An important apocalyptic document that provides insight into apocalyptic thinking and literature. It was popular reading in Paul's day and contains information about messianic expectations of the time.

2 Esdras. An apocalyptic document found in the Old Testament Apocrypha/Deuterocanon that predicts the Messiah will reign for four hundred years and then die and be raised again to participate in the last judgment.

Eschatological. The Greek word for "last" is *eschaton*, and eschatology is the study of last things. Eschatological people think that they are living in the last times. Most early Christians were eschatological (e.g., Acts 3:24; 1 Cor. 10:11), believing that Christ would return from heaven in the near future and judge the world.

Genizah. A storage room for old manuscripts found in synagogues. Jews did not want to destroy old and worn documents,

so they stored them away in these hidden rooms. Some very important historical documents were found in the *genizah* of the old synagogue in Cairo.

Messiah. Term means "the Anointed One."

Messianic banquet. Great meal that many Jews believed the Messiah would invite the righteous to attend when he came in power.

Psalms of Solomon. Collection of poems apparently written by Pharisees between 60–30 BCE. Valuable source for understanding Pharisaic piety.

Synagogue discipline. Public beating with a whip of a Jewish person who was found guilty of some offense viewed by the synagogue elders as meriting such punishment. In 2 Corinthians 11:24, Paul states that he received such beatings (39 lashes) five times, presumably for his proclamation of Jesus as the Messiah.

FURTHER READING
ON MESSIANIC EXPECTATIONS

Charlesworth, James H., ed. *The Old Testament Pseudepigrapha*, 2 vols. Garden City, NY: Doubleday, 1983–85. Standard collection of translations of ancient texts. Important for research in primary sources.

*Cook, Edward M. *Solving the Mysteries of the Dead Sea Scrolls: New Light on the Bible.* Grand Rapids: Zondervan, 1994. Very interesting. Initially like a detective novel. Good basis for understanding the significance of the Dead Sea Scrolls.

Fitzmyer, Joseph A. *The Dead Sea Scrolls: Major Publications and Tools for Study.* Sources for Biblical Study 8. Missoula, MT: Scholars Press, 1977. Bibliographic guide.

Hengel, Martin. *Judaism and Hellenism.* 2 vols. Philadelphia: Fortress Press, 1974. Technical. Volume 1 is the text; volume 2 has the footnotes.

Horsley, Richard A. *Bandits, Prophets, and Messiahs: Popular Movements in the Time of Jesus.* Minneapolis: Winston Press, 1985. Focuses on the miserable lives of the Jewish common people of the first century: overtaxed by Romans, driven off their land by wealthy landowners, and so forth—pushed to armed rebellion.

Josephus, Flavius. *The Works of Josephus.* Translated by Joseph Whiston. Updated version. Peabody, MA: Hendrickson Publishers, 1987. Older translation of Josephus's works. Readily available and reasonably priced. Also available on the Internet.

Schürer, Emil. *The History of the Jewish People in the Age of Jesus Christ.* Rev. ed. Vol. 1. Edinburgh: T&T Clark, 1973. Revised edition of the standard work on the time period. Packed with technical information from ancient texts, coins, inscriptions, and so forth.

Tomasino, Anthony J. *Judaism before Jesus: The Ideas and Events That Shaped the New Testament World.* Downers Grove, IL: InterVarsity Press, 2003. Review of history leading up to Paul's time. The last chapter, "Oppression, Resistance, and Messianic Hopes," deals with Jewish messianic expectations.

Vermes, Geza, trans. *The Complete Dead Sea Scrolls in English,* rev. ed. New York: Penguin Books, 2004. Good translation of the DSS.

Wise, Michael, Martin Abegg Jr., and Edward Cook, trans. and commentary. *The Dead Sea Scrolls: A New Translation,* rev. ed. New York: HarperCollins, 2005. Good translation of the DSS.

CHAPTER 4

Greek and Roman Religions of Paul's Day

Fertility cults were common among ancient Mediterranean peoples, and their worship practices were popular. These cults played an important role in society, because people believed that certain gods and goddesses aided with the reproduction of animals, crops, and humans. Members of agricultural societies are acutely aware of how much life depends on successful crops and livestock breeding—far more than most folks today who buy their food in grocery stores. Many Mediterranean men in Paul's day worshiped fertility deities by having sex with cult prostitutes who were associated with particular temples, and their wives did not complain. They believed the deities for whom the cult prostitutes worked would look favorably on such actions and grant fertility to the men's wives, animals, and crops.

From a pious Jewish perspective such idolatrous activities were grossly immoral, but from a Gentile perspective they were part of being a good citizen. Early Christian missionaries like Paul faced the difficult task of convincing Gentile converts to Christianity to abandon their devotion to **fertility cults** and other religions and to devote themselves to Christ. But deeply ingrained habits die hard, and some lapsed into former practices. Many Jewish Christians insisted that the only way to ensure a high level of ethics and morality in the church was to demand that all Christians, whether Jews or Gentiles, obey the laws of Moses. Paul chose a different path and suffered much criticism for it.

In this chapter you will read quotations from ancient sources describing various religious beliefs and activities common among the Gentiles of Paul's day. Knowledge of these sometimes peculiar practices will increase your ability to understand Paul's Letters. Indeed, some statements in Paul's Letters make no sense unless you know something about the religions common among the Gentiles of his time. As an apostle to the Gentiles, he felt called by God to proclaim the gospel to people whose religious experience would seem shocking to most Christians today. Paul had to figure out ways to make the message of Christ understandable to those who worshiped idols and who often made little connection between religious experiences and moral living—at least morals by Jewish standards.

How did he do it? How did Paul reach these people whose backgrounds differed so drastically from his devout Pharisaic heritage? Paul's missionary success owed a great deal to four historical factors: Diaspora Judaism, Koine Greek, Pax Romana, and a religious climate of despair.

According to Acts, Paul understood himself as an apostle to the Gentiles; yet whenever he initially entered a town, he went first to the synagogue to preach to the Jews. In the first century, many more Jewish people lived outside of Judea than inside, so he had a potentially enormous audience. In virtually every city of any consequence, Jews lived in sufficient numbers to support the building of a synagogue. Thus, when Paul entered a town he immediately had much in common with people at the local synagogue. Jewish people, unlike average Greeks and Romans, understood what he meant by Messiah and God's covenant promises to Israel. However, most of the Jews to whom he spoke rejected his message and even drove him violently from their synagogues. Yet one particular group of Gentiles tended to listen eagerly to his message.

In speeches in Acts 13:16, 26, Paul addresses himself to Israelites and "others who fear God." The second group, the **God-fearers**, consisted of Gentiles who were attracted to the monotheism and higher standard of morality taught in the synagogues. They seem to have attended the synagogues to hear the teaching, but they balked at becoming **proselyte** Jews, which involved circumcision. Greeks and Romans viewed circumcision as a mutilation of the body, and few would be willing to undergo the painful operation or the social stigma that accompanied it. Therefore, when Paul proclaimed that *all* could become full members of the covenant people of God by placing their faith in Jesus Christ, without taking on the weight of the laws of Moses, many of the God-fearers responded positively to his message. Thus, Jews living dispersed around the Roman Empire (**Diaspora Judaism**) provided, by their presence and influence on Gentile society, an excellent source of contacts for Paul and his missionary companions.

KOINE GREEK
AND PAX ROMANA

Regardless of his audience, however, the pervasive use of **Koine Greek** allowed him to communicate with people in the regions where he traveled. One legacy of Alexander the Great's conquests was a common language (**lingua franca**) across what was

The Temple of Hephaistos at Athens, completed in 415 BCE, is the best preserved Greek temple in the area. Located on the northwest side of the *agora* (market area), it illustrates the architecture of the time period. Hephaistos (or Hephaestus) was the patron-god of metal workers. (Courtesy of Michael Cosby)

now the Roman Empire. Because people all over the Mediterranean world spoke a generic form of Greek, Paul had no need to learn local dialects before he could preach the good news about Jesus Christ.

Another factor that enhanced Paul's movements was the widespread peace, termed Pax Romana, imposed by the Roman legions. He could move with relative safety from region to region—at least more safely than he could without the soldiers' presence. Paul confronted bandits and other dangers, as his list of sufferings in 2 Corinthians 11 vividly illustrates: "in danger from rivers, danger from bandits, danger from my own people, danger from Gentiles, danger in the city, danger in the wilderness, danger at sea, danger from false brothers, . . . through many a sleepless night, hungry and thirsty, often without food, cold and naked" (11:26–27). His journeys, rigorous as they were, were largely possible due to the Pax Romana.

WHAT DOES YOUR HOROSCOPE SAY?

Another key component to Paul's missionary success was the *religious climate of despair* present everywhere in the Greco-Roman world of his time. Many Gentiles saw the world as an uncertain and dangerous place, full of devastating events that one might experience not because of doing anything evil but merely from being in the wrong place at the wrong time. So they commonly worshiped the goddess **Fate** (Greek *Tychē*) as a means of avoiding her devastating and capricious actions. Such worship took a variety of forms, as witnessed by the writings and statuary produced during the centuries surrounding Paul's time. By worshiping and serving Fate, some people sought to convince her not to harm them; some sought protection from Fate through worship of savior gods and goddesses; others looked to the stars for guidance; and many took a syncretistic approach, seeking help through astrology, mystery religions, and any other means available that they could afford.

As people observed what seemed to be random and chaotic events in their world, feelings of helplessness and hopelessness abounded. Yet as they gazed upon the stars, they saw order and not chaos in the heavens. They perceived such order as divine in nature, and many believed that the stars were deities. To be in touch with such divine order might bring more harmony to their own experience, or at least enable them to cope with life's hardships. The following quotation from Vettius Valens, who lived in the second century CE, provides insight into the perceived benefits of **astrology**. Notice, however, that Valens did not share the belief of many that knowledge of astrology would *change* events in a person's life.

> Fate has ordained as a rigid law for all people the inalterable consequences of their horoscope. She controls the myriad causes of good and evil. Furthermore, two self-begotten goddesses, Hope [*Elpis*] and Fate [*Tychē*], are her ministers who watch over these matters. Not only do they reign over life, but by deception and compulsion they make completely sure that all obey the law. Hope reveals herself to everyone in the consequences of what has been preordained, whether good and pleasant or dark and cruelly painful. She deceitfully exalts some only to cast them down later. Others she initially hurls down into obscurity only to exalt them later in great splendor. (AT)

Valens goes on to describe Fate as a flatterer who lures people into desiring and attempting things that they cannot have or accomplish. She deceives them, yet they fall for her enticements. Only those trained in astrology can handle such situations properly and not be enslaved to Fate or Hope.

Those who expend the effort necessary to interpret the future by the predictions of astrology will learn the truth and live in freedom from bondage. They ignore Fate and devalue Hope, and thereby lose their fear of death and live focused lives free of distractions. They courageously discipline their souls and refuse to get too excited over good fortune or too depressed over adversity. Rather, they learn to live contented lives focused on the present moment. They do not pine away for things they cannot have but endure with discipline what Fate decrees for them. As good soldiers of Fate, they place no value in either pleasures or penalties.

They know that people cannot by praying or offering sacrifices alter their destinies, which have been set from the beginning. We cannot choose a destiny that is in accord with our own wishes. We cannot stop what has been decreed for us by praying about it, and we cannot cause something to happen that is not decreed—no matter how much we pray about it. We are like actors on a stage, changing our masks in accordance with the poet's script, following the mandates of the written drama. Sometimes the script demands that we play the role of kings; sometimes it dictates that we play robbers. Sometimes we play peasants and common people; sometimes we play gods. Whatever role Fate demands that we play, we put on the appropriate mask and accept our part—whether we like it or not. (AT)

LAMPOONING SUPERSTITION

Although there was a widespread feeling of despair among people in the first century, most saw human choice playing a much larger role than did Valens. The following sarcastic description of a superstitious man by the Greek philosopher Theophrastus (ca. 370–288 BCE) is meant to be humorous. Yet it reflects the lengths to which some of the frightened common folk went to protect themselves.

> Superstition appears to be a kind of cowardice with respect to the divine. The superstitious man is the sort that will not leave for the day before

he washes his hands and sprinkles himself at the nine springs, and places in his mouth a bay leaf that he obtained near a temple. And if a cat crosses his path, he will not continue on his way until someone else passes along before him, or until he throws three stones across the street. And if he sees a snake in his house, if it is reddish, he calls upon Sabazius.[1] But if the snake is a sacred type, he immediately builds a shrine. And if he goes past one of the shiny stones that people set up at crossroads, he anoints it with oil from his flask, and he will not continue on his way until he gets down on his knees and worships it. And if a mouse chews a hole in his sack of grain, off he runs to a wizard [exēgētēs] to ask what to do. But if the wizard tells him to take the sack to a harness maker to be sewn up, he rejects this advice and chooses instead to protect himself from bad luck by conducting a ceremony of aversion.

The superstitious man continually purifies his house because he fears that the dreadful **Hecate**[2] has been attracted there. If he is walking about and hears an owl hoot, he becomes agitated and will not continue on his journey until he cries, "**Athena**,[3] protect me!" He refuses to step on a tomb or come near to a woman who is giving birth, because he wants to keep himself from pollution. Each month, on the fourth and seventh days, he obtains spiced wine for his family; and going out he also buys myrtle boughs, frankincense, and holy pictures. Upon returning, he spends the rest of the day offering sacrifices to the hermaphrodites[4] and placing garlands on them. Whenever he has a dream, he sprints to the diviners or the soothsayers or the dream interpreters, asking what he must do to appease a god or goddess.

And when he is to be initiated into the mysteries of Orpheus,[5] he goes to the priests every

month and takes his wife with him. But if his wife does not have the time, he takes the nurse and children. He is among those who constantly go to the seashore to cleanse themselves. And when he see one of those figures of Hecate at the crossroads, the kind that have garlic wreaths, he runs home to wash his head and he summons priestesses, whom he asks to purify him by parading around him with a squill[6] or a puppy. And if he sees a madman or a person with epilepsy, he trembles and spits into his bosom. (*Characters* 16, "Superstitiousness," AT)

This parody of the superstitious man by Theophrastus is funny because it ridicules actual practices. Tragically, we could do similar satires of many people in the world today. **Superstition** makes illogical connections between events of life and supposed supernatural causes. If a superstitious fellow wears his lucky socks for every basketball game, perhaps the only problem for others is that he may reek of foot stench after a while. But if the same guy believes that all sorts of things in his life happen because he either did or did not give some deity the proper offerings, he becomes a problem not only for himself but also for those around him.

HOW TO GET DIVINE GUIDANCE

Theophrastus's humorous depiction of the superstitious man going to an **oracle** for dream interpretation is actually based

---

1. Greek god associated with wine and fertility. Supposedly his father was Zeus, who came to his mother, Persephone, in the form of a snake. Some mystery rituals in honor of Sabazius involved the use of models of snakes.

2. Hecate was the fertility goddess and protectress of witches.

3. Athena was a warrior goddess who guarded the city. She protected civilized life, the work of craftsmen, and agriculture. She was also known as a goddess of wisdom. Her city was Athens, and she was associated with the owl—which is the association made by Theophrastus in his description of the superstitious man.

4. Probably eunuch priests of a particular goddess.

5. In Greek mythology, Orpheus was the greatest musician and poet. He was also said to be the founder

of the Orphic mystery religion. He married Euridice, a nymph, who died shortly after the wedding due to a snake bite. Orpheus was grief stricken and went to the underworld to retrieve her. By his sweet singing he convinced Hades, god of the underworld, to let Euridice return to the land of the living. Hades agreed, with the condition that Orpheus could not look back until he was above ground. However, just before reaching the surface of the ground, Orpheus glanced back, so Euridice was taken back down to the underworld.

6. A bulbous European plant that resembles an onion.

on a common religious approach taken by Greeks and Romans. Certain priests and priestesses, particularly those associated with the god Apollo, were trained to receive or discern messages from a deity for people seeking guidance. These religious guides, called oracles, obtained divine messages in a variety of ways, including observing the flights of birds and analyzing the entrails of sacrificial animals.

Some priestesses went into trancelike states by inhaling volcanic fumes or chewing on certain kinds of leaves, and then they spoke ecstatic messages that were interpreted by nearby priests. Such "divine" messages were usually written in hexameter verse, often using such cryptic language that one could interpret them in numerous ways. These messages were also called oracles. The most famous center for divine guidance among the Greeks was the oracle at Delphi. Popular demand for such utterances was so high that those involved in securing them played a serious role in the life of the people. The following quotation from Pausanias (second century CE) demonstrates how average people viewed oracles and why their popularity remained high. Pausanias describes the sanctuary of Amphiaraus, a human hero to whom the Greeks began to give divine honors.

> The Oropians have a spring near the temple, which they call the spring of Amphiaraus. They neither sacrifice in it nor use it for purification rituals or for hand washing. But whenever a man is healed of a disease by the oracle's efforts, their custom is to throw gold or silver coins into the spring; because they say that Amphiaraus took this route when he rose up after becoming a god. Iophon the Cnossian, one of their interpreters, produced oracular responses in hexameter verse, saying that Amphiaraus directed the Argives to go against Thebes. These verses were very attractive to the general public.

> None of the seers actually uttered oracles, except for those whom Apollo is said to have inspired of old. However, the seers were good at explaining dreams and interpreting the flights of birds and the entrails of sacrificial victims. And I think that Amphiaraus was particularly good at giving divination by dreams. To be sure, when he became a god, he set up a dream oracle. When anyone comes to consult Amphiaraus, he must first purify himself according to custom. This purification means he must sacrifice to the god. However, they sacrifice not only to Amphiaraus but also to all those whose names are on the altar. And after the purification rites, they sacrifice a ram, spread out its skin, and go to sleep on it, expecting a dream that will provide divine direction. (*Description of Greece* 1, *Attica*, 34.4–5, AT)

Elsewhere Pausanias explains how worshipers went about receiving a message from a deity named Trophonius. His description provides significant insight into a religious worldview of the first century. Notice carefully the rituals of preparation for receiving the divine message:

> Here is what takes place at the oracle: When a man has decided to descend to meet with Trophonius, he resides for a certain number of days in a building consecrated to the Good Spirit and to Fate [*Tychē*]. While living there, he purifies himself, using no hot water but bathing only in the river Herkyna. He must provide an abundance of meat from the sacrifices, because when a man goes down to Trophonius, he must offer sacrifices to Trophonius and to his children, and to Apollo, and to Kronos, and to Zeus the King, and to Hera the Charioteer, and to Demeter, whom they call Europa and whom they believe was the nurse of Trophonius. A soothsayer is present at each sacrifice, and he examines the entrails of the animals, inspecting them to predict whether or not Trophonius will kindly and graciously receive the person who is descending. The entrails of most sacrificial animals do not reveal the mind of Trophonius so clearly as does a ram. So on the night when each inquirer descends [for divine guidance], he sacrifices a ram at a pit, while calling upon Agamedes [Trophonius's brother]. And even if the previous sacrifices provided good omens, it does not matter unless the ram's entrails indi-

cate the same. But if they do agree, the man can descend full of hope.

The inquirer's descent happens like this: First, two boys of about thirteen years of age—both the sons of local citizens—take him to the river Hercyna, where they wash him and anoint him with oil. These boys are called guides, and they wash the descender; and as his attendants, they act as his servants. Afterward, priests take him, not straight to the oracle but to springs of water that are very close together. Here he must drink the Water of Forgetfulness, to clear his mind of all that he has been thinking. Later he drinks the Water of Memory, which enables him to remember what he saw during his descent. He looks at the statue that they say Daedalus[7] made, which the priests show only to those who descend to Trophonius. He gazes at it and worships it, prays, and then goes to the oracle while wearing a linen tunic tied with ribbons and wearing boots made in that region.

The oracle is located on the side of a mountain, above a sacred grove of trees. A circular platform of white marble surrounds it, whose circumference is about the size of a small threshing floor and whose height is just under two cubits (= three feet). Bronze posts with crossbars holding them together are embedded in this platform, with doors to pass through. Within this enclosure is a man-made chasm in the earth, not a natural one, but one skillfully constructed from a careful design. The structure is shaped like a large stone oven having a diameter, I would guess, of about four cubits [six feet] and a depth of hardly more than eight cubits [twelve feet]. Because there is no way to descend, when a man goes to Trophonius, they provide for him a narrow, light ladder. When he gets down, he finds a hole between the wall and the floor that is about two feet wide and one foot high. The man who is descending lies down on the ground, holding honey cakes in his hands. He pushes his feet into the opening and tries to get his knees into the hole. After his knees are in the hole, the rest of his body is immediately sucked in as if the current of a large and swift river dragged him down.

After those who descend have entered the shrine, they learn the future, but not always in one and the same way. While one may hear, another may see as well. When they return, they ascend through the same hole, feet first. . . .

When a man returns from Trophonius, the priests have him sit on the Chair of Memory, located not far from the shrine. They ask him about everything that he saw and learned during his experience. After extracting this information, they return him to his friends, who pick him up and carry him to the building where he lived before with the Good Spirit and Fate. At this point he is still terrified and hardly conscious of himself or his surroundings. Later his senses return, however, and he is able to think clearly again and even to laugh.

I am not merely writing hearsay from others. I have not only inquired of Trophonius myself, but I have also interviewed others who have done so. Whoever descends to Trophonius is required to dedicate a tablet on which is written all that he heard or saw. (*Guide to Greece* 9, *Boeotia*, 39.5–14, AT)

GO TO SLEEP AND GET HEALED

Most of the initiation rituals for cults like those of Amphiaraus and Trophonius were conducted at night, often involving peculiar procedures. But cult initiation rituals and efforts to learn the future were not the only nocturnal religious practices. People also went to temples to seek healing from the deities that they believed had power in this area, and most of the Greco-Roman miracle stories recount healings that occurred at night. Worshipers consulted different deities for different life events because they believed that gods and goddesses had distinct spheres of influence.

The principal god of healing was **Asclepius**, son of Apollo and a woman named Coronis. Apollo entrusted Asclepius's education to a centaur named Chiron, who trained him in medical arts, music, and prophecy. Asclepius named one of his daughters Hygeia (symbolic of health) and another Panacea (symbolic of healing). He taught his healing arts to his sons, who

---

7. Daedalus was, according to Greek legends, a craftsman of extraordinary ability.

established temples called Asclepieions, with orders of priests devoted to healing. Statues and paintings often depict Asclepius holding a staff with a serpent entwined around it. In fact, priests used nonpoisonous snakes in healing rituals, letting them crawl on the dormitory floors where patients slept. When people were healed, they were supposed to leave a small model of whatever body part was healed.

The following healing stories are from ancient votive tables discovered in the Asclepieion at Epidauros. I have added subtitles for my translations of each.

The Long-Suffering Mother

When Cleo had been pregnant for five years, she sought help from the god and slept in the holy place. Upon leaving the holy place, she bore a son, and immediately after his birth he bathed in the spring and walked around with his mother. The thankful mother inscribed upon her gift offering the following:

The god, not the greatness of the tablet, is wonderful!
For five years Cleo bore her burden beneath her heart,
But when she slept here, the god healed her.

The Doubting Man

A man whose fingers were paralyzed (all but one) came to the god, seeking help; but after reading the tablets displayed in the temple, he scoffed at the accounts of healings and ridiculed the inscriptions. But during his sleep he dreamed the following. He was playing with dice in the temple, and while he prepared to throw the dice, the god appeared to him, sprang upon his hand, and stretched out his fingers. While still dreaming, the man got up and opened and closed his fist, stretching out first one finger and then another. After the man stretched out all his fingers, the god asked him if he still continued to disbelieve the inscriptions in the temple; and he answered, "No." Then the god said, "Because you formerly refused to believe accounts that

are not unbelievable, from now on you will be known as 'the Doubter.'" The next morning, when the man came out, he was cured.

The Doubting Woman

An Athenian woman named Ambrosia was blind in one eye. She came seeking help from the god, but when she read in the temple the many accounts of people being cured, she mocked the records. She said, "I cannot believe that it is possible for lame and blind people to be cured merely by dreaming." But as she slept, she dreamed that the god came and promised to make her whole. But in return she had to present the following votive offering in the temple: a silver pig in memory of her stupidity. After stating this, he cut open her faulty eye and poured in a potion. The next morning, she left healed.

The Little Boy

A boy from Epidaurus named Euphanes suffered from kidney stone. When he slept in the temple, he dreamed that the god stood over him and asked, "If I make you well, what will you give me in return?" The boy answered, "Ten dice." Laughing, the god promised to relieve his sufferings. The next morning he left healed.

The Blind Man

A blind man came to the god, seeking help. His condition was so far advanced that his eye sockets were completely empty; only his eyelids remained. Some onlookers in the temple said that he was completely stupid for believing that he would ever see again, for there was nothing left of his eyes; only empty sockets remained. But in a dream he saw the god prepare a drug of some sort, open his eyelids, and pour the drug into the eye sockets. The next morning when he left the temple, he could see with both eyes.[8]

8. Inscriptions recorded by Emma J. and Ludwig Edelstein, *Asclepius: Collection and Interpretation of the Testimonies* (Baltimore: Johns Hopkins University Press, 1945); also documented by Panagiōtēs Kavvadias, *To hieron tou Asklēpiou en Epidaurō kai hē therapeia tōn asthenōn* (Athens: The Brothers Perrē, 1900). For ET of numerous inscriptions and texts, see *Hellenistic Religions: The Age of Syncreticism*, ed. F. C. Grant (New York: Bobbs-Merrill, 1953).

This ancient depiction of a Roman sacrificial scene is preserved on an altar at Pompeii. The man officiating the event stands just to the left of the small altar. In accordance with tradition, he has his garment pulled up over his head. Imagine how much blood they would drain out of an animal this size. (Courtesy of The VRoma Project [www.vroma.org])

WASHED IN THE BLOOD OF A BULL

The religious climate of despair in the first century increased the popularity of religious cults that promised deliverance from the evils that Fate inflicts on a person. These cults did not demand exclusive allegiance to their particular organizations; people could belong to a number of different mystery religions if they could afford the initiation fees. Each had its own unique induction ceremony and community secrets, which initiates were forbidden to share with outsiders. Consequently our knowledge of their mysteries is limited.

Some mystical rites were elaborately expensive, such as the *taurobolium*, in which a person was drenched by the blood of a bull while standing in a pit underneath the animal. A fourth-century Christian writer called Prudentius describes one of these ceremonies for the consecration of a high priest (*Peristephanon Liber* [*Crowns of Mar-*

tyrdom] 10.1010–1050).[9] He explains that workers dug a pit into the earth, and the priest descended into it. The workers constructed a wooden platform over the pit and drilled many holes through the wood to provide openings for the bull's blood. Then other priests led a bull draped with flowers to the platform. There they took a sacred spear and cut open the bull's chest so that large quantities of blood gushed onto the boards and through the holes, flowing down onto the high priest below. The priest was completely drenched by the blood, and he threw back his head and reveled as the gore splashed onto him. When all the blood had been drained from the bull, the priest emerged dripping from the pit and paraded in front of the onlookers.

9. The Latin text and ET may be read in *Prudentius*, vol. 2, trans. H. J. Thomson, LCL (Cambridge, MA: Harvard University Press, 1953), 295–99. Other translations of this text are also available on various Web sites.

People who experienced these blood-baths were said to be *reborn* through the blood of the bull. The following inscription records this event for an esteemed man.

> To the Great Gods, to the Mother of the Gods, and to Attis: the honorable Sextilius Agesilaus Aedesius, the worthy Solicitor in the African court, Imperial Councilor, President of the Supreme Commission on Petitions and Investigations, Head of the Chancellery, Captain of the Prefects in Spain in all the most important matters, Father of Fathers of the Invincible Sun God Mithras, Hierophant[10] of Hecate, Chief Shepherd of Dionysus, reborn unto eternity through the sacrifice of a bull and a ram—[this man] has dedicated the altar, on the Ides of August, while Lords Valens, for the fifth time, and Valentinian the younger, the Augusti, were consuls. (An inscription found in Rome and dated August 13, 376 C.E.)[11]

PLEASING A GOD BY SELF-CASTRATION OR SACRIFICING YOUR CHILDREN

The rather gruesome spectacle of a man being drenched with the blood of a bull, believing that he thereby gained the favor of a god, illustrates common religious views held in Paul's time. Some of the priests identified with particular mystery cults participated in violent rituals. Lucian's account of religion in Syria (second century CE), for example, provides fascinating insight into the sometimes frenzied nature of religious acts and the debased depths that sacrificial devotion can reach.

> And during certain days the multitude assembles in the temple, and many Galli, the religious men that I previously spoke of, perform ceremonies there. They cut their arms and

10. One who interprets sacred mysteries.
11. Translation by Grant, *Hellenistic Religions*, 147.

beat each other's backs. And many who stand around play flutes, and many beat drums, and others sing holy and inspired songs. This happens outside the temple, and those who participate do not enter the temple.

> In these days also men become Galli. For when the others play flutes and perform orgies, the frenzy seizes many of them; and many who came merely to watch get caught up in the same frenzy. And I will describe what they do. The youth who is thus possessed casts off his clothes and goes into the middle of the crowd, crying with a loud voice, and picks up one of the swords which I suppose has been standing there for many years. And taking the sword at once he castrates himself and then runs through the city, holding his testicles in his hands. And into whatever house he chooses, he casts them, and from that house he takes female ornaments and clothing. This they do during their castration ceremonies. (*The Syrian Goddess* 50–51, AT)

Lucian goes on to describe various kinds of sacrifice offered by the Syrians, and then he recounts a truly tragic dimension to the religion of the area.

> There is also another manner of sacrifice. They drape their animal victims with garlands and throw them down from the heights at the entrance of the temple. When they hit the pavement, they die. And some men hurl down their own children in this place, but not like they do their cattle. They put them in a sack and sew the top shut, and as they throw them down, they say that these are not children but cattle. (*The Syrian Goddess* 58–59, AT)

MAKING MONEY BY SELF-FLAGELLATION

In a humorous novel called *The Golden Ass*, written by an ancient Roman author named Lucius Apuleius, there is an interesting description of a frenzied dance performed by mystery religion priests. Notice the monetary motivation behind the self-inflicted torture of these transvestites:

On the following day I saw the priests dressed in a variety of colors, their faces hideously smudged with paint and their eyes smeared with color, with turbans on their heads, saffron-colored cloaks, and silk and linen garments. Some wore white tunics painted with purple stripes that pointed every direction like spears, and belts around their waists, and they wore yellow shoes on their feet. They dressed the goddess [the idol of **Isis**] in a silk robe. . . . Then they set forth with their arms bare to their shoulders, carrying with them large swords and mighty axes, shouting and dancing like madmen to the sound of the pipe. After we had passed many small villages, we had the good fortune of coming to a certain rich man's house. As soon as they entered his place, they began to howl in great discord and scurried about here and there, as though they were crazy. They twirled feverishly with wild motions with their feet and heads. They bent down their necks and spun round so that their hair flew out in a circle. They even bit their own flesh. Finally, every one took his two-edged knife and cut his arms in various places.

Meanwhile one priest raved more insanely than the rest. Many deep sighs arose as from the bottom of his heart, as though a divine spirit possessed him, and he pretended to be injured and to swoon. (As if, indeed, the presence of the gods did not tend to make men better than before, but weak and sickly.) Yet notice how by divine providence he received a just and worthy reward. After he seemed to return to his senses, he shouted violent prophesies, devised and manufactured a great lie, and incessantly reproached and denounced himself, declaring that he had displeased the goddess by offending the order of their holy religion. Therefore, he prayed that he might inflict the just penalty upon himself. And then he grabbed a whip, the kind that these eunuch priests seem always to carry, having twisted knots and wool tassels, and strung with sheep's knucklebones. With these knotted thongs he brutally whipped his own body. He was able to endure the blows amazingly well.

The ground grew wet and stained with the blood of these effeminates as it squirted profusely from the sword cuts and the blows of the scourge. . . . After they at last grew weary, or at least weary of torturing themselves, they stopped this bloody business. And they began to receive their reward from the inhabitants, placing into the bosoms copper coins, and silver as well, which the crowd eagerly offered, together with containers of wine, milk, cheese, flour, and wheat. (*The Golden Ass* 8.27–28, AT)

ISIS: SAVIOR GODDESS WITH MANY NAMES

The most detailed account of an initiation ceremony into a mystery religion comes from the same adventure novel, **The Golden Ass** (Greek title *Metamorphoses*). The book is written in prose and is one of the earliest novels in history. In this story a young man named Lucius is changed into a golden-colored donkey when his curiosity causes him to dabble in magic. As a donkey/ass, he suffers many misfortunes during the tale, and in the end he regains his human form through the gracious savior goddess Isis. He has a vision of this goddess while asleep, and he observes her breathtaking beauty as she emerges out of the sea. Her gracious words to Lucius reveal that she is worshiped by people in many different countries, who call her a variety of different names. With her divine voice she says to him:

Behold, Lucius, I have come. Your weeping and prayers moved me to save you. I am the mother of all, mistress and governess of all the elements, first offspring of the world, chief of divine powers, queen of the dead, paramount of those who dwell in the heavens, in whom alone are combined all the characteristics of the gods and goddesses. By my will I reign over the planets in the heaven, the wholesome winds of the seas, and the sorrowful silences of the underworld. Throughout the entire world my deity is adored in various ways with various customs, and by many names.

The Phrygians, firstborn of all humans, call me the Mother of the gods, she who resides at Pessinus. The Athenians, who are sprung from their own soil, call me Cecropian Minerva. The Cyprians, who are circled by the sea, call me Paphian Venus. The Cretans, who carry arrows, call me Diana Dictynna. The Sicilians, who speak three languages, call me infernal Proserpine. The Eleusinians call me their ancient goddess Ceres. Some call me Juno, others Bellona, others Hecate, others Rhamnusia. But the Ethiopians, on whom shine the first rays of the morning sun, and the Egyptians, who are masterful in ancient lore, honor me with proper ceremonies and call me by my true name, Isis the Queen. (*The Golden Ass* 11.4–5, AT)

Notice that Isis does not mind various peoples calling her by different names; she is mainly concerned that she receives worship, regardless of what name the people use.

As the story proceeds, Isis explains to Lucius that he will regain his human form only if he goes to her local priests and follows certain directions. He does so, and after the transformation occurs, one of these priests explains to Lucius how Isis can save him from the capricious acts of Fate. The priest's exhortation is extremely important for understanding how many people of Paul's day perceived the benefits of being initiated into a mystery religion:

> O friend Lucius, after enduring so many labors and escaping so many tempests of Fate, you have now come at length to the port and haven of rest and mercy. . . . But however much blind Fate tormented you with diverse dangers, now by her thoughtless malice she has brought you to this present religious bliss. Let Fate go somewhere else and fume with fury. Let her find someone else to persecute. Fate has no power over those who have dedicated their lives to serve the majesty of our goddess. . . . Understand that you are now safe under the protection of that fate who is not blind but can see. By her clear light she illuminates the other gods. . . . Let those who are not devoted to the goddess see and acknowledge their error. [Let them say,] "Behold Lucius, liberated from his former, terrible miseries by the providence of the goddess Isis, and rejoice and triumph over his fate." And so that you may live more safe and secure, join this sacred order . . . and dedicate your mind to obey our religion. . . . For when you begin to serve and to honor the goddess, then you will understand more completely the fruit of your liberty. (*The Golden Ass* 11.15, AT)

INITIATION INTO A MYSTERY RELIGION

After his transformation, Lucius deeply desires to be initiated into the mysteries of Isis and become her devoted follower. In response to his prayers, Isis appears to him at night and gives clear commands for his initiation. She even specifies how much it will cost Lucius, explaining what he needs to purchase. In addition, she states that her high priest Mithras will administer the secret rites to Lucius, explaining that their two destinies are closely bound by the ordering of the planets (note the syncretism here with astrology). The following account of his preparation for the mysteries of Isis and initiation into them is extremely significant for giving us a window into the secretive world of ancient mystery cults. Note the details carefully.

> When I heard these and other instructions from the goddess, I felt exhilarated and arose before sunrise in order to go speak with the high priest. I fortunately spotted him just as he left his bedchamber. I greeted him and decided to be bold with my request to be initiated, now that the goddess had indicated it was time. However, as soon as he saw me, he spoke before I had a chance, saying, "O Lucius, I now know that you are most happy and blessed, because our great goddess mercifully extends her favor to you. Why are you idly standing there? What's the delay? The day you have earnestly longed and prayed for has come. The goddess of many names divinely commands that by my own hands you will be initiated into the secret orders of our holy religion." Then the old man took me by the hand and led me gently to the gate of the enormous temple, performed a solemn ritual, and then opened the gate. After the morning sacrifice was offered, out of a secret place in the temple he brought certain books that were written with undecipherable letters. (*The Golden Ass* 11.22–23, AT)

Lucius gives a vague description of these letters and then continues on with the rest of the initiation procedure:

I gave directions to some of my companions to purchase with liberality whatever was needed, and I paid for some of it myself. And now that the priest knew that the time had come, he conducted me to the nearest baths, accompanied by the rest of the religiously minded. When I entered the bath, he asked the gods to pardon me; then he washed me and purified me with pure water according to their custom. After this, when the day was two-thirds over, he led me back again to the temple, and he presented me at the feet of the goddess. There he privately entrusted certain secret information to me, which is unlawful for me to recount. Then openly, before all who were gathered around us, he ordered me to fast for ten consecutive days. I was not to eat any meat or drink any wine during this time. I carefully observed all these requirements.

At long last the day came for the sacrifice of dedication; and when the sun descended and evening came, a crowd of priests came from the whole surrounding area. According to their ancient tradition, they offered many gifts and presents to me. After this they commanded all those who were not initiated into Isis to leave. Then they placed upon me a new linen robe; the priest took me by the hand and led me to the most secret and most sacred part of the temple.

Perhaps your curiosity is strong, my studious reader, and you want to insist on knowing what was said and done there. Please understand that I would describe it if it were legal for me to do so, and you would learn it all if it were legal for you to hear. But my tongue and your ear would suffer the penalty for such rash curiosity. However, I will torment you no longer because some of your interest might be due to devout longings for religious devotion. Listen, therefore, and believe my message to be true. You will understand that I came near to hades, to the very gates of Proserpine [i.e., the underworld]. And after I was dragged through all the elements, I returned to my proper place. About midnight I saw the sun shining brightly. And I saw the celestial gods and the gods of the underworld, and I approached them and worshiped them. . . . I will only add a few more things that can be related to the uninitiated without incurring guilt.

When morning arrived and the solemn rites were completed, I came forth dressed in twelve gowns, which have religious significance for the initiate. I am not forbidden to speak of this clothing, even though it is most holy, because many people saw me wearing it after my initiation. I was made to stand on a platform in the middle of the temple, before the statue of the goddess, dressed in a linen robe. I was stunning in this garment, which was richly embroidered with flowers. A precious cape was attached at my shoulders and hung down my back all the way to the ground, and it was decorated with animal figures constructed with different colors. The cape had Indian dragons, griffins from the far north, and creatures like birds, but not of this world. Priests of Isis call this cape the Olympian stole.

In my right hand I carried a burning torch, and I had a garland of flowers around my head, with white palm leaves spiking out in every direction like rays of the sun. Thus, I was adorned like the sun and stood on the platform, resembling an image of a god. And when the curtains were drawn aside, people crowded around to stare at me. (*The Golden Ass* 11.23–24, AT)

At the end of his initiation, Lucius is lavishly dressed like a god and presented like an idol before the people. His identity has been merged into that of Isis. He is now her loyal follower. Paul's Gentile converts were well aware of the religious beliefs presented in the initiation of Lucius. Later we will ponder how such stories might have shaped their understanding of Paul's teaching that, by being baptized into Christ, a believer becomes one with Christ.

PRAISING ISIS AND ZEUS

The psychological intensity of a secret initiation into the mysteries of Isis in the dead of night brought the initiate into a powerful attachment to the deity. Furthermore, the community of other initiates supported this commitment. Together they formed a

Hymn by John Wesley (1739)

O for a thousand tongues to sing
My great Redeemer's praise,
The glories of my God and King,
The triumphs of His grace!

My gracious Master and my God,
Assist me to proclaim,
To spread through all the earth abroad
The honors of Thy name.

Jesus! the name that charms our fears,
That bids our sorrows cease;
'Tis music in the sinner's ears,
'Tis life, and health, and peace.

He breaks the power of canceled sin,
He sets the prisoner free;
His blood can make the foulest clean,
His blood availed for me.

He speaks, and, listening to His voice,
New life the dead receive,
The mournful, broken hearts rejoice,
The humble poor believe.

Hear Him, ye deaf; His praise, ye dumb,
Your loosened tongues employ;
Ye blind, behold your Savior come,
And leap, ye lame, for joy.

society with its own web of relationships. Lucius experienced a type of conversion, which is evident in the expressions of praise and thankfulness contained in the following paragraphs. Pay special attention to the attachment of Lucius to the priest who initiated him. It will be important background material for understanding the schisms in the church at Corinth (1 Cor. 1:10–17).

After his initiation he celebrated three days of feasting with the others, and then he remained a while longer, basking in the pleasure of being near to the image of Isis.

> My benefits from the goddess were more than I could ever repay. But at length she admonished me that it was time to go home. So I gave my sincerest thanks; and although they were inadequate to express my debt to her, they were quite sincere and to the best of my ability. My attachment to the goddess was so powerful that I could hardly be persuaded to break the chains of my devotion and begin my homeward journey. Before leaving I came into her presence and fell prostrate before her image and wiped her feet with my face. I found it difficult to speak because of my emotion and my tears, and my speech was interrupted by sighing and weeping. Nevertheless, I said something like this:
>
> O holy and blessed Lady, the eternal guardian of human beings, who by your abundance and grace you nourish and provide for all the world. Like a loving mother you care for the miserable and the adversities they suffered. You sleep neither at night nor during the day, but constantly watch over and bless people, whether they are on land or at sea. You are she who drives away all the storms of life by stretching out your right hand to help.
>
> You unweave even the inextricable and entangled web of Fate. You hold back the harmful courses of the stars. The celestial gods honor you; the gods of the underworld revere you. You give light to the sun and you control the turning spheres of heaven. You trample the power of the underworld. To your power the stars respond, the seasons change for you, the gods rejoice in you, and the elements serve you. The winds blow at your command, the clouds bring rain on the earth, the seeds sprout, and the fruits grow. Before your majesty, the birds in the sky, the beasts in the mountains, the snakes in the ground, and the monsters of the deep tremble.
>
> I am incapable of praising you adequately, and my wealth is inadequate to offer sufficient sacrifices. My lips cannot express with ample

Language of Praise

Note the similarities that the hymn of praise to Zeus have with expressions of praise to God in Christian hymnbooks, such as the following song written in 1876 by Walter C. Smith:

Immortal, invisible, God only wise,
In light inaccessible, hid from our eyes,
Most blessed, most glorious, the Ancient of Days,
Almighty, victorious, thy great name we praise.

Unresting, unhasting, and silent as light,
Nor wanting, nor wasting, thou rulest in might;
Thy justice, like mountains, high soaring above
Thy clouds, which are fountains of goodness and love.

To all, life thou givest, to both great and small;
In all life thou livest, the true life of all;
We blossom and flourish as leaves on the tree,
And wither and perish, but naught changeth thee.

Great Father of glory, pure Father of light,
Thine angels adore thee, all veiling their sight;
All laud we would render; O help us to see
'Tis only the splendor of light hideth thee.

eloquence what your majesty deserves—not even if I had a thousand mouths with a thousand tongues that were able to continue forever without tiring. Nevertheless, as a devout person who has limited ability, I will do what I can. Forever I will treasure your divine image in my memory; forever I will hold your holy deity within my heart.

After I finished my speech to the goddess, I went to embrace Mithras, the great priest who was now my spiritual father. Hanging upon his neck and giving him many a kiss, I asked for his forgiveness, because I was not able to repay him for all the good that he had done for me. But after numerous words of thanks and many a tearful farewell, I at last departed by the shortest route for home, to see my parents and my friends from whom I had been separated so long. And after a short while, exhorted on by

the goddess, I pressed on toward Rome. (*The Golden Ass* 11.25–26, AT)

Such expressions of praise are not uncommon in the pious literature of antiquity. Note the exalted praise of Zeus in the following hymn, credited to Ceanthes (ca. 330–ca. 230 BCE).

Most glorious of immortals, Zeus
The many-named, almighty evermore,
Nature's great Sovereign, ruling all by law—

Hail to thee! On thee 'tis meet and right
That mortals everywhere should call.
From thee was our begetting; ours alone
Of all that live and move upon the earth
the lot to bear God's likeness.
Thee will I ever chant, thy power praise!

For thee this whole vast cosmos, wheeling
    round
The earth, obeys, and where thou leadest
It follows, ruled willingly by thee.
In thy unconquerable hands thou holdest fast,
Ready prepared, that two-tined flaming blast,
The ever-living thunderbolt.
. . . .
Zeus, thou giver of every gift,
Who dwellest within the dark clouds, wielding
    still
The flashing stroke of lightning, save, we pray,
Thy children from this boundless misery.

Scatter, O Father, the darkness from their souls,
Grant them to find true understanding—
On which relying thou justly rulest all—
While we, thus honored, in turn will honor thee,
Hymning thy works forever, as is meet
For mortals, while no greater right
Belongs even to the gods than evermore
Justly to praise the universal law![12]

                            (via Stobaeus, *Eclogae* 1.1.12)

MYSTERIOUS ECSTASY

The Gentiles to whom Paul preached were quite familiar with various forms of **ecstasy** related to the worship of mystery deities in particular. In an ecstatic state, the worshiper experiences heightened sensory perceptions, sometimes resulting in visionary experiences. Ecstasy finds expression in a large number of religious traditions, including Christianity and Islam, and allows the ecstatic to feel a sense of union with the divine. Ancient mystery religions provided worshipers with a more personal relationship with a god or goddess, and many who found philosophical expressions of belief to be too stilted and sterile welcomed these personal experiences.

The Neoplatonist philosopher Iamblichus, who was born in Syria about 250 CE, provides an excellent description of the effects of ecstasy. He explains that when people are possessed by a god, they experience a kind of ecstasy that enables them not to be burned, although they have fire applied to them. He claims that the god who breathes within them either prevents them from being burned or causes them not to feel the pain. Furthermore, he says that people experiencing ecstasy sometimes have knives thrust through their flesh, or have their backs sliced with hatchets, yet do not feel the pain. Because the god sustains them, they might pass through fire without being burned, or they might walk barefooted over snow or on hot coals. According to Iamblichus, the fact that they are unaware of their actions shows that they are possessed by a divine life filling them and living in them.[13]

Iamblichus further explains that there are different kinds of divine possession and therefore different manifestations of divine spirits awakening within people. He calls this divine seizure and states that a person may be entirely possessed by a god (an experience of the highest level of power), become absorbed into the god (experience of middle power), or merely cooperate with the deity (experience of lowest power). Sometimes the soul is completely separated from the body; sometimes it remains connected to the body; and sometimes the person's entire nature is controlled by the deity. The manifestations of divine possession may include movement of the person's body parts, or complete relaxation, or divinely inspired singing and dancing.

---

12. Translation from ibid., 152–54.

13. For an ET of Iamblichus's account, see ibid., 173–74.

Iamblichus claims that the bodies of some divinely controlled individuals have been seen to rise into the air and move about; and they have been heard to utter speech in different languages and with different sounding voices.

Such descriptions probably sound eerily similar to what you have heard about some modern religious experiences. When we study 1 Corinthians and examine the way some of the Christians in Corinth emphasized ecstatic states, remember the material presented in this chapter on Gentile religions. As you imagine a group of new Christians bringing to their worship services some of the concepts learned from mystery religions, you will better understand what Paul had to address in his letters to Corinth.

FACTORS FOR SUCCESS

The quotations from ancient literature in this chapter increase our awareness of the diversity of religious beliefs and practices of Gentiles in Paul's day. Imagine being a missionary among people who held these beliefs, seeking both to convince them to embrace the good news about Jesus Christ and to lead them away from their polytheistic worldview. The Gentiles' lives were based on understandings of the divine that they shared with their family, friends, and colleagues; these convictions erected huge obstacles to their becoming Christians. Their family positions and economic livelihood would be placed at risk if they abandoned their beliefs and followed Jesus. They would be considered a hazard to the safety of the community because the city's patron deity might be offended if not receiving proper worship. Fellow citizens would place intense psychological pressure on them not to follow Jesus exclusively.

Yet in spite of these major problems, Paul's missionary efforts succeeded. Many Gentiles became Christians. In the following chapter on the book of Acts, you will follow Paul's three missionary journeys and notice how Jews and Gentiles responded to his preaching. You will read about the Holy Spirit leading and empowering Paul and the other missionaries, and you will see a few accounts of the beliefs of Gentiles that will remind you of those described above. As you study the stories in Acts, remember the four historical factors that greatly enhanced Paul's missionary work: Diaspora Judaism, Koine Greek, Pax Romana, and a religious climate of despair among the Gentiles.

Wherever Paul traveled, he could readily communicate with local inhabitants of an area, and the Roman road system made reaching these places possible with relative safety. When he arrived, he would find some measure of positive response initially among the God-fearers in particular. And the religious climate of despair so prevalent in the Greco-Roman world made people eager to hear a message of hope, of deliverance from the power of Fate and other deities who might want to harm them. But the downside of the Gentile response to the gospel is that they brought with them into the church many of their superstitious beliefs, immoral practices, and ideas about God. As we will readily see when studying Paul's Letters, he had many difficulties in trying to correct the pagan beliefs and practices of his converts.

GLOSSARY

Asclepius. The principal Greek god of healing—the son of Apollo and a woman named Coronis. Asclepius was educated by a centaur named Chiron, who trained him in medical arts, music, and prophecy. Statues and paintings often depict Asclepius holding a staff with a serpent entwined around it.

Astrology. Study of the stars in an attempt to know how they influence the lives of people on earth. Many in the first-century Mediterranean world studied astronomy/astrology, seeking to find order in the seemingly chaotic events of life. The practice of connecting earthly events with movements in the heavens apparently began in Babylon and was considered to be a scholarly enterprise.

Athena. Athena was a warrior goddess who guarded Athens. She protected civilized life, the work of craftsmen, and agriculture. She was also known as a goddess of wisdom, and she was associated with the owl.

Diaspora Judaism. In the first century, more Jews lived outside of Palestine than in Palestine. These Jews were considered to be part of the Dispersion, or Diaspora Jews. Their many synagogues provided ready places for Paul to begin his evangelistic efforts when he first entered a city.

Ecstasy. An ecstatic state in which the worshiper experiences heightened sensory perceptions, producing a sense of union with the divine and sometimes resulting in visionary experiences. Ancient mystery religions provided ecstatic worshipers with a more personal relationship with a god or goddess.

Fate (*Tychē*). Greek goddess worshiped by many Gentiles who thought that this capricious deity was responsible for much that happened in the world.

Fertility cults. In the ancient agricultural world in which Paul lived, people were extremely concerned with fertility. Their lives depended on successful harvesting of crops and breeding of farm animals. Fertility cults typically practiced ritualized forms of sexual intercourse (cultic prostitution) as part of their worship of the fertility deities, whom they believed were responsible for reproduction.

God-fearers. Gentiles who were attracted to Jewish teaching about God and moral living, but were unwilling to become proselyte Jews because of the requirements of keeping the laws of Moses and being circumcised. These people formed an important core of Paul's Gentile converts to Christianity.

Golden Ass, The. Early novel written by Lucius Apuleius, in which a young man named Lucius is changed into a golden-colored donkey when he dabbles in magic. As a donkey/ass, he suffers many misfortunes, but he finally regains his human form through the savior goddess Isis. The book gives excellent insight into initiation rites of mystery religions.

Hecate. Fertility goddess and protectress of witches.

Isis. Egyptian mystery religion savior goddess whose worship was popular in many areas of the Mediterranean world.

Koine Greek. The common Greek vernacular that was spoken in most areas of the Mediterranean world of the first century.

The conquests of Alexander the Great in the fourth century BCE paved the way for this widespread use of Koine (including most of the documents in the New Testament).

Lingua franca. Common language used by people living in a variety of locations. In the first-century Mediterranean world, Koine Greek was used as a common or trade language by many people around the Roman Empire. Wherever Paul traveled, he could communicate with people in Greek.

Oracles. Particular priests and priestesses, often those associated with the god Apollo, who were trained to receive or discern messages for those who were seeking divine guidance. Oracles typically wrote their "divine" messages in hexameter verse, and these messages are also called oracles.

Pax Romana. A Latin phrase meaning "Peace of Rome." The Roman legions imposed this order or peace, which allowed Paul to move in relative safety from region to region as he did his missionary work.

Proselytes. People who leave one form of belief to become members of another religious faith. For example, when polytheistic Romans converted to Judaism and sought to keep the laws of Moses, they became proselyte Jews.

Religious climate of despair. Prevailing attitude among many Gentiles of Paul's time. Many saw the world as an uncertain and dangerous place, and they often worshiped the goddess Fate (Greek *Tychē*) as a means of avoiding her capricious actions.

Superstition. Illogical belief in supposed connections between events of life and supernatural causes. Superstitious people in Paul's day believed that many things happened because they either did or did not give particular deities proper offerings. They rejected logical explanations in favor of fanciful ones.

Taurobolium. A ritual in which a person was drenched by the blood of a bull while standing in a pit under the sacrificed animal. It was believed that the blood washed away the person's sins and caused the person to be reborn unto eternity.

FURTHER READING ON THE RELIGIONS OF PAUL'S DAY

Apuleius, Lucius. *The Golden Ass.* Translated by W. Adlington. LCL. Cambridge, MA: Harvard University Press, 1958. This ancient novel provides an account of initiation into the mysteries of Isis that is important for understanding mystery religions.

Aune, David. *Prophecy in Early Christianity and the Ancient Mediterranean World.* Grand Rapids: Wm. B. Eerdmans Publising Co., 1983. Detailed, scholarly book. Good resource for research.

Barrett, C. K. *The New Testament Background: Selected Documents.* New York: Harper Torchbooks, 1961. Good selection of ancient texts that relate to NT passages. Arranged by topic.

Beard, Mary, John North, and Simon Price. *Religions of Rome.* Vol. 2, *A Sourcebook.* Cambridge: Cambridge University Press, 1998. Valuable collection of ancient sources and modern analysis of topics. Good bibliographies. Great resource.

Burkert, Walter. *Ancient Mystery Cults*. Cambridge, MA: Harvard University Press, 1987. Interesting study of ancient mystery religions.

Ferguson, Everett. *Backgrounds of Early Christianity*. 3rd ed. Grand Rapids: Wm. B. Eerdmans Publishing Co., 2003. Useful and well-written, 648-page book. Clear arrangement of contents according to categories. Easy to find what you want to know about Greek, Roman, and Jewish culture and practices.

Grant, F. C., ed. *Hellenistic Religions: The Age of Syncreticism*. New York: Bobbs-Merrill, 1953. Good collection of translations of ancient documents, inscriptions, and so forth. Now out of print. Locate in a library.

*Lohse, Eduard. *The New Testament Environment*. Nashville: Abingdon, 1976. Nice beginning book. Accessible information about history and culture.

Luck, Georg. *Arcana Mundi: Magic and the Occult in the Greek and Roman Worlds*. Baltimore: Johns Hopkins University Press, 1985. Technical, as the title suggests.

Meeks, Wayne A. *The First Urban Christians: The Social World of the Apostle Paul*. New Haven, CT: Yale University Press, 1983. Social analysis of early Christianity. Scholarly book.

*Tripolitis, Antonia. *Religions of the Hellenistic-Roman Age*. Grand Rapids: Wm. B. Eerdmans Publishing Co., 2001. Brief overview of the philosophies and religions of the Hellenistic-Roman Age (from Alexander the Great to the Christian Roman Empire of the fourth century CE). Well written and easily accessible. Good choice for beginners in this field.

Turcan, Robert. *The Cults of the Roman Empire*. Translated by Antonia Nevill. Oxford: Blackwell Publishers, 1996. Written to be understandable for the nonspecialist in this field. Good presentation of the religious practices that characterized the lives of common people during the time.

———. *The Gods of Ancient Rome: Religion in Everyday Life from Archaic to Imperial Times*. Translated by Antonia Nevill. New York: Routledge, 2001. Provides an introduction to the nature of classical religions. Like *The Cults of the Roman Empire*, this book is not difficult to follow. Readable style.

CHAPTER 5

The Fearless Apostle of Acts

The book of Acts chronicles Paul's transformation from a fierce opponent of the church to the foremost apostle to the Gentiles. In the narrative of Acts, Paul is larger than life, fearlessly proclaiming the gospel of Jesus Christ in region after region. Oblivious to pain and persecution, he pushes forward relentlessly. In his Letters, however, we see a more vulnerable side of Paul. His emotions are raw in some Epistles, and his words express frustration, anger, sarcasm, discouragement, and fear. How should we reconcile such details? Should we reconcile them? Determining what role Acts should play in a careful study of Paul is an important matter.

Although Paul's Letters provide our closest glimpse of him as a man, Acts gives an indispensable description of his mis-sionary journeys. Without the itinerary recounted in Acts, we would be at a loss to determine when Paul wrote his Letters. Consequently, as a means of becoming acquainted with his missionary endeavors, it is advantageous to read the Acts of the Apostles before studying Paul's Epistles. This sequence raises certain difficulties, such as reconciling the heroic portrait of Paul in Acts with the emotional image of him that emerges from his Letters. Acts also provides a highly selective outline of Paul's movements that needs to be supplemented with additional information from his Letters. In spite of such obstacles, however, the chronological framework given in Acts helps us make sense out of Paul's Letters. In addition, Acts recounts reasons for some of the turmoil experienced by the early church because of Paul's mission to the Gentiles.

WHAT DO WE KNOW ABOUT THE AUTHOR OF ACTS?

Uncertainty exists over the identity of the author of the Acts of the Apostles, although clearly the same man also wrote the Gospel of Luke. Luke and Acts combine to form a two-volume work (more accurately "two-scroll") on Jesus' ministry and on the development of the early church. The Gospel prologue (Luke 1:1–4) dedicates the book to Theophilus, who was probably the author's literary patron—the one who paid the bills while he was researching and writing. Similarly, the prologue of Acts begins by addressing this same man: "In the first book, Theophilus, I wrote about all that Jesus did and taught." Acts picks up the narrative where the Gospel account left off, describing the early Christian movement.

Although Luke and Acts are anonymous documents, there is a fairly strong tradition from the late second century that the physician Luke, Paul's sometime traveling companion, is the author. One of the earliest claims for Luke's authorship comes from a Christian leader named Irenaeus (ca. 180 CE), who says, "Luke also, the companion of Paul, recorded in a book the Gospel preached by him" (*Against Heresies* 3.1.1; *ANF*). Likewise the Muratorian Canon (a list of books found in Rome that many think dates back to about 200 CE) asserts the following: "The third Gospel book, that according to Luke. This physician Luke after Christ's ascension, since Paul had taken him with him as an expert in the way

(of the teaching), composed it in his own name according to (his) thinking."[1]

Yet these sources were written a century after the composition of Acts, and mistakes could easily have been made in ascribing authorship to Luke. Irenaeus is accurate in some of his claims, but at times he declares as facts some rather odd assertions. For example, in *Against Heresies* 2.22.6, he states that Jesus was almost fifty years old when he was crucified. Some of the traditions passed on by Irenaeus and other second-century teachers go back to the early days of the church and represent authentic materials. Others do not. With the available evidence, we cannot positively say that Luke wrote Acts, but we can observe many details on how the author constructed his narrative. For convenience we will simply call the author Luke, bracketing for now the question of authorship.[2]

1. Translation from *New Testament Apocrypha*, vol. 1, *Gospels and Related Writings*, rev. ed., ed. E. Hennecke and W. Schneemelcher (Louisville, KY: Westminster John Knox Press, 2006), 43.
2. We also will not explore other difficult historical issues at this stage. Some scholars, such as Ernst Haenchen (*The Acts of the Apostles* [Philadelphia: Westminster, 1971]), relentlessly subject every story in Acts to intense historical scrutiny, speculating on what really happened and what did not. Such investigations lie beyond the scope of this study. Our goal now is to observe carefully the portrait of the early church in Acts, to see what the author says about the early Christians and about Paul's missionary activities. Until we carefully interact with the text on its own terms, seeking to see its message, we are not ready to explore multiple issues pertaining to historicity. In this regard, our approach matches what we did in the last chapter when reading the Hellenistic miracle stories, mystery religion initiation stories, and so forth. Our concern is to focus on deciphering the beliefs of the authors and then to ponder the implications of these beliefs. Hard-core historical analysis is a stage beyond our purpose at this point.

Lively debates center on these questions, and commentaries on Acts forcefully argue various perspectives. Although these matters are important in their

The author of Acts was a well-educated man who worked comfortably with the literary conventions of his day when telling about the early church.[3] His ability becomes immediately obvious in his prologues, which he wrote in a highly refined style of Greek prose. Yet he also has the ability to move easily from long and complicated sentences, which are typical of historical prologues of that time period, to a Greek vernacular that sounds very Semitic. When describing characters in a Jewish setting at the Jerusalem temple, for example, the story sounds as if it were spoken in Hebrew or Aramaic and translated literally into Greek. Such passages resemble the syntax often seen in the Septuagint, the Greek translation of the Hebrew Bible made in Alexandria, Egypt, beginning about 250 BCE.

However, when Luke recounts events in Gentile settings, such as Paul's speaking with philosophers in Acts 17, the language fits these settings (in this case sounding like what one would expect to hear in Athens). This aspect of his work resembles that of good novelists whose story characters speak in distinct patterns. For example, in a novel an author might have a Southerner

speak with southern speech forms, whereas a character from New Jersey would speak with distinct northeastern idioms.

By patterning the language for the occasion, so that in one story the speech sounds like Septuagintal Greek while in another it is refined and highly rhetorical, Luke uses a Greco-Roman tradition that goes back at least to the historian **Thucydides** (ca. 472–395 BCE). In the *History of the Peloponnesian War*, Thucydides describes what later came to be a widely used literary technique among Greek and Roman authors that we call the **historical speech**. Note carefully how he explains his method:

> As to the speeches that were made by different men, either when they were about to begin the war or when they were already engaged therein, it has been difficult to recall with strict accuracy the words actually spoken, both for me as regards that which I myself heard, and for those who from various other sources have brought me reports. Therefore the speeches are given in the language in which, as it seemed to me, the several speakers would express, on the subjects under consideration, the sentiments most befitting the occasion, though at the same time I have adhered as closely as possible to the general sense of what was actually said. (1.22.1 [Smith, LCL])

Lucian, a second-century CE author, makes a similar comment in *How to Write History* 58: "If a person has to be introduced to make a speech, above all let his language suit his person and his subject" (LCL). In this way, ancient authors employed speeches in their stories as a means of giving their readers important information about the events they described. Thus, the person delivering a speech in the narrative was in fact speaking what the author wanted readers to know at that point in the account. But as Thucydides said, he also tried to report

---

own right, exploring them now would sidetrack our particular study. The approach taken in this book is to read Acts in light of what ancient historians explained about their craft, and not to agonize over the identity of the author of Acts, when exactly he wrote, or the accuracy of every story he recounts. Our concern is more with understanding his portrait of Paul and the early church. In this regard understanding more about his writing style also proves to be helpful.

3. See Bruce W. Winter, *The Book of Acts in Its Ancient Literary Setting*, vol. 1, *The Book of Acts in Its First Century Setting* (Grand Rapids: Wm. B. Eerdmans Publishing Co., 1993). Also, Henry J. Cadbury's *The Making of Luke-Acts* (London: Allenson, 1958) remains an important study on these issues.

what he imagined that the speakers in his history should or would have said in the occasions he describes.

Ancient historians were moderately concerned with accuracy—within the information-gathering constraints of their time. Although the speeches in these history books may sound as if they are quotations of what the speakers literally said, the authors often did not personally hear these orations. Some they made up entirely. Some they loosely constructed on the basis of third-party accounts. Luke, as a man educated in the first century, naturally used this prevalent literary approach. Recognizing this historical practice helps us to interpret Acts responsibly and keeps us from asking absurd questions about where he got some of his information. For example, when we read abbreviated versions of discussions by members of the Sanhedrin (Acts 5:33–39) or governmental officials (25:13–22) where no Christians were present to hear the speakers, we will know not to speculate on how Luke got the transcript of what was said. He might simply have written what he believed that certain characters would have said in each situation.

THE EARLY CHURCH EXPLODES ONTO THE SCENE (ACTS 1–8)

Because of his commitment to the Pharisees' messianic expectations, Saul of Tarsus violently opposed the idea of a crucified Messiah. But what about Jesus' inner circle? What were the messianic expectations of Peter and the other followers of Jesus?

Prelude to Pentecost (Acts 1:1–26)

1. Even forty days after Jesus' resurrection (1:3), what does the disciples' question in 1:6 reveal about their expectations of what the Messiah should accomplish?

2. What does Jesus' answer in 1:7–8 reveal about his intent for their mission after his departure? Instead of military power, what sort of power will they receive to accomplish their mission?

The missionary movement in Acts largely follows the agenda set forth in 1:7–8, tracing the gospel's progress from Jerusalem to Rome. Thus 1:7–8 provides a foreshadowing of coming events in the story.

Here are several details that will assist in understanding the story. The Sabbath day's journey mentioned in 1:12 is a distance of about half a mile. Jewish teachers had established this distance as the maximum one could walk on the Sabbath day and not be guilty of working. A clever interpretation of Exodus 16:29 on the basis of Numbers 35:5 provides the rationale for specifying that a Sabbath's day journey is about 2,000 cubits (= ½ mile; Mishnah, *Sotah* 5.3).

Jesus' disciples, "together with certain women, including Mary the mother of Jesus, as well as his brothers" (1:14), gather in an upper room to pray and await the baptism of the Spirit. Peter quickly emerges as the leader of the Christian movement (1:15), and the early chapters of Acts focus on him. Most of the twelve apostles listed in 1:13–14 are not mentioned again by name in the narrative. Acts concentrates on a few major figures in the church and leaves untold the stories of the rest.

3. What qualifications does Peter give for the apostle selected to replace Judas? What method do they use for selecting him?

4. The book of Acts almost never calls Paul an apostle. How does 1:21–22 clarify why the author reserves this title for the Twelve?

Fiery Tongues from Above (Acts 2)

The large number of people who witness this event may well indicate that it happened in the temple (2:5–11)—which would fit Luke's emphasis on the disciples spending substantial time in the temple precincts (Luke 24:52–53; Acts 3:1–11; 5:12, 25, 42).

This 1:50 scale-model reconstruction of the first-century Jerusalem temple complex is located by the Holyland Hotel, near Jerusalem. The courtyard around the central shrine provided a location for people to gather. (Courtesy of David Pettegrew)

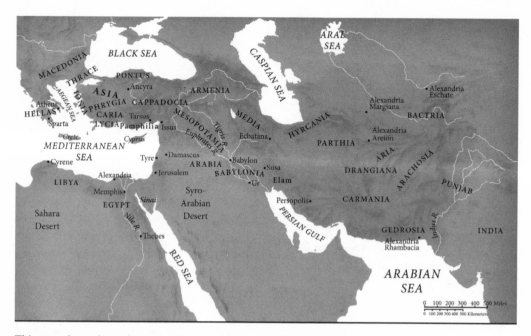

This map shows the various countries (except for Rome) from which Jewish pilgrims came to Jerusalem for the feast of Passover.

1. Locate on a map of the Mediterranean region where the Jews listed in 2:8–10 lived before coming to Jerusalem. How far have some of them journeyed to celebrate Pentecost?

Two different words in 2:5, 10 describe the circumstances of these Jews. The term "living" in 2:5 translates a participial form of the verb *katoikeō*, specifying permanent residence. In 2:10,[4] however, the word "visi-

4. The NIV incorrectly places "visitors" in Acts 2:11.

tors" in the phrase "visitors from Rome" translates a participial form of the verb *epidēmeō*, which describes people dwelling in a land that is not their native country. Hence it can be translated "to sojourn" or "to live as a foreigner." Also, "Jews" in 2:10 designates those who are Jews by birth, whereas **"proselytes"** indicates non-Jewish people who have become Jews by conversion.

Note that these people hear Jesus' disciples praising God in their native languages (2:11), and the result is *confusion* (2:12). Not until Peter stands up to preach in a language they all understand (probably Greek, but possibly Aramaic) do they comprehend the significance of the event. The speaking in tongues in 2:4–12 functions not as a set of missionary proclamations but as praise to God in a host of different languages. This function of tongues resembles Paul's own description in 1 Corinthians 12–14, which we will study later.

Comparing proclamations of the gospel in Acts with Paul's teaching in his Letters can be an interesting study. Analyze the public address Peter gives in response to the charge by bystanders that those who are speaking in tongues are drunk.

2. What are the main points of Peter's speech in 2:14–36?

3. According to 2:43–47, what characterized the early Christian movement in Jerusalem?

Growth Pains in the Early Church (Acts 3–5)

Peter and the other apostles continue to attend religious functions in the Jerusalem temple (3:1). Following Jesus Messiah does not separate them from their Jewish heritage.

1. Peter's healing of the lame man at the gate of the temple draws a crowd of confused people, somewhat like tongues did in Acts 2. How do the main points in Peter's sermon in 3:12–26 compare with the main points in his sermon in 2:14–36?

The view expressed in 3:24 was typical among the early Christians. When Peter says, "All the prophets, as many as have spoken, from Samuel and those after him, also predicted these days," he expresses their understanding that all of the Scriptures speak of the time of the end. This viewpoint partially explains why early Christians seldom paid close attention to the context of the biblical quotations they employed. They believed that *all* of the Scriptures were, as Paul says, "written down to instruct us, on whom the ends of the ages have come" (1 Cor. 10:11; see also 1 Cor. 7:29, 31; Rom. 13:12). Peter's use of Scripture in Acts 1:20 (cf. Pss. 69:25; 109:8) and 2:17–21 (cf. Joel 2:28–32) and 2:25–28 (cf. Ps. 16:8–11) also shows the first-century Jews' common lack of concern to understand the historical context of the passages they quoted. We will study this phenomenon further when dealing with Paul's use of Scripture in his Letters.

Peter's boldness in 4:8–12 sharply contrasts with his fearful denials in Luke 22:57–62. The Jewish leaders are amazed at his fearless proclamation of Jesus as the Christ, for they recognize that he is "uneducated" (4:13). Being uneducated by their definition does not necessarily mean that he could not read and write, but that he had not received the formal training of a scribe. A fisherman like Peter should not be able to debate successfully with the more educated Jewish leaders in Jerusalem.

As you read the early chapters of Acts, also notice the theme of predestination. When the disciples say in 4:28 that those who killed Jesus were doing "whatever your hand and your plan had predestined to take place," they echo the theme that God is in control of the birth and expansion of the church. In 2:23 Peter said, "This man, handed over to you according to the definite plan and foreknowledge of God, you crucified and killed by the hands of those outside the law." All had been foretold in the Scriptures; none of these things happened outside of God's plan. As Jesus explained in Luke 24:44, "Everything written about me in the law of Moses, the prophets, and the psalms must be fulfilled."

2. In Acts 4:32–37 we meet **Barnabas**, who will become a long-term traveling companion and partner in ministry with the apostle Paul. What does this passage tell about his background and personality?

3. In Acts 3–5 what primary reasons contribute to the developing tension between the church and the synagogue?

Hellenistic Christians under Siege (Acts 6–7)

In the early days when the Christian movement was relatively small, the structure remained simple. Increased size brought the need for greater organization. It also multiplied sources for conflict.

1. What dispute erupts among the early Christians, and how do the apostles deal with the problem?

2. The seven deacons appointed in 6:5 all have Greek names, indicating that they were "Hellenists" (see 6:1). What does this detail indicate about the apostles' strategy in appointing them to serve?

3. With which Jews does Stephen come into conflict in Jerusalem, and what charges do they launch against him?

4. How does Stephen's speech in 7:2–53 demonstrate that God is not limited to the confines of the Jerusalem temple? How does his speech confirm for his adversaries the charge they brought against him in 6:13?

5. What role does Saul of Tarsus play in Stephen's death?

Meanwhile, Philip begins to fulfill what Jesus said in 1:8, "You will be my witnesses in Jerusalem, in all Judea and Samaria, and to the ends of the earth." Yet the motivation for preaching to Samaritans comes not from planned outreach, but because persecution in Jerusalem drove him out of the city. Regardless of the motivation, however, Philip's preaching was very unusual, given the long-standing animosity between Jews and Samaritans. For centuries these people had fostered ill will against each other, as illustrated in the story where Jesus asks the woman at the well for water in John 4:7. The narrator clarifies her shocked response by explaining in John 4:9 that "Jews do not share things in common with Samaritans." Another example of this tension may be seen in Luke 9:54: in reaction to Samaritans refusing to provide lodging, James and John ask Jesus, "Lord, do you want us to command fire to come down from heaven and consume them?"

1. The Samaritans respond positively to the gospel message preached by Philip, a Jewish Christian. When do they actually receive the Holy Spirit: before or after they are baptized?

Driven from Jerusalem (Acts 8:1–40)

According to 8:1 the apostles did not leave Jerusalem during the persecution that scattered many Christians out of the city—which seems to indicate that they continued to attend temple functions. They apparently remained loyal to the laws of Moses and were not challenging the law and the temple as did Stephen.

As you continue to read through Acts, try to see if there is any set pattern with regard to when people receive the Holy Spirit. Later we will study what Paul says on this subject in his Letters.

TAKING THE GOSPEL TO THE GENTILES (ACTS 9–14)

Radical Reversal on the Road to Damascus (Acts 9:1–31)

In chapter 3, "Messianic Expectations Turned Upside Down," we analyzed the account of Saul's conversion, baptism, and early preaching ministry in Acts 9. Now we return to this account and notice the effects of his activities on the early Christian movement.

1. According to Acts 9, Barnabas introduces Saul to the disciples at Jerusalem, who are skeptical about the former persecutor. What results from Saul's preaching activities in Jerusalem?

2. When do the Gentiles at Cornelius's house receive the Holy Spirit? How does this timing compare with when the Samaritans received the Spirit in 8:14–17?

3. Note the amazement of the Jewish Christians in 10:45 when they witness the Gentiles receiving the Spirit. When the other apostles in Jerusalem first hear about Peter's activities among the Gentiles, how do they respond? What does their response reveal about the Jewish Christians' beliefs concerning who was worthy of the salvation offered in Jesus Christ?

Dirty Animals in a Clean Sheet (Acts 9:32–11:18)

This section reveals much about the difficulties the early Christian leaders had with understanding and implementing Jesus' words in Acts 1:8.

1. How does the vision of the sheet full of animals help Peter to overcome his hesitation over dealing with Gentiles?

The Gospel Goes to the Gentiles (Acts 11:19–14:28)

1. Jewish Christians coming from which two locations break with the normal policy of preaching only to Jews (11:19–20) and begin to preach the gospel also to the Gentiles at Antioch? (Find these places on the map.)

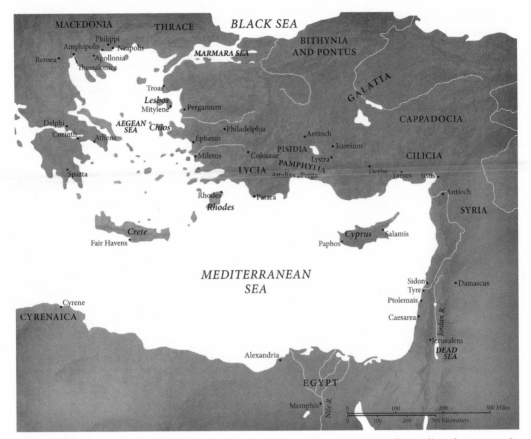

This map shows the regions in which Paul conducted his missionary journeys. By reading the account in Acts, you can plot his journeys.

Barnabas, who was appointed by Jerusalem apostles to oversee the Christians in Antioch, journeyed to Tarsus to recruit Saul to help him with the work of ministry (11:25–26). Later, about 47–48 CE, these two men, along with John Mark (12:25; 13:5), were called upon to depart on a missionary journey (13:1–3). On a map, trace their travels from Antioch to the island of Cyprus, to Perga on the coast of Pamphylia (where John Mark quit the team and returned to Jerusalem), to Pisidian Antioch, to Iconium, to Lystra, to Derbe, and back around through the towns to the coast at Attalia and by ship back to Syrian Antioch.

2. In Acts 13–14, observe the pattern of where Barnabas and Paul go first when entering a new city. What sort of strategy do they seem to develop for their missionary work?

3. Why do the Jews predominantly reject the gospel message, and what actions do they take against Paul and Barnabas?

4. Gentiles are the main ones who believe the gospel. What problems would the establishment of predominantly Gentile churches have for the Christian movement?

The **God-fearers** mentioned in 13:16 were Gentiles who were attracted to the high moral and ethical teaching, as well as the monotheism, proclaimed by Jewish elders in the synagogues. But they were unwilling to take on the full weight of the laws of Moses and become Jewish proselytes. Circumcision in particular was a major obstacle keeping them away from full participation with the Jewish community. Paul's message of salvation by faith alone, that one can be part of God's covenant community apart from circumcision, proved to be very attractive to these people. They heard the gospel gladly.

MAJOR DEBATE AS THE GOSPEL SPREADS TO GENTILES (ACTS 15:1–18:22)

Fiery Argument in Jerusalem (Acts 15:1–35)

The success of Paul and Barnabas's missionary journey sparked strong opposition. Jewish Christians from Judea traveled to the Gentile churches to correct what they believed to be the false teaching of Paul and Barnabas (15:1). The resulting debate with Paul finally resulted in the Jerusalem council of 49 CE, a major meeting to decide what should be done about Gentile converts in the church (15:2–29).

At the council meeting, Pharisees continued to insist that Gentile converts should be circumcised and follow the laws of Moses. Notice in 15:7 that there was considerable debate. Nearly twenty years after the crucifixion of Jesus, the idea that God would welcome Gentiles was still a difficult concept for many Jewish Christians to accept.

1. What finally settled the debate in favor of Paul and Barnabas?

2. What compromise solution do the delegates reach in 15:20, and what does the explanation in 15:21 indicate about the reason behind the details of the compromise?

3. Why was it wise to send Judas and Silas with Paul and Barnabas (15:22)?

Determining the Will of God

Some individuals mistakenly think that early Christians did not wrestle as much as people do today with understanding and doing the will of God. They naively imagine that God regularly gave directions through visions, and so forth. However, in Acts 15 when the apostles struggle to make a major decision that affects the entire church, what steps do they follow before finally concluding what they accept to be God's will pertaining to Gentiles obeying the laws of Moses? How could you apply these steps in your own experience of making major decisions in life?

Angry Apostles Go Separate Ways
(Acts 15:36–16:40)

1. Why do Paul and Barnabas get angry with each other and part company at the beginning of the second missionary journey?

2. Why, after winning the battle over not having to circumcise Gentile Christians, would Paul circumcise Timothy in 16:3?

A Long, Dusty Road

Calculate on a map the distance Paul, Silas, and Timothy walked across what today is the country of Turkey, being thwarted every time they tried to enter an area for evangelism. Not until they reach Troas on the Aegean coast does Paul receive direction in a vision (Acts 16:9–10). How long would you estimate such a journey would take?

When they tried to go southwest into the Roman province of Asia, they could not go on. So they tried to go north into Bithynia, and again their way was blocked (Acts 16:6–7). Given what you know about Paul at this point, how frustrating do you think these delays might have been for him? How frustrated would you be if you departed on a missionary journey of this length, only to be thwarted repeatedly?

"We" Passages in Acts

Periodically in the narration of Acts 16–28, the author writes in the first-person plural. Instead of describing the travels of Paul and his companions with the third-person "they," he switches to "we." In Acts 16:1–7, for example, the author describes the travels of Paul and Timothy, but suddenly in 16:10, he says, "When he had seen the vision, *we* immediately tried to cross over to Macedonia." This detail seems to indicate that the author joined Paul at certain times and traveled with him for a while; and when the author described these journeys, he included himself in the story because he witnessed the events he recorded. Thus, in 16:10–16 the author seems to be part of the group, but from 16:18 to 20:4 the first-person pronouns drop out. At 20:5 "we" resumes—"We sailed from Philippi . . . , and in five days we joined them in Troas"— and continues through their arrival in Jerusalem (see 20:13; 21:1, 7, 15). There is no further use of "we" until 27:1–28:16—the account of Paul's sea voyage to Rome. After the sea voyage ceases at 28:17, the use of "we" vanishes from Acts.

The presence of these **"we" passages** has played a significant role in scholars' arguing that Paul's sometime traveling companion Luke wrote Luke-Acts. Modern readers often appeal to the following passages as further evidence: Philemon 23–24 ("Epaphras . . . sends greetings to you, and so do Mark . . . and Luke, my fellow workers"); Colossians 4:14 ("Luke, the beloved physician, and Demas greet you"); and 2 Timothy 4:11 ("Only Luke is with me"). Vernon Robbins, however, argues that the "we" passages in Acts occur in the context of sea voyages, and he postulates that Luke's use of "we" simply represents a well-established tradition of recounting sea voyages by using first-person pronouns.[5]

Robbins cites passages from a number of ancient Mediterranean documents and argues that the author of Acts was merely following a literary convention, not using the first-person style to describe events that he personally observed. One of the problems with this theory is that Acts 13:4–5, 13; 14:26; 15:39; and 18:18–21 mention sea voyages but do not use first-person pronouns. Furthermore, the "we" passages are not strictly limited to describing sea voyages. For example, whereas all of 16:10–17 uses "we," only verse 11 speaks of sailing. The rest describes events in Philippi, which is not a seaport; and the story of Paul's activities at Philippi continues through 16:18–40.

Further challenges to Robbins's theory have arisen with respect to descriptions of sea voyages. S. M. Praeder, for example, has analyzed the narration styles of ancient Mediterranean stories and found more accounts of sea voyages recounted in third person than he found narrated in first person.[6] Finding a pattern that provides the proper context for understanding Acts 16–28 remains a problem. A. J. M. Wedderburn explains:

> We have a number of Greek and Roman histories written by persons who had actually participated in at least some of the events which they described; examples like the histories of Thucydides, Julius Caesar and Josephus spring readily to mind. However, these writers mostly do not narrate those events in the first person, but in the third person, and speak even of their own actions in the third person. . . . If they use the first person at all it is in the introductions to their works (as is also the case in Luke 1,1–4 and Acts 1,1) or their conclusions or in comments on the events, not in the actual descriptions of the events themselves. . . . [And] whereas such historical writers say plainly who they are, mostly in the foreword to their work, . . . and that in the first person singular, not plural, the fact remains that the work which we have does not identify the author, and this is a surprising omission if he were in fact an eyewitness of, and a participant in, at least some of the events which he describes. Such coyness does not seem to match the conventions of ancient writing.[7]

Some creative attempts to unravel this problem of the "we" passages and the authorship of Acts have been attempted, but none has won a consensus among New Testament scholars.

At this time we simply do not know enough to give a definitive explanation for the presence of the "we" passages in Acts. Do they indicate the presence of eyewitness accounts at certain points, or do they represent a literary technique whose origin and purpose we do not yet understand? Fortunately, for our analysis of the portrait of Paul in Acts, we do not have to answer this question in order to proceed with our work. We can postpone a decision on this matter and continue our investigation of Paul's second missionary journey.

Note that Lydia, the first convert in Philippi, comes from Thyatira (16:14), which is located in Asia, where Paul was

---

5. V. K. Robbins, "By Land and by Sea: The We-Passages and Ancient Sea Voyages," in *Perspectives on Luke-Acts*, ed. Charles H. Talbert (Edinburgh: T&T Clark, 1978), 215–42.

6. S. M. Praeder, "The Problem of First Person Narration," in *Novum Testamentum* 29 (1987): 193–218.

7. ·A. J. M. Wedderburn, "The 'We-Passages' in Luke Acts: On the Horns of a Dilemma," *Zeitschrift für die neutestamentliche Wissenschaft* 93 (2002): 81. See also Praeder, "Problem of First Person Narration," 208: "If Acts is a first person ancient history, then it is alone in its lack of first person singular participation."

forbidden to go in 16:6. In Acts, be aware of when Paul actually does missionary work in Asia.

1. The owners of the slave girl at Philippi are furious over their loss of money. On an ethnic charge ("They are Jews") they get Paul and Silas beaten and imprisoned. How do Paul and Silas turn this nasty situation into a redemptive occasion?

2. How does Paul use his Roman citizenship to force an apology from the Philippian magistrates?

Fierce Opposition to the Gospel
(Acts 17:1–18:22)

At Thessalonica and Beroea, Paul continues to encounter intense opposition from Jewish opponents similar to what he experienced during his first missionary journey (17:1–15).

The Importance of Obscure Details

When Acts 18:12 specifies that the Jewish attack on Paul occurred when Gallio was proconsul, this minor detail provides a significant anchor for assigning approximate dates to various events during Paul's missionary activities. Gallio, a son of the well-known Spanish rhetorician Marcus Annaeus Seneca, was the younger brother of Lucius Annaeus Seneca, the famous Stoic philosopher. He did not serve long as proconsul (his brother wrote in *Moral Epistles* 104.1 that he had to leave Achaia because of a fever). An inscription found at Delphi states that the emperor Claudius appointed Gallio as proconsul of Achaia in the year 51 (probably by July 1).

By working backward from this date, we can estimate when Paul started his second missionary journey, that the Jerusalem council of Acts 15 occurred in approximately 49, that the first missionary journey took place in 47–48, and so forth. By working forward from this date, we can assign approximate dates to the third missionary journey and the times when he wrote most of his Letters. Sometimes small details have major implications in biblical scholarship.

The Temple of Zeus in Athens was enormous. Note the size of the person in the foreground. The Acropolis, with the Parthenon, is in the background. (Courtesy of Michael Cosby)

1. How does the content of Paul's speech to the philosophers at Athens (17:22–31) differ from the sermons he proclaims in the synagogues?

2. Paul remained at Corinth for eighteen months (18:11), during which time he had considerable success among Gentiles. Why does Gallio, who was proconsul of Achaia in 51, refuse to condemn Paul?

In 49 the emperor Claudius expelled all Jews from Rome because of rioting in the Jewish sectors. As we will see when we study Romans, these riots apparently resulted when Christians tried to evangelize their fellow Jews. Aquila and Priscilla (18:2) seem to have been Christians before Paul met them, and they became his long-term friends.

3. On a map follow the route Paul took on the return to his home church at Syrian Antioch (18:18–22). Approximately how many miles was this sea voyage?

IMPRISONED FOR HIS EFFORTS
(ACTS 18:23–22:29)

Sweating across Asia
(Acts 18:23–19:41)

1. How does Paul's journey in 18:23 and 19:1 differ from the route taken at the beginning of his second missionary expedition in 16:6–8?

2. Note how and when the disciples of John receive the Holy Spirit (19:1–7). How does this timing compare with that experienced by the Samaritans (8:14–17) and those in Cornelius's household (10:44)?

3. For two years Paul proclaims Jesus Christ to those in a lecture hall in Ephesus. What causes the riot in 19:23–41? What does this detail reveal about the effectiveness of Paul's preaching?

The fact that Paul encounters a group of John the Baptist's disciples in Ephesus (19:1–4) in approximately 52 reveals how influential the Baptist's ministry was. It also shows how slowly news traveled in the ancient world, for these disciples had not yet heard the good news about Jesus.

The spectacular theater at Ephesus seated 25,000 people and is still used for concerts today. Acts 19:28–41 describes a two-hour riot that occurred in the Ephesus theater, resulting from Paul's effective preaching and the resulting loss of revenue by silversmiths. (Courtesy of Michael Cosby)

A Long Journey and a Lethal Sermon
(Acts 20:1–21:14)

Using the narrative in this section and a map, trace Paul's voyages for the duration of his third missionary journey.

1. In Acts 20:1–21:14, Christians repeatedly warn Paul against going to Jerusalem. How does he respond to their concerns?

2. Paul's long-winded sermon at Miletus proves to be deadly (20:7–12). What does the speech in 20:18–35 emphasize about the apostle Paul?

Violence in the Holy City
(Acts 21:15–22:29)

1. Why are the Jerusalem apostles hesitant about Paul's coming to town?

2. What do the apostles tell Paul about the attitude of Christians in Jerusalem toward the laws of Moses?

3. What does Paul's participation in the purification ritual in the temple reveal about his own relationship to Jewish customs and the Mosaic law? How does his action stand in tension with his belief about Gentiles and the law?

4. What causes the riot during which Paul is beaten by the Jews and finally arrested by the Romans?

5. During Paul's speech in 22:1–21, the Jews listen attentively to his story until what point?

Note how Paul begins his speech by emphasizing his faithfulness to Mosaic law as a means of getting a sympathetic hearing. He also says that Ananias, a devout Jew, was sent to restore his sight, and that he received *God's commission* to go to the Gentiles while he was *in the Jerusalem temple* (22:17).

6. How does Paul's Roman citizenship again come to his aid when he is arrested?

How far did they travel the first night from Jerusalem? What does this distance tell you about the endurance of Roman soldiers?

3. In the letter from Claudius Lysias to Felix, what is his assessment of Paul's guilt or innocence?

BUSTED AND DEPORTED
(ACTS 22:30–28:31)

"We Hate His Guts!"
(Acts 22:30–24:27)

1. In his trial before the Sanhedrin, how does Paul gain the support of the Pharisees on the council? (22:30–23:10)

Felix, the governor of Judea, was a freedman known for brutality. Tacitus, a Roman historian, says that "he practiced every kind of cruelty and lust, wielding the power of a king with all the instincts of a slave" (*Annals* 12.54). He ruled over Judea from about 52 to 59 CE, and his arrogant and brutal treatment of Jewish people finally resulted in the emperor removing him from office.

4. Notice the way the orator Tertullus begins his speech in 24:2–9. How does he seek to gain a sympathetic hearing from Felix?

2. Paul's nephew warns the Roman tribune of the Jewish plot to murder Paul (23:16–22), and the tribune sends Paul to Caesarea to stand trial. Locate Antipatris on a map (23:31).

5. Why does Felix keep Paul in prison for two years? What does this treatment tell you about the legal system?

"I Appeal to the Emperor" (Acts 25–26)

Nero appointed Porcius Festus to be **procurator** of Judea in 60 CE. A Roman procurator served as a personal agent of the emperor, and in small provinces like Judea they functioned like governors. In the larger imperial provinces, they served under provincial governors as overseers of revenue (chief financial officers). The little we know about Festus comes from Acts 25–26; Josephus, *Antiquities* 20.182–197; and *War* 2.271. According to

Josephus, Festus was more honest and a better administrator than either his predecessor or successor. Apparently he died while in office in 61 or 62, but during his time as ruler he quickly eliminated a number of lawless elements, especially the *sicarii*, the dagger men. (According to Acts 21:38, the Roman tribune connected Paul with the *sicarii*, thinking he was one of these assassins.)

Upon Festus's coming into Judea, it happened that Judea was afflicted by the robbers, while all the villages were set on fire, and plundered by them. And then it was that the *sicarii*, as they were called, who were robbers, grew numerous. They made use of small swords, not much different in length from the Persian *acinacae*, but somewhat crooked, and like the Roman *sicae* [or *sicles*], as they were called; and from these weapons these robbers got their name; and with these weapons they slew a great many; for they mingled themselves among the multitude at their festivals, when they were come up in crowds from all parts to the city to worship God, as we said before, and easily slew those that they had a mind to slay. . . . So Festus sent forces, both horsemen and footmen, to fall upon those that had been seduced by a certain impostor, who promised them deliverance and freedom from the miseries they were under, if they would but follow him as far as the

Remains of this theater at Caesarea are smaller than the one at Ephesus. Herod the Great built a spectacular harbor and city, some of the remains of which may still be seen. Imagine watching a performance in this theater with the Mediterranean Sea as the backdrop. (Courtesy of Michael Cosby)

wilderness. Accordingly those forces that were sent destroyed both him that had deluded them, and those that were his followers also. (*Antiquities* 20.8.10 [Thackeray, LCL])

Festus sought the good favor of the Jewish ruling elite, and eliminating the *sicarii* was one thing that endeared him to them. The account in Acts 25 indicates that he responded quickly to their request to try Paul. Paul had Roman law on his side, for he had done nothing to deserve imprisonment; yet on the practical level, Roman procurators were often perfectly willing to let the social elite have their way as a means of gaining their cooperation. Mediterranean cultures often function on the basis of doing favors and expecting favors in return, and Paul was well aware of how the system worked. Festus would be tempted to get rid of a problem lingering from his predecessor's rule.

After spending two years in jail (24:27), Paul soon realizes that Festus intends to deliver him to the Jews. So Paul exercises his right as a Roman citizen to have his case heard before Caesar. Festus was responsible to send a document with him, describing the charges that merited the emperor taking the time to hear the case. Because he did not fully understand the case against Paul, he ran the risk of causing the emperor to question his competence. Festus therefore requested Agrippa, a local dignitary who had come to pay a visit, to help him with the situation.

Herod Agrippa II, the son of Agrippa I, the great-grandson of Herod the Great, lived from 27 to 100. Agrippa grew up in Rome in Claudius's court, and the emperor liked him. In 50 Claudius named Agrippa king over this young man's native region northeast of Judea, and in 53 he updated his former decision and made Agrippa ruler over an expanded version of Herod Philip's former area (the emperor Nero enlarged his rule in 56 to include part of Galilee). Because Agrippa was well liked by Claudius, if his name were included in the letter that Festus had to send to the emperor, this connection would help to make him look good to his superior.

Accompanying Agrippa was his younger sister, Bernice. She had previously married her uncle, but he died in 48, so she moved to her brother's estate. Rumors spread that she was living incestuously with her brother, so she married Polemon, king of Cilicia, in 63. This marriage of convenience was a bad one, and after only three years she returned to live with Agrippa. During the Jewish war with Rome, Bernice became the mistress of Titus, the Roman general in charge of the war. When he returned to Rome, she accompanied him, which caused quite a scandal that he was living with a Jew and even wanted to marry her. Roman anti-Semitism was so strong that Titus later dismissed Bernice because her presence hindered his political aspirations.

1. When addressing the gathering of important people (see 25:23), Paul seeks to demonstrate his innocence and emphasize the divine nature of his calling. What else does he seek to accomplish in his speech?

2. What does Agrippa conclude after listening to Paul's defense?

Slow Boat to Rome (Acts 27–28)

The sea voyage recounted in Acts 27 represents the most sustained use of elegant Greek prose in all of Luke-Acts. Luke's more classical Greek in this account probably results from the fact that stories of sea voyages were popular in Greek and Roman literature and tended to be told in certain ways. Heroes like Odysseus in the *Odyssey* go on sea voyages, but such material is not limited to fiction. Historians recount such stories as well (e.g., Thucydides' *History of the Pelopponesian War* 2.6.26; 8.24.31; etc.; and Herodotus's *Persian Wars* 3.138; 7.188). Luke, as a literary man of the first century, patterns his language to fit the genre.

On a map trace Paul's journey from Caesarea to Rome, noting from the places mentioned that ancient sailors often kept fairly close to the coastline as a safety precaution. Winter travel for sailboats on the Mediterranean is treacherous, and after a certain time in the fall, sailors remain in a port until spring.

On this map, plot the perilous sea journey that Paul experienced on his way to Rome.

1. To have a better place to spend the winter, the captain ignores Paul's warning not to leave Fair Havens on the island of Crete (27:9–12). The resulting disaster of being driven out to sea by a northeasterly wind dearly costs the ship, its crew, and passengers. On the map calculate the distance from Crete to the island of Malta, where they come ashore. In what activities is Paul engaged during the three months on the island?

On the map trace Paul's journey from Malta to Rome the next spring. Note that there are already Christians in Rome and the surrounding countryside (28:14–15), and they seem to know something about Paul. Remember that Priscilla and Aquila were expelled from Rome, according to 18:2.

2. What sort of reception does Paul receive from the Jews when he arrives at Rome? Do they seem to know about him already, or do they learn about him from his own words?

3. Under what conditions does Paul live for his two years in Rome?

The conclusion of Acts leaves Paul's fate uncertain. It does not specify whether he was released or executed after the two years. Remember, however, that Lysias (23:29), Festus (25:25), and Agrippa (26:31) all concluded that Paul had done nothing deserving death or imprisonment. The main point the closing chapter makes is that Paul freely preached the gospel during his time of captivity in Rome. Later, as we study the last Epistles attributed to Paul, we will consider whether he was released and made further missionary journeys, or whether he was executed under Roman law.

Portrait of Paul in Acts

1. Overall, what portrait of the apostle Paul does Acts paint? Page through Acts and notice details that are particularly significant. Then list the main characteristics of the apostle in Luke's account.

GLOSSARY

Barnabas. Significant leader in the early church. He was from the island of Cyprus and belonged to the tribe of Levi. For years he was a coworker with Paul.

God-fearers. Gentiles who were attracted to Jewish teaching about God and moral living but were unwilling to become proselyte Jews because of the requirements of keeping the laws of Moses and being circumcised. These people formed an important core of Paul's Gentile converts to Christianity.

Historical speech. A widely used literary technique in which Greek and Roman authors composed speeches so as to sound like what the character in a narrative would have said under the conditions given in the story. This writing technique goes back at least to the historian Thucydides (ca. 472–395 BCE), who included many speeches in his *History of the Peloponnesian War.*

Procurator. Roman procurators served as personal agents of the emperor, and in small provinces like Judea they functioned like governors. In the larger imperial provinces, they served under provincial governors as overseers of revenue (chief financial officers).

Proselytes. People who leave one form of belief to become members of another religious faith. For example, when polytheistic Romans converted to Judaism and sought to keep the laws of Moses, they became proselyte Jews.

Sicarii. Jewish zealots who were assassins. They were called *sicarii* ("dagger men"; see Acts 21:38) because of the daggers they used to murder people. Their tactic was to mingle among crowds during festivals, stab prominent citizens in the back, and then disappear into the crowd.

Thucydides. Greek historian who lived about 472–395 BCE. In his *History of the Peloponnesian War,* Thucydides implemented what later came to be a widely used literary technique among Greek and Roman authors that we call *historical speech.* This technique of having characters in a story serve as mouthpieces to express what the author wants to say at key points in the narrative is used frequently in the Acts of the Apostles.

"We" passages. Passages in Acts where the narration is set in first-person plural form: "We . . ." There is debate over whether these indicate where the author actually joined Paul on his missionary journeys, or whether they are simply part of a literary technique used to describe ancient sea voyages.

FURTHER READING ON THE BOOK OF ACTS

Barrett, C. K. *A Critical and Exegetical Commentary on the Acts of the Apostles.* ICC. Edinburgh: T&T Clark, 1994. Technical work. Good resource.

Bruce, F. F. *Commentary on the Acts of the Apostles.* NICNT. Grand Rapids: Wm. B. Eerdmans Publishing Co., 1954. Semitechnical work. Readable. Dated.

Chance, J. Bradley. *The Acts of the Apostles.* Macon, GA: Smyth & Helwys, 2007. Uses more engaging format than normal commentaries. Has pictures and colorful sidebars.

Dunn, James D. G. *The Acts of the Apostles.* Narrative Bible Commentaries. Valley Forge, PA: Trinity Press International, 1996. Good source of information about authorship, themes, date of writing, and purpose of Acts.

Fitzmyer, Joseph A. *The Acts of the Apostles.* AB. New York: Doubleday, 1998. Technical, demanding commentary in a well-established series.

Gasque, W. Ward. *A History of the Criticism of the Acts of the Apostles.* Grand Rapids: Wm. B. Eerdmans Publishing Co., 1975. Survey of scholarship on Acts up to 1975. Explains the interpretive questions with which scholars grapple.

Gaventa, Beverly R. *The Acts of the Apostles.* Nashville: Abingdon Press, 2003. Clear and understandable.

González, Justo L. *Acts: The Gospel of the Spirit.* Maryknoll, NY: Orbis Books, 2001. Social analysis/commentary by a Latin American author. Reflections on the implications of the message of Acts.

Haenchen, Ernst. *The Acts of the Apostles: A Commentary.* Philadelphia: Westminster Press, 1971. Influential commentary in its day. Haenchen was skeptical of the historicity of most of Acts.

Hengel, Martin. *Acts and the History of Earliest Christianity.* Philadelphia: Fortress Press, 1978. Hengel contrasts with Haenchen with respect to his assessment of the historicity of Acts.

Johnson, Luke Timothy. *The Acts of the Apostles.* Collegeville, MN: Liturgical Press, 1992. Thorough. Good for close, exegetical analysis.

Levine, Amy-Jill, and Marianne Blickenstaff, eds. *A Feminist Companion to the Acts of the Apostles.* New York: T&T Clark International, 2004. A collection of essays about the women in Acts.

Marshall, I. Howard. *The Acts of the Apostles: An Introduction and Commentary.* Grand Rapids: Wm. B. Eerdmans Publishing Co., 1982. In part seeks to refute Haenchen and assert the historicity of Acts. Fairly readable.

Porter, Stanley E. *Paul in Acts.* Peabody, MA: Hendrickson Publishers, 2001. Literary analysis. Good resource for comparing the portrait of Paul in Acts with the portrait of Paul that emerges from his own letters.

Robbins, Vernon K. "By Land and by Sea: The We-Passages and Ancient Sea Voyages." *Biblical Research* 20 (1975): 5–18. Also in *Perspectives on Luke-Acts.* Edited by Charles Talbert. Edinburgh: T&T Clark, 1978. Argues that ancient sea-voyage accounts used first-person plural pronouns ("we" passages in Acts are not evidence that the author joined Paul at various times and used "we" when describing these events).

Talbert, Charles H. *Reading Acts: A Literary and Theological Commentary on the Acts of the Apostles.* New York: Crossroad, 1997. Good literary analysis of Acts.

Witherington, Ben, III. *The Acts of the Apostles: A Socio-Rhetorical Commentary.* Grand Rapids: Wm. B. Eerdmans Publishing Co., 1998. Explores sociological and rhetorical dimensions of Acts. Helps readers see its stories in light of ancient Mediterranean thought and cultural practices.

CHAPTER 6

Reading Other People's Mail

PHILEMON

Letters sometimes expose fragments of people's broken lives. The following letter, written on June 17 in 1 BCE and discovered in an ancient trash dump in Egypt, reveals a sordid situation that would easily capture the interest of afternoon talk-show producers today. Filled with misspellings and sloppy grammar, this brief message exposes a tragic situation that was probably not uncommon during that time period:

Hilarion to Alis his sister, many greetings. Also to Berus my lady and Apollonarin. Be aware that we are still in Alexandrea [sic]. Don't be distressed if when the others return I remain in Alexandrea. I ask you and encourage you to take care of the little child. And if I soon receive my wages I will send you up [i.e., send for you]. . . . If when you have the baby it was a male, allow it to live. If it was a female, throw it out. You said to Aphrodisias, "Don't forget me." How am I able to forget you? I ask you, there-fore, not to be distressed. 29th year of Caesar, Pauni 23[1]

I find it difficult not to be infuriated at the oaf who sent this letter. He appears to have been a laborer who was away from home, working in Alexandria, Egypt. His pregnant wife, Alis, whom he calls "sister" (a common term used for one's wife in Egypt), thinks he has abandoned her; and she told this to a common friend named Aphrodisias. Hilarion, her husband, talks as if he is concerned for Alis and her baby, yet he callously orders her to kill the child if it happens to be a girl. As the father, he

1. My translation of the letter is based on the Greek text provided by Adolf Deissmann, *Light from the Ancient East* (London: Hodder & Stoughton, 1927), 167–68.

MS 1644/1
Teaching of the Apostle Addai. Syria, 9th-10th c.

Papyrus was a less expensive writing surface than parchment, so people tended to use it for letters. But it also decayed faster, so fewer papyrus documents have survived the centuries. This Syriac text from the ninth century CE shows the way perpendicular strips of papyrus were pressed together to form the writing surface. (Courtesy of Schøyen Collection, MS 1644/1)

had the right to decide if his child lived or died. By law he could have the child taken to the trash dump and exposed (left to die). Too bad Alis could not dump him, as she appears to have done with the letter!

Hilarion's letter was written on a piece of papyrus. Because of the extremely dry climate of Egypt, it did not disintegrate during the nearly two thousand years it lay buried in sand. Curiosity causes me to wonder what kind of man could be so matter-of-fact about killing his own child. There is so little to know about him. And I can only wonder about what happened to Alis and her baby.

Reading other people's mail can be both intriguing and frustrating, for such letters reveal only bits and pieces of their lives. Piecing together accurate pictures of the people involved is impossible. Fortunately, our information about Paul is less fragmentary, yet substantial obstacles still remain. Although we have a collection of his letters, they reveal only part of his complex personality and theology. Understanding the letter form used by Paul helps in the process of interpretation. By learning about ancient Mediterranean letters, we better understand not only Pauline Epistles but also much of the rest of the New Testament.

Early Christians found letters to be important for the ongoing work of the church. To date more than nine thousand letters written by Christians in antiquity

Business Letter Form

Business Letter Form	
Name and address of letter writer	Mattson Contracting Company 1142 South River Drive Upstate, PA 17029
Date of writing	August 10, 2009
Name and address of letter recipient	Charles Hanson 5487 North Purgatory Midstate, PA 17068
Salutation	Dear Mr. Hanson:
Body of letter, stating business	We apologize for destroying your house. The carpenters we assigned to renovate your kitchen are slightly inexperienced. Although they did not intentionally start the fire before they left for lunch, we fired them anyway. When we settle with the insurance company in several years, we will rebuild your home.
Closing	Sincerely,
Signature of letter writer	*K.C. Mattson*
Typed name of letter writer	K. C. Mattson, President
Initials of letter writer and typist	KCM: eln

have been discovered.[2] Within the New Testament alone, twenty-one of the twenty-seven documents are written in letter form, and two of the remaining six, Acts and Revelation, contain letters. Understanding the form and function of letters in Paul's day is vital for understanding Christian theology. Without knowledge of his letter format, we can easily misinterpret some of his sayings. A few examples from our own time will illustrate what I mean.

Letters today follow traditional forms that have been in use long enough that we accept them without question. If, for example, you receive a letter that uses the illustrated

2. Stanley K. Stowers, *Letter Writing in Greco-Roman Antiquity*, Library of Early Christianity (Philadelphia: Westminster Press, 1986), 15.

format, you know immediately that it is a business letter. When people write such letters, they do not ponder the precise meaning of words traditionally used in the openings and closings. Consequently, we would think it very quaint if people from another culture read too much into such words as Dear and Sincerely. If they conclude that K. C. Mattson likes Mr. Hanson because he begins "Dear Mr. Hanson," or that Mattson is a very sincere person because he concludes the letter "Sincerely," they misunderstand. These words are merely part of the conventional way in which people write letters. They probably reveal nothing about their author.

Even our personal letters follow a fairly set pattern, although their tone and structure are less formal than business letters. For example, our imaginary Mr. Hanson might write the letter below to his parents.

Some informal business letters and personal letters are written with a more business-like tone, but these are only variations of the normal forms. We have considerable freedom of expression in letters, but we show this freedom by modifying known forms of writing. So it was for the apostle Paul. He modified the forms of his day, and his Epistles are more understandable when we read them in light of the standard Greco-Roman forms that he creatively altered.

HOW ANCIENT GREEKS AND ROMANS WROTE THEIR LETTERS

The conquests of Alexander the Great in 333–323 BCE provided an important developmental stage for letter writing. The vastness of his empire necessitated more efficient methods of communication.

Personal Letter Form

Date of writing

Greeting

Body of letter
(gives news in an informal tone)

Closing
First name or nickname of writer

Aug. 15 2009

Dear Mom and Dad,

Please send any letters you may write to me to Uncle George's address. I'm staying with him until I can deal with the bunch of incompetent bozos who torched my house and went to Burger King for lunch. I think I will have to find a mean lawyer to get the contractors to take care of the mess they created. Meanwhile, I'm suffering for their mistakes.

Love,
Chuck

Consequently, letter writing developed at an accelerated rate during the several centuries after Alexander. Yet, because of the haphazard nature of mail delivery and the expense of writing materials, letters written by average people tended to be short, vague, and rather superficial. Furthermore, if letter writers could have a friend deliver their mail, they often entrusted longer, oral versions of their messages to their letter carriers, who were able to elaborate on the written text they carried. Aspects of Paul's Epistles that remain vague to us now would become clear if we could only talk to those who delivered his mail!

Letters in Paul's time fulfilled a wide variety of functions. But in spite of their diversity, for the most part they used the format outlined below.

The letter from Antonius Maximus (see sidebar) is a message from a soldier to people in his hometown, and it nicely illustrates the way the health wish followed the greeting. Writers often specified the god Serapis, a deity recognized as one who provided health and safety. The following excerpts from three different letters illustrate this. Observe the formal and repetitive nature of these greetings.

> Apion to Epimachus his father and lord, many greetings. Before all things I pray that you are healthy, asking that in all things you prosper, along with my sister and her daughter and my brother. I give thanks to the lord Serapis

---

Greco-Roman Letter Form

Introductory Salutation
(A) Sender to addressee
(B) greetings (*chairein* in Greek)
(C) a wish for good health, often indicating that sender prays to a certain deity on behalf of the addressee

Body of letter usually introduced with characteristic formulae

Conclusion
(A) final greetings, often including people other than addressee
(B) good wishes, especially for people other than addressee
(C) concluding greeting or prayer sentence
(D) sometimes a date

Address on reverse side of the letter, which was usually folded

---

Antonius Maximus to Sabina the sister, many greetings.

Before all else, I pray that you are healthy, for I myself also am healthy.

After praying for you to the gods here, I received a short letter from our fellow-citizen Antoninus. And when I heard that you are doing fine, I rejoiced greatly. And I will be diligent to write to you concerning my health [literally, "salvation"] and that of my family.

Greet Maximus warmly, and also Copres my lord. My life's partner, Aufidia, greets you, as does Maximus my son, . . . and Elpis and Fortunata. Salute my lord. . . .

because, being in peril in the sea, he immediately saved me. . . .

Antonis Longus to Nilus his mother, many greetings. I pray continually that you are healthy. Day after day I intercede for you to the lord Serapis. . . .

Sempronius to Saturnila his mother and lady, many greetings. Before all things, I pray that you and my brothers fare well, safe from the evil eye. Daily I intercede for you to the lord Serapis. . . .[3]

Delivering letters to their intended recipients could be frustrating. In the absence of a postal service and street addresses, people had to make their own arrangements for mail delivery. Note how the sender of the following letter dealt with this situation.

To Isidorus, my brother, greetings. Upon reaching Antinoöpolis, I received your letter, through which I experienced the feeling of seeing you. I therefore urge you to keep writing continually, for in this way our friendship will be increased. When I am slow to write to you, this happens easily because I am not able to find anyone traveling your way. Write to me about any need you might have since you know that I will comply without delay. If you write me a letter, send it to my friend Hermes at the house of Artemis so that he may deliver it to me. Hermes himself and his sister Tausiris send you many greetings. Farewell. [Verso] Deliver to my friend Isidorus in Philadelphia from [. . .][4]

The word "brother" in the first line was often used as a term of affection for friends, and the tone of the letter seems to indicate that Isidorus was the writer's good friend. This brief message illustrates how ancient Mediterraneans considered correspondence to be a means of maintaining friendship with those who were geographically separated from them. The letter writer says that when he received a letter from Isidorus, "I experienced the feeling of seeing you." Another man begins a letter, "You have come! . . . Although absent, you have appeared by means of your letter."

The Roman politician (and Stoic philosopher) Seneca (4 BCE–65 CE) says the following about his approach: "I prefer that my letters should be just what my conversation would be if you and I were sitting in one another's company or taking walks together, . . . spontaneous and easy" (*Letters* 75.1). In another correspondence Seneca states, "I never receive a letter from you without being in your company forthwith" (*Letters* 40.1).[5]

Although most of the ancient letters sent by common people were far too short and formulaic to simulate actual conversation, they nevertheless did provide an infrequent means of connecting people. And given the difficulties involved in sending mail, receiving letters was an anticipated event. In the letter above, for example, the writer indicates that before he can send mail to Isidorus, he must first find someone who is traveling to the town where Isidorus lives. Then he probably had to negotiate an appropriate fee for the traveler to deliver the letter. He could not just put a stamp on it and drop it in a mailbox. By contrast, in our own culture, we can communicate with people almost instantaneously by telephone or text messaging. In Paul's day, to receive a letter was an exciting event worth sharing with extended family and neighbors.

3. My translations based on the Greek texts provided by Deissmann, *Light from the Ancient East*, 179, 187, 192–93.

4. Stowers, *Letter Writing in Greco-Roman Antiquity*, 62–63.

5. Ibid., 62.

HOW PAUL WROTE HIS LETTERS

Paul's letters are not like the brief, stereotyped, impersonal notes so characteristic of his time period. Emotional expressions fill his Epistles. And although Paul used the Hellenistic letter form, he gave it characteristic changes that usually result in the following format:

Pauline Letter Form

Salutation

(A) Paul (sometimes specifies "an apostle of Jesus Christ"; sometimes includes coworkers with him at time of writing) to addressee (either a church or an individual)

(B) "grace (*charis*) to you and peace" (*eirēnē*, the Greek form of the Jewish greeting *shalom*)

Thanksgiving section states how he thanks God for particular characteristics of their particular group (e.g., faithfulness, evangelization efforts) and perhaps says what he prays for them. The reason for rejoicing is not for the physical safety of the addressees. He does not thank the lord Serapis for rescuing them from danger or illness, but he thanks God for their work in the gospel of the Lord Jesus Christ. Often the thanksgiving section provides a sort of brief introduction to some of the major themes of the letter, and commonly it ends with some sort of eschatological climax (e.g., "to wait for his Son from heaven, whom he raised from the dead—Jesus, who rescues us from the wrath that is coming" [1 Thess. 1:10]).

Body of the letter begins with an introductory formula (e.g., "You yourselves know, brothers and sisters" [1 Thess. 2:1]; "I want you to know, beloved" [Phil. 1:12]; "Now I appeal to you, brothers and sisters" [1 Cor. 1:10]). In this main part of the letter, Paul presents his *mission theology* (= the theological instructions that form the basis for actions that the addressees need to take). He also gives exhortations, ordering the people to do certain things and not do others. The exhortation is based on the mission theology and sometimes forms a distinct section following the statement of mission theology; at other times the two are mixed.

Closing usually includes formulaic benedictions and greetings to certain individuals in the church as well as greetings from certain people with Paul. At times the writing process itself is mentioned (as when Paul's scribe adds a note [in Rom.16:22], "I Tertius, the writer of this letter, greet you in the Lord"). On some occasions Paul comments about his concluding signature ("I, Paul, write this greeting with my own hand" [1 Cor. 16:21]; "See what large letters I make when I am writing in my own hand!" [Gal. 6:11]).

Philemon: Turning Up the Heat on a Good Friend

To see the parts of a Pauline letter, read through Philemon and highlight the beginning of the salutation, the thanksgiving, the body, and the closing. Then interact with the following questions on the content of the letter.

1. What positions in society do Philemon and Onesimus occupy?

2. What has occasioned the writing of this letter?

3. What is Paul's relationship to Philemon?

to Onesimus?

4. In order to mediate between Philemon and Onesimus, what pressure tactics does Paul use on Philemon? What difference does it make for Philemon that the letter is to be read to the entire house church?

5. What seems to be Paul's attitude toward slavery?

6. What insights into Paul does this brief letter give?

How Were Slaves Treated?

Onesimus means "useful" or "beneficial" and was a common slave name. Thus, when Paul says in verse 11 that Onesimus was formerly useless but now is useful, he is making a pun. Slavery was extremely common in the Roman Empire. Slaves were so numerous in Rome, for example, that when a senator proposed that all slaves be required to wear distinctive dress, his

Philemon

[1]Paul, a prisoner of Christ Jesus, and Timothy our brother,

To Philemon our dear friend and co-worker, [2]to Apphia our sister, to Archippus our fellow soldier, and to the church in your house:

[3]Grace to you and peace from God our Father and the Lord Jesus Christ.

[4]When I remember you in my prayers, I always thank my God [5]because I hear of your love for all the saints and your faith toward the Lord Jesus. [6]I pray that the sharing of your faith may become effective when you perceive all the good that we may do for Christ. [7]I have indeed received much joy and encouragement from your love, because the hearts of the saints have been refreshed through you, my brother.

[8]For this reason, though I am bold enough in Christ to command you to do your duty, [9]yet I would rather appeal to you on the basis of love—and I, Paul, do this as an old man, and now also as a prisoner of Christ Jesus. [10]I am appealing to you for my child, Onesimus, whose father I have become during my imprisonment. [11]Formerly he was useless to you, but now he is indeed useful both to you and to me. [12]I am sending him, that is, my own heart, back to you. [13]I wanted to keep him with me, so that he might be of service to me in your place during my imprisonment for the gospel; [14]but I preferred to do nothing without your consent, in order that your good deed might be voluntary and not something forced. [15]Perhaps this is the reason he was separated from you for a while, so that you might have him back forever, [16]no longer as a slave but more than a slave, a beloved brother—especially to me but how much more to you, both in the flesh and in the Lord.

[17]So if you consider me your partner, welcome him as you would welcome me. [18]If he has wronged you in any way, or owes you anything, charge that to my account. [19]I, Paul, am writing this with my own hand: I will repay it. I say nothing about your owing me even your own self. [20]Yes, brother, let me have this benefit from you in the Lord! Refresh my heart in Christ. [21]Confident of your obedience, I am writing to you, knowing that you will do even more than I say.

[22]One thing more—prepare a guest room for me, for I am hoping through your prayers to be restored to you.

[23]Epaphras, my fellow prisoner in Christ Jesus, sends greetings to you, [24]and so do Mark, Aristarchus, Demas, and Luke, my fellow workers.

[25]The grace of the Lord Jesus Christ be with your spirit.

proposal was quickly voted down. Most senate members feared that serious problems would result if the slaves realized how many others there were (Seneca, *De clementia* 1.24.1).

In earlier centuries many people became slaves as a result of warfare, with captives of conquered cities forced into slavery. By the first century, however, political conditions were more stable, and a greater percentage of slaves were homebred. Children inherited the condition of their mothers, so the offspring of slave women were born slaves. Sometimes people even sold their children into slavery in order to pay debts, and some people were subjected to slavery as punishment for crimes. Regardless of the reason, slaves were considered property, and their lot in life largely depended on the kindness or severity of their masters. Some were treated quite well, while others existed in terrible conditions.

Owners could treat their slaves however they wished. In the fourth century BCE, Aristotle called slaves living tools (*Nicomachean Ethics* 8.11), and many after his time agreed with this assessment: they were things, objects to be used. Their duties varied from brutal labor in mines, which resulted in short life expectancy, to highly responsible duties in Roman government (bureaucratic functions), which were often a source of pride for these slaves. Some worked as farmhands, others as housekeepers. Some functioned as teachers, others as craftsmen. Enslaved people did much of the work in the Roman Empire.

According to Roman custom, slaves could potentially earn a certain amount of money, which they could accumulate until they were able to purchase their freedom. Liberated slaves were called freedmen, and they typically had certain responsibilities toward their former owners, who now functioned as their benefactors.

One particular Roman custom might lie behind the story of Onesimus in Paul's Letter to Philemon. If a slave had done something to incur the wrath of the master, the slave might flee to one of the master's respected friends, who would then function as an intermediary to help settle the problem. Perhaps Onesimus deliberately sought out Paul because he believed

that the apostle garnered enough respect that he would be able to exert influence on Philemon to reduce the penalty he expected due to stealing his master's money, or whatever it was that he did. While visiting Paul in prison, he evidently became a Christian himself, and Paul later sent Onesimus back to Philemon with a letter concerning him.[6]

Assembling the Broken Pieces

Reconstructing Paul's life is somewhat like trying to reassemble the fragments of a broken pottery vase that is missing a number of pieces. As we painstakingly see which pieces fit with which other pieces, we slowly reconstruct the basic shape of the vase. Perhaps a more familiar example would be assembling a jigsaw puzzle that is missing numerous pieces. We have to fill in the gaps as best we can. Although Paul's Letters reveal only fragments of his busy life, they do allow for fascinating insights into his personality and his ministry. His short letter to Philemon, for example, reveals his ability to pressure people. It also shows his deep love and concern for a slave in need of assistance and mercy.

In the chapters that follow, we will examine each of the existing pieces of Paul's life as they are represented by his Letters, and then seek to reconstruct a larger view of the apostle. Our reconstruction will be

---

6. Colossians and Philemon might have been written at the same time and delivered by the same letter carrier, Tychicus, who accompanied Onesimus (Col. 4:7–9). Paul's companions are identical in the two letters (cf. Col. 4:10–14 with Phlm. 23–24; and Col. 1:1 with Phlm. 1:1).

tentative because we are missing much information. But as we study each letter, we will see how he addresses pressing issues of concern among specific Christian groups. We will explore Paul's communications to his original readers in light of their historical context, and then we will ask what relevance his words have for us today.

Exercise on Letter Writing

1. Write a brief letter to a friend using the standard Greco-Roman letter form.

2. Now write the same letter using the Pauline letter form.

FURTHER READING ON LETTER WRITING IN ANTIQUITY

Deissmann, Adolf. *Light from the Ancient East.* Reprint, Grand Rapids: Baker Book House, 1978. Originally published in 1927. Important for understanding Paul's Letters in light of the common letters of his day. Contains pictures of ancient letters, translations, and comments.

*Doty, William G. *Letters in Primitive Christianity.* Philadelphia: Fortress Press, 1973. Short book for beginners in this field of study. Explains letter structure and summarizes the implications for interpreting Paul's Letters.

Klauck, Hans-Josef. *Ancient Letters and the New Testament: A Guide to Context and Exegesis.* Waco, TX: Baylor University Press, 2006. ET of a 1998 German text. Although detailed (504 pages), this book is readable.

Malherbe, Abraham J. *Ancient Epistolary Theorists.* Atlanta: Scholars Press, 1988. Technical work. Good for research.

O'Brien, Peter Thomas. *Introductory Thanksgivings in the Letters of Paul.* Leiden: E. J. Brill, 1977. Explores the construction of thanksgiving sections and explains implications for interpretation.

Schubert, Paul. *The Form and Function of the Pauline Thanksgiving.* Berlin: Alfred Topelmann, 1939. Groundbreaking study. Dated, but valuable.

*Stowers, Stanley K. *Letter Writing in Greco-Roman Antiquity.* Philadelphia: Westminster Press, 1986. Helpful and accessible. Filled with examples of ancient letters, categorized by form and function.

White, John L. *Light from Ancient Letters.* Philadelphia: Fortress Press, 1986. Good survey of insights gleaned from the discovery of ancient letters.

FURTHER READING
ON PHILEMON AND SLAVERY

Barth, Marcus. *The Letter to Philemon: A New Translation with Notes and Commentary.* Eerdmans Critical Commentary. Grand Rapids: Wm. B. Eerdmans Publishing Co., 2000. Scholarly commentary.

Bradley, K. R. *Slaves and Masters in the Roman Empire: A Study in Social Control.* New York: Oxford University Press, 1984. Detailed study of the tensions between masters and slaves, the brutality that often surrounded slavery, and how slaves could gain their freedom.

*Bruce, F. F. *Epistles to the Colossians, to Philemon, and to the Ephesians.* NICNT. Grand Rapids: Wm. B. Eerdmans Publishing Co., 1984. Good balance between scholarship and readability.

Callahan, Allen Dwight. *Embassy of Onesimus: The Letter of Paul to Philemon.* Valley Forge, PA: Trinity Press International, 1997. Short work (96 pages) argues an unusual position: that Onesimus was Philemon's estranged brother, not his slave.

Fitzmyer, Joseph A. *The Letter to Philemon: A New Translation with Introduction and Commentary.* AB. New York: Doubleday, 2000. Scholarly commentary.

Lohse, Eduard. *Colossians and Philemon.* Philadelphia: Fortress Press, 1971. Technical commentary.

Wall, Robert W. *Colossians and Philemon.* IVP New Testament Commentary Series. Downers Grove, IL: InterVarsity Press, 1993. Scholarly analysis plus pastoral application. Good example of contemporary application based on a historical reading.

Wiedemann, Thomas. *Greek and Roman Slavery: A Sourcebook.* Baltimore: Johns Hopkins University Press, 1981. English translations of 243 ancient texts and inscriptions dealing with slavery. Valuable for studying slavery in the Roman world.

CHAPTER 7

1 Thessalonians

PROBLEMS WITH PROPHECY

Early Christians believed that they were living at the end of world history. When Paul proclaimed salvation in Jesus Christ, he also preached that the Lord would soon return to judge the living and the dead. For Paul, time on earth was about over, and this greatly affected his views on life. As we will see in 1 Corinthians, for example, his anticipation of the end heavily influenced the advice he gave to engaged couples on whether they should marry, or to slaves on whether or not to seek freedom. And here in 1 Thessalonians, probably his earliest letter, answering questions his converts raised about the second coming of Christ occupies much of his attention.

Some Christians at Thessalonica concluded that because Christ was going to return soon, they should not concern themselves with work. Their reasoning went something like this: "If the Lord is coming soon, why shouldn't the wealthy Christians in our group freely support the rest of us? Why worry about food and possessions if we won't need them much longer? Why work?" In 1 Thessalonians, Paul seeks to correct this end-time laziness, as well as to comfort those who are troubled by the fact that some of their number had died before the Lord's return.

AN IMPORTANT PORT CITY OF MACEDONIA

When Paul journeyed from Philippi to **Thessalonica** on his second missionary journey, he most likely traveled along the

Review Acts 17:1–10 on what happened to Paul and his companions at Thessalonica during his second missionary journey, in approximately 49 or 50.

1. Approximately how long did Paul spend in Thessalonica, and under what circumstances did he leave?

2. What might the husbands of the women in 17:4 have said to their wives about Paul, the itinerant Jewish preacher of the strange new deity, Jesus Christ?

Via Egnatia (Egnatian Way), an important road for trade and troop movement. Cassander, king of Macedonia, founded Thessalonica in 315 BCE, largely because he needed a good harbor for expanded trade with port cities in other regions. He named the city after his wife, Thessalonikē, daughter of Philip II and half sister of Alexander the Great. It became a cultural and trade center and played a significant role in the political history of Macedonia.

When Macedonia became a Roman province in 148 BCE, Thessalonica was the Roman administrative center of the region, the headquarters of the proconsul. The Via Egnatia ran through the city, providing the main line of communication between Rome and the eastern provinces. In 42 BCE, Mark Antony (Marcus Antonius) granted Thessalonica the status of a free city, and this allowed it to be governed by its own rulers, called politarchs (Acts 17:6, 8). In the first century CE, Thessalonica was one of the major cities of the region.

The main religious cult there when Paul arrived was that of Cabirus, and loyalty to this deity was considered part of being a good citizen. Also, emperor worship was well established in the first century, and this helped to foster good relationships with Rome. When Paul began to preach belief in Jesus Christ to the exclusion of local and national deities, his actions were considered subversive and threatening to the social order of the city. To attack such worship was seen as a threat

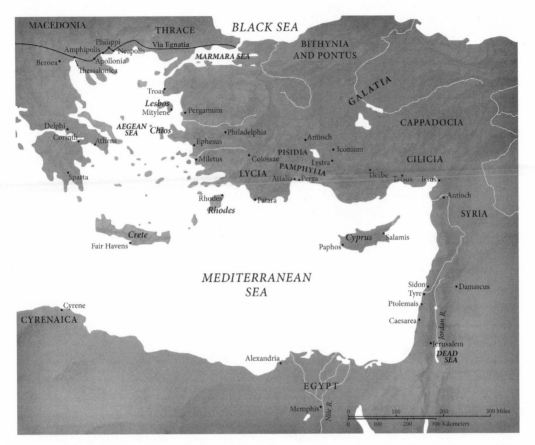

The Via Egnatia was named after Gaius Ignatius, who ordered its construction. Romans developed this road for rapid troop movement and for commerce.

to the security of Thessalonica and invited reprisals.

A WARM, PARENTAL LETTER (1 THESS. 2:17–3:13)

Like the letter to Philemon, 1 Thessalonians was to be read to the assembled believers (5:27). Try to imagine what these new converts might think as they heard the letter read aloud.

1. What do Paul's comments in 2:17–3:13 reveal about his feelings toward the Thessalonians? What steps has he taken to care for them?

"YOU GUYS ARE DOING GREAT" (1 THESS. 1:2–10)

Following the greeting in 1:1, Paul's thanksgiving in 1:2–10 reveals quite positive feelings toward these new believers, thanking God for their spiritual growth in spite of persecution.

1. Identify which verses in 1:2–10 contain the standard elements of Pauline thanksgiving sections that are detailed in chapter 6.

2. In light of conditions described in Acts 17:1–10, why might non-Christians at Thessalonica have leveled these charges against him?

3. Note the parental terms used in 2:7, 11. How has Paul been like a mother to these Christians? (Think of how mothers are with their infants. Why does Paul use this imagery in this context?)

"NO! I'M REALLY NOT LIKE THAT!" (1 THESS. 2:1–12)

After the opening formula in 2:1 ("You yourselves know"), Paul mentions the difficult conditions under which he proclaimed the gospel to the Thessalonians. Then he explains how honorable his behavior was among them.

1. Against what false charges does Paul defend himself in 2:3–12?[1]

---

provide role models for ethical behavior: "Exhortation in First Thessalonians," *Novum Testamentum* 25 (1983): 238–56; and *Moral Exhortation: A Greco-Roman Sourcebook*, Library of Early Christianity (Philadelphia: Westminster, 1986), 135–38. See also Stanley K. Stowers, *Letter Writing in Greco-Roman Antiquity*, Library of Early Christianity (Philadelphia: Westminster Press, 1986), 25–26, 99–100; and Charles A. Wanamaker, *The Epistles to the Thessalonians: A Commentary on the Greek Text*, NIGTC (Grand Rapids: Wm. B. Eerdmans Publishing Co., 1990), 91–108. However, the examples given by these scholars are not pertinent parallels to what Paul states in 1 Thess. 2:1–12 and do not give adequate evidence that Paul merely used a stock list of moral virtues. Note that 2:2 refers to a concrete historical event, and 2:9 references their hard work in contrast with the idleness of some Thessalonian Christians whom Paul seeks to correct in 4:11–12 and 5:14. In addition, the use of female nurse imagery in 2:7–8 does not fit the standard, male examples cited by Malherbe and others.

Philip F. Esler argues that Malherbe's treatment of a passage from the Cynic philosopher Dio misconstrues what the ancient author meant to communicate. Esler believes that Malherbe anachronistically reads Dio in a modern, intellectual manner that divorces him from his "conflict-ridden Mediterranean culture." He concludes by saying, "Malherbe essentially depends upon verbal similarity between a section of Dio Chrysostom's *Oration* 32 and 1 Thess. 2 without closely examining the meaning of the language in these distinct contexts": *Galatians*, New Testament Readings (New York: Routledge, 1998), 66.

---

1. Some scholars argue that the behaviors Paul lists in 1 Thess. 2:3–12 are merely a catalog of moral behaviors. Abraham Malherbe compares 2:3–12 with lists of moral examples in Greco-Roman literature, which

4. What does Paul consider to be his fatherly role to them?

"THEY'RE SLIMY SNAKES, AND GOD WILL BLAST THEM!" (1 THESS. 2:13–16)

1. These new converts could easily assume that something was wrong with their new faith, for they soon began to experience hardships because of it. What reassurance does 2:13–16 offer?

Modern Christian sensitivities cause some to be uneasy with Paul's aggressive verbal attack against Jews in 1 Thessalonians 2:14–16. His words, however, are typical of the argumentation style of his day.[2] Ancient Mediterranean people freely used overstatement when describing their opponents. Examples of **hyperbole** in the

New Testament can include racial stereotypes ("Cretans are always liars, vicious brutes, lazy gluttons" [Titus 1:12]) as well as regional stereotypes ("Can anything good come out of Nazareth?" [John 1:46]). Expressions that were considered typical in Paul's culture might seem like slanderous defamations of opponents to modern Western Christians. To get a close approximation of their word choices, we might compare them with the mudslinging that goes on in tight political races in our own country. Adversaries often do not present fair evaluations of their opponents; they paint them as incompetent, dishonest, immoral, and unethical. Paul's frequent use of aggressive language when blasting his adversaries represents a common form of argumentation.

Luke T. Johnson illustrates how ancient Greeks, Romans, Jews, and Christians used hyperbolic language when slamming their opponents.[3] Dio of Prusa, for example, was a rhetorician turned philosopher, and he became viciously critical of rhetoricians.

> He calls the *sophistai* [rhetoricians]: "ignorant, boastful, self-deceived" (*Or.* 4:33), . . . "unlearned and deceiving by their words" (4.37), . . . "evil-spirited" (4.38), . . . "impious" (11.14), . . . "liars and deceivers" (12.12), . . . "preaching for the sake of gain and glory and only their own benefit" (32.30). They are flatterers, charlatans and sophists (23.11); . . . they profit nothing (33.4–5); . . . they are mindless (54.1), boastful and shameless (55.7), deceiving others and themselves (70.10), demagogues (77/78.27). He can say all this though he grudgingly admits that some sophists act for good (35.9–10). In other words, the polemic has nothing to do with specific actions, but typical ones.[4]

2. Carol J. Schlueter, for example, explores this passage in light of the use of hyperbole in Paul's day: *Filling up the Measure: Polemical Hyperbole in 1 Thessalonians 2.14–16.* JNTS Supplement Series 98 (Sheffield: Sheffield Academic Press, 1994).

3. Luke T. Johnson, "The New Testament's Anti-Jewish Slander and the Conventions of Ancient Polemic," *Journal of Biblical Literature* 108 (1989): 419–41.

4. Ibid., 430.

Johnson explains how Mediterraneans took generalized criticisms and applied them liberally to opponents, especially if these adversaries posed a direct threat to the authors' positions in society. In other words: Did they pose a challenge to the author's honor?

If people were not considered threats, open-minded writers might be magnanimous in their remarks about them. For example, "Plutarch, a priest of Apollo at Delphi, was the most urbane of ancient philosophers, encyclopedic in learning, vast in sympathy." Johnson reports that when this priest described Jewish people, he was somewhat generous, and this proves that "*their* version of philosophy was unimportant to him." By contrast, when responding to an attack in which Plutarch's heroes were labeled "buffoons, charlatans, assassins, prostitutes, nincompoops," he responded that the attackers were charlatans whose "eminent men write with such shameless arrogance" (*Moralia* 1124C).[5] Similarly, Epictetus, a Stoic philosopher, said of Epicureans, "Your doctrines are bad, subversive of the state, destructive of the family, not even fit for women" (*Dissertations* 3.7.21).[6]

As so often in Hellenistic rhetoric, these charges became standardized. . . . Certain things are conventionally said of all opponents. Their teaching was self-contradictory, or trivial, or it led to bad morals. . . . Either they preached but did not practice (in which case they were hypocrites), or they lived as they taught and their corrupt lives showed how bad their doctrine was (like the Epicureans). Certain standard categories of vice were automatically attributed to any opponent. They were all lovers of pleasure, lovers of money, and lovers of glory.[7]

Slanderous accusations meant that an author viewed certain people as a threat to be squashed. Furthermore, most of these harangues were written to be read by members of their own groups—not by members of the opposition. Frequently authors considered persuasion to be more important than precision.

The Jewish historian Josephus, for example, calls the *Sicarii* (assassins) "imposters and brigands" (*War* 2.8.6), "slaves, the dregs of society, and the bastard scum of the nation" (5.8.5), who are more wicked than Sodom in being godless (5.13.6) and "outdo each other in acts of impiety toward God and injustice to their neighbors, . . . [leaving] no word unspoken to insult, no deed untried to ruin" (7.8.1).[8] Similarly, a passage from the Dead Sea Scrolls accuses a rival Jewish group of "greed and . . . wickedness and lies, haughtiness and pride, falseness and deceit, cruelty and abundant evil, . . . abominable deeds committed in a spirit of lust" (1QS 4.9–14). Such attacks were common, and Paul's words in 1 Thessalonians 2:14–16 should be read in light of this cultural tendency. If we look for polite, generous descriptions of opponents in the New Testament, we will be disappointed. Members of ancient Mediterranean cultures were verbally aggressive in their competition for honor, and Paul was no exception.

Paul's contemporaries knew how to insult each other, and they did so with zest. If we could hear or read the accusations that were directed against Paul, they would

---

5. Ibid., 431.
6. Ibid., 432.
7. Ibid.; footnote 47 provides examples of each category of accusation.

8. Ibid., 437. For an examination of similar techniques used by Romans in their political speeches, see J. Roger Dunkle, "The Greek Tyrant and Roman Political Invective of the Late Republic," *TAPA* 98 (1967): 151–71.

have been sizzling. Such language was common to all sides of these debates. Indeed, matching insults with opponents is an art form with a long history. The great Protestant reformer Martin Luther sometimes attacked his antagonists with vivid language. In 1511 he defamed Duke Heinrich von Braunschweig-Wolfenbüttel by saying, "You shouldn't have written a book, unless you had heard a fart from an old sow, when you should have opened your mouth wide to it and said, 'Thank you very much, beautiful nightingale; that will make good text for me.'"[9] In Paul's day leaders sought to gain the loyalty of their followers by defaming those with whom they disagreed. Periodically such attacks surface in the New Testament. We should not be shocked by them so much as read them in light of first-century norms and sensitivities—which means not taking every word literally.

THE WIDE-OPEN ATTITUDE TOWARD SEX AMONG GENTILES (1 THESS. 4:1–12)

Sexuality among Gentile Christians posed difficulties for the early church. We have seen how, during the Jerusalem council meeting described in Acts 15, part of the compromise solution to the problem of Gentiles in the church was that these new Christians must abstain from fornication (15:20, 29). This transition would not be easy, because Greeks and Romans had sensitivities about sexual matters quite different from Jewish people. The Greek author Athenaeus, for example,

praises a group of women called *hetairai*, whom wealthy men employed as female companions. "We keep mistresses [*hetairai*] for pleasure, concubines for daily concubinage, but wives we have in order to produce children legitimately and to have a trustworthy guardian of our domestic property" (*Deipnosophistae* 13.573b [Gulick, LCL]).[10]

> In Greek culture . . . husbands were allowed to have extramarital intercourse, and this was not considered to be a violation of marriage. . . . There was, nevertheless, a distinct double standard in sexual matters, since the Greek wives were forbidden to have extramarital intercourse. The sexual liberties denied the women were considered to be perfectly legitimate for the men, with society frowning only on excess.[11]

Observant Jews abhorred such Gentile customs, and many Jewish Christians criticized Paul for not demanding that his Gentile converts become **proselyte** Jews and obey the laws of Moses.

1. According to 1 Thessalonians 4:1–8, Paul is pleased with the way the Thessalonians are maintaining the sexual ethics that he taught them. What guidelines does Paul give on sexual matters in 4:1–8?

9. Martin Luther, *Wider Hans Worst* (1541), quoted from Gerhard Ebeling, *Luther: An Introduction to His Thought* (Philadelphia: Fortress, 1970), 54.

10. Wealthy Greek wives typically led a secluded life at home and did not go out into public with their husbands or even visibly appear to their husband's guests who were being entertained in their own homes. Poorer-class wives had more freedom to be in public spaces like the marketplace.

11. Michael R. Cosby, *Sex in the Bible: An Introduction to What the Scriptures Teach Us about Sexuality* (Englewood Cliffs, NJ: Prentice-Hall, 1984), 118.

2. In 4:9–12, why does Paul insist that these Christians work and live respectable lives?

2. From 4:15, 17, does Paul expect to be alive or dead when the Parousia occurs?

3. In 5:1–2 Paul indicates that he previously taught them about these things. Which people will be surprised by the Parousia? Which people will not be surprised?

THE NOISY RETURN OF CHRIST FROM HEAVEN (4:13–5:11)

During his brief stay in Thessalonica, Paul evidently placed considerable emphasis on the second coming of Christ (also called the **Parousia**) in his preaching to the new converts (note the references in 1:10; 2:19; 3:13 and the lengthy treatment in 4:13–5:11). After his departure from Thessalonica, however, confusion arose about this matter, especially with regard to the destiny of those who had died since Paul left the city. In the following passage determine the questions that Paul was apparently answering and note the verbs he uses to describe the Parousia.

1. Paul reassures his readers in 4:13–18 that the dead in Christ will participate in the Parousia. Note carefully the description of this event in 4:15–17. What sights and sounds does Paul's explanation employ?

The image of labor pains in 5:3 is common in apocalyptic writings, and some Old Testament authors used it for portraying the trials associated with divine judgment (e.g., Isa. 13:6–8; 26:16–19; Jer. 6:22–26; Hos. 13:13; Mic. 4:9–10). **First Enoch**, an important **apocalypse**, applied it to end-time wrath against godless rulers.

> On the day of judgment, all the kings, the governors, the high officials, and the landlords shall see and recognize him—how he sits on the throne of his glory, and righteousness is judged before him. . . . Then pain shall come upon them as on a woman in travail with birth pangs. . . . They shall be terrified and dejected; and pain shall seize them when they see that Son of Man sitting on the throne of his glory. (62.3–5)[12]

12. Translation from *The Old Testament Pseudepigrapha*, vol. 1, *Apocalyptic Literature and Testaments*, ed. James H. Charlesworth (Garden City, NY: Doubleday, 1983), 43.

Eschatological Jewish authors of the first century largely believed that, just before the end of what they called the **present evil age**, God's faithful will experience a time of unprecedented stress. They called this time the **woes of the Messiah** and used analogies such as labor pains to describe it. As a woman suffers while giving birth to her baby, so they believed that the earth would suffer during the birth of the new age. They called the future time of eternal bliss the **age to come**: an era of the blessed reign of God on earth, which would be ushered in by the Messiah. They believed that, whereas the present evil age is a time of suffering due to evil, the age to come will be free from sin, suffering, and death. The following illustration depicts this idea visually.

JEWISH VIEW OF THE TWO AGES

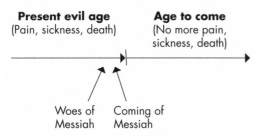

Christians adopted this concept of the two ages, and we see it periodically in the New Testament. For example, Ephesians 1:21 mentions Christ being "far above . . . every name that is named, not only in this age but also in the age to come." They also adopted the imagery of childbirth with respect to the dawning of the new age. Thus Jesus' disciples ask him in Mark 13:4, "Tell us, when will this be, and what will be the sign that all these things are about to be accomplished?" Jesus replies, "When you hear of wars and rumors of wars, do not be alarmed; this must take place, but the end is still to come. For nation will rise against nation, and kingdom against kingdom; there will be earthquakes in various places; there will be famines. This is but the beginning of the birth pangs" (13:7–8).

Christians believed that this end-time stress would come just before the Parousia. Like labor pains, the intensity of Christian suffering would get worse and worse until, just when all looked hopeless, Jesus would return from heaven with fiery judgment to vindicate the righteous and punish the wicked (so 1 Thess. 1:10: "Jesus, who rescues us from the wrath that is coming"; and 5:3: "When they say, 'There is peace and security,' then sudden destruction will come upon them, as labor pains come upon a pregnant woman, and there will be no escape"). Because Christians believed that Jesus Messiah had already come, they modified Jewish expectations of when the Messiah would usher in the age to come. The following illustration shows how they did so:

CHRISTIAN MODIFICATION OF THE JEWISH VIEW OF THE TWO AGES

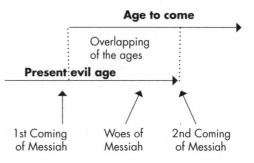

Jesus' followers believed that his Parousia would be a universally visible event that would begin the age to come in its fullness. Already they experienced some of the benefits of God's rule, as we have seen from the miracle accounts in Acts. But they believed that when Christ returned, all remnants of the present evil age would be wiped out. As we have seen in 1 Thessalonians, Paul associated the Parousia with both judgment and salvation. He wanted the Thessalonian Christians to experience Christ's vindication, not his wrath (see 5:9, 23).

4. According to 5:8–21, how should knowledge of Christ's return affect the way Christians live?

End-Time Enthusiasm

Some Christians today are convinced that Jesus Christ is going to return to earth within the next few years (or months). What are the dangers of radical commitment to this belief?

HOW TO THROW A PARTY WHEN THE KING COMES TO TOWN

In Paul's time it was customary to conduct a formal greeting ceremony when an emperor or other famous dignitary came to one's city. In preparation for the reception (Greek *apantēsis*), the city officials would sometimes levy a tax on the local citizens in order to fashion a golden crown for the dignitary. On the day of his arrival, the citizens went out beyond the city walls and stood waiting alongside the road. The city officials ceremoniously met the dignitary as he approached, and the people cheered and welcomed him. After this grand welcoming ceremony, the dignitary led the citizens in procession back into the city, where typically he would offer sacrifices on the local altars.

The Jewish historian Josephus describes one of these receptions when he recounts the return of Vespasian to Rome. Observe the wild enthusiasm of the crowd.

> Amidst such feelings of universal goodwill, those of higher rank, impatient of awaiting him, hastened to a great distance from Rome to be the first to greet him. Nor, indeed, could any of the rest endure the delay of meeting, but all poured forth in such crowds—for to all it seemed simpler and easier to go than to remain—that the very city then for the first time experienced with satisfaction a paucity of inhabitants; for those who went outnumbered those who remained. But when he was reported to be approaching and those who had gone ahead were telling of the affability of his reception of each party, the whole remaining population, with wives and children, were by now waiting at the road-sides to receive him; and each group as he passed, in their delight at the spectacle and moved by the blandness of his appearance, gave vent to all manner of cries, hailing him as "benefactor," "savior," and "only worthy emperor of Rome." The whole city, moreover, was filled, like a temple, with garlands and incense. Having reached the palace, though with difficulty, owing to the multitude that thronged around him, he offered sacrifices of thanksgiving for his arrival to the household gods. (*War* 7.68–72 [Thackeray, LCL])

When Paul describes Christ's coming in 4:15–17, this Greco-Roman practice of enthusiastically greeting an arriving dignitary is part of the cultural background (cf.

Roman citizens sometimes conducted elaborate receptions when a king or a victorious general came to their city. This arch of triumph, located near the forum in Rome, commemorates the victory of Titus over Jewish insurrectionists in Palestine in 70 CE. (Courtesy of Michael Cosby)

Acts 28:15 where Christians go out of Rome to greet Paul).

Although Greco-Roman formal receptions provide valuable background for Paul's description of the Parousia, they do not give a blueprint for it, for he reverses most of the standard expectations. Unlike the planned receptions when citizens knew when to go out to greet the dignitary, Christ returns abruptly, at an unexpected time (although Christians are not surprised at the coming [5:1–4]). As Christ the great king approaches the world, those who belong to him are suddenly caught up to meet him in the clouds. Instead of bringing gifts to the king, however, they receive their resurrection bodies as a gift from him. Instead of human heralds announcing Christ's arrival, he proclaims his own descent from heaven, accompanied by an angelic trumpet blast and the shout of an archangel (4:16). The dead in Christ are joined by those who are still alive, and together they join in a grand procession down to the earth, where the returning king pronounces judgment on those who have not believed in him. The earsplitting blast from the heavenly trumpet and the shout of the archangel make this event eminently public, taking the non-Christians by surprise and vindicating the Christians. One could humorously say that there will be enough noise to raise the dead (4:16). But there is no humor in it for those who dwell in darkness. The Parousia involves God's wrath (1:10; 5:3, 9), for it involves Christ's descent to earth to judge the wicked (2:19; 3:13; 5:23).[13]

Ironically, some Christians today teach that this spectacular public display will be what they call the secret rapture of the

13. For a detailed investigation of the practices involved in ancient receptions of dignitaries and how Paul's description of the Parousia compares with them, see Michael R. Cosby, "Hellenistic Formal Receptions and Paul's Use of ΑΠΑΝΤΗΣΙΣ in 1 Thessalonians 4:17," *Bulletin for Biblical Research* 4 (1994): 15–33.

church, a quiet snatching of Christians up into heaven to deliver them from the coming tribulation. According to this teaching, non-Christians will suddenly realize that Christians have mysteriously vanished, and the world will enter a time of confused chaos. This teaching about a secret rapture, called the "blessed hope" by some, is recent in the history of the church. Yet it has spawned a growth industry among those who develop charts depicting end-time events and who give confident predictions of what will happen in the near future.

You can assess the magnitude of this prophecy movement by typing "Bible prophecy" into an Internet search engine and clicking on some of the multitude of links to Web sites that will appear. The consistent inaccuracy of claims they make regarding future events largely results from a failure to read the New Testament in its historical context. In the case of 1 Thessalonians 4:13–18, the loud and universally visible event that Paul describes becomes a secret snatching up of Christians into the clouds so that they might avoid the great tribulation.[14] Paul would be stunned if he saw what people are doing with his words!

How the sound and light display described briefly in 4:14–18 can provide one of the key texts to teach the secret rapture of the church is itself a mystery. If we pay attention to Paul's description and read this passage in the context of 1 Thessalonians as a whole, we see that it describes Christ's coming to gather his people while he is on his way to earth for the final judgment.

14. See Michael R. Cosby, "The Danger of Armageddon Theology," in *The Covenant Quarterly* 51 (August 1993): 37–45.

LETTER CLOSING
(1 THESS. 5:23–28)

1. How does this closing compare with the description of Pauline conclusions provided in chapter 6, "Reading Other People's Mail"?

WHAT DID YOU LEARN
ABOUT PAUL?

1. What does 1 Thessalonians reveal about Paul the man? How does he view himself?

How does he view his work?

How does he view those to whom he ministers?

GLOSSARY

Age to Come. Phrase used to describe the future age of bliss promised to God's faithful. The Messiah was to come and bring an end to the present evil age; and following the last judgment, he would usher in the eternal age to come, which would be characterized by the absence of sin, evil, suffering, and death.

Apantēsis. Greek technical term for the loud and festive, formal reception of a dignitary into a city. Paul incorporates some of the imagery of such receptions into his description of the second coming of Christ in 1 Thessalonians 4–5.

Apocalypse. Title for works supposedly written to reveal the mysteries of the end times. It comes from the Greek word *apocalypsis*, meaning "revelation." Apocalypses are known for their use of bizarre imagery, angelic revealers, pseudonymous authorship, telling history as if it were prophecy, determinism, pessimistic view of history, cosmic battles between the forces of good and evil, and the triumph of God in the end.

Eschatological. The Greek word for "last" is *eschaton*, and eschatology is the study of last things. Eschatological people think that they are living in the last times. Most early Christians were eschatological (e.g., Acts 3:21, 24; 1 Cor. 10:11), believing that Christ would return from heaven in the very near future and judge the world.

1 Enoch. An important apocalypse that provides insight into apocalyptic thinking and literature. It was popular reading in Paul's day and contains information about messianic expectations of the time.

Hetairai. Women whom wealthy Greek men employed as female companions (call girls) when they attended parties.

Hyperbole. Overstatement for effect. A common speech technique in the Mediterranean world of Paul's day—one that Paul uses with some frequency to present his messages in his various letters.

Parousia. Term used by Christians to refer to the second coming of Christ. The word means "coming" or "presence."

Present evil age. Term used to describe the present age, which is characterized by sin, evil, suffering, and death. It was to come to an end when the Messiah came to usher in the age to come.

Proselytes. People who leave one form of belief to become members of another religious faith. For example, when polytheistic Romans converted to Judaism and sought to keep the laws of Moses, they became proselyte Jews.

Thessalonica. The Roman administrative center of Macedonia, the headquarters of the proconsul. It was an important harbor city that functioned as a center of culture and commerce. Paul visited the city on his second missionary journey.

Via Egnatia. The Egnatian Way, an important road for trade and troop movement that provided the main overland line of communication between Rome and the eastern provinces.

Woes of the Messiah. A time of unprecedented stress experienced by the righteous just before the end of the present evil age. Often the analogy of labor pains is used to describe this time. As a woman suffers while giving birth to her baby, so the earth and its inhabitants would suffer during the birth of the new age.

FURTHER READING ON 1 THESSALONIANS

See bibliography under 2 Thessalonians.

CHAPTER 8

2 Thessalonians

GET TO WORK, YOU LAZY MOOCHERS!

According to 2 Thessalonians, the problems that surfaced in Thessalonica with the teaching about the nearness of Christ's second coming continued to plague Paul. Most of this letter pertains to events surrounding the Parousia; and 2 Thessalonians 3:6–15 gives further instructions on dealing with the idlers, the fainthearted, and the weak, also mentioned in 1 Thessalonians 5:14.

Some aspects of 2 Thessalonians seem a bit unusual if 2 Thessalonians is one of Paul's earliest Letters. In 2:1–3, for example, Paul indicates that someone has written a false letter in his name, claiming that the Parousia is already past. So he assures his readers not to be alarmed by this deception. In 3:17 he also calls attention to his signature as a sign of authenticity in all of his Letters. In addition, he reminds them

of the "oral traditions" that he taught them (2:15).

Why would anyone forge a letter in his name to a new group of Gentile Christians living in an area where Paul was hardly known? At this early stage, why would anyone produce a literary deception claiming that "the day of the Lord is already here" (2:2)? Typically such forgeries are produced after a person has become well known and has an established reputation. Consequently, numerous scholars believe that someone wrote 2 Thessalonians in Paul's name after the apostle's death in order to address a theological issue that Christians debated decades later: the **delay of the Parousia** (Christ not returning soon as expected). Entertain this idea as a possibility while you study the Letter.

Few Romans believed in an afterlife. Many of their tombstones display the saying "I was not; I am not; I care not." The weathered faces on this sarcophagus at Aphrodisias, Turkey, ironically reflect their philosophy: When you die, that is all she wrote. You cease to exist. Some Romans found Paul's preaching about the resurrection of the dead to be quite attractive. (Courtesy of Michael Cosby)

THEY PERSECUTE YOU BECAUSE YOU ARE GOOD, BUT PAYBACK TIME IS COMING (2 THESS. 1:1–12)

1. How do the main concerns expressed in the thanksgiving section in 1:3–12 compare with 1 Thessalonians 1:2–10?

2. What is the attitude toward persecution and persecutors expressed in 1:3–12?

EVIL WILL ONLY GET WORSE (2 THESS. 2:1–17)

1. Before the Parousia, the "lawless one" (Greek "man of lawlessness") appears. What evil things will this man do?

2. According to 2:1–12, what else must happen before the Parousia?

Paul expected the Parousia *soon* (while he was still alive) *but not immediately*. He anticipated the horrible coming of the **lawless one** (elsewhere called the **antichrist**) before Christ's second coming. When this arrogant individual arrived, he was to exalt himself and even perform false miracles. But according to 2:7, this could not happen until "the one who [or, that which] now restrains" the mystery of lawlessness is removed. The exact meaning of this phrase is difficult to determine, but it seems to refer to the present rule of the emperor Claudius, who had not as yet launched any campaigns against Christians. The belief may well be that the present Roman rule held in check the full expression of lawlessness, but it would be overthrown and replaced by a completely demonic ruler. This final, rebellious leader would cause tremendous persecution of Christians (woes of the Messiah) and would be destroyed by Christ at the second coming.

NO WORK—NO FOOD
(2 THESS. 3:1–15)

The problem mentioned in 1 Thessalonians 4:11–12 and 5:14 of Christians living in idleness because they believed that the Parousia was coming very soon receives more attention in 2 Thessalonians 3:6–15.

1. What commands are given in 3:6–15 concerning work, and how are the Thessalonian Christians to pressure their idle members into providing for themselves?

Personal Reflection

1. How does the situation addressed in 3:10–12 differ from the problem of people in our society who want to work but are unable to find employment?

2. Do you believe that Paul's teaching here has any relevance for making decisions on the nature of welfare benefits and who receives them? Why, or why not?

WHICH CAME FIRST:
1 OR 2 THESSALONIANS?

If Paul wrote 2 Thessalonians, he may have written it before or after 1 Thessalonians. The order of his letters in the New Testament is based more on their length than on chronological considerations. Thus, 1–2 Thessalonians could be in the reverse order of their composition merely because 2 Thessalonians is the shorter of the two. Scholars argue for both options.

Arguments for the priority of 1 Thessalonians often appeal to 2 Thessalonians 2:15 ("So then, brothers and sisters, stand firm and hold fast to the traditions that you were taught by us, either by word of mouth *or by our letter*" [emphasis added]), which might be a reference to 1 Thessalonians. Also, 1 Thessalonians 1:6 describes persecution as a *past* experience, and 3:3 as a possibility, whereas in 2 Thessalonians 1:4–6 the Christians are presently enduring persecution. This could indicate that what Paul feared would happen had indeed come about. Similarly, in 1 Thessalonians 4:10–12 and 5:14, Paul warns against idleness, but in 2 Thessalonians 3:6–15 he deals with this problem quite harshly (e.g., "Anyone unwilling to work should not eat. For we hear that some of you are living in idleness, mere busybodies, not doing any work" [3:10–11]).

Perhaps his first warning proved to be insufficient, and the problem worsened. Furthermore, although Paul mentions his earlier, oral instruction in 1 Thessalonians 5:1, he says nothing of a previous letter as he does in 2 Thessalonians 2:2. First Thessalonians gives no indication that there was an earlier letter. And the mention of the way Paul makes his signature in 2 Thessalonians 3:17 is somewhat pointless if his readers did not already have a previous example of it. Finally, some scholars believe that Paul's information about himself and Timothy in 1 Thessalonians 2:17–3:10 only makes sense if it is his first correspondence with the Christians in Thessalonica.

Reasons for believing that 2 Thessalonians is the earliest include the following: 2 Thessalonians 1:4–7 speaks of a present persecution, whereas 1 Thessalonians 2:14 seems to speak of persecution as a thing of the past. Perhaps a more intense initial opposition had mellowed. And whereas 2 Thessalonians says nothing about the issue of what happens when Christians die before the Parousia, 1 Thessalonians 4:13 indicates that some have died, which might hint at a later date. The idleness described as a recently reported phenomenon in 2 Thessalonians 3:11–15 is perceived by some scholars as an established pattern in 1 Thessalonians 4:10–12.

Others see Paul's comment that these believers do not need instruction on the time of the Parousia in 1 Thessalonians 5:1 as based on his prior teaching on this in 2 Thessalonians 2:1–12. Still others judge the teaching on the Parousia in 2 Thessalonians to be more primitive than that found in 1 Thessalonians. Finally, some say that, since the expression "now concerning" in 1 Thessalonians 4:9 and 5:1 is a formula used elsewhere by Paul to begin answers to questions asked by his audience (e.g., 1 Cor. 7:1; 8:1), he might be answering a few questions that were raised by the Thessalonian Christians in response to an earlier letter.

Most New Testament scholars who view 2 Thessalonians as authentically Pauline believe that 1 Thessalonians is the earlier of the two letters. Yet both viewpoints must make significant assumptions that are not verifiable, and careful examination of the arguments reveals problems with both positions. How one re-creates the historical situation surrounding the letters largely determines which way one goes with the evidence.

Many scholars, however, believe that this whole argument is a waste of time because they view 2 Thessalonians as post-Pauline, written by someone else in his name. They postulate literary dependence of 2 Thessalonians on 1 Thessalonians and claim that what is said about the end times in 2 Thessalonians 2:1–12 simply does not agree with 1 Thessalonians 4:13–5:11 or 1 Corinthians 15:20–52. Some also do not believe that Paul would say such violent things as 2 Thessalonians 1:5–10 asserts will happen to the wicked, or state that God deludes people into believing what is false, as 2 Thessalonians 2:11–12 asserts. Finally, some claim that the strong appeal to Paul's authority in 2 Thessalonians (beware of letters purporting to be from him [2:2], the teachings by word of mouth or through letter [2:15], and the authoritative letter material in 3:14, 17) are evidence that the Epistle is a forgery from a later time period.

At this point in our study, we will not interact in detail with the issue of **pseudonymity** (writing in someone else's name). Later we will devote careful attention to this special problem. We will ponder how to be both cautious of cultural assumptions and fearless in dealing with credible evidence. Some arguments against Pauline authorship of certain New Testament documents are based on careful observation of details

of his letters. Some, however, reflect the modern sensitivities of particular scholars (what *they* find acceptable for Paul to say and do and therefore what *they* believe Paul would or would not have done). Cultural sensitivities differ, and we should avoid deciding in advance what biblical authors considered acceptable. For example, the violent predictions in 2 Thessalonians 1:5–10 are not that different from the rhetoric against Jews in 1 Thessalonians 2:14–16.

In the case of the authenticity of 2 Thessalonians, as well as whether it was written before or after 1 Thessalonians, we need to evaluate the evidence honestly and then formulate positions. In this process, recognizing and acknowledging our own biases helps us to accomplish our investigation with greater integrity. But in the present study we are still in the beginning stages of becoming familiar with Paul, so to concentrate too heavily now on issues that call for considerable finesse would be counterproductive. With respect to the authorship of 2 Thessalonians, it is sufficient at this stage to know that scholars debate this issue. We have plenty of time to revisit the matter later.

GLOSSARY

Antichrist. Called the "lawless one" in 2 Thessalonians 2:3–10, this evil ruler was expected to persecute Christians and lead the majority of people astray in the end times.

Delay of the Parousia. The problem faced by early Christians that arose when Jesus did not return to earth soon after his death as expected. As the decades rolled by and more and more first-generation Christians died, those who remained had to adjust to the idea that Christ's return was not imminent.

Lawless one. *See* Antichrist.

Pseudonymity. Writing using a false name (pseudonym). Apocalyptic writings nearly always were attributed to an important person who died long before the actual author wrote the work. There are also instances of letters written in someone else's name. For a full explanation, see chapter 16, "Monsters in the Closet: The Problem of Pseudonymity."

FURTHER READING ON 1–2 THESSALONIANS

Bailey, John A. "Who Wrote II Thessalonians?" *New Testament Studies* 25 (1978): 131–45. Technical study.

Gaventa, Beverly Roberts. *First and Second Thessalonians.* Interpretation. Louisville, KY: Westminster John Knox Press, 1998. Written for practical use by pastors and educated laypeople. Applies text to today's world (138 pages).

Jewett, Robert. *The Thessalonian Correspondence: Pauline Rhetoric and Millenarian Piety.* Foundations and Facets. Philadelphia: Fortress Press, 1986. Do not be scared off by the title.

Koester, Helmut. *Introduction to the New Testament.* Vol. 2, *History and Literature of Early Christianity.* Philadelphia: Fortress Press, 1982. Technical intro-

duction to the NT. On pp. 241–46. argues against Pauline authorship of 2 Thessalonians.

Kümmel, Werner G. *Introduction to the New Testament.* 17th ed. Nashville: Abingdon, 1975. Technical and tedious introduction to the NT. Argues for Pauline authorship of 2 Thessalonians on 264–69.

Malherbe, Abraham J. *The Letters to the Thessalonians: A New Translation with Introduction and Commentary.* AB. New York: Doubleday, 2000. Technical commentary (528 pages).

Marshall, I. Howard. *1 and 2 Thessalonians.* Grand Rapids: Wm. B. Eerdmans Publishing Co., 1983. Evangelical scholar argues for Pauline authorship of 2 Thessalonians.

Richard, Earl J. *First and Second Thessalonians.* Sacra Pagina 11. Collegeville, MN: Liturgical Press, 1995. Detailed and technical (432 pages). Good resource.

Schlueter, Carol J. *Filling Up the Measure: Polemical Hyperbole in 1 Thessalonians 2:14–16.* JSNT Supplement Series 98. Sheffield: JSOT Press, 1994. Provides cultural background information on hyperbole. Challenges reading Paul's words in this passage as literally stating what he meant. Dissertation. Technical.

Wanamaker, Charles A. *The Epistles to the Thessalonians: A Commentary on the Greek Text.* NIGTC. Grand Rapids: Wm. B. Eerdmans Publishing Co., 1990. Assumes knowledge of Greek. Argues for Pauline authorship of 2 Thessalonians and that Paul wrote it prior to 1 Thessalonians. Technical but readable. Summarizes different positions.

Witheringon, Ben, III. *1 and 2 Thessalonians: A Socio-Rhetorical Commentary.* Grand Rapids: Wm. B. Eerdmans Publishing Co., 2006. Clear explanations of the rhetorical structure. Helpful historical and cultural background information.

Wright, N. T. *Paul for Everyone: Galatians and Thessalonians.* Louisville, KY: Westminster John Knox Press, 2004. Clear, insightful, short. Easy to read but not simplistic.

Yarbrough, O. Larry. *Not Like the Gentiles: Marriage Rules in the Letters of Paul.* Atlanta: Scholars Press, 1985. Published dissertation. Technical. Valuable information.

CHAPTER 9

Galatians

A FURIOUS APOSTLE STRIKES BACK

When Paul dictated Galatians, he erupted like a volcano, spewing forth molten accusations and condemnations. In this letter we see the apostle at his most volatile, even his most vulgar. His anger burns so hot that in a blast against Jewish Christian opponents in Galatians 5:12 he declares, "I wish those who unsettle you would castrate themselves!" Yet despite the emotionally charged nature of this letter, Galatians has functioned as one of the most important theological documents in the New Testament. Protestants in particular have mined Galatians for an immense amount of doctrinal ore, at times seemingly oblivious to its emotional heat.

Martin Luther, the great Protestant reformer, said that in Galatians "Paul goeth about to establish the doctrine of faith, grace, forgiveness of sins, . . . to the end that we may have a perfect knowledge and difference between Christian righteousness, and all other kinds of righteousness."[1] Such accolades are common. Richard Longenecker, for example, describes the importance of Galatians:

> Historically, Galatians has been foundational for many forms of Christian doctrine, proclamation, and practice. And it remains true today to say that how one understands the issues and teaching of Galatians determines in large measure what kind of theology is espoused, what kind of message is proclaimed, and what kind of lifestyle is practiced.[2]

Christians often become so involved in digging for doctrine in Galatians that they miss much of the emotion. As you read

1. *A Commentary on St. Paul's Epistle to the Galatians*, trans. P. S. Watson (London: James Clark, 1953), 21.
2. Richard Longenecker, *Galatians*, Word Biblical Commentary 41 (Dallas: Word Books, 1990), xliii.

121

this letter, seeking to understanding what Paul believed about salvation by faith and about the nature of true spirituality, try to feel the intensity of his language. Seek to perceive what upset Paul so dramatically, and look for the major themes he pursues in response. Begin by reading quickly through the entire letter to gather a feeling for his argument as a whole.

1. What seems to have upset Paul and motivated him to write this letter?

"HOW DARE YOU CHALLENGE MY AUTHORITY!" (GAL. 1–2)

As we saw in the chapter on 1 Thessalonians, ancient Mediterranean people used very pointed language when condemning others or defending themselves. Defense of **honor** was a major concern in these cultures,[3] and because opponents were calling Paul's apostolic authority into question, he vigorously defended his honor standing. Honor is a public matter, granted by members in society. By publicly challenging Paul's credibility, his opponents challenged his apostolic honor. Paul had no choice, culturally speaking, but to counterattack.

In Mediterranean societies, challenge-and-response situations involved social equals.[4] Aristotle explains this matter in terms of envy and rivalry, saying "no man tries to rival . . . those who, in his own opinion or in that of others, are either far inferior or superior to him; and the people and things which one envies are on the same footing; . . . whence the saying, 'Potter [being jealous] of potter'" (*Rhetoric* 2.10.5–6 [Freese, LCL]). If someone made a derogatory comment to a person of higher social status, the higher-class individual need not bother to respond. It was no real challenge to that person's honor. Therefore, Paul's vigorous response to the charges of his detractors seems to indicate that he considered them legitimate threats to his authority. If they were insignificant nuisances, Paul's converts would not be so tempted to reject his teaching and follow theirs. Notice the intensity with which he addresses the challenge.

1. Compare the salutation in 1:1–5 with the one in 1 Thessalonians 1:1. What do Paul's additions in Galatians emphasize?

---

3. For an introduction to honor and shame for ancient Mediterraneans, see Bruce J. Malina, *The New Testament World: Insights from Cultural Anthropology* (Louisville, KY: Westminster/John Knox Press, 1993), 28–62.

4. Ibid., 35.

2. Notice that there is no thanksgiving section in Galatians. Why do you think he omitted it and begins the body of his letter with a forceful confrontation in 1:6–9?

3. In light of Paul's overall argument in Galatians, what reason would his Jewish-Christian opponents have for accusing him of seeking to please people and not God (1:10)?

Paul calls Peter **Cephas** (Gal. 1:18), the Aramaic form of the name "Peter." Both words mean "rock" or "stone." Except for Galatians 2:7–8, Paul always uses the name Cephas for this important Jerusalem apostle. Elsewhere in the New Testament, except for John 1:42 (which includes an explanation that *Cephas* means *Petros*), other biblical authors use the Greek name Peter (*Petros*).

4. Paul includes an autobiographical section in 1:13–2:14 to defend himself against charges leveled against him. In 1:13–24 he stresses his former zeal for the law as a way of deflect-

ing criticism from his opponents. Why does he stress the brevity of his visits with Peter and James in 1:18–19?

5. By the time Paul went to Jerusalem (1:18; 2:1), he had been a Christian for at least seventeen years. In 2:1–14, how does he demonstrate his equality with the Jerusalem apostles?

6. In Paul's account of the confrontation with Peter in Antioch (2:11–21), he accuses Peter of hypocrisy in ceasing to eat with Gentile Christians. But Paul's traveling companion, Barnabas (2:13), sided with Peter in this matter. How might Peter's account of the confrontation have differed from Paul's?

7. Given the agreement that Peter and Paul reached concerning where each would evangelize (2:7–9), Peter possibly faced a difficult situation upon the arrival of the men from Jerusalem (2:12). How might eating with Gentile Christians have jeopardized Peter's main missionary work in Jerusalem?

8. What insight does 2:15–21 give into why the issues addressed in this letter are so important to Paul and why he is so upset over them?

WHY DIDN'T JEWS EAT MEALS WITH GREEKS AND ROMANS?

As we saw in Acts 15, Jewish Christians debated whether or not Gentile Christians should be required to obey the laws of Moses. In Galatians this debate reaches a flash point, and Paul responds with emotional intensity to his detractors. For the Gentile Christians in Galatia to consider being circumcised, Jewish Christians must have been pressuring them. Culturally speaking, it had to do with Jews separating themselves from Gentiles. Remember that in Acts 10, Peter hesitated to eat with Gentiles, even though Cornelius was a godly man. Jews were not only concerned about eating **kosher** foods but also about proper food preparation.

Deuteronomy 14:3–21 and Leviticus 11 provide lists of animals that Jewish people may and may not eat. Pork, for example, is strictly forbidden, as are shellfish. Romans loved pork, however, and assumed that their deities did also. They considered pigs to be good sacrificial animals. The matter of sacrifices caused considerable problems with Gentiles and Jews eating together. Gentiles slaughtered most of their animals in honor of their gods or goddesses, and they typically dedicated their wine to a deity. Jews were sensitive about eating or drinking anything touched by a Gentile for fear that they would be committing idolatry by partaking of food or drink that had been sacrificed to pagan deities.

This social separation created problems for Jews living in Gentile communities. Many Greeks and Romans considered Jews to be disgustingly antisocial. The Roman historian Tacitus, for example, says of them, "Towards all others [they feel] hatred and enmity. They sit apart at meals and they sleep apart, and although they are a race most given to lust, they abstain from intercourse with foreign women; among themselves nothing is unlawful" (*Histories* 5.5.2). His evaluation, although obviously bigoted, reveals social tension over the Jewish practice of not eating with Gentiles.

The church was not exempt from these social tensions, especially when Christians gathered for **Communion** (or **Eucharist**), their sacred meal to honor Jesus' sacrificial death on the cross. When Jewish Christians sat at table with Gentiles, they broke their inherited social taboos. Such behavior created problems for them in their own Jewish communities. They were accused of idolatry, apostasy against God, and betrayal of their religious and cultural heritage. And the tendency of Greek and Roman Christians to bring into the church their customs about how to conduct social gatherings exacerbated the problem.

Gentile Christians also experienced ostracism for their faith. Families, friends, and associates pressured them if they stopped attending social functions. Because these events were dedicated to some deity, Christian missionaries discouraged followers of Jesus from participating in them. But refusal to attend created social displacement, with sometimes devastating economic results for Christians. It is difficult for us to realize how much polytheistic thinking permeated the structures of Gentile society, or how participation in rituals to honor various gods and goddesses was considered vital to the health of the city. Citizens were expected to attend fraternal meals, where the focus was fellowship, but which always included paying homage to patron deities.

Greeks held communal meals in special rooms in which social equals reclined two per couch on between seven to fifteen couches and all drank wine mixed with water from a large jar called a **kratēr**. The first part of the meal focused on food, but the second part, called the *symposion*, began with **libations** (liquid offerings) to their gods and then focused on "serious drinking, talking and entertainment."[5] All guests received wine from the *kratēr*. The conclusion of these male-only meals involved a procession through town that showed the unity of the group.

Roman banquets differed from Greek meals. The Roman dining room (called a triclinium) had three couches (each holding up to three people), on which participants reclined. Guests were arranged according to a hierarchy, and honorable women were sometimes present. Although participants focused on the food rather than the wine drinking, the central mixing jar (*kratēr*) was still present.[6]

When Paul preached salvation in Jesus Christ for all who believe—regardless of race, religion, or social standing—problems surfaced. Jewish Christians felt pressure to sit apart from the Gentile believers, eating their own food and drinking their own wine from separate utensils. If they refused to partake from a common *kratēr* of wine that the Greeks and Romans used, or to partake of the same food as their Gentile brothers and sisters in Christ, fellowship suffered. Paul insisted that during the eucharistic meal *all* partake of the same food and drink from the same serving vessels, as we will see in 1 Corinthians. This practice made Jewish Christians nervous. He also insisted that the communion meals be conducted without drunkenness or overindulgence, which forced Gentiles to rethink their approach to social gatherings. Paul did not want them celebrating Christ with the heavy drinking that characterized some of the religious festivals that they formerly attended.

5. Philip F. Esler, *Galatians* (New York: Routledge, 1998), 102.

6. Ibid., 103.

"FOOLS! WHO BEWITCHED YOU TO BELIEVE SUCH NONSENSE?" (GAL. 3)

Paul's opponents considered faith in Christ to be necessary but not totally sufficient for salvation. Their logic must have been persuasive, because Paul fears that the Galatians are turning away from what he taught them. With exasperation he declares, "You foolish Galatians! Who has bewitched you?" (3:1). It deeply offends the apostle that his opponents are persuading these Gentile Christians of the need to be circumcised and obey the laws of Moses in order to be truly spiritual and pleasing to God. His use of "bewitched" probably refers to the Mediterranean belief in someone casting the **evil eye** on another.[7] This type of sorcery, which brings evil upon its victim, is feared even today in Mediterranean cultures. Palestinians, for example, frequently wear jewelry with an eye on it as a way of warding off the evil eye. The fact that Paul equates Gentile Christian submission to the laws of Moses with being bewitched reflects the depth of his feeling about this matter.

1. What main point against his opponents' position does Paul make in 3:1–5?

Ancient Mediterraneans feared the evil eye curse from others and took steps to protect themselves from it. Actually, many people in modern Mediterranean societies fear the evil eye. All over Turkey (in airports, cafes, buses, cars, homes), you will see versions of the amulet shown in this picture. (Courtesy of Michael Cosby)

7. John H. Elliott has published a number of articles on this practice: e.g., "Paul, Galatians, and the Evil Eye," *Currents in Theology and Mission* 17 (1990): 262–73; "The Fear of the Leer: The Evil Eye from the Bible to L'il Abner," *Forum* 4 (1988): 77–85; "The Evil Eye and the Sermon on the Mount: Contours of a Pervasive Belief in Social Scientific Perspective," *Biblical Interpretation* 2 (1994): 51–84.

2. Using Abraham as an example of faith in 3:6–9 adds credibility to Paul's argument against Jewish Christian opponents. According to 3:10–14, what problems arise when

relying on works of the law in order to gain acceptance with God?

texts, and compare these with the meanings Paul gives to them.)

3:6–9 ⇨ Genesis 15:1–6

3. Paul argues that the promise God gave to Abraham was fulfilled in those who have faith, not in the physical descendants of Abraham. According to 3:15–20, what function did the law play in the history of salvation?

3:11 ⇨ Habakkuk 2:4

3:12 ⇨ Leviticus 18:5

4. In 3:21–29, what does Paul say is the actual value of the laws of Moses for Christians?

3:13 ⇨ Deuteronomy 21:22–23

3:16 ⇨ Genesis 12:7 and 22:17–18

5. Paul's use of Scripture in Galatians is fascinating. How does he use the Old Testament in the following passages? (Look up the verses and see what they mean in their original con-

Male and Female in the Church

Galatians 3:27–28—"As many of you as were baptized into Christ have clothed yourselves with Christ. There is no longer Jew or Greek, there is no longer slave or free, there is no longer male and female; for all of you are one in Christ Jesus"—plays a central role in Christian debates over women exercising leadership roles in the church. Look carefully at these two verses in their context. Do you think that they should be applied to social equality for men and women?

WHICH CAME FIRST: THE WORLD OR THE LAWS OF MOSES?

For Pharisaic teachers of Paul's day, the laws of Moses played such a central role that they could not imagine existence without it. The origins of their thinking trace back to about 180 BCE, when a Jewish wisdom teacher named Jesus Ben Sira wrote what is now called Ecclesiasticus, or **Sirach**, a book found in the Old Testament Apocrypha/Deuterocanon. Ben Sira associated the laws of Moses (Torah) with Wisdom as personified in Proverbs 8:22–31, a passage that describes wisdom as an elegant woman who worked with God in creating the universe. Symbolically this text teaches that God used wisdom to create the world, so people should guide their lives by wisdom. Sirach 24:23 connects divine wisdom with Torah (cf. 15:1–10). In other words, God's wisdom is expressed in the laws of Moses. Later Jewish teachers reinforced Ben Sira's connection of the law and wisdom. By Paul's day, many Jewish teachers asserted that the laws of Moses predated the creation of the world.

They believed that God first formulated Mosaic law and then used it as the basis for creating the world. "As the ground plan for the universe it could not but be perfect and unchangeable; . . . no prophet could ever arise who would change it, and no new Moses should ever appear to introduce another Law to replace it."[8] A later rabbi named Hosha'ya explained the role of Torah in creation with the following analogy: "When a king builds a palace, he does not do it himself, but with the help of 'the knowledge of a master builder.' And the master builder in turn considers plans and drawings: in just the same way, 'God looked into the Torah when he created the world.'"[9] Rabbis simply could not fathom life without Torah, either in this time or in the age to come. They believed that Torah would even govern the afterlife, so that in heaven people would obey the laws of Moses perfectly. Given their emphasis on Torah, therefore, we can see why Paul's view of the law infuriated Jews (including Jewish Christians) who believed in the eternity of the law.

The following diagram illustrates their belief visually:

8. W. D. Davies, *The Setting of the Sermon on the Mount* (Cambridge: Cambridge University Press, 1964), 157–58.

9. Martin Hengel, *Judaism and Hellenism*, vol. 1 (Philadelphia: Fortress Press, 1974), 171.

JEWISH VIEW ON THE ETERNITY OF THE LAW

God formed the law	→	God created the world according to the law	→	God gave the law on Mt. Sinai	→	Messiah will bring an authoritative interpretation of the law	→	Age to come (law will be kept perfectly)

The view of law that Paul presents in Galatians 3 radically rejects this notion. Paul relegates the law to the status of an add-on, something temporary that was given between God's promise to Abraham and the fulfillment of the promise in the coming of Jesus Messiah—something given in response to sin, not the perfect expression of God's will for human good.

PAUL'S VIEW OF THE LAW IN SALVATION HISTORY

Creation of the world	→	Promise given to Abraham	→	430 years later, law added because of sin	→	Messiah comes to fulfill the promise given to Abraham and ushers in the Age of the Spirit

Paul's vigorous and fundamental challenge to the dominant Jewish view of the importance of Mosaic law put him in radical conflict with many Jewish Christians.

LIFE UNDER THE LAW IS SLAVERY! (GAL. 4)

1. Paul's opponents were evidently teaching that spiritual maturity comes through obeying the laws of Moses. According to 4:1–11, what happens when Christians rely on the law for acceptance with God?

The words translated "elemental spirits of the world" in 4:3, *ta stoicheia tou kosmou*, may also be translated "basic principles of the world" or "rudiments of the world." The term *stoicheia* basically designates elements in a series, and it could refer to earth, water, air, and fire, which ancient Greeks thought to be the basic elements comprising the world. Paul might be using *stoicheia* to designate elemental teachings, the ABCs, so to speak, of religion.

2. Paul compares following the laws of Moses with Gentile enslavement to the elemental spirits (or basic principles) of the world (4:3, 8–9). In 4:1–11, what kind of relationship with God does Paul insist that Christians should experience?

Paul mentions a physical problem that was instrumental in his preaching the gospel to the Galatians at first (4:13), but he does not say what it was. In 4:15 he admits that his condition could have brought their scorn and abuse (4:14), and people down through the centuries have speculated on what sort of ailment he endured. Because Paul goes on to say in 4:15 that the Galatians would have torn out their eyes and given them to him, and in 6:11 he mentions signing his name with large letters, some conclude that Paul had some sort of debilitating eye problem. Perhaps it is the same problem that he calls a thorn in the flesh in 2 Corinthians 12:7–9 and begs God to remove from him. We do not know for sure. His comment about eyes may simply have been symbolic of something supremely precious. All we can do is speculate on the nature of his physical infirmity.

Earning God's Favor

What does Galatians 4 reveal about Paul's understanding of the effect of relying on the laws of Moses either for acceptance by God or for righteousness before God?

3. In the allegory of Hagar and Sarah in 4:21–31, how does Paul describe the condition of people who rely on the law? (See Gen. 16:1–16; 17:15–22; 21:1–21 for the story of Hagar and Sarah and their children.)

"DON'T THROW AWAY YOUR FREEDOM FOR SLAVERY!" (GAL. 5)

1. What does Paul warn will happen if the Galatian Christians submit to the yoke of living under the laws of Moses?

The effort to force Gentiles to keep the law, symbolized by the act of **circumcision**, upsets Paul terribly and causes him to respond with considerable emotion. In 5:12, for example, he expresses his wish that those who preach circumcision would go all the way and castrate themselves (Greek *apokoptō*). He seems to be enraged because some Jewish Christian missionaries told his converts that he is not a true apostle and that he does not understand the Christian faith as taught by the "real" leaders of the church in Jerusalem.

However, Paul's insistence that the law plays no role in the salvation of a person does not mean that he believes Christians can be lax in their moral and ethical conduct—as his opponents charged. For Paul, good behavior comes as a *result* of salvation; it is not the *cause* of it. Freedom in Christ must never be seen as a license for self-indulgence. On the contrary, it should liberate Christians to become servants of one another (5:13).

2. According to Paul, what does true fulfillment of the law involve?

3. What does Paul associate with "the flesh" in 5:16–26, and what does he say that one should do to overcome its negative influences? (If you use the New International Version, your text reads "sinful nature" instead of "flesh." This translation is a questionable, interpretive paraphrase of the Greek word *sarx*, which means "flesh.")[10]

4. How does Paul's warning in 5:21 ("Those who do such things will not inherit the kingdom of God") reconcile with his fervent insistence in Galatians that salvation comes strictly through faith, not by works?

5. What do you think he means in 5:24 when he says that Christians have crucified the flesh (cf. 2:19)?

---

10. James D. G. Dunn explains that when Paul uses *sarx*, he means the human condition of weakness due to our being connected to the physical world. Flesh does not designate a kind of hereditary/innate human sinfulness, as the NIV indicates, but a human tendency to be weak before the temptations of sin. To live for the flesh is to exist on the level of merely gratifying physical desires, which severely limits the freedom brought by the Spirit (*The Epistle to the Galatians*, Black's New Testament Commentary [Peabody, MA: Hendrickson Publishers, 1993], 287). Similarly, Ben Witherington III argues that in this context flesh refers to an inclination in humans to desire evil—not to a corrupt nature due to the effect of evil. Fallen humanity has not lost the image of God but has effaced it. Christians may choose either to stifle the sinful inclination by the power of the Spirit or allow the sinful inclination to rule in their lives. The human body is weak and generates sinful urges that may be progressively controlled but never entirely eliminated. Thus the term "flesh" is connected to the physical body. It does not mean "sinful nature," a totally corrupt spiritual condition that people inherit as a result of the sin of Adam and Eve in the garden of Eden. Christians continue to live in a state of tension between the sinful urging of the flesh (physical) and the leading of the Spirit (*Grace in Galatia: A Commentary on Paul's Letter to the Galatians* [Grand Rapids: Wm. B. Eerdmans Publishing Co., 1998], 377–78).

FULFILL THE LAW OF CHRIST
(GAL. 6)

Life is filled with conflicts, and learning how to deal with them is vitally important. What Paul commands in 6:1–2 indicates that he did not always take the harshly confrontational approach that he employs in writing this letter.

1. What guidelines does 6:1–5 give for how to deal with the problem of someone who has fallen into sinful behavior (cf. Matt. 18:15–17)?

In 6:12, Paul seems to claim that the Jewish Christians who are trying to make proselyte Jews out of the Galatian Christians are doing so for the selfish reason of being able to boast.

2. According to Paul, what is vastly more important than whether or not a person submits to the Mosaic law of circumcision?

Christian Confrontation

1. How do you deal best with conflict situations?

2. How did you personally respond when you read Paul's intense and angry reaction to those who questioned his gospel message?

3. In 6:16 Paul redefines who belongs to the "Israel of God." Of what significance is this redefinition for his larger argument?

WHAT DOES IT MEAN
TO BE SPIRITUAL?

1. In Galatians, how does Paul understand the meaning of true spirituality?

WHO WERE THE GALATIANS,
AND WHEN DID PAUL
WRITE TO THEM?

Although New Testament scholars do not question Paul's authorship of Galatians, they do disagree concerning when and to whom he wrote this Epistle. Many older books in particular promote the **North Galatian hypothesis**, arguing that "Galatians" designates the ethnic Galatian inhabitants of the area north of Pamphylia, Pisidia, and Lycaonia (see map). Many scholars today, however, affirm the **South Galatian hypothesis**, arguing that "Galatians" refers to the large Roman province whose northern extremity bordered the Black Sea and whose southern end bordered the Mediterranean Sea (see map). Although no definitive resolution to this debate over the intended audience is presently possible, the available evidence favors the South Galatian theory.

The Galatian people migrated from Central Europe and settled in North-Central Asia Minor, and Ancyra became their capital city (Ankara, the modern capital of Turkey, occupies the same location). In 25 BCE, Augustus Caesar made their territory part of a Roman province, which he called Galatia; this province stretched south to the Mediterranean Sea, far beyond the actual ethnic homeland of the Galatian people. According to the Roman historian Pliny, in the first century the province of Galatia extended from the Black Sea to the Mediterranean (*Natural History* 5.147).

Thus, in Paul's day the province of Galatia included the cities of Iconium, Lystra, and Derbe, where he and Barnabas established churches on their first missionary journey (ca. 47–48 CE; Acts 13–14). According to Acts 15, the Jerusalem council (ca. 49) met to decide whether or not Gentile Christians should be circumcised in obedience to the law of Moses; not long after that meeting, Paul left on his second missionary journey, traveling overland from Syrian Antioch to Lystra, where he picked up Timothy as a traveling companion (16:1–4). They traveled on "through the *region* of Phrygia and Galatia, having been forbidden by the Holy Spirit to speak the word in Asia" to the southwest (16:6, stress added). The Greek text, τὴν Φρυγίαν καὶ Γαλατικὴν χώραν, uses the singular "region" to include both Phrygia and Galatia in the same area, to describe the same location, not two different provinces.

The Acts account indicates that, after trying unsuccessfully to go north into Bithynia, they proceeded west until they reached the Aegean Sea: "When they had come opposite Mysia, they attempted to go into Bithynia, but the Spirit of Jesus did not allow them; so, passing by Mysia, they went down to Troas" (16:7–8). Thus, they apparently did not travel north into ethnic Galatia. Similarly,

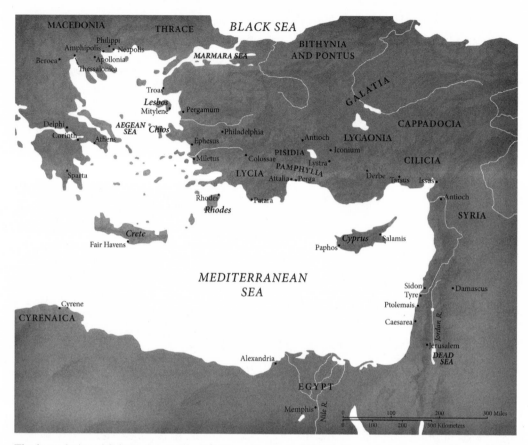

The boundaries of Galatia changed in 137 CE and again in 297 CE. These changes resulted in confusion among later Christian commentators, who assumed that the smaller boundaries of Galatia in their own day were the same as those in Paul's time.

the account of Paul's third missionary journey states that he left Syrian Antioch and "went from place to place through the *region* of Galatia and Phrygia, strengthening all the disciples" (18:23, stress added). This follow-up trip shows Paul going back to the churches that he previously established, strengthening disciples. Acts gives no indication that he ever journeyed north into ethnic Galatia, yet for centuries most scholars believed that Paul sent his letter to churches in North Galatia. Why?

The reason seems fairly simple: by the time Christians began writing commentaries on Galatians, the boundaries of Galatia had been redrawn, and this affected their understanding. In 137 CE the Lyconian area of the Roman province of Galatia (which includes Iconium, Lystra, and Derbe) was incorporated into the province of Cilicia (see map), and in 297 the rest of the southern part of the former province of Galatia was attached to a new province of Pisidia. Thus, during the time when early Christian leaders were writing their commentaries, Galatia referred to what was only the northern part of the region of Galatia in Paul's day. When they read "Galatia," they merely assumed (incorrectly) that it referred to the same geographical location as the Galatian province of their own time. Once established in Christian tradition, however, this North Galatian theory exercised a powerful influence on later thinking.[11]

Much debate also focuses on *when* Paul wrote Galatians. Some who endorse the South Galatian theory argue that if he wrote Galatians before the Jerusalem council of 49 CE, this explains why Paul never uses the decision of the council, that circumcision is not necessary for Gentile

Christians (Acts 15), as part of his argument. One would think that this decision by the Jerusalem apostles would annihilate the argument of his opponents in Galatia—who denied Paul's authority by pitting him against Peter and the other apostles, and who asserted that Gentiles need to keep the law of Moses and be circumcised. F. F. Bruce, for example, states that Paul did not use the council's decision because the council meeting was still in the future. According to Bruce, Paul wrote Galatians before his second missionary journey, before the Jerusalem council, and thus it is the earliest extant Letter of Paul.[12]

This argument has merit; but since the parallels between Galatians and Romans are so numerous, most scholars conclude that Paul probably wrote Galatians shortly before he wrote Romans, in Corinth just before he left for Jerusalem, at the end of his third missionary journey (Rom. 15:25–32). The fact that he does not mention the Jerusalem council's decision might merely reflect his resistance in Galatians 1–2 to view his own apostolic authority as in any way subservient to Jerusalem. He asserts that God called him to be an apostle; he gained no authority from Peter and the others.

Because we cannot know for sure when Paul dictated Galatians, I have vacillated on where to place this chapter on Galatians. Perhaps it should come before 1 Thessalonians; perhaps it should come just before Romans. The decision to place it right before 1 Corinthians represents a

---

11. Scholars today who argue that Paul wrote Galatians for churches in North (or tribal) Galatia typically do so for different reasons than Christians used in former times. Esler, for example, argues that those who hold the South Galatian theory do so out of a need to maintain the historical accuracy of Acts. He asserts that the account in Acts of what Paul encountered in provincial south Galatia does not coincide with the issues debated in Galatians, and that we cannot harmonize Gal. 1:13–2:14 with Acts anyway (*Galatians*, 32–33). Esler believes that Acts contains valuable historical information. But in the case of the Jerusalem council, he thinks that this event happened later than 49 CE. "Acts 15 has too many features in common with the Jerusalem council as described by Paul in Gal. 2.1–10 to be based on another meeting in the holy city. Luke seems to have moved it back into an earlier period in Paul's career and to have conflated with it information of a later compromise on the problems of table fellowship between Gentiles and Israelites, which produces an impression of harmony on this issue much earlier than it *ever* could have been established" (33–34). However, using Acts 16:6–7 as an *accurate* historical reflection, Esler states that Paul made a brief excursion into tribal Galatia, probably to the town of Pessinus (here he relies heavily on Jerome Murphy-O'Connor, *Paul: A Critical Life* [Oxford: Clarendon Press, 1996], 159–62, 191–92). Speculation of this type abounds in such reconstructions. Scholars have an easier time pointing out problems with others' positions than with proving their own.

12. F. F. Bruce, *The Epistle to the Galatians: A Commentary on the Greek Text*, NIGTC (Grand Rapids: Wm. B. Eerdmans Publishing Co., 1982), 43–56. See also Richard Longenecker, *Galatians*, lxiii–lxxxviii; or Witherington, *Grace in Galatia*, 8–24.

compromise stemming from theological considerations, not historical ones. Studying Galatians provides important insights into what Paul taught about salvation by faith. Interacting with his views on Christian freedom from the law of Moses gives insight into how the Corinthian Christians misunderstood his teaching and misapplied it to form a deviant lifestyle. As some of the Christians at Thessalonica misappropriated Paul's teaching on the Parousia to adopt a lifestyle of laziness, so some at Corinth overextended his teaching on grace to form a perverted kind of immoral and unethical lifestyle. Their behavior undoubtedly strengthened the conviction of Paul's Jewish Christian opponents that his rejection of the relevance of the law of Moses for Gentiles was a mistake of immense proportions. But Paul continued to fight for his position.

GLOSSARY

Cephas. The Aramaic form of the name Peter. It means "rock" or "stone." Peter (Greek *Petros*) also means rock or stone.

Circumcision. Minor operation to remove the foreskin from the male penis. Jews perform this operation on their boys when they are eight days old, and in Philippians 3:5 Paul states that he was so circumcised. The Romans viewed circumcision as a form of mutilation and frowned upon the practice. But Jews saw it as an important sign of loyalty to God and to the laws of Moses. Many Jewish Christians in the first century insisted that all Gentile Christian men be circumcised in obedience to God's covenant. Paul argued vigorously against Gentiles being subjected to this (esp. in Galatians).

Communion. Sacred meal celebrating the death and resurrection of Jesus; also called the **Eucharist**. Among early Christians it involved eating a meal together, but over time the celebration became mostly symbolic, with participants receiving one bite of unleavened bread and one sip of wine or grape juice. First Corinthians 8–10 indicates that the church at Corinth had many problems with the selfish way in which some of the Christians there celebrated their communion meals.

Evil eye. Common type of sorcery practiced in the Middle East in which someone casts a spell on another (bewitches the person; see Gal. 3:1).

Honor. One's reputation or honor standing was a major concern for people in Mediterranean cultures. If someone challenged their honor, they were expected to defend themselves vigorously. Because honor is a public matter, granted by members in society, it must be defended publicly.

Kosher. Jewish term for foods considered proper to eat. Deuteronomy 14:3–21 and Leviticus 11 provide lists of animals that Jewish people may and may not eat. Pork, for example, is strictly forbidden, as are shellfish. Jews of Paul's time were sensitive about eating or drinking anything prepared by a Gentile for fear that they would be committing idolatry by partaking of food or drink that had been sacrificed to pagan deities. This cultural separation caused problems between Jewish and Gentile Christians.

Kratēr. A large jar containing wine mixed with water that was used during meals by the Greeks and Romans to fill the wine glasses of participants.

Libations. Liquid offerings, usually of wine, symbolically dedicated to certain deities before people drink the wine during a meal.

North Galatian hypothesis. Theory that Paul wrote Galatians to Christians living among the ethnic Galatian inhabitants of the region north of Pamphylia, Pisidia, and Lycaonia (i.e., the central region of modern Turkey).

Sirach. A wisdom book consisting of proverbial material and found in the Apocrypha/Deuterocanon; also called Ecclesiasticus or the Wisdom of Ben Sira. Written by Jesus Ben Sira, this document connects the wisdom of God with the laws of Moses.

South Galatian hypothesis. Theory that Paul wrote Galatians to residents of the southern area of Roman provincial Galatia (area around Pamphylia, Pisidia, and Lycaonia, which Paul visited on his first missionary journey). In Paul's day the borders of the Roman province of Galatia extended from the Black Sea in the north to the Mediterranean Sea in the south.

Torah. Typically a title for the Pentateuch, the first five books of the Hebrew Bible, although sometimes it was used to refer to the Scriptures as a whole. The term "torah" comes from Hebrew and means "instruction."

Triclinium. The Roman dining room (called a triclinium) had three couches (each holding up to three people) on which participants reclined. Guests were arranged according to a rather strict hierarchy, and honorable women were sometimes present. Although participants focused on the food rather than the wine drinking, the central wine-mixing jar (*kratēr*) was still present.

FURTHER READING ON GALATIANS

Betz, Hans Dieter. *Galatians: A Commentary on Paul's Letter to the Churches in Galatia.* AB. Philadelphia: Fortress Press, 1979. Groundbreaking commentary that set the stage for considerable debate over the rhetorical composition of Galatians. Technical.

Brinsmead, Bernard H. *Galatians: Dialogical Response to Opponents.* Chico, CA: Scholars Press, 1982. Technical analysis.

Bruce, F. F. *The Epistle to the Galatians: A Commentary on the Greek Text.* NIGTC. Grand Rapids: Wm. B. Eerdmans Publishing Co., 1982. Technical but readable analysis of the Greek text of Galatians.

Dunn, James D. G. *The Epistle to the Galatians.* Black's New Testament Commentary. London: A&C Black, 1993. Technical and fairly dry. Puts a different twist on Paul's opponents and the nature of his theological argument.

———. *The Theology of Paul's Letter to the Galatians.* New York: Cambridge University Press, 1993. Pays attention to Paul's emotions and speaks of his words in Galatians as "theology in the raw."

Esler, Philip F. *Galatians.* New York: Routledge, 1998. Fairly readable. Focuses on Mediterranean rhetoric and social values (norms for public meals, etc.).

Hanson, G. Walter. *Galatians*. IVP New Testament Commentary Series. Downers Grove, IL: InterVarsity Press, 1994. Readable. Seeks to apply Galatians to modern concerns.

Hays, Richard B. *The Faith of Jesus: An Investigation of the Narrative Substructure of Galatians 3:1–4:11*. Chico, CA: Scholars Press, 1984. Reprint with introduction by Luke T. Johnson. Grand Rapids: Wm. B. Eerdmans Publishing Co., 2001. Published dissertation—therefore technical. Stirred debate by insisting that, although most translations of Galatians 2:16 and 3:22 read "faith in Christ," it should be "the faith of Christ."

Jervis, L. Ann. *Galatians*. NIBCNT 9. Peabody, MA: Hendrickson Publishers, 1999. Readable 172-page commentary, showing insight into Paul's emotions.

Longenecker, Richard. *Galatians*. Word Biblical Commentary 41. Dallas: Word Books, 1990. Technical. Deals with rhetorical strategies.

Martyn, J. Louis. *Galatians: A New Translation with Introduction and Commentary*. AB. New York: Doubleday, 1997. Detailed and tedious. Speculative reconstruction of events in Galatia.

Matera, Frank J. *Galatians*. Sacra Pagina 9. Collegeville, MN: Liturgical Press, 1992. Technical. Argues that Paul's opponents sought to impose Jewish cultural norms on Gentiles.

Nanos, Mark D. *The Irony of Galatians: Paul's Letter in First-Century Context*. Minneapolis: Fortress Press, 2002. Sociological investigation of ancient Mediterranean norms.

Smiles, Vincent M. *The Gospel and the Law in Galatia: Paul's Response to Jewish-Christian Separatism and the Threat of Galatian Apostasy*. Collegeville, MN: Liturgical Press, 1998. Written for scholars. Argues that Paul expresses deep emotions in the Letter.

*Williams, Sam K. *Galatians*. Abingdon New Testament Commentaries. Nashville: Abingdon Press, 1997. Understandable and engaging. Seeks to help the reader feel what it would be like to be a Galatian Christian hearing this letter read aloud.

*Witherington, Ben, III. *Grace in Galatia: A Commentary on Paul's Letter to the Galatians*. Grand Rapids: Wm. B. Eerdmans Publishing Co., 1998. Fairly readable commentary (although detailed: 494 pages). Argues that Paul wrote Galatians before the Jerusalem council in 49 CE. Deals with sociological reconstructions and with Greco-Roman rhetoric.

Wright, N. T. *Paul for Everyone: Galatians and Thessalonians*. Louisville, KY: Westminster John Knox Press, 2004. Clear, short, and insightful. Easy to read but not simplistic.

CHAPTER 10

1 Corinthians

SEX, BOOZE, AND ECSTATIC WORSHIP

Prostitution thrived in ancient Corinth, a business enriched by sailors visiting the city. Rampant sexuality and greed permeated the society, but in this city was a small religious group who endorsed practices that shocked even the immoral Corinthian culture. They were the Christians.

On the basis of their motto "Freedom in Christ," they proudly endorsed an incestuous living arrangement that the crudest sailors would condemn. They bragged about their spiritual enlightenment while bickering with each other and dividing into competing factions. They sued each other before local magistrates; they attended wild parties in local temples; they turned communion services into opportunities to pig out and get drunk; they threw aside dress codes; they sought to draw attention to themselves by engaging in ecstatic demonstrations of speaking in tongues during their worship services; they rejected Paul's teaching because they judged him not to be a spiritual-enough leader. They drove the apostle crazy.

Ironically, they based their warped theology and practice on Paul's own teaching of freedom in Christ that we just saw him vehemently defend in his letter to the Galatians. Their perverse behavior provides a vivid illustration of the worst-case scenario that many Jewish Christians used to argue against Paul's insistence that Gentile converts must not be compelled to keep the laws of Moses. "What will happen to the moral and ethical quality of the church if we allow these pagans to become Christians and do not insist that they live in obedience to Mosaic law?" they wanted to know. "Will we not be degraded and displeasing to God if we do not insist that our converts keep the laws of God?" The church at Corinth validated their viewpoint. "If we do not maintain high standards," they reasoned, "how will we be distinguished from the wicked culture that surrounds us?" Paul's argument in Galatians suggests that their case convinced many Christians, including a number of Gentiles.

How did Paul deal with the errant believers at Corinth? How did he try to guide them into lives of holiness while still maintaining that salvation comes by faith alone? Before analyzing his Letter to see what methods he used to correct them, we should know more about the city in which they lived.

AN AFFLUENT HARBOR CITY

Corinth had a long and colorful history. Located strategically with respect to shipping and commerce, it was a wealthy city. And like many harbor towns, Corinth was a center for vice and sexual excess. Before the Roman general L. Mummius completely destroyed it in 146 BCE, Corinth was known for its worship of Aphrodite. According to the ancient geographer **Strabo**, the temple of Aphrodite had over a thousand cult prostitutes in "temple service."

> And the temple of Aphrodite was so rich that it owned more than a thousand temple-slaves, courtesans, whom both men and women had dedicated to the goddess. And therefore it was also on account of these women that the city was crowded with people and grew rich; for instance, the ship captains freely squandered their money, and hence the proverb, "Not for every man is the voyage to Corinth." (*Geography* 8.6.20 [Jones, LCL])

He probably exaggerated this number, and he may have been wrong about the presence of cult prostitution. "The ancient city of Corinth had such a long-standing reputation for vice that the Athenian dramatist Aristophanes (ca. 448–380 BCE) apparently coined the expression 'to corinthianize' [κορινθιάζεσαι] as a term for describing profligate living"[1] (*Fragment* 354; cf. Plato, *Republic* 404d). Athenian authors tended to stereotype Corinthians, portraying them in comedies as drunks, prostitutes, and lechers.

Yet all these sources describe the city before 146 BCE. After Mummius reduced the city to ashes and slaughtered its inhabitants, the site remained largely in ruins, with modest habitation, for a hundred years. In 44 BCE, Julius Caesar established a Roman colony there and named it *Colonia Laus Iulia Corinthus*. He gave much of the land to Roman settlers (many of them retired soldiers) and emancipated Greeks from Italy. At first, Latin was the official language, but as more Greeks settled in the area, Greek replaced Latin. A variety of religions flourished in Corinth—including Judaism, as attested by the discovery of an inscription reading "Synagogue of the Hebrews." Due to its location on an important trade route, Corinth again grew and prospered, and in 27 BCE it became the capital of the province of Achaia.

Corinth enjoyed a constant influx of money because merchants used the narrow **Isthmus of Corinth** to transport goods from the Gulf of Corinth to the Saronic Gulf and on to mainland Greece and back. Use of the

---

1. Michael R. Cosby, *Sex in the Bible: An Introduction to What the Scriptures Teach Us about Sexuality* (Englewood Cliffs, NJ: Prentice-Hall, 1984), 118.

Temple of Apollo at Corinth, with Acro-Corinth in the background. The Doric columns of this temple were each carved from a single block of stone, which was quite unusual. These columns are about six feet in diameter and 21 feet high. (Courtesy of Michael Cosby)

isthmus eliminated the lengthy sea voyage around the southern tip of Achaia, much like using the Panama Canal eliminates the need for ships today to go completely around South America. But the short, overland transit across the isthmus meant unloading the ships' cargoes onto wagons and hauling them along a rock-paved road to the other side. Workers also placed the ships on wheeled vehicles and transported them overland on the same road. This expensive process was faster and cheaper than sailing around Achaia. Because Corinth controlled this important transit site, considerable wealth flowed into the city from trade centers both to the east and to the west. Shortly after the time of Paul, in 67 CE, the emperor Nero ordered that a canal be dug across the Isthmus of Corinth; but when he died the work ceased. Not until 1881 was the project resumed, and in 1893 the canal was finished, allowing ships to float across the six kilometers to the other side.

Due to the destruction of Corinth in 146 BCE, most of the remains of the city today are of Roman construction. Archaeological excavation of the site has revealed the remnants of an impressive city. Corinth had a gymnasium, a large theater, an *ōdeion* (smaller, covered theater), and a number of basilicas (buildings used for assemblies), bath houses, and monuments. A large marketplace (**agora**) provided focus for commerce, and a variety of temples provided diverse worship possibilities.[2]

As a harbor town, Corinth differed little from similar cities around the Mediterranean world. Its greed, corruption, and immorality were not unique. Rome, for example, had a terrible reputation for vice. The satirist Juvenal (ca. 55–140 CE) describes female lust and perversity in *Satires* 6, as he humorously warns a friend of his not to marry. After

2. For detailed information, see Jerome Murphy-O'Connor, *St. Paul's Corinth: Texts and Archaeology* (Wilmington, DE: Michael Glazier, 1984).

saying that chastity used to dwell on earth but has long since retreated to heaven, he gives the following advice:

> To bounce your neighbor's bed, my friend, to outrage
> Matrimonial sanctity is now an ancient and long-
> Established tradition. All other crimes come later,
> With the Age of Iron; but our first adulterers
> Appeared in the Silver Era. And here you are in *this*
> Day and age, man, getting yourself engaged.
> . . . Postumus, are you *really*
> Taking a wife? You used to be sane enough
> —what
> Fury's got into you, what snake has stung you up?
> Why endure such bitch-tyranny when rope's available
> By the fathom, when all those dizzying top-floor windows
> Are open for you, when there are bridges handy
> To jump from? Supposing none of these exits catches
> Your fancy, isn't it better to sleep with a pretty boy?
> . . . You were once the randiest
> Hot-rod-about-town, you hid in more bedroom cupboards
> Than a comedy juvenile lead. Can this be the man now
> Sticking his silly neck out for the matrimonial halter?
> And as for your insistence on a wife with old-fashioned
> Moral virtues—man, you need your blood-pressure checked, you're
> Crazy, you're aiming over the moon.[3]

Juvenal's sarcastic descriptions of lewd behavior, although exaggerated for the sake of humor, nevertheless reflect the sad reality of moral decay in Rome. Horace's *Odes* and Petronius's *Satyricon* also lampoon

women's outrageous behaviors, probably indicating that truth lay behind the exaggerations. Juvenal's comic assertions that marriages no longer existed wherein either the husband or the wife were faithful to the other are more tragic than funny.

Although Corinth was probably no worse than many other cities in the first century, it was filled with immorality. And a number of the Christians there refused to separate themselves from the rampant vice. They even developed religious reasons to justify their outrageous behaviors. Before studying how the apostle confronted this difficult group of Christians, a brief review of what Acts says about Paul's time in Corinth helps to set the historical context.

DRAGGED BEFORE GALLIO THE PROCONSUL (ACTS 18:1–18)

According to Acts 18:11, during Paul's second missionary, he stayed eighteen months at Corinth. After his initial effort to evangelize local Jews met with stiff resistance, he focused on preaching the gospel to Gentiles and enjoyed much more success. In Corinth he met a Jewish couple, Aquila and Priscilla, who were tentmakers like Paul. According to Acts 18:2, they had to leave Rome, along with all the other Jews, due to the **expulsion edict of Claudius** (49–50 CE). Because Acts 18:12 mentions Gallio, who was proconsul of Achaia in 51 CE,[4] we esti-

---

3. *Juvenal: The Sixteen Satires*, trans. Peter Green, Penguin Classics (New York: Penguin Books, 1967), 127–28.

4. The time of Gallio's tenure as proconsul in Corinth is known from an inscription found at Delphi that records an edict made by Emperor Claudius sometime between the end of 51 and the middle of 52 (it also mentions Claudius being acclaimed "imperator" for the twenty-sixth time). This inscription specifies Gallio as proconsul of Achaia about July 51. For a photo

mate that Paul first ministered in Corinth in 50–52. In addition, Acts 18:24–26 explains that Priscilla and Aquila instructed an Alexandrian Jew named Apollos, who later went to Corinth and proclaimed the gospel of Jesus Christ (18:27–28).

Paul wrote 1 Corinthians during his third missionary journey, probably in 55. In this Letter he mentions Priscilla and Aquila once, in 16:19, and the eloquent Apollos seven times (1:12; 3:4, 5, 6, 22; 4:6; 16:12).

1 CORINTHIANS 16 REVEALS PAUL'S CIRCUMSTANCES WHEN HE WROTE THIS LETTER

1. What project is Paul directing (16:1–4)?

2. According to 16:5–9, where is Paul when he writes, and what time of year is it?

3. What does 16:10–11 reveal about the attitude of some of the Corinthian Christians toward Paul's companion Timothy?

4. What does 16:12 reveal about the attitude of Apollos toward the Corinthians?

YOU ARE FOOLISH, LOW, AND DESPISED (1 COR. 1:1–2:13)

1. What differences do you notice between the salutation in 1:1–3 and that found in 1 Thessalonians 1:1?

2. What might the differences in detail between the thanksgiving section in 1:4–9 and that found in 1 Thessalonians 1:2–10 tell you about the Corinthian Christians?

---

of the inscription, see Adolf Deissmann, *Paul: A Study in Social and Religious History* (New York: Harper & Row, 1957), plate 1. The reconstructed text is on 261–86.

In addition to the letter from the Corinthians, Paul has a further source of information about the church: a delegation of people who came to him from the house of Chloe (1:11). "Chloe's people" may refer to a house church similar to the one that met in the home of Aquila and Prisca (=Priscilla; 16:19), or perhaps it merely designates Chloe's children or her servants.

3. Delegates from Corinth bring a disturbing message to Paul about divisions in the church. Notice that the loyalty given by the various factions to their designated leaders (1:12) seems to be largely linked to who baptized them (1:12–16). How does Paul respond to this situation?

Oh! Wait a Minute!

1 Corinthians 1:16 provides a good example of the mistakes that people often make when writing letters. After making a strong point in 1:14–15 that he baptized no one other than Crispus and Gaius, Paul corrects himself in 16 with an "Oh, wait a minute" clarification as he suddenly realizes that his comment in 1:14–15 is not completely accurate.

When writing with pen and ink, such corrections are typical. No doubt you have had similar experiences of writing something and suddenly realizing that what you just penned has problems with it. Do you cross out what you wrote, or do you write a qualifier? Personal preferences differ. Paul's correction provides a vivid example of the fact that 1 Corinthians is a real letter, written in the heat of dealing with a difficult situation.

Remember the loyalty that mystery-religion members had for the priests who initiated them, such as Lucius's bond with Mithras, who initiated him into Isis (chap. 4, "Greek and Roman Religions of Paul's Day"). Perhaps the Corinthian Christians brought to their new faith a similar perspective on baptism.

4. According to 1:17–25, what seems to impress the Corinthian Christians? In light of 1:26–27, why is this rather ironic?

5. Why would Paul's message of a crucified Messiah be a stumbling block for Jews to believe his gospel? Why would it be foolishness to Greeks?

6. In 2:1–5 Paul states that he refused to use rhetorical skills or human wisdom when he proclaimed the gospel to them. How does the wisdom that Paul preaches differ from the wisdom of this age (2:6–13)?

2. "You" in 3:16–17 is a plural form (like the southern "y'all"), and Paul's reference to God's temple refers to the group as a whole. What warning, therefore, does his assertion in verses 16–17 give to those who want to exercise leadership in Corinth? How are some of the people "destroying God's temple" (3:17)?

GROW UP, YOU SPIRITUAL BABIES! (1 COR. 2:14–4:21)

Apparently some of the Corinthians called themselves *pneumatikoi* (Greek πνευματικοί, "spiritual ones"), viewing themselves as superior to other Christians. Paul calls them *sarkinoi* (Greek σαρκίνοι, "fleshly ones") in 3:1 and *sarkikoi* (also "fleshly ones") in 3:3, asserting that they are so immature that they cannot eat solid food but still need milk like babies.

1. Using the imagery of farming (3:6–8) and building (3:9), Paul explains the responsibilities other leaders have when they build on the foundation he established at Corinth (3:10–15). How will subsequent teachers be judged?

The Importance of Context

Some people interpret 3:16–17 as an ethical exhortation directed to individual Christians concerning what they do with their own physical bodies (smoking, overindulgence, etc.). How does interpreting these two verses in their context rule out this use of the passage?

3. As we will see in 9:1–3, some Corinthians judged Paul to be inadequate as an apostle. He does not think much of their evaluation (4:3). How does Paul judge himself? (4:3–5)

Paul's belief that Christ will judge at the Parousia, so prevalent in 1 Thessalonians, appears in 3:13–15 ("the Day" of judgment is connected with fire) and 4:5 ("Do not pronounce judgment before the time, before the Lord comes, who will bring to light the things now hidden in darkness and will disclose the purposes of the heart").

4. Some Corinthian Christians are arrogant (4:6), and Paul sarcastically puts them in their place (4:7; cf. 3:1–4). In 4:8–13, how does Paul use sarcasm to expose further their misguided pride?

5. Their tendency to appropriate new leaders ("ten thousand guardians in Christ" [4:15]) and their condescending attitude cause Paul to respond to their challenge. What ultimatum does he deliver in 4:18–21?

6. Notice that Paul mentions sending Timothy to them in 4:17 (cf. the warning in 16:11 not to despise him). In light of 1 Corinthians 1–4, what seems to have happened during Timothy's last visit?

Dealing with Insubordination

How does Paul's style of confronting the rebellious Corinthian Christians compare with his means of confronting the Galatian Christians? How effective would his approach be in your church? Why?

Reflecting on 15:12 ("Some of you say that there is no resurrection of the dead") increases our understanding of 1 Corinthians 5–14. Paul defends his belief in the **resurrection** of the body in chapter 15, apparently in response to a challenge from some of the Corinthians. Unlike Paul, whose Pharisaic parents and teachers taught him that the righteous will live forever in a resurrected body, most Greeks and Romans found such a belief to be amusing. Many distinguished between the soul and the body, believing that the afterlife will not be a bodily existence.

Greek beliefs in afterlife varied somewhat. Some held a bleak view, such as that pictured in Homer's *Odyssey*, book 11, where the dead are pitiful, bodiless shades who endure a kind of pseudoexistence in darkness below the surface of the earth. Others, like Plato, believed in a type of reincarnation. In the "Myth of Er" (*Republic* 10.614b–621d), he recounts a tale about a seriously wounded warrior whose soul supposedly went to the place where the souls of the dead undergo journeys, some to a thousand years of torment and others to a shorter time of blissful existence. In this myth the souls keep going back to earth to live in other bodies (animal or human) until they finally reach a stage of purity that liberates them from this cycle. In another of Plato's dialogues called *Phaedo*, Socrates argues at length that the soul is eternal and therefore his students and friends should not mourn his coming death.

Similarly, in *Phaedrus*, Plato includes the following argument that all souls are immortal, because they are ever in motion:

> Soul [considered collectively] has the care of all that is inanimate, and traverses the whole universe, though in ever-changing forms. Thus when it is perfect and winged it journeys on high and controls the whole world, but one that has shed its wings sinks down until it can fasten on something solid and settling there it takes to itself an earthly body which seems by reason of the soul's power to move itself. . . . The natural property of a wing is to raise that which is heavy and carry it aloft to the region where the gods dwell. (*Phaedrus* 246b–d)[5]

Some Greeks strove through philosophy to rid their souls of weight so that after death

their purified souls could soar upward, escaping the physical realm to join the unchanging realm of the divine. They looked forward to being rid of their changing human body. Greeks had a saying, ***sōma sēma***, which means "the body—a grave." For example, in Plato's *Cratylus*, Socrates responds to a question by saying,

> For some say that the body [*sōma*] is the grave [*sēma*] of the soul, which may be thought to be buried in our present life; or again the index of the soul, because the soul gives indications to [*sēmainei*] the body; probably the Orphic poets were the inventors of the name, and they were under the impression that the soul is suffering the punishment of sin, and that the body is an enclosure or prison in which the soul is incarcerated, kept safe [*sōma, sōzētai*], as the name *sōma* implies, until the penalty is paid. (400 b–c)[6]

The idea of bodily resurrection was foreign to Greeks. Acts 17:32, for example, records a negative reaction to this belief by an audience in Athens: "When they heard of the resurrection of the dead, some scoffed." As a general rule, Greeks had little notion of a blessed afterlife. For them, religion primarily assisted one to live better in the present world.

Among Romans there was also skepticism about afterlife. On ancient Roman tombstones the bleak saying **"I was not; I am not; I care not"** recurs with such frequency that those who carved the epitaphs typically just abbreviated this Latin expression: ***NFNSNC***. Thus, Paul preached a gospel of hope to people who largely were not optimistic about eternal life. His message appealed to a fair number in Corinth, yet his belief in a physical, resurrected body seemed quaint to many. Some of the new

5. Translation by R. Hackforth, *Plato's Phaedrus* (Cambridge: Cambridge University Press, 1952); also found in *The Collected Dialogues of Plato*, ed. E. Hamilton and H. Cairns (Princeton, NJ: Princeton University Press, 1961).

6. Translation by Benjamin Jowett, in Hamilton and Cairns, *The Collected Dialogues of Plato*.

Christian converts modified his teaching about the resurrection into a purely spiritual phenomenon, thus maintaining their separation of body and soul. Echoing the belief "the body—a grave," they held a much lower view of the physical body than did Paul.

One group, whom we will call the **libertines**, took this view to the extreme of saying that whatever one does in the body does not matter since it does not affect the important part of the person, the soul. Their motto is best expressed in 6:12, where Paul quotes their slogan: "All things are lawful for me." Another way of saying this would be *"If it feels good, do it!"* They distanced themselves from their own bodies, seeing the body as external to the real self. Apparently they had the following attitude: "If the body wants to do something, let it do as it pleases. Only what pertains to the soul is important. And we who are spiritual (*pneumatikoi*) understand these things much better than poor Paul, who is terribly confused."

Their beliefs combine a Greco-Roman view of the person with a misunderstanding of Paul's proclamation of Christ's second coming and of his teaching on freedom in Christ. Apparently the libertines believed that they had already experienced some sort of spiritual resurrection, perhaps when they were baptized (cf. 1:12–17). Consequently they considered themselves above earthly ethics and morality, things that pertain to fleshly people but not to those who have transcended the physical. They saw Paul's denunciation of their view as evidence of his own lack of spirituality. Their self-centered arrogance led to aberrant behavior.

PROUD OF THE MAN HAVING SEX WITH HIS STEPMOTHER (1 COR. 5)

The first example is the "man living with his father's wife" in 5:1, most likely referring to a member of the Corinthian church living with his stepmother. In Greek and Roman society it was not uncommon for men to marry younger women, especially if their first wives died. Apparently, the father of one of the Christians had died, leaving behind a widow who could easily have been younger than his children. His son found the stepmother attractive and began living with her. This action shocked even the citizens of Corinth. Jews, Greeks, and Romans all considered such relationships to be incestuous and forbade them.

Jewish law forbids men from having sexual relations with women who belonged or had belonged to their fathers: "You shall not uncover the nakedness of your father's wife" (Lev. 18:8). "A man shall not marry his father's wife, thereby violating his father's rights" (Deut. 22:30). "Cursed be anyone who lies with his father's wife, because he has violated his father's rights" (Deut. 27:20). Mishnah *Sanhedrin* 7.4, although written after Paul's time, also reflects this prohibition: "These are they that are to be stoned: he that has connection with his mother, . . . his daughter-in-law, a male. . . . He that has connection with his father's wife, . . . whether in his father's lifetime or after his father's death, whether after betrothal [only] or after wedlock."[7]

---

7. Translation by Herbert Danby, *The Mishnah* (Oxford: Oxford University Press, 1933), 391–92.

Roman law also forbids such unions (Gaius, *Institutes* 1.63). The Roman author Cicero denounces the union of a woman with her son-in-law: "Oh! to think of the woman's sin, unbelievable, unheard of in all experience save for this single instance! To think of her wicked passion, unbridled, untamed!" (*Pro Cluentio* 14 [LCL]). Greek literature contains similar prohibitions, and sometimes such unions enter into their tragedies. Sophocles (ca. 430 BCE) develops a tragic plot around an incestuous union between a man and his biological mother in *Oedipus Rex*. However, these texts never explain why Greeks, Romans, and Jews considered sexual relationships between a man and his stepmother to be incestuous. They simply assume that readers will all share the author's horrified response to such unions.

1. According to 5:2, 6, what attitude do some of the Corinthian Christians have toward the incestuous union?

2. What is Paul's evaluation of the situation, and what action does he demand in response? (Note that Paul mentions nothing about disciplining the woman. She probably was not a Christian.)

3. Compare 5:6–8 with 16:8. Why would the imagery of the Passover lamb and getting rid of yeast be appropriate for him to use at this time of year? (You might want to read about the Passover ritual in Exodus 12:1–20.)

Shunning

On the basis of 5:11, some Christians practice shunning. What are the pros and cons of refusing to speak or eat with Christians who commit the sins listed in this verse?

When, in your opinion, should an immoral person be kicked out of the church, as Paul demands in 5:13? How is the effectiveness of shunning limited by the number of churches in most communities today, as well as the specter of lawsuits?

4. In 5:9 Paul refers to a letter he previously wrote to the Corinthians. What instructions in that letter seem to have confused them?

5. What do his new instructions in 5:9–13 reveal about problems in the church?

1. Especially in light of the Corinthian emphasis on wisdom (cf. 1:17–31), 6:1–6 is a sarcastic, shaming argument. With what attitude would Paul have them replace their self-centered greediness?

2. How does 6:9–11 refute the libertine belief that what one does with the body is of no real consequence?

FREE IN CHRIST FOR FRIVOLOUS LAWSUITS AND SEXUAL IMMORALITY (1 COR. 6)

In the ancient Mediterranean world, court cases often involved efforts to shame someone publicly and to gain honor for oneself. Through bribes and hiring good lawyers, the wealthy were able to make themselves virtually unassailable by people from lower social strata. Dio Chrysostom, writing about 100 CE, said that Corinth had countless lawyers "perverting justice"; he laments younger lawyers displaying their oratorical skills at athletic contests in an effort to gain more business (*Or.* 8.9). For a contemporary parallel, look at the number of pages of listings under "Attorneys" in the Yellow Pages of your phone book.

3. How do Paul's words in 6:9–11 and 5:7 ("as you really are unleavened") compare with his teaching in Galatians 2:19–20; 5:24?

Paul rejects the libertine slogan "All things are lawful for me" (6:12a), replying, "But not all things are beneficial," and "I will not be dominated by anything" (6:12b). The close connection between hunger for food and desire for sexual intercourse in

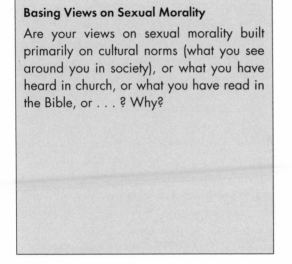

Basing Views on Sexual Morality

Are your views on sexual morality built primarily on cultural norms (what you see around you in society), or what you have heard in church, or what you have read in the Bible, or . . . ? Why?

6:13 suggests that the libertines placed both on the same "physical level." If a man is hungry, he eats food; if he is sexually stimulated, he finds a woman. Ultimately, this philosophy places women on approximately the same level as a plate of food: they are means to gratify a bodily desire. According to the libertines, all bodily desires are below the spiritual level on which they live. But Paul refuses to equate sex with food.

4. What is Paul's view of sexual relations between men and women (6:14–20)?

Archaeologists discovered a woman's sandal at Corinth that somehow escaped the normal deterioration of time. A wooden plate was fastened to the sole with

nails, and on the plate was written in Greek ΑΚΑΛΟΥΘΕΙ ΜΟΙ (*akolouthei moi*), "Follow me."[8] Whenever the owner of this sandal walked on dusty streets, she left her message for any men who might want to follow her. Perhaps she was a higher-class prostitute whose clientele could read.

SEX, CELIBACY, MARRIAGE, AND DIVORCE (1 COR. 7)

In 7:1 Paul begins to answer a series of questions posed to him in the letter from Corinth: "Now concerning the matters about which you wrote." Caution is needed when reading his answers, however, because one can easily misread his quotations of Corinthian slogans as expressions of his own viewpoints instead of ideas that he seeks to correct. For example, people often mistakenly read Paul's statement in 7:1b as his own view of human sexuality: "It is well for a man not to touch a woman." However, in the words that follow, he argues *against* this view, not for it.

Thus 8:1–7 clearly illustrates Paul's approach of first quoting a Corinthian slogan and then correcting it. He begins by stating another question asked in their letter: "Now concerning food sacrificed to idols." Then he quotes a Corinthian slogan: "We know that 'all of us possess knowledge'" (8:1)—a view that he proceeds to refute: "It is not everyone, however, who has this knowledge" (8:7).

In 7:1–7 Paul disputes an ascetic belief that sexual intercourse, even between

8. Hans Licht, *Sexual Life in Ancient Greece* (New York: Barnes & Noble, 1963), 338.

married couples, is wrong. Obviously, in light of the libertine views he corrects in chapters 5–6, a different faction must have promoted such a belief. Unfortunately for Paul, people who promoted both extremes struggled for dominance in the same church. The libertines said, "If it feels good, do it." Another group, commonly called **ascetics**, seemed to promote the motto *"If it feels good, it must be sin"* (note particularly in 7:28, 36 how he rejects their teaching that getting married is sin). Paul had to refute both extremes in the same letter.

Chapter 7 deals first with the ascetic view: that sexual intercourse is beneath the will of God for truly pious individuals.

1. What are the main points of Paul's argument in 7:1–7 against the idea that married couples should not engage in sexual intimacy?

Paul's words in 7:4, "The wife does not have authority over her own body, but the husband does," accurately reflect Mediterranean cultural norms. However, when he asserts in the same verse, "Likewise the husband does not have authority over his own body, but the wife does," he probably raised many eyebrows. Such an assertion would shock and perhaps offend numerous men.

Some Jewish writings provide interesting background information for the Corinthian ascetics' insistence that husbands and wives refrain from sexual intercourse so that they can devote themselves to prayer. For example, *Testament of Naphtali* says, "There is a time for having intercourse with one's wife, and a time to abstain for the purpose of prayer" (8.8).[9] In later rabbinic writings, similar comments may be found, complete with time limits. According to Mishnah *Ketubboth* 5.6, the school of Shammai teaches that a man may take a vow of abstinence for up to two weeks, but the school of Hillel limits such vows to one week unless the man needed extended time to study Torah. Scholars could expand the time to thirty days for intensive study, and they could do so without consulting their wives for permission. On the other hand, the same regulations stipulate that if a wife refuses sexual intercourse with her husband, he has the right to reduce her dowry. Paul stretched cultural norms by asserting that wives had authority over their husband's bodies.

2. In 7:6–7, what is Paul's attitude toward his own celibacy?

9. Translation by H. C. Kee, in *The Old Testament Pseudepigrapha*, vol 1, *Apocalyptic Literature and Testaments* (Garden City, NY: Doubleday, 1983), 814.

3. What advice does Paul give for those who have strong sexual urges and are not content with celibacy?

6. According to 7:29, 31, how much longer does Paul expect the world to last (cf. 10:11)?

From 7:10–16 it appears that the ascetics urged Christians to separate from their mates as a way of pursuing purity.

4. In 7:10–16, what instructions does Paul give pertaining to separations or divorces?

As we saw in 2 Thessalonians, early Christians expected a time of intense persecution just before the second coming of the Lord. They believed that during this end time, many would die as martyrs when the forces of evil convulsed the world.

7. How does Paul's view of the coming end of the world influence his advice in 7:25–35 concerning marriage or remarriage?

Among the new Christians at Corinth were those whose mates chose not to follow Christ. The ascetics evidently told them that remaining married to nonbelievers would cause their children to be unclean. Paul rejects this view and asserts that the believing parent makes the children holy (7:14).

5. What do Paul's examples of circumcision and slavery in 7:17–24 contribute to his main point about whether or not one should seek marriage or celibacy?

In 7:34 Paul distinguishes between women who have never married ("virgins," Greek *parthenoi*) and those who once were married but presently are not, whom he simply calls "unmarried" (Greek *agamoi*). In Classical Greek, *agamoi* can refer either to virgins or to those who have lost their mates through death or divorce. Yet in 1 Corinthians 7 Paul seems to use *agamoi* in a more limited way to describe those who were once married but presently are not (as distinguished from virgins). This minor detail possibly provides insight into Paul's own marital status, for in 7:8 he seems to include himself with the unmarried men (*agamois*) and the widows (*chērais*). Although we cannot know for sure, it is entirely possible that Paul had been married and either his wife died or he lost her when he became a Christian and was then branded a heretic by those in the larger Jewish community.

Celibacy was rare among Jewish men. With the exception of members of a few fringe sects, such as the Qumran community, Jewish males typically married by age twenty. They considered it their duty to propagate their race. A statement in the Mishnah (ca. 200 CE) shows how strongly they believed that marriage and childbirth were necessary.

> No man may abstain from keeping the law *Be fruitful and multiply*, unless he already has children: according to the School of Shammai, two sons; according to the School of Hillel, a son and a daughter, for it is written, *Male and female created he them*. If he married a woman and lived with her ten years and she bore no child, it is not permitted him to abstain. If he divorced her she may be married to another and the second husband may live with her for ten years. If she had a miscarriage the space [of ten years] is reckoned from the time of the miscarriage. The duty to be fruitful and multiply falls on the man but not on the woman. R. Johanan b. Baroka says: Of them both it is written, And God blessed them and God said unto them, Be fruitful and multiply. (Mishnah, *Yebamot* 6.6) [10]

Because Paul was a Pharisee, part of the Jewish cultural mainstream, he once shared the belief that he was responsible to fulfill the commission of Genesis 1:28: "And God said to them, 'Be fruitful and multiply and fill the earth and subdue it.'" We

10. Translation by Danby, *The Mishnah*.

do not know how much the prescriptions contained in the Mishnah reflect practice in Paul's day. But the attitude of these Rabbis was that, aside from a possible delay for intense study of the Scriptures, men should marry by age twenty (Mishnah *Abot* 5.21).

8. In light of 7:29, 31, why does Paul advise betrothed couples in 7:36–38 that it is better for them if they do not marry? [11]

YOUR VIEW ON THE ISSUE OF DIVORCE

Problems associated with divorce convulse our culture, and the divorce rate among Christians reflects that of the general population. Imagine that you are appointed to serve on a church committee assigned the task of formulating a policy statement on divorce. In preparation, study the following passages, noting the differences between the Gospel stories (some are boldfaced or italicized to call attention to them).

11. A few translations of this passage word it as if Paul is speaking of a father worrying about his single daughter and trying to decide whether or not to give her in marriage. Although it is possible to translate the verb *gamizō* in 7:37 to mean "give in marriage," the context argues against it. *Gamizō* is a rare verb, and there are ample examples of its being used to mean "enter into marriage" (see J. H. Moulton and W. F. Howard, *A Grammar of New Testament Greek*, vol. 2 [Edinburgh: T&T Clark, 1929], 409–10; Hans Conzelmann, *1 Corinthians*, Hermeneia [Philadelphia: Fortress Press, 1975], 131, 136; C. K. Barrett, *The First Epistle to the Corinthians* [New York: Harper & Row, 1968], 185).

Mark 10:1–12

He left that place and went to the region of Judea and beyond the Jordan. And crowds again gathered around him; and, as was his custom, he again *taught* them.

² Some Pharisees came, and to test him they asked, "Is it lawful for a man to divorce his wife?" ³ He answered them, "What did Moses *command* you?" ⁴ They said, "Moses *allowed* a man to write a certificate of dismissal and to divorce her." ⁵ But Jesus said to them, "Because of your hardness of heart he wrote this *commandment* for you. ⁶ But from the beginning of creation, 'God made them male and female.' ⁷ 'For this reason a man shall leave his father and mother and be joined to his wife, ⁸ and the two shall become one flesh.' So they are no longer two, but one flesh. ⁹ Therefore what God has joined together, let no one separate."

¹⁰ **Then in the house** the disciples **asked him again about this matter**. ¹¹ He said to them, "Whoever divorces his wife and marries another commits adultery against her; ¹² **and if she divorces her husband and marries another, she commits adultery.**"

Matthew 19:1–12

When Jesus had finished saying these things, he left Galilee and went to the region of Judea beyond the Jordan. ² Large crowds followed him, and he *cured* them there.

³ Some Pharisees came to him, and to test him they asked, "Is it lawful for a man to divorce his wife **for any cause**?" ⁴ He answered, **"Have you not read** that the one who made them at the beginning 'made them male and female,' ⁵ and said, 'For this reason a man shall leave his father and mother and be joined to his wife, and the two shall become one flesh'? ⁶ So they are no longer two, but one flesh. Therefore what God has joined together, let no one separate." ⁷ They said to him, "Why then did Moses *command* us to give a certificate of dismissal and to divorce her?" ⁸ He said to them, "It was because you were so hard-hearted that Moses *allowed* you to divorce your wives, but from the beginning it was not so. ⁹ And I say to you, whoever divorces his wife, **except for unchastity**, and marries another commits adultery."

¹⁰ His disciples **said** to him, **"If such is the case of a man with his wife, it is better not to marry."** ¹¹ **But he said to them, "Not everyone can accept this teaching, but only those to whom it is given.** ¹²**For**

there are eunuchs who have been so from birth, and there are eunuchs who have been made eunuchs by others, and there are eunuchs who have made themselves eunuchs for the sake of the kingdom of heaven. Let anyone accept this who can."

Luke 16:18

"Anyone who divorces his wife and marries another commits adultery, and whoever marries a woman divorced from her husband commits adultery."

Deuteronomy 24:1–4

Suppose a man enters into marriage with a woman, but she does not please him because he finds something objectionable about her, and so he writes her a certificate of divorce, puts it in her hand, and sends her out of his house; she then leaves his house ² and goes off to become another man's wife. ³ Then suppose the second man dislikes her, writes her a bill of divorce, puts it in her hand, and sends her out of his house (or the second man who married her dies); ⁴ her first husband, who sent her away, is not permitted to take her again to be his wife after she has been defiled; for that would be abhorrent to the LORD, and you shall not bring guilt on the land that the LORD your God is giving you as a possession.

1 Corinthians 7:10–16

¹⁰ To the married I give this command—not I but the Lord—that the wife should not separate from her husband ¹¹ (but if she does separate, let her remain unmarried or else be reconciled to her husband), and that the husband should not divorce his wife.

¹² To the rest I say—I and not the Lord—that if any believer has a wife who is an unbeliever, and she consents to live with him, he should not divorce her. ¹³ And if any woman has a husband who is an unbeliever, and he consents to live with her, she should not divorce him. ¹⁴ For the unbelieving husband is made holy through his wife, and the unbelieving wife is made holy through her husband. Otherwise, your children would be unclean, but as it is, they are holy. ¹⁵ But if the unbelieving partner separates, let it be so; in such a case the brother or sister is not bound. It is to peace that God has called you. ¹⁶ Wife, for all you know, you might save your husband. Husband, for all you know, you might save your wife.

Compare the issues that Paul tackles in 1 Corinthians 7 with those addressed in Mark, Luke, and Matthew. And notice that Deuteronomy 24:1–4, the casuistic law mentioned in Mark 10:4 and Matthew 19:7–8, actually deals with remarriage. It assumes a man's right to divorce his wife but cautions against exercising it hastily. If she remarries and then becomes single again, her first husband cannot take her back. Jewish women did not have the same right to divorce their husbands. Consequently, Jesus' statement against divorce in Matthew 19 and Luke 16:18 speaks only to men. The fact that Mark 10:12 includes women in the warning is good evidence of a Gentile audience for the Gospel, particularly Roman women.

Roman women enjoyed more freedom than the secluded upper-class Greek women. Indeed, the male double standard with regard to fidelity among Romans had eroded significantly in the first century. During Paul's time some Roman women divorced their husbands merely to marry men who were making swifter political progress. They also attained more economic freedom, which contributed to briefer marriages, because they became less dependent on men.[12] Consideration of such historical/cultural factors results in more nuanced attempts at determining contemporary relevance.

In your policy statement on divorce, consider the following:

1. How do the biblical authors' varied audiences and circumstances influence your analysis and conclusions? For example, how does knowing Paul's reason for counseling betrothed couples not to marry (1 Cor. 7:36–38) influence what you do with his advice today?

2. What role do you think Scripture should play in formulating a divorce policy? Why?

3. What role do you believe reason and experience should play in making decisions on this painful issue? Should your reasons for divorce be limited to the ones specified in the Bible, or should you include others? Do you view these passages as *case studies* on which to reflect and use in formulating the best way to live, or do you consider them *laws* to be implemented strictly as stated?

What is the difference between viewing Scripture as a *case book* or as a *law-code book*? Do you take the approach that the Bible gives exhaustive mandates for all major issues of life (i.e., only reasons specified in the Bible are legitimate reasons for divorce)? Or do you believe that Scripture does not specifically address some important issues? For example, is it legitimate for a wife to divorce her husband if he is an alcoholic who beats her and their children, even though this exact reason is not specified in the Bible?

4. Review the steps that the apostles took in Acts 15 when reaching a major decision. How might their approach help you formulate your divorce policy?

---

12. William H. Leslie, "The Concept of Women in the Pauline Corpus in Light of the Social and Religious Environment of the First Century" (PhD diss., Northwestern University, 1976), 416–17.

State Your Policy on Divorce

"WHY CAN'T WE GET DRUNK DURING COMMUNION?" (1 COR. 8–10)

In cities such as Corinth, Gentile sacrifices often involved communal meals—which contributed to the social fabric of society. Some were held in temples, some in homes. Some were cultic meals, some were family celebrations or fraternal gatherings. Papyri discovered in Egypt that extend invitations to such meals indicate that the occasions varied from birthday parties and coming-of-age celebrations to official religious gatherings with invitations from a patron god or goddess.[13]

Sacrificial meat for these celebrations was divided into three parts: (1) a portion for the god or goddess, which was burned on an altar; (2) a portion for the worshipers, which comprised the dominant amount of the animal; and (3) a portion dedicated to the deity, which was placed upon a special table. Theoretically the deity ate the third portion, but practically the worshipers and/or cult officials consumed it.[14] They placed the deity's portion on a table called a *trapeza*, the word that Paul uses in 10:21 when he speaks of "the *table* of the Lord" and "the *table* of demons."

When Gentiles gathered for social occasions, they would nearly always pray to a god or goddess and pour out a **libation**. They assumed the presence of a deity, regardless of the occasion. Most trade guilds and athletic groups were named after a deity. When members assembled, they gave proper respect to the patron deity; but the primary purpose for gathering was social in nature.[15]

Some ancient inscriptions describing sacrificial meals express concern that participants receive fair portions of food, so that no one is left out. Other inscriptions specify rules of orderly conduct, forbidding participants from being too loud, acting in disorderly ways, using abusive language,

13. See Wendell Lee Willis, *Idol Meat in Corinth: The Pauline Argument in 1 Corinthians 8 and 10*, Society of Biblical Literature Dissertation Series 68 (Chico, CA: Scholars Press, 1985), 39–43.

14. David Gill, "*Trapezōmata*: A Neglected Aspect of Greek Sacrifice," in *Harvard Theological Review* 67 (1974): 117–37; and Willis, *Idol Meat in Corinth*, 8–10, 15–17.

15. Willis, *Idol Meat in Corinth*, 47–52.

or starting fights. Apparently the amount of wine consumed during such gatherings created problems. The main reason for attending the celebrations was to have a good time, and some got carried away with their drinking. The Greek author Aristophanes indicates that drunkenness characterized the cult festivals of Bacchus.[16] On a somewhat lesser level, the same situation existed for festivals dedicated to other deities.[17]

The Gentile Christians at Corinth had probably attended many such cultic celebrations. As we will see in 11:17–22, some brought their party habits into the newly founded church, turning communion meals into raucous feasts. But in chapter 8 Paul addresses the issue of whether or not Christians may attend cult gatherings in local temples with their friends and extended family. His insistence that Christian faith excludes honoring the gods and goddesses of one's family, guild, and city posed problems for Gentile converts.

1. What does Paul's summary of the libertine position in 8:1, 4–6 reveal about why they believed it was OK to attend feasts in local temples?

2. What reasons does Paul give for why Christians should not attend such feasts?

LIBERATED TO SERVE OTHERS (1 COR. 9)

1. What indications does Paul give in 9:1–3 that some Corinthian Christians reject him as an apostle?

2. What does Paul say he has given up for the sake of his ministry to others (9:4–14)? (His method of using Scripture in 9:8–10 is called *pesher*. We will examine this approach when we study Romans 10.)

3. How does Paul's description of his lifestyle in chapter 9 illustrate his point in chapter 8

---

16. Bacchus was the Roman god of wine and revelry, who was equivalent to the Greek god Dionysus.
17. Willis, *Idol Meat in Corinth*, 54–61.

about not living selfishly (as opposed to the self-centered lives of the libertines)?

4. What philosophy of life and ministry does Paul endorse in 9:15–27?

1. How does Paul use the story of the rebellious and idolatrous Israelites (10:1–13) to show that the complacency of the libertines is dangerously misguided?[18]

Marriage is one of the sacrifices that Paul consciously made (9:5). His endorsement of celibacy in 7:7 ("I wish that all were as I myself am") does not indicate that he viewed marriage as a concession for lesser Christians. He viewed marriage as a positive good that he willingly gave up for the sake of serving others.

STAY OUT OF PAGAN TEMPLES! (1 COR. 10)

The libertines believed that their freedom in Christ liberated them to do whatever they pleased—including attending feasts in idol temples. Paul, in an effort to combat this belief, appeals to Scripture as he argues against their practies.

18. The reference to Christ being a spiritual rock that followed the Israelites in the wilderness (10:4) is probably based on a legend that Paul learned during his Pharisaic training. Later rabbinic writings, for example, speak of a well that followed Moses and the Israelites up over mountains and down through valleys (e.g., Tosefta *Sukka* 3.11 [196]; *Targum Onqelos* on Num. 21:17; *Midrash Sifre* on Num. 11:21). Some texts call it Miriam's well and explain that when she died, it disappeared (Babylonian Talmud *Shabbat* 35a; *Ta'anit* 9a). Although knowing exactly what Paul meant in 10:4 is difficult, it is clear that he intends his readers to view his command as part of a severe warning to turn from their sins. See Conzelmann, *1 Corinthians*, 166–67; Willis, *Idol Meat in Corinth*, 133–42.

Head coverings in the Middle East today go from burkas that hide the entire head to mere scarves. These Egyptian schoolgirls are wearing moderate head coverings and obviously have their own sense of dressing in style. (Courtesy of Lynne Cosby)

2. How does Paul's view in 10:11 of how much longer the world will last compare with what he said in 7:29, 31?

Paul's use of the term *koinōnia* ("fellowship" or "sharing") in 10:16–21 reflects the widespread use of the term in his day. Some ancient texts and inscriptions use this word to describe cultic meals, and they depict the congenial sharing of things. Other sources use *koinōnia* to denote business partnerships, kinship relationships, political associations, marriage, and even sexual intercourse.[19] Paul uses *koinōnia* in this chapter to describe religious meals held by Christians (10:16), Jews (10:18), and Gentile idol worshipers (10:20). The people in each group share fraternal meals; and when eating meat, they participate in the worship of the deity in whose name the animal was killed. Paul bans participation in idol worship, but he has a different view on sharing meals in people's homes.

After repeating the libertine slogan "All things are lawful" (10:23), Paul addresses the issue of Christians eating meat purchased in the marketplace. Some meat sold in the markets had been sacrificed to idols—which raises an important question: Should Christians completely avoid such food?

19. Willis, *Idol Meat in Corinth*, 167–181.

3. Why does Paul believe that it is OK to eat meat sacrificed to idols so long as one is in a private home, but not OK to eat it in a worship setting in a public temple?

ship. Whether these were veils or some other type of covering, we do not know for sure. Unlike his approach in Galatians, here Paul stresses *continuity* with the traditions he received from others as a way of arguing for conformity with customary practices.

1. What view of male and female participation in worship does 11:2–16 seem to presuppose?

WHY WOMEN MUST WEAR HEAD COVERINGS (1 CORINTHIANS 11:2–16)

In this passage Paul deals with the problem of women wanting to remove their head coverings during communal wor-

---

Appropriate Clothing for Worship

Christians differ on what they consider to be appropriate church attire. Using Paul's instructions to women in 11:2–16, what principle would you formulate as a guideline for this issue?

Dealing with Different Cultural Norms

What are the implications for applying Paul's Letters if we conclude that at times the best way to obey his *intended* message is to do the opposite of what he says (e.g., because of cultural differences, not wearing a head covering instead of wearing one)?

2. To what different sources of authority does Paul appeal in 11:2–16 in his attempt to convince the Corinthians to respect the tradition of wearing head coverings?

4. Practically speaking, if a woman wearing a veil entered an average church in a Western culture today, what effect would it have on other people's focus? How would this response differ from a Middle Eastern context where expectations differ?

3. If men were accustomed to women wearing head coverings in public, what probably happened to their focus on worshiping God when the coverings began coming off?[20]

WHY PEOPLE DIE AFTER TAKING COMMUNION (1 COR. 11:17–34)

1. How were some Corinthian Christians abusing the communion meal? (11:17–34) How were the wealthier members a particular problem in these matters?

20. Ben Witherington III, *Conflict and Community in Corinth: A Socio-Rhetorical Commentary on 1 and 2 Corinthians* (Grand Rapids: Wm. B. Eerdmans Publishing Co., 1995), 232–35; on the basis of ancient artwork, he argues that Roman women did not wear veils in public. He contends that, among Roman men and women, the wearing of a head covering meant that the individual was in the process of offering a sacrifice. On an ornately carved altar housed in the Louvre, none of the participants in a sacrificial parade wears a head covering except one woman, and she is the one who is about to offer a sacrifice. Witherington also states that men who were reading the entrails of sacrificial animals wore head coverings (Livy, *History of Rome* 10.7.10), as did women involved in similar activities (Varro, *The Latin Language* 5.29.130). What Witherington does not explain with sufficient clarity is why, on the basis of nature and tradition, Paul insists that men pray and prophesy with heads uncovered and women pray and prophesy with heads covered. More work needs to be done on this topic before anything close to certainty can emerge.

2. How does recognizing these problems help in understanding the meaning of "discerning the body" in 11:29?

Points to Ponder

How might such abuses have contributed to Communion (the Eucharist) becoming a symbolic meal consisting only of a bite of bread and a sip of wine or juice instead of the actual meal celebrated by early Christians?

When Gentile Christians gathered for "the Lord's Supper," their previous experiences with fraternal meals seem to have influenced their view of what was appropriate.

3. In light of the symbolic meaning of the eucharistic meal (Christ sacrificed himself for others), why are these abuses so ironic?

CONTROLLING CHARISMANIA
(1 COR. 12–14)

In 12:1 Paul begins to address the next question contained in the letter he received from the Corinthian Christians. Their confusion over the function of spiritual gifts in worship services produced a confused, riotous spectacle that embarrassed Paul. So he explains in chapter 12 the source and function of spiritual gifts. Then in chapter 13 he asserts the superiority of love and how it must provide the motivation for use of such gifts. In chapter 14 he provides practical advice for the use of prophecy and tongues, the two gifts evidently most coveted by the Corinthian Christians who wanted to show themselves to be more spiritual than the rest.

In 12:1–3 Paul asserts the difference between the idolatrous experiences that these Gentile converts previously associated with "inspired utterances" and what is acceptable for Christians gathered for worship. As we saw in the descriptions of ecstatic speech associated with some of the mystery religions (chap. 4, "Greek and Roman Religions of Paul's Day"), those involved were caught up in a kind of frenzy. Evidently someone informed Paul that an ecstatic person, supposedly speaking under the inspiration of the Spirit, had said, "Let Jesus be cursed!"—which had caused quite a stir. Some of the Corinthian Christians were prone to exhibitionism, so Paul corrects their emphasis on tongues and prophecy.

1. Note that Paul repeatedly says the "same Spirit" is the source for all spiritual gifts (12:4–11). Why does he emphasize that God arranged the parts of the body and that all these parts are important? (12:12–26)

2. Why does Paul stress a numerical order of the various gifts in 12:28 ("first apostles, second prophets, . . . various kinds of tongues")?

The structure of Paul's questions in 12:29–30 presupposes a "No" answer for each: "Are all prophets? No! . . . Do all speak in tongues? No! Do all interpret? No!" Each question begins with *mē* (Greek μή), a Greek construction that demands a negative response.

2. What is the "complete" (or "perfect") that Paul expects in 13:10? Why will this event put an end to the need for spiritual gifts?

THE MORE EXCELLENT WAY OF LOVE (1 COR. 13)

In 13:1–3 Paul devalues the significance of merely possessing and using a spiritual gift. He asserts that, unless love motivates the use of spiritual gifts, they possess no value. To use such gifts merely to call attention to oneself makes a mockery of their function to edify the group.

PROPHECY AND TONGUES (1 COR. 14)

1. What evidence in 1 Corinthians indicates that the libertines were envious, boastful, arrogant, insisted on their own way, and so on (13:4–6)?

1. Why, according to 14:1–5, is prophecy a greater gift than speaking in tongues?

2. According to 14:6–12, what is the problem with speaking in an unknown tongue while in a communal worship service?

4. In what ways are the Corinthian Christians abusing the gift of tongues (14:20–25)?

3. According to 14:13–19, what is the proper use of tongues?

5. What practical advice does Paul give for orderly use of prophecy in 14:26–33a, 37–40?

An Exercise in Textual Criticism (14:33b–36)

1. How does the comment in 14:33b–36 stand in tension with 11:2–16?

2. How does 14:33b–36 break the flow of thought in 14:26–40? (Note that if you remove this paragraph, Paul's thought flows nicely from 14:33a to 14:37.)

3. Do you think that 14:33b–36 is original to 1 Corinthians or is an early scribal addition to the Epistle? Why?

4. What difference does your decision make for what relevance you believe this passage has for the contemporary church?

THE RESURRECTION
OF THE BODY (1 COR. 15)

1. Why are the eyewitness accounts of Jesus' resurrection important for Paul's argument in 15:3–11?

2. How does Paul's insistence that he stands in unity with the Jerusalem apostles (15:3–11), when he argues for belief in the resurrection, differ from his rhetorical strategy in Galatians 1:18–2:14? Why the change?

3. In Paul's mind, why is the position of some Corinthians that there is no physical resurrection from the dead an inconsistent and destructive belief for Christians?

4. In Paul's explanation of the final subjection of all God's enemies, including death (15:20–28), what is his view of Christ's relationship with God the Father?

In 15:29, a notoriously difficult passage, Paul is hopefully pointing out a problem with Corinthian logic. In other words, if they do not believe that God will raise Christians from the dead, why are they conducting a ritual of baptism for the dead? However, if the Corinthians who do believe in the resurrection are advocating this practice—and if Paul uses their ritual as further confirmation of his viewpoint and does not object to baptizing for the dead—then we have some difficult questions to answer concerning his belief system.

Belief in the Resurrection

When you think of the afterlife, do you envision a spiritual (bodiless) existence or a resurrected physical body? Or do you believe that when you die, existence ceases? Why? Of what significance is your belief in terms of daily living?

5. When describing the resurrection body (15:35–49), Paul relies on metaphor. What does he claim about the afterlife in this passage?

1. In 1 Corinthians 16, where does Paul tell the Corinthians that he plans to journey in the near future? Map his planned itinerary.

6. How does his description of the Parousia in 15:50–52 compare with what he expressed in 1 Thessalonians 4:14–17?

SUMMARY QUESTIONS ON 1 CORINTHIANS

1. What characterizes Paul's approach to dealing with his rebellious converts in Corinth? What does this letter contribute to your understanding of him?

TRAVEL PLANS AND FINAL GREETINGS (1 COR. 16)

In 16:1–4, Paul addresses the issue of a collection of money for Christians in Jerusalem. This effort at benevolence becomes a contentious issue in 2 Corinthians. At this earlier stage, however, Paul simply directs them to set aside money when they gather for worship each Sunday ("first day of the week" [16:2]). Part of the contention that surfaces in 2 Corinthians 1–2 and 7 pertains to Paul's changing itinerary and his motives for altering his plans.

2. What were the major beliefs and practices of the libertines?

3. What were the beliefs and practices of the ascetics?

4. How does a low view of the body influence both libertine and ascetic views on proper Christian living?

Today, the morals of many Christians differ little from society as a whole. Living with someone without being married to that person is so common that it hardly raises an eyebrow. Christian participation at nightclubs and other places where parties are wild and immoral often goes unchallenged. Some television evangelists proclaim that following Christ leads to wealth, and their message of greed and self-indulgence finds open reception in many homes. People seek to enrich themselves by means of frivolous lawsuits. Divorce among Christians is statistically as common as it is in the rest of society.

Paul's critique of the Corinthian Christians therefore has much relevance to the church today. Understanding how his Letter addressed a distorted set of beliefs and practices can help us to consider how to deal with similar situations today.

LEARNING FROM THE PAST

Rampant sexuality and greed permeated ancient Corinth; and, tragically, some Corinthian Christians were virtually indistinguishable from the society in which they lived. The libertines applauded an incestuous relationship, sued each other over trivial matters, gave a theological justification for participating in wild parties at pagan temples, used church gatherings as an excuse to gorge themselves and get drunk, and misused the gifts of tongues and prophecy to turn worship services into a circus. The ascetics degraded the institution of marriage, encouraging Christians to divorce their mates.

GLOSSARY

Agora. Greek and English word for "marketplace." Central place of commerce in ancient cities.

Ascetics. Christian group at Corinth who believed that spirituality is increased by denying physical pleasure to the body. They held a philosophy opposite from the Libertines, although both groups had a low view of the human body.

Communion. Sacred meal celebrating the death and resurrection of Jesus. Also called the **Eucharist**. Among early Christians it involved eating a meal together, but over time the celebration became mostly symbolic, with participants receiving one bite of unleavened bread and one sip of wine or grape juice. First Corinthians 8–10 indicates that the church at Corinth had many problems with the selfish way in which some of the Christians there celebrated their communion meals.

Expulsion edict of Claudius. In 49–50 CE, the Roman emperor Claudius ordered all Jews to be expelled from Rome because of rioting in the Jewish sectors of the city. This expulsion is mentioned in Acts 18:2. These riots quite likely happened as a result of Jewish Christians trying to evangelize the Jewish population of Rome.

Fertility cults. In the ancient agricultural world in which Paul lived, people were extremely concerned with fertility. Their lives depended on successful harvesting of crops and breeding of farm animals. Fertility cults typically practiced ritualized forms of sexual intercourse (cultic prostitution) as part of their worship of the fertility deities, whom they believed were responsible for reproduction.

Isthmus of Corinth. A narrow strip of land east of Corinth over which people in Paul's time transported goods from the Gulf of Corinth to the Saronic Gulf and on to mainland Greece and back. Use of the isthmus eliminated the lengthy sea voyage around the southern tip of Achaia.

Koinōnia. Greek word meaning "fellowship" or "sharing." Often used by early Christians to describe their gathering together for worship and sharing a meal.

Libations. Liquid offerings, usually of wine, symbolically dedicated to certain deities prior to the drinking of the wine during a meal.

Libertines. Christian group at Corinth who believed that what people do with their body has nothing to do with their spirit. Their motto was "All things are lawful for me" (1 Cor. 6:12, i.e., "If it feels good, do it").

NFNSNC. Latin abbreviation found on many Roman grave stones. It abbreviates the phrase *Non fui, non sum, non curo*: **"I was not; I am not; I care not."** It reveals how skeptical many Romans were about any sort of afterlife.

Pneumatikoi. Greek word meaning "spiritual ones," which some Corinthian Christians arrogantly used to describe themselves—viewing themselves as superior to other Christians. Paul calls them *sarkinoi* ("fleshly ones") in 1 Corinthians 3:1.

Resurrection. Raising of the dead to new life in an exalted, heavenly body. Pharisees and Christians believed that God would give a new body (at least to the righteous) at the time of the last judgment. Many Greeks considered the belief in eternal existence in a physical body to be absurd.

Sarkinoi. Greek word meaning "fleshly ones." Paul uses the term in 1 Corinthians 3:1 and *sarkikoi* (also "fleshly ones") in 3:3 to assert that some Corinthian Christians are so spiritually immature that they cannot eat solid food but still need milk, like babies.

Sōma sēma. Greek expression that means "the body—a grave." It expresses the view of some Greek philosophers that the body is the grave or prison of the soul and keeps the soul tied to the physical world. They did not associate bodily existence with afterlife.

Strabo. Greek geographer who lived 64 BCE–23 CE. His writings provide valuable information about the areas in which Paul did his missionary work.

FURTHER READING
ON 1 CORINTHIANS

Barrett, C. K. *The First Epistle to the Corinthians.* New York: Harper & Row, 1974. Fairly accessible commentary.

Conzelmann, Hans. *First Corinthians.* Hermeneia. Philadelphia: Fortress Press, 1975. Technical commentary. Wealth of information.

Fee, Gordon D. *The First Epistle to the Corinthians.* NICNT. Grand Rapids: Wm. B. Eerdmans Publishing Co., 1987. Huge commentary (904 pages). Good resource.

Grant, Robert M. *Paul in the Roman World: The Conflict at Corinth.* Louisville, KY: Westminster John Knox Press, 2000. Excellent source of background information about Corinth and the Greco-Roman culture of the city. Many insights into the social, religious, and moral setting of this church, which gave Paul such troubles.

*Hays, Richard B. *First Corinthians.* Interpretation. Louisville, KY: John Knox Press, 1997. Attempts to apply 1 Corinthians to contemporary situations.

Horsley, Richard A. *1 Corinthians.* Nashville: Abingdon Press, 1998. Interesting commentary.

Hurd, John C., Jr. *The Origin of 1 Corinthians.* London: SPCK, 1965. Groundbreaking study of Paul's use of Corinthian slogans (e.g., "All things are lawful").

Murphy-O'Connor, Jerome. *St. Paul's Corinth: Texts and Archaeology.* Wilmington, DE: Michael Glazier, 1984. Technical presentation of what archaeology has revealed about Corinth.

Ramsay, William M. *The Cities of St. Paul, Their Influence on His Life and Thought: The Cities of Asia Minor.* Grand Rapids: Baker, 1960. Older study that has value for understanding the history of interpretation of Paul's Letters.

Soards, Marion L. *1 Corinthians.* Peabody, MA: Hendrickson Publishers, 1999. Interacts with recent trends in Pauline interpretation.

Talbert, Charles H. *Reading Corinthians: A Literary and Theological Commentary on 1 and 2 Corinthians.* New York: Crossroad, 1987. Interesting and fairly nontechnical.

Thiselton, Anthony C. *The First Epistle to the Corinthians: A Commentary on the Greek Text.* NIGTC. Grand Rapids: Wm. B. Eerdmans Publishing Co., 2000. An exhaustive study containing 1,424 pages.

Willis, Wendell L. *Idol Meat in Corinth: The Pauline Argument in 1 Corinthians 8 and 10.* SBL Dissertation Series 68. Chico, CA: Scholars Press, 1981. Valuable collection of materials related to public, religious meals. Great background information for studying 1 Corinthians 8–10.

*Witherington, Ben, III. *Conflict and Community in Corinth: A Socio-Rhetorical Commentary on 1 and 2 Corinthians.* Grand Rapids: Wm. B. Eerdmans Publish-

ing Co., 1995. Fairly readable. Much information about social norms and ancient rhetoric.

*Wright, N. T. *Paul for Everyone: 1 Corinthians.* Louisville, KY: Westminster John Knox Press, 2004. Clearly written for a general audience. Many helpful illustrations.

CHAPTER 11

2 Corinthians

APOSTOLIC BASKET CASE

We have seen a wide range of emotions expressed in Paul's letters thus far, from warm and gentle encouragement in 1 Thessalonians to furious reprimand in Galatians. But we have not yet observed the depth of discouragement conveyed in 2 Corinthians. The Corinthian Christians severely taxed Paul's patience, causing him to scold them sarcastically in 1 Corinthians. But his confrontational letter did not bring repentance. These rebellious Christians did not stop judging Paul, or yield to his authority, or obey his instructions on moral and ethical living. They remained obstinate, causing him considerable stress. After he sent 1 Corinthians, the situation reached a flash point, and 2 Corinthians provides clues of what happened between Paul and his detractors.

PAINFUL VISIT— PAINFUL LETTER (2 COR. 1–4)

1. The content of Paul's thanksgiving section in 1:3–7 differs strikingly from that of 1 Corinthians 1:4–9. What is the focus of 2 Corinthians 1:3–7?

2. How does Paul's description of the terrifying experience he suffered in Ephesus (1:8–11) clarify his focus in 1:3–7?

5. How do his travel plans compare with his actual travel itinerary in 2 Corinthians 1:23–2:4, 12–13; 7:5–16? Plot his route on the map.

3. In 1:3–11, what value does Paul find in going through difficult times?

After stressing his sincerity in 1:12, in 1:17–2:13 Paul refutes an accusation that he vacillates on his travel plans. Apparently some accused him of dishonesty and planning trips to suit his personal whims, not their best interests.

4. How do Paul's travel plans in 1 Corinthians 16:1–9 differ from what he says he planned to do in 2 Corinthians 1:15–16? Plot both routes on the map.

Deciphering Paul's journeys is difficult, partly because what he says in 2 Corinthians does not correspond with the description of his third missionary journey in Acts. His somewhat lengthy stay in Ephesus (Acts 19:10; 20:31) matches Paul's designation of Ephesus as his place of residence when writing 1 Corinthians (see 1 Cor. 16:8), but thereafter things become more muddled. In Acts 19:21–22 he plans to go from Ephesus to Macedonia, then down to Achaia (to Corinth), then on to Jerusalem, and finally to Rome. This in fact happens in Acts 20–24, although he ends up going to Rome as a prisoner. In 1 Corinthians 16:1–8, Paul's plans match the itinerary in Acts, but after sending this letter things began to change.

In 2 Corinthians 1:23 Paul explains that he avoided traveling to Corinth to spare them *another* painful visit (2:1). Instead, he wrote them a *painful letter* (2:3–4), sent it via Titus, and waited for the results. This letter must have been a real scorcher, for after he sent Titus to deliver it, Paul was so emotionally distraught that he could not keep his mind on his work. Evidently it was also getting late enough in the year that Titus could not return across the Aegean Sea due to rough

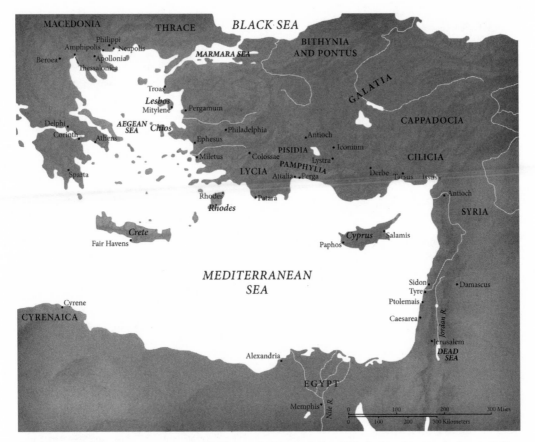

On this map of the Aegean area, plot Paul's travel plans in 1 Cor. 16:1–9, then his travel plans in 2 Cor. 1:15–16, and then his actual travels in 2 Cor. 1:23–2:4, 12–13; and 7:5–16.

winter weather. He would have to return via the land route north through Macedonia. The longer Paul waited for Titus, the more agitated he became. Instead of remaining in Ephesus until Titus arrived with news of how the Corinthians had responded to his letter, Paul journeyed north to Troas. While there a door for effective ministry opened, but he was so preoccupied with the Corinthian situation that he left it behind and went on to Macedonia (2:12–13). There he met Titus.

The fact that he speaks so much of pain and consolation indicates the depth of his conflict with the rebels at Corinth. Paul admits in 2 Corinthians 7:5 that even in Macedonia he could find no rest from his emotional turmoil. Not until Titus arrives with good news does Paul's anxiety give way to joy (7:6–7). He confesses how much he regretted writing the **Painful Letter** (7:8), but he adds that the effect was redemptive, so he no longer regrets sending this powerful epistle (7:9–11).

Apostolic Basket Case

You have witnesseed Paul's frustration and anger in Galatians and 1 Corinthians. Now in 2 Corinthians he recounts being so distraught that he could not keep his mind on his work. For you, do his emotions detract from his stature as an apostle? Why or why not?

Apparently sending Timothy with 1 Corinthians did not work. So he fulfilled his warning in 1 Corinthians 4:19, 21: "I will come to you soon, . . . and I will find out not the talk of these arrogant people but their power. . . . What would you prefer? Am I to come to you with a stick, or with love in a spirit of gentleness?" He crossed the Aegean Sea and confronted the guilty parties (**painful visit**, 2 Cor. 1:23; 2:1). The excursion ended badly, and Paul returned to Ephesus with the matter unresolved. From there he wrote the Painful Letter and sent it by way of Titus—and this time it worked. The Corinthians took decisive actions against a man who strongly opposed Paul, one whom Paul now asks them to forgive (2:5–11). With a great sense of relief, he dictates another letter. We call it 2 Corinthians, but it was at least his fourth letter to this church:

> Corinthians A = letter mentioned in 1 Corinthians 5:9–13
>
> Corinthians B = 1 Corinthians
>
> Corinthians C = Painful Letter mentioned in 2 Cor. 2:3–4; 7:8
>
> Corinthians D = 2 Corinthians

Paul's allusion to the triumphal procession in 2:14 presupposes knowledge of the way Romans received their generals when these men returned home from a victorious battle. The Jewish historian Josephus provides a vivid example of one such enthusiastic greeting. Writing about 75 CE, he describes the citizens of Antioch flocking out of their city to greet Titus, the general who commanded the assault on Jerusalem and ended the Jewish rebellion in Palestine.

> The people of Antioch, on hearing that Titus was at hand, through joy could not bear to remain within their walls, but hastened to meet him and advanced to a distance of over thirty furlongs (3.75 miles), not only men, but a crowd of women and children also, streaming out from the city. And when they beheld his approaching, they lined the road on either side and greeted him with extended arms, and invoking all manner of blessings upon him returned in his train. (*Jewish War* 7.100–102 [Thackeray, LCL])

During these riotous receptions it was common to parade captives before the crowd, some of whom would be executed as part of the celebration. Thus the smell of incense that filled the air was for the crowd a symbol of divine favor as they honored their heroes and worshiped their gods for victory. The captives who were facing execution, however, associated the same smell with death. Therefore, Paul's use of this image in 2:14–17 contains an odd twist, for he envisions himself as one who was conquered by Christ and led in a triumphal procession. His participation in this procession is part of the sweet smell of life for those who believe his message, but it is the foul smell of death for those who reject it. His altering of the details of a Roman custom resembles the way in which, in 1 Thessalonians 4:14–5:11, he reversed the details of formal receptions of dignitaries.

LETTERS OF RECOMMENDATION

People in Paul's day used letters of recommendation to solicit patronage from residents of cities to which they traveled. Paul sometimes recommended friends in his Letters, such as in Philemon, where he advocated for Onesimus, the runaway slave. In Romans 16:1–2 he said, "I commend to you our sister Phoebe, a deacon of the church at Cenchreae, so that you may . . . help her in whatever she may require from you, for she has been a benefactor of many and of myself as well" (see also Phil. 2:25–30). In 2 Corinthians 8:16–24, Paul recommended Titus and another man, whom he said was famous for preaching the gospel (for other examples, see 3 John 5–8, 12).

Thus, what Paul belittles in 2 Corinthians 3:1–3 is what he considers to be an abuse of this practice. Apparently some self-asserting teachers arrived in Corinth with letters of recommendation from recognized authority figures. They derided Paul for having no such commendations and insisted that

people should not believe him. From Paul's perspective, these men were arrogant, self-serving, and unethical individuals who took money from the Corinthian Christians. Later in 2 Corinthians we will see his sarcastic description of them.

1. In 3:6–11, what contrasts does Paul make between the old covenant based on Mosaic laws and the new covenant that he preaches?

Old covenant   New covenant

In 3:12–18 Paul allegorizes the Exodus 34:29–35 account of Moses veiling himself. In the Exodus story, after coming down from Mount Sinai with the Ten Commandments, Moses discovers that his face is shining. His appearance frightens the Israelites. So after delivering the law to the people, Moses veils his face. Then whenever he enters the tabernacle to speak with God, he takes the veil off again.

2. Paul's interpretation of Exodus 34 makes a creative connection with his own ministry. How does he contrast his approach to preaching the gospel with that used by his opponents?

3. Why, according to 4:16–18, does Paul not become depressed by the opposition he faces and the hardships he endures?

"I DON'T WANT TO BE FOUND NAKED" (2 COR. 5–7)

1. Paul's metaphors for the physical body and the resurrection body in 5:1–5 emphasize the temporary nature of the one and the permanence of the other. What is his attitude toward being "bodiless" (= naked)?

shell-like growth which encased him, was being stripped away and the soul laid bare (lit., 'made naked') and yearning for its natural removal hence" (*On the Virtues* 76 [LCL]).

2. When he wrote 1 Thessalonians 4:15, 17 and 1 Corinthians 15:51–52, Paul clearly expected to be alive when Jesus would return from heaven. What hints do you see in 2 Corinthians 5:1–10 perhaps indicating that he has changed his mind?

3. How might the experience mentioned in 1:8–9 have shaped his present belief about whether or not he will be alive at the Parousia?

Paul describes existence without a body as being *naked* in 5:3. As we saw in the chapter on 1 Corinthians, some Greek philosophers viewed the body as an impediment to true existence, hence the expression *sōma sēma* ("the body—a grave/prison"). They viewed bodilessness (i.e., nakedness) as desirable. Even some Jews held such a view of the soul and body. Philo of Alexandria thus wrote of Moses' death: "He began to pass over from mortal existence to life immortal and gradually became conscious of the disuniting of the elements of which he was composed. The body, the

To deal with the mortality of others is one thing; to deal with your own is another. Paul's words in 5:1–10 contain an element of struggle. Continue to be aware of what he says about his own death in future letters, especially Philippians, and how he resolves the issue.

4. According to 5:14–21, how are people reconciled with God?

APPEAL FOR RECONCILIATION

1. What does 7:5–13 reveal about Paul's emotional condition when he met Titus in Macedonia?

5. What approach does Paul use to defend his integrity in 6:1–10?

2. What does Paul view as evidence that the Corinthian Christians have experienced godly grief?

An Exercise in Textual Criticism (6:14–7:1)

Paul's flow of thought continues smoothly if you go directly from 6:13 to 7:2, leaving out the material in between.

1. How does the content of 6:14–7:1 differ from what comes before and after it?

2. Paul does not discuss the matters addressed in 6:14–7:1 previously in 2 Corinthians. Do you believe that this passage is a later, scribal insertion or part of the original letter? Why?

TURNING UP THE HEAT
TO GIVE MONEY (2 COR. 8–9)

In 1 Corinthians 16:1–4 Paul gave instructions pertaining to the collection of money for poor Christians in Jerusalem. Now the time has come to complete this charitable offering. Paul is in Macedonia, preparing to go south to Corinth. To prepare for his arrival, he sends Titus and a well-known preacher to deliver 2 Corinthians. Soon he will follow, and some Macedonian Christians might come with him. He seems nervous about what the Macedonians might discover when they arrive, so Paul sends Titus ahead to make sure the money is collected before he gets to Corinth.

1. Note the contrast between the financial condition of the Macedonian Christians and their level of generosity. What motivated their generosity (8:2–5)?

2. To motivate the Corinthian Christians to give generously, Paul tells about the Macedonians' giving and about Jesus' free gift (8:8–9). What are his guidelines for how the Corinthians should give?

3. What does Paul want Titus to accomplish in Corinth before his own arrival (8:16–24)?

4. In 9:1–2, what else does Paul say played an important role in motivating the Macedonian Christians to give so generously?

5. According to 9:3–5, what does Paul fear will happen when he arrives in Corinth?

6. What further incentive for giving do Paul's words in 9:6–15 provide?

Put yourself in Paul's place for a moment. Think of how he motivated the Macedonians to give generously, and how they responded beyond his expectations.

7. Given Paul's past experiences with the Corinthians, what dilemma does he face in seeking to make sure that they complete their offering for the poor in Jerusalem?

the tithe (for different traditions, see Lev. 27:30–33; Num. 18:21–32; Mal. 3:8–10).

1. If church leaders followed the directives specified in Deuteronomy 14:22–29, how would they exhort Christians to use their tithe, and for what things would they say it should not be used?

SHOULD CHRISTIANS TITHE?

Requests for money during church services typically begin with a formulaic saying such as, "We will now receive your tithes and offerings." Interestingly, the New Testament rarely even mentions tithing (Matt. 23:23; Luke 11:42; Heb. 7:5), which was part of the Israelite agricultural system. Several Old Testament passages give insight into the nature of the **tithe**, which was not money but animals, grain, and fruit. The tithe did not pay for construction or upkeep of the worship center. All Hebrew males were required to give a half-shekel temple tax each year in March to finance the temple (Exod. 30:11–16; cf. Matt. 17:24–27). Ancient Israelites made no distinction between religion and government that remotely resembles the separation of church and state in the United States.

Read **Deuteronomy 14:22–29**, which provides the best window into the functions of

2. Which uses of the tithe specified in Deuteronomy 14:22–29 are often provided in our society by the government and financed by taxes?

3. Do you believe that the church should continue to use the expression "tithes and offerings," or should it adopt another designation? Explain.

4. What guidelines do you suggest for Christian giving? On what do you base them?

3. In 11:1–4, how does Paul shame the arrogant Corinthians?

SARCASM AS A WEAPON OF DEFENSE (2 COR. 10–12)

The conciliatory tone in chapters 1–9 dramatically changes at 10:1. Paul's language becomes confrontational as he defends himself against accusations that some at Corinth launched against him.

1. In light of the unsuccessful painful visit and the successful painful letter mentioned in 1:23–2:13; 7:2–13, why would Paul's opponents say what he sarcastically reports in 10:1, 10–11?

4. Given his comments in 11:5–6 and 10:1, 10, what is one of the main ways in which Paul's opponents assert their superiority over him?

"WHY WON'T YOU TAKE OUR MONEY?"

1. Evidently some at Corinth are offended that Paul will not accept money from them, although his opponents readily accept their support. What reason does Paul give for refusing their money?

2. According to 10:12, Paul's opponents validate their own ministry by boasting of their accomplishments. How does Paul undermine their boasting in 10:13–18?

2. Paul sarcastically calls the rival teachers at Corinth **superapostles** in 11:5. How does he characterize them in 11:12–15?

1. What sort of experience does Paul depict in 12:1–5?

3. Note Paul's use of sarcasm to ridicule their boasting in 11:16–21. Instead of boasting about rhetorical eloquence, of what sorts of things does Paul boast in 11:22–33?

2. Paul admits that he prayed three times for relief from his condition but was not healed. How does his report affect your personal view of divine healing?

TRANSPORTED
TO THE THIRD HEAVEN

At first reading, 12:1–5 seems to describe an experience of someone Paul knows. But in 12:6–7 he speaks of the exceptional nature of revelations that *he* received, and in 12:7–10 he explains that he has endured a physical problem that kept him from becoming arrogant over his experiences. Paul is probably stepping back from his boasting in 12:1–5 by describing his own experiences as if someone else had them. It is in keeping with his theme of boasting in weakness.

Paul's perception of levels of heaven between the physical earth and the abode of God is characteristic of first-century Jewish beliefs. Although the number of levels ranges from three to ten in documents written in this era, there is a recurring belief that lower angelic beings inhabit lower levels of heaven; as one gets closer to God, the beings represent higher and higher orders. Ancient apocalypses often claim that angels took the men who supposedly wrote these texts on tours of the heavens. For example, *2 Enoch* 7.1 says that angels took Enoch to the second heaven: "And they set me down on the second heaven. And they showed me prisoners under guard, in measureless judgments. And there I saw the condemned angels, and I said to the men who were with me, 'Why are these ones being tormented unceasingly?'"[1] Going on from the lower levels where rebellious angels are tortured, Enoch describes his ascent to the third heaven, where he sees paradise with all its beautiful trees, including the tree of life from the garden of Eden (*2 Enoch* 8).

Many Jews believed that God created the **cosmos** with multiple levels. *Second Enoch* 11, for example, describes Enoch being taken to the fourth heaven, where he sees the solar and lunar tracks and measures their movements: "And I saw that the sun has a light seven times greater than the moon. And I saw his circle and his wheels on which he always goes, going past always like the wind with quite marvelous speed. . . . And 150,000 angels accompany him in the daytime, and at night 1,000. And 100 angels go in front of the sun's chariot, six-winged, in flaming fire" (11.1–5). Enoch's journey continues until he finally reaches the tenth heaven, where he sees God, whose "face is not to be talked about, it is so marvelous and supremely awesome and supremely frightening" (22.1–2).

Similarly, *3 Baruch* recounts a journey up through five levels of heaven. Documents like *2 Enoch* and *3 Baruch* clarify the fact that many Jews and Christians in the first century did not conceive of a hell below the earth, and sky above the earth, and then heaven above the sky. They believed that a number of levels of heavens separated them from God, and that hostile beings inhabited the lower levels, and some of these bad angels were being tormented for their crimes. In

keeping with this view of the cosmos, when 1 Peter 3:19 speaks of Jesus preaching to the "spirits in prison," the author most likely envisions a place in one of the lower levels of heaven that he believed Jesus visited while ascending to heaven to "the right hand of God" (1 Pet. 3:22). Those who wrote the Apostles' Creed in the fourth century evidently did not understand this cosmology when they included the phrase "he descended into hell."

ONE LAST, PARTING PUNCH (2 COR. 13)

Paul's warning in 13:1–4 resembles the ultimatum he gave in 1 Corinthians 4:18–21, where he told them he was coming to find out whether his arrogant detractors had anything to back up all their tough talk: "What would you prefer? Am I to come to you with a stick, or with love in a spirit of gentleness?" Now he stresses once more: "If I come again, I will not be lenient" (2 Cor. 13:2).

1. How does Paul's attitude toward the Corinthians in 13:1–13 compare with his attitude toward them in chapters 1–9?

1. Translation by F. I Anderson, in *The Old Testament Pseudepigrapha*, vol. 1, *Apocalyptic Literature and Testaments*, edited by J. H. Charlesworth (Garden City, NY: Doubleday, 1983).

Note that in 12:14 and 13:1, Paul mentions that he is coming to them the *third* time. If his initial time there during the second missionary journey was the first time, then his second time might be the painful visit mentioned in 2:1. Many scholars believe that 2 Corinthians 10–13, because of its harshly confrontational tone, is actually part of the Painful Letter that Paul mentions in 2:3–4 and 7:8, and was therefore written prior to chapters 1–9 and later appended to this letter.

2. Evaluate the theory that 2 Corinthians 10–13 is part of the Painful Letter and later combined with 2 Corinthians 1–9.

In 2 Corinthians we see an avalanche of emotions. On the one hand, Paul deeply loved these wayward Christians, and his conflict with them caused him considerable stress. Indeed, in the days leading up to the writing of chapters 1–9, he was an emotional basket case. On the other hand, his frustration with them brought intense anger and defensiveness, which he vents in chapters 10–13. As their spiritual parent, he experienced alternating desires to hug them and to beat them. They drove him crazy, yet he loved them intensely. Fortunately for the apostle, not all of his converts were such problems. The contrast in tone between 2 Corinthians 10–13 and Philippians is dramatic.

GLOSSARY

Cosmos. Greek word for the world or universe.

Painful Letter. Highly confrontational letter written by Paul and delivered by Titus to the Corinthian church following the failure of the painful visit to bring about repentance among rebellious Christians.

Painful visit. Paul's confrontational trip to Corinth. After 1 Corinthians failed to bring about repentance and modified behavior among the rebellious Corinthian Christians, Paul left Ephesus and crossed the Aegean Sea to confront the rebels. The trip evidently ended in failure for Paul.

Superapostles. A derogatory title that Paul uses in 2 Corinthians 11 to describe Christian leaders who were telling the Christians at Corinth that he lacked rhetorical skills and that his physical presence was weak/wimpy.

Tithe. Practice among ancient Hebrews of setting aside 10 percent of their agricultural produce to be used for extended family celebrations and for social concerns such as caring for orphans and widows. See, for example, **Deuteronomy 14:22–29**.

FURTHER READING ON 2 CORINTHIANS

Barrett, C. K. *The Second Epistle to the Corinthians.* New York: Harper & Row, 1975. Fairly accessible commentary.
Belleville, Linda L. *2 Corinthians.* IVP New Testament Commentary Series. Downers Grove, IL: InterVarsity Press, 1996. Seeks to show the

relevance of the letter for Christians who live in commercial and hedonistic cultures.

Best, Ernest. *Second Corinthians*. Interpretation. Atlanta: John Knox Press, 1987. Written for pastors and educated laypeople to show contemporary relevance.

Betz, Hans Dieter. *2 Corinthians: A Commentary on Two Administrative Letters of the Apostle Paul*. Philadelphia: Fortress Press, 1985. Technical, analytical commentary.

Furnish, Victor Paul. *Second Corinthians*. AB. New York: Doubleday, 1984. Technical, 648-page commentary. Wealth of information.

Hafemann, Scott J. *2 Corinthians*. NIV Life Application Commentaries. Downers Grove, IL: InterVarsity Press, 2001. A 544-page commentary devoted to giving background material to show the relevance of 2 Corinthians.

Harris, Murray J. *Second Epistle to the Corinthians*. NIGTC. Grand Rapids: Wm. B. Eerdmans Publishing Co., 2005. Exhaustive study of the Greek text (989 pages). Good for research. Somewhat disjointed organization.

Keener, Craig S. *1–2 Corinthians*. New Cambridge Bible Commentary. Cambridge: Cambridge University Press, 2005. Valuable historical/cultural background information.

Lambrecht, Jan. *Second Corinthians*. Collegeville, MN: Liturgical Press, 2007. Accessible and scholarly.

Martin, Ralph P. *2 Corinthians*. Word Biblical Commentary 40. Waco, TX: Word Books, 1986. Very detailed commentary (591 pages).

Scott, James M. *2 Corinthians*. NIBCNT 8. Peabody, MA: Hendrickson Publishers, 1998. Emphasizes Paul's Jewishness. Some unusual interpretations.

Shillington, V. George. *2 Corinthians*. Believers Church Bible Commentary. Scottdale, PA: Herald Press, 1998. Emphasizes peace-and-justice issues.

Talbert, Charles H. *Reading Corinthians: A Literary and Theological Commentary on 1 and 2 Corinthians*. New York: Crossroad, 1987. Clear analysis in nontechnical language.

Thrall, Margaret E. *A Critical and Exegetical Commentary on the Second Epistle to the Corinthians*. ICC. Edinburgh: T&T Clark, 1994. Thorough (544 pages) and thoughtful summaries of interpretations given by other scholars.

*Witherington, Ben, III. *Conflict and Community in Corinth: A Socio-Rhetorical Commentary on 1 and 2 Corinthians*. Grand Rapids: Wm. B. Eerdmans Publishing Co., 1995. Readable. Good source of information about social norms and ancient rhetoric.

*Wright, N. T. *Paul for Everyone: 2 Corinthians*. Louisville, KY: Westminster John Knox Press, 2004. Easy-to-read 176 pages, yet scholarly. Many helpful illustrations.

CHAPTER 12

Philippians

THANKS FOR THE MONEY

Following Paul's furious rebuke in Galatians, his forceful and often sarcastic reprimand in 1 Corinthians, and his caustic self-defense in 2 Corinthians 10–13, Philippians comes as a welcome relief. Although these Macedonian Christians were experiencing significant problems, and Paul's own situation was bleak, this Epistle has a remarkably positive tone. As you read his words, be alert to indications of Paul's relationship with the Philippians. Look for clues that indicate how they felt about the apostle and what he felt toward them.

CITIZENS OF A GRAND CITY

In the first century, **Philippi** was one of the leading cities of Macedonia. According to Acts 16:11–12, Paul first went there during his second missionary journey. He and his companions left Troas aboard a boat and crossed the Aegean Sea to the port town of Neapolis. When Paul left Neapolis to make his way inland, he had to climb the steep hills that rise from the seacoast. Philippi, located ten miles to the northwest of Neapolis, was on the **Via Egnatia**, the major overland trade route of that region in Roman times. Originally a small Thracian village called Krenides occupied the site; its name comes from the Greek *krēnē*, which means spring (today the small town located near the ancient ruins is called Krinides). In 356 BCE, Philip II, king of Macedonia and father of Alexander the Great, expanded the village and named it after himself. Some of the archaeological remains, including the city wall and the theater, may date back to his time, but most of the ruins date from later periods.

The Romans conquered Macedonia in 168/67 BCE and divided it into four districts. Philippi remained a fairly modest-sized settlement until Octavian (Octavius) and Antony defeated the army of Julius Caesar's assassins (Brutus and Cassius) in the Battle of Philippi in 42 BCE. They settled some of their army veterans at the site and established the city as a Roman colony. Later, when Octavian and Antony were at war with each other, Philippi grew rapidly due to an influx of people from Rome. Octavian defeated Antony in 31 BCE, expelled from Rome many who had sided with Antony, and gave their property to those who had been loyal to him. Some of the exiles were allowed to settle in Philippi, which Octavian (Augustus Caesar) named after himself: Colonia Iulia Augusta Philippensis. He granted Philippi the distinction of becoming a Roman principality (*Ius Italicum*), governed by Roman law. The citizens of Philippi enjoyed Roman citizenship, with all its rights and privileges. The mixed population of this growing city worshiped a number of different deities, a situation much in evidence when Paul arrived about 49 CE.

"SO GOOD TO HEAR FROM YOU!" (PHIL. 4:10–20)

1. Philippians 4:10–20 reveals that Paul's main reason for writing this letter to the Christians at Philippi was to thank them for money. What does this passage indicate about the history of his relationship with the Philippian Christians?

In 2 Corinthians 11:7–12 Paul mentions his refusal to accept money from the Corinthians, but he indicates that friends from Macedonia brought financial help to him. His refusal to take money from Corinthian Christians seems to have been a point of tension with them (the "superapostles" certainly followed no such policy). From Philippians 4:15–16 we see that his Macedonian friends were probably the Philippians.

COMPARING SALUTATIONS (PHIL. 1:1–2)

1. Do Paul's designations for himself and Timothy compare more closely with what he uses in 1 Corinthians 1:1; 2 Corinthians 1:1; and Galatians 1:1; or with what he uses in 1 Thessalonians 1:1? In light of Philippians 4:10–20, how might his relationship with the Philippians have determined his choice of the word "servants" in 1:1?

The fact that Paul calls the leaders bishops (or overseers: Greek *episkopoi*) and deacons (*diakonoi*) in 1:1 indicates a more advanced organizational structure. This church is not a group of recent converts.

SO THANKFUL FOR YOU ALL (PHIL. 1:3–11)

1. What does the thanksgiving in 3:1–11 reveal about Paul's feelings toward the Philippians?

The eschatological climax to the thanksgiving (1:10–11) appears in other Pauline Letters (e.g., 1 Thess. 1:10). Also, the theme of needing to be pure and upright because the Parousia will be a day of judgment (1:10) is repeated in 2:16 (cf. 1 Thess. 1:10; 2:19; 3:13; 5:2–10, 23).

I CAN'T DECIDE IF I WANT TO LIVE OR DIE (PHIL. 1:12–30)

1. In 1:12–18 Paul's attitude toward his imprisonment for preaching the gospel is remarkably positive. What is his attitude toward his Christian opponents, who are taking advantage of his imprisonment? Why does he feel this way about their work?

The **Praetorian Guards** (*Praitōrion* [1:13]) were elite troops stationed at important government centers around the Roman Empire, not just in Rome near Caesar. Acts 23:35, for example, uses *Praitōrion* to describe the governor's residence of Herod in Caesarea, on the seacoast northwest of Jerusalem. On the basis of Paul's use of this word, there thus is no justification to conclude that he wrote Philippians from Rome.

2. Compare Philippians 1:13 with 4:22. What do these statements reveal about Paul's activities during the hours he was watched by various members of the Praetorian Guard?

3. According to 1:19–26, what does Paul now believe about his own death?

How does it compare with his view in 1 Thessalonians 4:13–18 and 1 Corinthians 15:51–52?

Singing the Blues?

If you were in prison for doing missionary work, and rival evangelists were taking advantage of your absence, what attitude would you have toward your situation? Why?

4. How do his feelings about his death differ from what he expressed in 2 Corinthians 5:1–10?

fore set off its lines as poetry. How does this poem assert the deity of Christ?

Paul exhorts his readers to work out their salvation (2:12). He adds, however, that God gives them the desire and the power to do so (2:13); they are not on their own as they prepare for the great judgment on the day of Christ, the day of the Parousia (2:16).

2. Working without murmuring and arguing (2:14) causes Christians to stand out in society like stars in the night sky. How does Timothy's attitude toward self and others (2:19–24) compare with Jesus' attitude (2:5–11)?

SELFISHNESS VERSUS
SELFLESSNESS (PHIL. 2:1–3:1)

In this letter that acknowledges disunity among Christians (e.g., 1:15–18; 3:2–4; 4:2–3), Paul stresses unity through sensitivity to each other's needs (2:1–4).

1. Jesus' sacrificial death provides for Paul a primary example of unselfishness. Philippians 2:6–11 is quite likely a quotation of an early Christian hymn, and most translations there-

By contrast, what motivates Paul's opponents (1:15–17; cf. 3:18–19)?

Paul is ready to pour out his life as a sacrifice for the sake of the Philippian Christians (2:17). His ultimate goal is not his personal

In Philippians 3:12–16, Paul uses the athletic imagery of running a race to describe the discipline needed for successful Christian living. Stadiums were found throughout the Roman Empire in Paul's day. One of the more impressive is this one at Aphrodisias, Turkey. (Courtesy of Michael Cosby)

freedom or safety, nor is it to advance his own stature and career. His greatest reward will be in presenting pure and obedient converts to God the eternal Judge on the day of Christ (2:16). To be able to boast of his faithfulness on judgment day transcends his present needs and desires.

3. Who was Epaphroditus, and what job did he do for the church at Philippi (2:25–30; 4:18)? How does his attitude toward others compare with Timothy's?

"MY RIGHTEOUSNESS IS CRAP" (PHIL. 3:2–4:1)

In 3:2–3 Paul contrasts Christians who serve God by the Spirit, and place no confidence in the flesh, with Jewish Christians who insist that people keep the laws of Moses.

1. Calling his opponents dogs (considered unclean) and mutilators of the flesh in 3:2 is obviously ironic/sarcastic in light of their insistence on circumcision for all Christians. Why does Paul proceed to give his own credentials in 3:4–6?

2. What is Paul's attitude toward his former accomplishments under the laws of Moses (3:7–9)?

4. What guideline for Christian living does Paul present in 3:12–16? (Lest you think that he doubts his eternal reward in light of 3:10–11, compare what Paul says in 1:20–21.)

When he says in 3:8 that he considers all his achievements to be "rubbish," he uses the word *skybala*. Polite translations of this word include "refuse," "dirt," and "dung." Given Paul's heated defense here, however, and the way he uses *skybala* as a slang expression of contempt, a more appropriate translation into our cultural context would probably be "crap" or even "shit." He is not seeking to be delicate but to assert a point. As with his reference to castration in Galatians 5:12, Paul can be quite earthy in his attacks on theological opponents.

3. According to 3:8–11, what important goals motivate Paul's actions?

"YOU TWO WOMEN NEED TO START GETTING ALONG" (PHIL. 4:2–20)

Two women who have done important work with Paul are having an argument, and he seeks their reconciliation (4:2–3).

1. How would adopting the guidelines given in 4:4–9 help Euodia and Syntyche be reconciled (see also 2:1–5)?

INTERPRETING AND APPLYING OVERSTATEMENTS

Christians often fail to recognize Pauline overstatement. When reading "Rejoice in the Lord always" (4:4) and "Do not worry about anything" (4:6), some mistakenly conclude that Paul condemned worry and failure to rejoice as sin. But as we have seen in 2 Corinthians in particular, Paul worried about problems he had with his churches (e.g., "And, besides other things, I am under daily pressure because of my *anxiety* for all the churches" [11:28]).

Such angst also plagued Paul when he wrote Philippians, which becomes obvious when reading his description of Epaphroditus recovering from illness: "I am the more eager to send him [to you], . . . that I may be *less anxious*" (2:28, stress added). And according to 2:26, Epaphroditus "has been *distressed* because you heard that he was ill" (stress added). Recognizing **hyperbole** in 4:4–6 helps us to decipher Paul's message. His admonitions are encouragements to be positive and to avoid excessive worry, not literal demands for Christian responses to all situations.

Focusing on the negative fosters problems, and Paul encourages positive thinking in 4:8–9. His own example of a positive attitude while in prison would be inspirational for the Philippian Christians, and in 3:17 he tells them to imitate him and his coworkers.

CONCLUDING THOUGHTS ON A POSITIVE LETTER

1. What beliefs does Paul express in Philippians that helped him to have a positive attitude even under his circumstances?

2. How would Paul's Letter have helped the Philippian Christians to surmount the problems they were facing?

WHEN AND FROM WHERE DID PAUL WRITE PHILIPPIANS?

In Philippians, Paul says he was in prison, but he does not say where. Acts mentions three imprisonments of Paul: Philippi (16:23–40), Caesarea (23:35–26:32), and Rome (28:16–31). But he experienced more than these. The selective account in Acts does not describe many of the hardships that Paul lists in 2 Corinthians 11:23–27; nor does it mention his painful visit to Corinth described in 2 Corinthians 2:1–4. The imprisonments narrated in Acts simply do not fit the situation described in Philippians.

For centuries a standard theory was that Paul wrote Philippians from house arrest in Rome, following his appeal to Caesar (Acts 28:30–31). But problems with this theory render it highly unlikely. First, the Roman imprisonment described in Acts 28 is a more comfortable house arrest, in which Paul entertains guests and preaches to those who freely come to visit him. In Philippians 1:12–13, however, his circumstances are harsher, and he only mentions witnessing to the Praetorian Guard. In 1:19–23 he expresses uncertainty over whether or not he will receive the death sentence. Second, the number of communications between Paul and the Philippian Christians excludes a Roman imprisonment. Philippians presupposes a total of five different communications back and forth between Paul and the church at Philippi, and another four trips that Paul plans for the future.

Consider the following details on messengers and messages: (1) the Philippian Christians received word that Paul was in jail and in need of help (4:14); (2) Epaphroditus journeyed from Philippi to bring money to Paul in prison (4:18); (3) while with Paul, Epaphroditus became gravely ill, and word traveled back to the Philippians of his condition (2:26); (4) word then traveled back to Paul that they were quite concerned about Epaphroditus, who then became distressed because they were worried about him (2:26); (5) Paul now plans to send Epaphroditus back to Philippi (2:28); (6) Paul also plans to send Timothy to them soon, in order to find out how they are doing (2:19); (7) Timothy will bring news back to Paul from Philippi (2:19); and (8) Paul plans to come to Philippi soon himself, if he gets out of prison (2:24). In light of the distance between Philippi and Rome, the frequency of these communications poses immense difficulties for those who claim that he was in Rome when he wrote the Letter.

For news to travel from Philippi to Rome, a messenger would probably walk 380 miles on the Via Egnatia to the port city of Dyrrachium, take a two-day boat trip to Brundisium in Italy, and then travel another 360 miles on the Via Appia (Appian Way) to Rome (see map). At a rate of 15 miles a day, such a trip would require

about 50 days. However, Paul's comments in Philippians indicate that he was much closer to Philippi, because communication was going back and forth much too rapidly for a round-trip time of over 100 days. We must look elsewhere for a place of imprisonment. The best option is Ephesus.

First Corinthians, which Paul wrote from Ephesus, indicates that he had experienced difficulties. In 4:9 he states, "For I think that God has exhibited us apostles as last of all, as though sentenced to death, because we have become a spectacle [Greek *theatron*] to the world, to angels and to mortals." And in 15:32 he asks, "If with merely human hopes I fought with wild animals at Ephesus, what would I have gained by it?" We do not know whether he means that he actually experienced some sort of public display in a Roman arena with animals, or whether he means these comments symbolically. Yet 2 Corinthians indicates that at a later time he endured a terrifying experience in Ephesus.

In 2 Corinthians 1:8–9 Paul says, "We do not want you to be unaware, brothers and sisters, of the affliction we experienced in Asia; for we were so utterly, unbearably crushed that we despaired of life itself. Indeed, we felt that we had received the sentence of death." Paul received such brutal treatment that he doubted he would survive. Although he does not specify where in Asia the ordeal occurred, the probable location was Ephesus. The fact that Acts is silent about an imprisonment in Ephesus does not pose a problem because Acts is highly selective in what it records of Paul's activities.

The communications between Paul and the Philippian Christians make much more

Calculating the distance a messenger would have to travel from Philippi to Rome and back raises serious problems with the theory that Paul was in Rome when he wrote his letter to the Philippians.

sense if he was imprisoned in Ephesus. The distance between the two cities is not nearly so great as from Philippi to Rome. Acts 16:11–12 reports Paul took three days to travel from Troas to Philippi, and 20:13 states that he took five days to return from Philippi to Troas (two days longer because of headwinds?). If it took another four days to journey from Troas to Ephesus, the entire trip would require only seven to nine days of continuous travel. This time framework fits Paul's words in Philippians.

Not only do the distances involved match what is said in Philippians, but other factors also corroborate this location. Acts 19:22 claims that Timothy was with Paul in Ephesus, as do Philippians 1:1 and 2:19–23; but Acts never mentions Timothy being in Rome with Paul. Philippians 4:10 speaks of the Philippians being concerned for Paul but having no opportunity to send aid. Yet this scenario would hardly be the case if he were in prison in Rome some twelve years after he first visited Philippi, not to mention the fact that Acts 20:6 says that Paul was again in Philippi toward the end of his third missionary journey.

His comment in Philippians 4:10 makes sense only if Paul wrote Philippians earlier in his journeys. Paul probably wrote Philippians from Ephesus, and he was released from his imprisonment as he thought he would be ("I know that through your prayers and the help of the Spirit of Jesus Christ this will turn out for my deliverance" [1:19]; "Since I am convinced of this, I know that I will remain and continue with all of you for your progress and joy in faith, so that I may share abundantly in your boasting in Christ Jesus when I come to you again" [1:25–26]; "I trust in the Lord that I will also come [to you] soon" [2:24]).

Although we cannot account for many of the details, it appears that during this trip to Philippi (and later Thessalonica), Paul met Titus somewhere in Macedonia as his messenger returned from delivering the Painful Letter. In response to the good news Titus brought, Paul composed 2 Corinthians, including his directions in 2 Corinthians 8–9 on giving money. After a while he proceeded south to Corinth to finish collecting funds for Christians in Jerusalem. Then, before his departure to Jerusalem with the offering, he wrote from Corinth his longest and most theologically complete letter: Romans. To this important document we now turn our attention.

GLOSSARY

Hyperbole. Overstatement for effect. A common speech technique in the Mediterranean world of Paul's day, one that Paul uses with some frequency to present his messages in his various letters.

Philippi. One of the leading cities of Macedonia, which Paul first visited during his second missionary journey. Philippi was located on the Via Egnatia, a major trade route of that region in Roman times. It was a Roman principality governed by Roman law, and its people enjoyed Roman citizenship.

Praetorian Guards. Elite Roman troops stationed at important government centers around the Roman Empire, not just in Rome near Caesar. Acts 23:35, for example, uses *Praitōrion* to describe Herod's governor's residence in Caesarea, on the seacoast northwest of Jerusalem.

Via Egnatia. The Egnatian Way, an important road for trade and troop movement that provided the main overland line of communication between Rome and the eastern provinces.

FURTHER READING ON PHILIPPIANS

Bakirtzis, Charalambos, and Helmut Koester, eds. *Philippi at the Time of Paul and after His Death.* Harrisburg, PA: Trinity Press International, 1998. Essays by archaeologists and New Testament scholars who met at Kavalla, Greece, for a symposium.

Bockmuehl, Markus. *The Epistle to the Philippians.* Black's New Testament Commentary Series. Peabody, MA: Hendrickson Publishers, 1998. Examines the rhetorical structure of Philippians and gives historical and cultural backgrounds of the Letter.

Bruce, F. F. *Philippians.* NIBCNT 11. Peabody, MA: Hendrickson Publishers, 1989. Accessible reading. Informative.

Cousar, Charles B. *Reading Galatians, Philippians, and 1 Thessalonians: A Literary and Theological Commentary*. Reading the New Testament Series. Macon, GA: Smyth & Helwys, 2001. Focuses on the literary dimensions of these three Letters.

Craddock, Fred B. *Philippians*. Interpretation. Atlanta: John Knox Press, 1985. Applies the Letter to contemporary situations.

Edwards, Mark J., ed. *Galatians, Ephesians, Philippians*. Ancient Christian Commentary on Scripture: New Testament 8. Downers Grove, IL: InterVarsity Press, 1999. Translations of comments on Philippians made by early Christian writers. Helpful insights into the history of interpretation.

Fee, Gordon D. *Paul's Letter to the Philippians*. NICNT. Grand Rapids: Wm. B. Eerdmans Publishing Co., 1995. Thorough (543 pages). Examines the content and structure of Philippians in light of Greco-Roman letter writing and Mediterranean cultural norms. Numerous applications of passages.

Getty, Mary Ann. *Philippians and Philemon*. New Testament Message 14. Wilmington, DE: Michael Glazier, 1980. Short (93 pages). Easy but informative read.

Hawthorne, Gerald F. *Philippians*. Word Biblical Commentary 43. Waco, TX: Word Books, 1983. Clear and thorough analysis of the Greek text. For scholars.

O'Brien, Peter T. *The Epistle to the Philippians: A Commentary on the Greek Text*. NIGTC. Grand Rapids: Wm. B. Eerdmans Publishing Co., 1991. Thorough (638 pages) examination of the Greek text, yet the tone is almost conversational.

Osiek, Carolyn. *Philippians, Philemon*. Nashville: Abingdon Press, 2000. Good material on Mediterranean customs and societal structures.

Saunders, Stanley P. *Philippians and Galatians*. Louisville, KY: Westminster John Knox Press, 2001. Brief. Re-creates what it would be like for those who received the letters to listen to them being read aloud.

Thielman, Frank. *Philippians*: NIV Application Commentary. Grand Rapids: Zondervan, 1995. Emphasizes contemporary relevance. Lacks thorough analysis.

*Witherington, Ben, III. *Friendship and Finances in Philippi: The Letter of Paul to the Philippians*. Valley Forge, PA: Trinity Press International, 1994. Focuses on Greco-Roman rhetoric and sociological matters. Readable and informative.

*Wright, N. T. *Paul for Everyone: The Prison Letters: Ephesians, Philippians, Colossians, and Philemon*. Louisville, KY: Westminster John Knox Press, 2004. Brief, readable, and insightful.

CHAPTER 13

Romans

THEOLOGY ON THE EDGE OF CONFLICT

Paul's Epistle to Rome deals with the same controversial issues addressed in Galatians, but without the heated and sharply confrontational tone. As Paul's most lengthy and formal letter, Romans explores a central issue: the place of Jew and Gentile in the church. Paul endured criticism for his insistence that Gentile Christians need not obey the laws of Moses, and Romans provides his most detailed defense of this position. It is theology on the edge of conflict—not delivered in the heat of battle as was Galatians.

Romans lacks many of the personal references so obvious in earlier letters. 1 and 2 Corinthians brim full of references to conflicts between Paul and these Christians; 1 and 2 Thessalonians speak of the problems faced by young Christians encountering opposition and experienc-ing confusion over the second coming of Christ; Galatians rebukes people for being swayed from their commitment to Paul's teaching; Philippians expresses thanks for money sent to Paul. Each of these letters abounds in references to specific individuals, groups, and situations. By comparison, Romans seems almost detached.

In this Letter, Paul seldom lashes out at opponents (see 3:8). He does not attack particular people; rather, he explores issues pertaining to salvation. Compared with his earlier Letters, Romans offers fewer clues as to the condition of its intended audience.

Consequently, scholars put forward a number of hypotheses to explain its purpose.[1] Some say that Paul was introducing

1. W. S. Campbell summarizes theories of composition in "Why Did Paul Write Romans?" *Expository Times* 85 (1974): 264–69. For a longer treatment, see

his theology to the Romans. Others claim that Paul sought to assert his apostolic authority by sending this treatise to the capital of the Gentile world. Still others maintain that Paul's thinking about Jerusalem dominates Romans, so even though he sends it to Rome, the message is more for Jerusalem. Yet another theory is that the formal style of Romans shows it to be a circular letter, with Rome as only one of its destinations. From this perspective, it could just as well have been sent elsewhere since it is a summary of Pauline theology, not a personal letter. Since Martin Luther's time in the 1500s, a popular approach has been to view Romans as an exposition of salvation by grace through faith in Jesus Christ.

Today, however, many New Testament scholars view Romans as Paul's effort to correct a serious problem at Rome: tension between Jewish and Gentile Christians—dissension that does not become obvious until Romans 14. The emerging consensus is that, like other Pauline Epistles, Romans represents mission theology. Many now believe that Paul's major emphasis in Romans on salvation by faith stems from his effort to explain the place of Jews and Gentiles in God's larger purpose in history. In other words, Romans addresses the argument over the place of Jew and Gentile in the church and what it means to be a faithful Christian. The formal style and extensive explanation of theology emanate partly from the fact that Paul had never been to Rome (1:13) and partly from the magnitude of the issue addressed.

Karl P. Donfried, ed., *The Romans Debate*, rev. ed. (Peabody, MA: Hendrickson Publishers, 2005).

PAUL AND THE CHURCH AT ROME

Paul composed Romans as he prepared to depart for Jerusalem with money for Jewish Christians. The offering came from predominantly Gentile churches in Macedonia and Achaia. Paul mentioned it in 1 Corinthians 16:1–3 and gave it substantial attention in 2 Corinthians 8–9; now it is successfully completed (Rom. 15:25–27). As the time drew near to depart for Jerusalem, the apostle dictated an epistle to Tertius, his scribe (16:22). The prospects of what might happen at Jerusalem caused him anxiety, which he expressed briefly in Romans 15.

"PRAY THAT THEY WILL TAKE THE MONEY" (ROM. 15:22–33)

1. What is Paul's planned travel itinerary at this time?

2. Why is Paul worried (15:31b) that the Jerusalem Christians might not receive the offering he brings? (Review Acts 21:17–21 in this regard.)

The once grand Colosseum in Rome, completed in 80 CE with capacity to seat 50,000 people, is only a shell today. For centuries, people in the area plundered bricks from it to build houses and other structures. Imagine a floor over the lower storage areas, the arena filled with bloody action, and the stands filled with screaming people. But remember that Paul wrote Romans before the Colosseum was built. (Courtesy of Michael Cosby)

3. If the Jerusalem Christians take the money from the churches in Macedonia and Achaia, what are they affirming about the Gentile Christians? Why might they resist this?

Mutual hostility and exclusion existed in the churches at Rome, and Paul counsels the Christians there: "Welcome one another, therefore, just as Christ has welcomed you, for the glory of God" (15:7). The verses that follow indicate that the hostile parties are "the circumcised" and "the Gentiles" (15:8–12), and Romans 14 reveals the cause of the problems.

RESOLVING CONFLICTS IN THE CHURCH (ROM. 14–15)

Tension between Jewish and Gentile Christians seems to have caused trouble also at Rome. Arguments over keeping or not keeping the laws of Moses posed problems from the earliest efforts to evangelize Gentiles. The early chapters of Acts reveal this struggle to a limited extent, and Galatians explodes with the anger Paul felt over the issue. Romans confronts it, but in a calmer manner. Not until Romans 14–15 does Paul directly address the problems raised by Jew and Gentile belonging to the same church.

1. In Romans 14–15, what characterizes those people whom Paul calls "weak" or "weak in faith"? Are they Jews or Gentiles?

2. What characterizes the other group, whom Paul describes in 14:2–6 and calls "strong" in 15:1? Are they Jews or Gentiles?

4. Why would the "strong" despise the "weak" (14:3, 10)?

5. According to Romans 14, why can some Christians participate in certain actions and in so doing please God, whereas if others do the same things, they would be sinning and displease God?

Church Fights

Which lifestyle issues do you see dividing Christians? Which people in these debates *judge* those who differ with them? Which people *despise* those who differ with them?

How might following Paul's advice in Romans 14–15 help to settle such disputes?

6. What guidelines for how to live harmoniously in the church does Paul give in these chapters?

3. Why would the "weak" pass judgment on the "strong" (14:3, 10)?

MAKING SENSE OF THE HISTORICAL SITUATION BEHIND THE LETTER

During the first century a large number of Jewish people lived in Rome. H. J. Leon estimates the number to be from forty to fifty thousand.[2] Jewish dealings with Rome date back officially to the days of the Maccabean Rebellion, when Judas Maccabeus established an alliance with Rome (ca. 160 BCE) in an effort to aid in his battle against the Syrians (1 Macc. 8:17–32). Problems later arose with the alliance, however, and in 62 BCE the Roman general Pompey captured Jerusalem and subjugated its people (Josephus, *Ant.* 14.54–76).

Over time, many Jews came to live in Rome. One comment made by Cicero (106–43 BCE) in a lawcourt indicates their presence. He was defending a certain Lucius Valerius Flaccus against the charge of not allowing Jews to convey their temple tax to Jerusalem while he was proconsul of Asia. During the trial, to make a point, Cicero said in a hushed tone so as not to be overheard by Jews outside the courtroom, "For you know how numerous they are and how clannish, and how they can make their influence felt" (*For Flaccus* 66).

Twice in the first century Jews were expelled from Rome, and one of these times directly affects our understanding of Romans. In 19 CE Tiberius Caesar decreed that all Jews must leave Rome because four of them swindled a wealthy Roman citizen named Fulvia out of a substantial amount of money (Josephus, *Ant.* 18.81–84; Tacitus, *Annals* 2.85.5; and Suetonius, *Life of Tiberius* 36). She had become a Jewish proselyte and had given a large gift for the Jerusalem temple, but these four used it for their own gain.

After a few years, imperial wrath diminished and the Jewish population in Rome regained its previous size—until 49 CE.

The emperor Claudius experienced problems with Jews in various places around the empire, especially Egypt and Rome. The Roman historian Dio Cassius, who lived ca. 150–235 CE, wrote that Claudius sought to eliminate the trouble in Rome initially by forbidding them "to meet together in accordance with their ancestral way of life" (*History* 60.6). About eight years after this edict, riots broke out in the Jewish sectors of Rome, and Claudius issued a decree in 49 CE ordering all Jews to leave the city. According to the Roman historian **Suetonius** (ca. 69–140 CE), the riots erupted because of a certain "Chrestos" (*Life of Claudius* 25.4).

Suetonius wrote approximately 120 CE (seventy years later) and appears to have mistakenly identified the cause of the riot. Although Suetonius says the trouble started "at the instigation of one Chrestos" (Latin *impulsore Chresto quodam*), it probably erupted over one "Christos." *Chrestos* was a common slave name meaning "good" and could easily be confused with *Christos.* Apparently Christians were proclaiming Jesus as Messiah (Christ) among the Jews at Rome during this time. Those in the Jewish community who considered the proclamation of a crucified Messiah to be heresy reacted to the message much as those we read about in Acts. As Paul's preaching started riots in such places as Thessalonica (Acts 17:5–9), Beroea (17:13), and Corinth (18:12–17), similar trouble erupted at Rome, resulting in an important friendship.

According to Acts 18:2, when Paul first went to Corinth, "there he found a Jew

---

2. H. J. Leon, *The Jews of Ancient Rome,* updated version (Peabody, MA: Hendrickson Publishers, 1995), 135–36. See also the helpful summary by James D. G. Dunn, *Romans 1–8,* Word Biblical Commentary 38A (Dallas: Word Books, 1988), xlvi.

This excellent depiction of a sacrificial scene, preserved in the Louvre Museum in Paris, shows that Romans valued pigs as sacrificial animals. One of their most sacred rituals, the *Suovetaurila*, involved offering a pig (*sus*), a ram (*ovis*), and a bull (*taurus*) to Mars to ask for purification of land. Gentile Christians in Rome grew up thinking that pigs were not only good food but also good sacrificial animals. Jewish Christians, however, were appalled at such an idea. In Romans, Paul seeks to reconcile Jewish and Gentile Christians, who quarreled over food laws. (Courtesy of The VRoma Project [www.vroma.org])

named Aquila, . . . who had recently come from Italy with his wife Priscilla, because Claudius had ordered all Jews to leave Rome." Yet Romans 16:3–5 indicates that this Jewish Christian couple was again residing in Rome: "Greet Prisca and Aquila; . . . greet also the church in their house." Relaxation of the ban followed the death of Claudius in 54. His successor, Nero, had a wife who liked the Jews, and she convinced Nero to allow them to return to Rome. Thus, by the time Paul wrote Romans about 57, Jewish Christians once again lived in Rome. Their return heightened the problem that Paul addresses in his lengthy Epistle.

We know little of the first efforts by Christians at evangelizing Rome, but apparently it occurred when Jewish Christians sought to convert their fellow Jews. Before Claudius expelled Jews in 49, the church in Rome was predominantly Jewish in composition.

Afterward, however, the church became a Gentile institution. During the next five or six years before the Jewish Christians could return, the church under Gentile leadership developed differently than it would have under its former Jewish leaders. When the Jews returned, therefore, some found themselves in conflict with the present leadership.

These Gentile Christians were unconcerned with keeping the laws of Moses, and some looked with disdain on the religious sensitivities of Jewish Christians. On the other hand, some of the Jews judged the Gentiles as disobedient to God because of not keeping kosher food laws or observing the Sabbath (Rom. 14:1–6). When this controversy came to Paul's attention, he wrote a theological response to the problem. Throughout his Letter to Rome, Paul addresses the place of Jew and Gentile in the purpose of God. Initially he asserts that both are sinners. In chapters 1–3 Paul speaks like a prosecutor, arguing for universal guilt. First he condemns the Gentiles and then the Jews as guilty before God and in need of saving grace.

GUILT AND GRACE (ROM. 1–3)

Comparing Salutations (Rom. 1:1–7)

1. Paul's salutation includes a succinct and formulaic christological addition in 1:3–4, which may be part of an early Christian creedal statement. What do these two verses affirm about Jesus?

Comparing Thanksgivings (Rom. 1:8–15)

1. How does this thanksgiving section compare with those we have studied in 1 Thessalonians 1:2–10; 1 Corinthians 1:4–9; 2 Corinthians 1:3–7; and Philippians 1:3–11?

2. What insight does 1:13–17 give into Paul's understanding of his ministry?

Knowing precisely where the body of this Letter begins is difficult because the sentences from 1:13–20 connect into a progression of thought. Each verse from 16 to 20 begins with *gar*, a connecting word in Greek normally translated "for." Thus 1:16 further explains 1:15, and 1:17 further explains 1:16, and so on. Such close connection between the thanksgiving section and the body of the Letter may also be seen in 2 Corinthians 1:8 and 1 Thessalonians 2:1, where the body begins with a formula of disclosure starting with *gar* ("For we do not want you to be ignorant, brothers," and "For you yourselves know, brothers" [AT; NRSV leaves out "for" in both passages]). Seeking to make a rigid division between the thanksgiving section and the body of Romans diminishes the continuity of Paul's thought.

Exchanging Natural Sex for Homosexual Acts (Rom. 1:16–32)

In Romans 1–3 Paul speaks like an attorney, and his argument builds to the assertion in 3:19–20 that *everyone* has sinned and is in need of God's grace. To accomplish this verdict he gives different reasons for Jews and Gentiles being guilty. For the Jews, he appeals to their failure to keep Mosaic laws. However, for Gentiles who do not have the laws of Moses, he appeals to nature and conscience to establish their guilt. Paul initially asserts the centrality of faith in his gospel message (1:16–17), and then he begins his explanation of the good news by stating the bad news in 1:18: God's wrath is revealed.

1. What does 1:19–20 say people can know about God from observing the world around them?

According to the following verses, what happens to them when they reject this natural revelation?

2. God's wrath in 1:24–32 allows people to do what they want to do. Why is this expression of wrath unusual?

3. Note the use of the terms "exchanged" in 1:23, 25, 26 and "gave up" in 1:24, 26, 28. How does the refusal to acknowledge God (1:18–21) result in the exchanges made in 1:23 and 25?

How do the exchanges in 1:23 and 25 lead to God's giving them up in 1:24 and 26?

4. According to Paul, therefore, what is the underlying cause of homosexual acts? Why does he view such acts as expressions of God's wrath?

Paul probably chose homosexual acts for his examples because they fit his argument from natural order. Such activities were common among the Greek and Roman men of his day, and they provided for him a vivid illustration of Gentile perversity. In ancient

Greek and Roman literature, many passages speak of older men courting boys who were entering puberty. These men, typically married and with children, found young males quite attractive and became rather giddy in their pursuit of them. The accounts exhibit behavior similar to that often observed in Western cultures with teenage boys courting girls. Plato's *Protagoras* opens with Socrates' companion asking him about the handsome young Alcibiades:

> **Companion:** Where do you come from, Socrates? And yet I need hardly ask the question, for I know that you have been in chase of the fair Alcibiades. I saw the day before yesterday; and he had got a beard like a man— and he is a man, as I may tell you in your ear. But I thought that he was still very charming.
>
> **Socrates:** What of his beard? Are you not of Homer's opinion, who says "Youth is most charming when the beard first appears"? And that is now the charm of Alcibiades.
>
> **Companion:** Well, and how do matters proceed? Have you been visiting him, and was he gracious to you?
>
> **Socrates:** Yes, I thought that he was very gracious; and especially to-day, for I have just come from him, and he has been helping me in an argument. But shall I tell you a strange thing? I paid no attention to him, and several times I quite forgot that he was present.
>
> **Companion:** What is the meaning of this? Has anything happened between you and him? For surely you cannot

have discovered a fairer love than he is; certainly not in this city of Athens. (309a–c)[3]

Plato's *Symposium* also describes what Greeks considered to be the positive relationships between mature men and boys. *Symposion* was the Greek title for a drinking party, and the guests of this particular party decided to take turns at seeing who could give the best speech in honor of Love. One of these speeches in particular praises the benefits to society of the "divinely inspired" love relationships between men and boys:

> Phaedrus began by affirming that Love is a mighty god, and wonderful among gods and men, but especially wonderful in his birth. For he is the eldest of the gods. . . .
> And not only is he the eldest, he is also the source of the greatest benefits to us. For I know not any greater blessing to a young man who is beginning life than a virtuous lover or to the lover than a beloved youth. For the principle which ought to be the guide of men who would nobly live at principle, I say, neither kindred, nor honour, nor wealth, nor any other motive is able to implant so well as love. Of what am I speaking? Of the sense of honour and dishonour, without which neither states nor individuals ever do any good or great work. And I say that a lover who is detected in doing any dishonourable act, or submitting through cowardice when any dishonour is done to him by another, will be more pained at being detected by his beloved than at being seen by his father, or by his companions, or by any one else.
> The beloved too, when he is found in any disgraceful situation, has the same feeling about his lover. And if there were only some way of contriving that a state or an army should be made up of lovers and their loves, they would be the very best governors of their own city, abstaining from all dishonour, and emulating

3. Translated by Benjamin Jowett from *The Collected Dialogues of Plato*, ed. Edith Hamilton and H. Cairns (Princeton, NJ: Princeton University Press, 1963), 309; also at The Internet Classics Archive, http://classics.mit.edu/Plato/protagoras.html.

one another in honour; and when fighting at each other's side, although a mere handful, they would overcome the world. For what lover would not choose rather to be seen by all mankind than by his beloved, either when abandoning his post or throwing away his arms? He would be ready to die a thousand deaths rather than endure this. Or who would desert his beloved or fail him in the hour of danger? The veriest coward would become an inspired hero, equal to the bravest, at such a time; Love would inspire him. That courage which, as Homer says, the god breathes into the souls of some heroes, Love of his own nature infuses into the lover. . . .

And greatly as the gods honour the virtue of love, still the return of love on the part of the beloved to the lover is more admired and valued and rewarded by them, for the lover is more divine; because he is inspired by God. Now Achilles was quite aware, for he had been told by his mother, that he might avoid death and return home, and live to a good old age, if he abstained from slaying Hector. Nevertheless he gave his life to revenge his friend, and dared to die, not only in his defence, but after he was dead. Wherefore the gods honoured him even above Alcestis, and sent him to the Islands of the Blest. These are my reasons for affirming that Love is the eldest and noblest and mightiest of the gods; and the chiefest author and giver of virtue in life, and of happiness after death. (*Symposium* 178a–180b)[4]

Such speeches indicate that mature men not only courted their favorite boys for sexual purposes, but they also trained them in warfare, rhetoric, and other dimensions of social responsibility. Sexual acts between males were considered ignoble only if money were the motivating reason. If the boy sold himself, he was dishonorable.[5]

Jewish people, on the other hand, exhibited profound revulsion toward homosexual acts. The Jewish *Sibylline Oracles* 3.584–606, for example, speaks of God's judgment falling on Greeks, Romans, and others who transgress God's laws by having "unholy intercourse with boys." Also, *2 (Slavonic) Enoch* 10.4–6 describes hell as a place prepared in part for those who practice "sin against nature, which is child-corruption after the sodomic fashion."[6] Jewish authors typically connected homosexual acts with idolatry, much as Paul does in Romans 1:18–32. They drew not only from the story of God's destruction of Sodom in Genesis 19:1–25, but also from the prohibitions in the Old Testament law codes: "You shall not lie with a male as with a woman; it is an abomination" (Lev. 18:22). "If a man lies with a male as with a woman, both of them have committed an abomination; they shall be put to death; their blood is upon them" (20:13).[7]

In Romans 1:18–32, Paul joins this chorus against homosexual acts, connecting them with the worship of idols, leading to God's judgment. The closest approximation of Paul's argument may be seen in Wisdom of Solomon 13–14. This first-century BCE document may well provide the background for Paul's thought in Romans 1:18–32. Wisdom 13 condemns idolatry and 14:12 connects it with all forms of immorality: "For the idea of making idols was the beginning of fornication, and the invention of them was the corruption of life."

---

4. Translation by Benjamin Jowett; also at The Internet Classics Archive, http://classics.mit.edu/Plato/symposium.html.

5. For more quotations from ancient literature that describe the acceptance of homosexual acts among Greek and Roman males, see Michael R. Cosby, *Sex in the Bible: An Introduction to What the Scriptures Teach Us about Sexuality* (Englewood Cliffs, NJ: Prentice-Hall, 1984), 154–62.

6. Translations from R. H. Charles, *The Apocrypha and Pseudepigrapha of the Old Testament in English*, vol. 2 (Oxford: Clarendon Press, 1913).

7. See Cosby, *Sex in the Bible*, 142–54, for references to ancient sources that describe Jewish abhorrence of homosexuality.

Paul and Modern Morals

How do you respond to Paul's description of homosexual acts as perverse, degrading, and evidence of the wrath of God? Can one endorse civil rights for homosexuals while still maintaining a position like Paul's on the immorality of homosexual acts? What is your position on gay and lesbian persons functioning in such roles as schoolteachers and pastors? Why?

one's own judge. No written law is needed in such cases. People are condemned by their own standards of right and wrong.

1. How does the wrath of God in 2:5–11 differ from the wrath of God in 1:18–28?

2. In light of Paul's insistence in Galatians that salvation is by faith alone and not by works, what seems odd about God's judgment in 2:1–11?

Paul, like other Jewish writers of his day, includes a list of additional vices with his condemnation of Gentile sexual aberrations. In Romans 1:29–31 notice his catalog of common sins, which he asserts will result in God's judgment.

Be Careful How You Judge!
(Rom. 2:1–16)

This passage begins with "therefore," showing that Paul is drawing a conclusion from the preceding material. Yet the conclusion is not what we might expect. Instead of summarizing his point, Paul provides another criterion used for divine judgment: what we might call the *principle of self-condemnation*. According to 2:1–3, anyone who sees another do something and judges the action to be wrong, but then does the same sort of thing at a later time, becomes

3. What principle of judgment does Paul teach in 2:12–16?

Jews Are Just as Guilty as Gentiles
(Rom. 2:17–29)

1. On what basis does Paul pronounce Jews guilty in 2:17–24? (His "rob temples" comment in 2:22 might allude to the two Jewish men who swindled the Roman matron Fulvia; see above.)

2. How does Paul redefine the meaning of Jewishness in 2:25–29?

They're All Filthy Sinners!
(Rom. 3:1–31)

1. Compare 3:1–2 with 3:9. How are the Jews better off than the Gentiles? How are they no better off than the Gentiles?

2. What accusation against Paul's teaching does he mention in 3:5–8?

3. How does the content of 3:9–20 function in Paul's argument?

4. In the context of Romans 1–3, why does Paul want to eliminate boasting in human achievement in 3:27?

Paul uses several key terms in 3:21–26. **Redemption** was often used in the context of slavery. Slave owners commonly allowed slaves to receive their freedom if someone paid a price, a **ransom**, to compensate the owner for the value of the slave. This fee could be paid by a third party, or some slaves were allowed to save money until they were able to pay the amount themselves. When the slaves received their freedom, they were

redeemed from bondage. In Romans, Paul speaks of Christ's death on the cross as the ransom price paid to redeem sinners from their slavery to sin.

Closely connected to the term "redemption" are the words **justify** and **righteousness** of God (3:21–26). As we noted previously, the Greek noun for righteousness is *dikaiosynē*, and the verb for justify is *dikaioō*. Because in English we have no corresponding verb for righteousness, we do not say that people are *righteoused*; we say that they are *justified*. But what did Paul mean when he spoke of someone being justified?

Down through the years Christians have put forward three basic options for the meaning of justification:

1. *pronounced righteous*—although people are sinners, God views them as righteous and treats them as if they were such;
2. *made righteous*—God gives a new nature to Christians and literally makes them into righteous men and women by a powerful work of grace; and
3. *covenant relationship*—Christians have entered into a covenant relationship with God.

In option 1, God exhibits divine myopia, not seeing what Christians are actually like because God looks at them only through the sacrificial death of Jesus. This view at times contributes to a lax attitude toward holy living. Option 2, on the other hand, may lead to a belief in sinless perfection, wherein Christians think that they have ceased to sin because God has removed their sin nature and thus their tendency to do wrong. Such perfect living, although a wonderful goal, does not withstand the test of everyday, practical experience. People who claim such perfection are self-deluded.

If, however, Paul meant a covenant relationship with God (option 3) when he spoke of righteousness, he acknowledged individual failings, such as what we saw among the Corinthian Christians, yet he trusted the Holy Spirit to lead believers into holy lives. As an example consider the story of David in the Old Testament. Throughout 1–2 Kings the narrator repeatedly says that David was true to God and followed God with all his heart. For example, in 1 Kings 14:8 God says that David "kept my commandments and followed me with all his heart, doing only that which was right in my sight" (see also 1 Kings 11:4, 33, 38; 15:3, 11; 2 Kings 14:3; 16:2; 18:3; 22:2). Yet 1–2 Samuel recounts David's atrocities. In the narrative God judges him for his sin; yet because David never worshiped idols or served other gods, he is highly praised as a loyal servant of God. To put it in a Christian perspective: God clearly sees peoples' faults but also continues to work with them to bring about improvement.

5. Explain in your own words how 3:21–31 answers the problem of human sinfulness that Paul raises in 1:18–3:20.

SALVATION BY GRACE THROUGH FAITH (ROM. 4–6)

Abraham Our Ancestor (Rom. 4:1–12)

In Romans 1–3 Paul argues that all people deserve condemnation by God. All need God's mercy and experience salvation through faith in Christ. No one is able to stand before God and boast of earning the right to enjoy God's favor. The apostle insists that all people must respond in faith, whether they are Jews or Gentiles (3:28–30). Reacting against his teaching, Jewish opponents concluded that Paul abolished the Mosaic law with his teaching on faith (3:31). So he asserts that, to the contrary, he upholds the law, giving it the true significance that God intended (3:31). Its significance, however, is far less in scope than most Jews believed.

To prove his point, he appeals to **Abraham**, the father of the Jewish people. By claiming that even the progenitor of the chosen people was justified by faith, he strengthens his argument.

1. What major distinction does Paul make between justification by works and justification by faith in 4:1–5?

In Genesis 12:2–3 God promised Abraham: "I will make of you a great nation, and I will bless you, and make your name great, so that you will be a blessing; . . . and in you all the families of the earth shall be blessed." Years later Abraham still had no male heir, for Sarah remained barren. Yet God communicated to him, "Look toward heaven and count the stars, if you are able to count them. . . . So shall your descendants be" (15:5). Abraham's response to this promise is essential to Paul's argument: "And he believed the LORD; and the LORD reckoned it to him as righteousness" (15:6).

2. How does Paul demonstrate in 4:6–12 that the blessing of God's promise to Abraham is for both Jews and Gentiles? (The theme of Abraham being the father of all who have faith will play a major role in Rom. 9–11.)

Hoping against Hope (Rom. 4:13–25)

To demonstrate that Abraham was righteous by faith, Paul cites the example of Isaac's miraculous birth. The one-hundred-year-old Abraham and his ninety-year-old wife, Sarah, were physically unable to produce an heir. A miracle was necessary.

1. By what means does Paul argue in 4:13–25 that God's promise to Abraham is for all people, not just for Abraham's physical descendants, those who are under the laws of Moses?

2. Read Genesis 16:1–4, a story taking place *after* the description of Abraham's faith being reckoned as righteousness (15:6). What does Abraham do in this passage about the problem of still having no heir?

3. Now read Genesis 17:15–21. How does Abraham respond to God's promise pertaining to Sarah? (Cf. 18:9–15.) What problems do these stories raise with Paul's version in Romans 4:18–22?

Obviously Paul's view of Abraham's faith dramatically exceeds that described in Genesis. As a trained rabbi, he knew the story of Abraham, so to think that Paul was ignorant of Abraham's laughing at God's promise does not seem reasonable. He deliberately focused on what he wanted to prove and left out other details that would compromise his position. This approach is not unlike his blanket condemnation of Gentiles and Jews in Romans 1–3. There his goal is to demonstrate that all are guilty, so he makes unqualified assertions to argue his case. He does not hint that not all Gentile men worship idols or chase boys, although he knew such to be true due to his extensive work among Gentiles. And when he speaks of Jews in Romans 2, one would gain the impression that they all were guilty of stealing, committing adultery, and so forth (2:21–24). Indeed, in his series of Old Testament quotations in 3:10–18, he depicts all people as completely evil and incapable of doing anything good. If taken at face value, it does not match his more generous view of Gentiles, for example, in 2:14–15, where he says, "When Gentiles, who do not possess the law, do instinctively what the law requires, . . . they show that what the law requires is written on their hearts."

Paul's language abounds with hyperbole. He does not qualify his arguments. Perhaps he thought that doing so would weaken his case. As we have seen previously in such comments as "Rejoice in the Lord always. . . . Do not worry about anything" (Phil. 4:4–6), we interpret the meaning of his overstatements in light of the overall intent of his argument. Like most people, what Paul *says* is not always exactly what he *means*. The difficult task is to determine when he is overstating. There is no formula.

Peace with God (Rom. 5:1–11)

After arguing that all people need to be justified by faith, Paul now describes the implications of justification. Beginning 5:1 with "therefore" ties this section solidly to the preceding material. Jesus died for our sins and was raised from the dead for our justification (4:24–25). Therefore we have peace with God (5:1).

1. According to 5:1–5, how does faith enable us to view the everyday problems of life?

2. In 5:6–11, what terms does Paul use to describe the condition of people before they place their faith in Christ?

God Gave the Law to Increase Sin (Rom. 5:12–21)

Paul again uses "therefore" (5:12) to connect his ideas to the previous material. Tracing human sinfulness back to the original sin of Adam, he explains the way God has dealt with this all-pervasive problem.

1. In 5:12–21, what connection does Paul make between sin and human mortality?

2. What contrasts does Paul give between the results of the actions of Jesus and those of Adam?

Adam   Christ

3. According to Paul, sin increased as a result of the law (5:20). Why is this understanding so radical for a man who was trained as a Pharisee?

Paul's interpretation of salvation history by using the typology of Adam and Christ as the two major events stands in stark contrast to the way in which the Jewish community normally viewed history. The following chart summarizes his argument (cf. the chart on Jewish belief regarding the law's age and purpose in the chapter on Galatians).

Creation →	Adam →	No Law	→	Law (condemnation) →	Christ
No sin or death in the beginning.	Death enters because Adam sins.	Death rules through sin. People are sinners even though they do not break God's command as Adam did.		Law increases sin, defines sin, and brings guilt, for people now knowingly do wrong.	Christ died for sinners. Grace makes sinners into saints and breaks the rule of death.

Does Paul's Theology Corrupt the Church? (Rom. 6:1–11)

One of the major issues that arises from Paul's explanation of salvation by faith alone and not by works of the law is the problem of **antinomianism**. Jewish Christians in particular complained that accepting Gentiles into the church simply on the basis of faith opens the door to multiple corrupting influences. They reasoned that requiring Christians to keep the Mosaic law brings a greater degree of control. If belief is the crucial factor, they complained, what is to keep people from living corrupt lives and thereby destroying the credibility of the church?

In 6:1 Paul responds to his critics: "What then are we to say? Should we continue in sin in order that grace may abound?" This caustic comment resembles 3:8: "And why not say (as some people slander us by saying that we say), 'Let us do evil so that good may come'? Their condemnation is deserved!" Scholars translate Paul's explosive answer in 6:2, *mē genoito*, in various ways: "By no means!" (NRSV); "God forbid!" (KJV); "May it never be!" (NASB); "No, No!" (NEB); "What a terrible thought!" (Phillips); "Hell, no!" (Clarence Jordan's *Cotton Patch Version of Paul's Epistles*). Each trans-

lator tries to capture Paul's disgust at such accusations. So although Romans is much calmer than Galatians or 1–2 Corinthians, at times it expresses strong emotion. Paul is not boiling, but in several paragraphs he vents some heat.

1. How does Paul use baptism in 6:2–4 to explain why the idea that a Christian could continue to live in sin is a contradictory notion?

2. According to 6:5–11, what happens when people place faith in Christ and are baptized?

3. Why would Christians who believe that justification means "made righteous" focus on this passage in 6:1–11?

Paul describes non-Christians as slaves to sin (6:6) and Christians as free from the tyranny of sin. The diagram below summarizes his teaching.

Refuse to Let Sin Control You (Rom. 6:12–23)

Since Christians no longer live under the old order of sin and condemnation, they should present themselves to God as those who are alive from the dead. The old order of life is buried now, and the Christian is free to live under grace (6:12–14). Yet if justification destroys human slavery to sin (6:6), and the Christian has been raised

to a whole new existence (6:7–8), why do Christians still struggle with sin? In 6:11 Paul says that believers should *consider* themselves dead to sin and alive to God. But what does this mean? Why were some of the Corinthian Christians, for example, so morally and ethically corrupt? If Christians have died to sin, why do they generally struggle with sin?

1. Although Paul considers sinning to be normal for nonbelievers, in 6:12–14, what sort of life does he say is possible for Christians?

2. According to 6:15–19, what possibilities are open to believers that they did not have before conversion?

Old Order	Death of Christ	New Order for Christians (Grace)
"Old self" or "body of sin" is enslaved to sin (6:6)	Christ died for sin, once for all, and now lives with God (v. 10). He rose from the dead. Death no longer rules over him (v. 9).	Old self is crucified with Christ, and the body of sin is destroyed (v. 6). Christians died to sin (v. 2), are buried with Christ by baptism into his death (v. 4), and now live with Christ (v. 8). Therefore it is a contradiction to live in sin (v. 11); sin is no longer Christians' master (v.12).

From 6:20–23 we must assume that, although Christians are slaves of God (v. 22), they still exercise freedom of choice in matters of obeying their Lord. Dying and rising with Christ liberates from the tyranny of sin, but it does not make righteous living automatic. Individual choice remains. The difference is that Christians have the power to live in a way that pleases God, their new master.

NEW LIFE IN THE SPIRIT (ROM. 7–8)

We Are Dead to the Law That Enslaved Us (Rom. 7:1–6)

Paul's analogy from marriage illustrates what he means by being liberated from sin and the law. At this point he might be primarily addressing the Jewish Christians at Rome, for he specifies: "I am speaking to those who know the law" (7:1). We cannot be sure of this, however. His subtle interpretations of the law in Galatians, a letter sent to a predominantly Gentile church, assume that they have heard the Scriptures.

1. The death of her husband frees a woman to marry another man (7:2–3). How does participation in the death and resurrection of Jesus change one's relationship to the laws of Moses (7:4–6)?

2. What is the result of belonging to Christ instead of to the law?

Paul's marriage analogy is not exactly parallel. In the example of the woman in 7:2–3, the death of her husband liberates her to marry another. She experiences a transfer of ownership from one man to another. In the explanation of 7:4–6, however, believers are freed to belong to God not because the law has died but because of their own death, as described in Romans 6. Nevertheless, the meaning is clear. Death severs servitude to the former husband (master) and liberates one to belong to Christ and bear fruit for him. The new means of service is by the Spirit, not the law (7:6).

Enslaved to Sin—Helpless to Do Right (Rom. 7:7–25)

After hearing Paul's argument in the preceding material, one might conclude that he has a low view of the law, although he protests this conclusion in 3:31. In 5:20 he asserts, "But law came in, with the result that the trespass multiplied," and in 6:14 he says, "For sin will have no dominion over you, since you are not under law but under grace." So closely does he connect sin and law that in 7:1–6 he speaks of the Christian's conversion experience as dying to that which held one captive:

"While we were living in the flesh, our sinful passions, aroused by the law, were at work in our members to bear fruit for death. But now we are discharged from the law, dead to that which held us captive" (7:5–6).

In 7:7, therefore, Paul insists that he is not saying the law is sin. The following verses, however, are among the most debated in the entire Letter. For centuries scholars have puzzled over the perspective Paul intends to communicate in 7:7–25. His sustained use of the first-person pronouns "I" and "me" in 7:7–25 appears to indicate that this section is autobiographical in nature. Yet in light of 6:1–11, many readers question this interpretation. This passage is where the meaning of justification becomes so debatable.

1. In 7:7–12, what connection does Paul make between law and sin?

2. According to 7:13–25, what effects does sin have on Paul?

3. According to Paul, why can he not do the good that he wants to do?

4. Review what Paul says about being liberated from slavery to the law and sin in 6:2–11, 17–18, 20–22; 7:1–6, and about Christians not allowing sin to rule in their bodies in 6:12–14, 19. In light of these affirmations, do you believe Paul is describing his Christian experience in 7:14–25 (esp. 7:14, 18, 23–24)? Why or why not?

Following Paul's logic in Romans 7 is difficult. In Romans 6 he asserts that Christians have been freed from the tyranny of law and sin by dying and rising with Christ. Paul's account of helplessness in 7:14–25 defies his description of empowerment in 6:1–7:6. Yet Christians identify with both extremes. People empathize with the struggle expressed in 7:14–25. We want to do what is right, but sin lurks ever close at hand. We know something is wrong and that if we do it we will feel guilty, but we find ourselves doing it anyway.

Personal identification with this dilemma causes many to conclude that Paul was describing his ongoing struggle with sin. They conclude that, although Romans 6 says Christians have died to sin, Romans 7 reveals that sin is always a struggle while we live in the present evil age. Some scholars, however, do not think that Paul had such introspective struggles.

Krister Stendahl, for example, rejected the belief that Paul struggled with his conscience. Stendahl argued that such interpretations of Paul's Letters come more from the legacy of interpretation handed down by such influential Christians as Martin Luther, who agonized with his conscience before coming to believe in justification by faith.

> A fresh look at the Pauline writings themselves shows that Paul was equipped with what in our eyes must be called a rather "robust" conscience. In Phil. 3 Paul speaks most fully about his life before his Christian calling, and there is no indication that he had any difficulty in fulfilling the Law. On the contrary, he can say that he had been "flawless" as to the righteousness required by the Law (v. 6).... When he says that he now forgets what is behind him (Phil. 3:13), he does not think about the shortcomings in his obedience to the Law, but about his glorious achievements as a righteous Jew, achievements which he nevertheless now has learned to consider as "refuse" in the light of his faith in Jesus as the Messiah.[8]

Stendahl asserted that "we look in vain for any evidence that Paul the Christian has suffered under the burden of conscience concerning personal shortcomings which he would label 'sins.'"[9]

To explain away Romans 7 with an appeal to Philippians 3, Stendahl diminished the emotional language Paul uses in Romans 7 to describe the experience of sin and guilt. Is he justified in so doing? Romans 1–3 argues that *everyone* is guilty and in need of grace because everyone is disobedient, either to conscience or to the law. Christian conversion is the result of liberation from enslaving sin by an act of God's grace (6:1–7:6), not from human achievement of keeping the law (which results in pride). Paul makes it clear in 3:27 that *no one* can boast before God; in 3:22–23 he asserts that "there is no distinction, since *all* have sinned and fall short of the glory of God"; and in 4:5 he declares that God "justifies the *ungodly.*" So although Paul claims in Philippians 3:6 that he kept the law, he says in Romans 3:20 that "through the law comes the knowledge of sin."

Paul includes himself in the indictment that he, like all others, needed to be justified by faith. Romans 7:7–25 describes either his Christian or pre-Christian experience, unless he is simply using first-person pronouns and present-tense verbs as a rhetorical way of describing the plight of everyone. Perhaps Paul is summarizing the pitiful condition of everyone apart from Christ by universalizing Adam's experience. If so, he could be explaining what captivity to sin and the law is like, a captivity that is broken only by conversion (6:1–7:6). In other words, Paul may be building on the argument of 5:12–21, where he describes the way sin entered the world through Adam's choice to disobey God. The experience of Adam becomes the experience of everyone. Before the fall, Adam lived apart from sin and death. With the command not to eat from the tree of the knowledge

---

8. Krister Stendahl, "Paul and the Introspective Conscience of the West," in *Paul among Jews and Gentiles* (Philadelphia: Fortress Press, 1976), 80.

9. Ibid., 82.

of good and evil came the temptation to sin (cf. 7:9), and the resulting disobedience brought death.

A better avenue for research, however, is to recognize that Paul frequently employs overstatement as a rhetorical technique in Romans. Although we should take his comments seriously, if we always interpret them literally, we misinterpret his intent. In other words, we must look for what Paul *means*, which is not always exactly what he *says*. He uses hyperbole in Romans 1–3 to demonstrate that all are guilty and in need of God's grace, and in 4:18–20 to assert that Abraham never weakened in faith as he waited for God to fulfill the promises delivered to him. It may well be that Paul also uses overstatement in Romans 6–8 to describe what happens when people become Christians. When he says that Christians have died with Christ and risen to a new life, where all has become new, he may mean that they have had a significant encounter with God, the Holy Spirit has come to dwell in them, and they now have resources at their disposal that were previously missing.

By asserting with finality a break with the old life, he defends himself against his opponents' charge that if his teaching were correct, one could sin brazenly because justification with God results only from grace and not from works. Through such absolute language he shows Gentile Christians that they must make a complete break with their old lives of idol worship and immorality and live new lives guided by the Spirit of God. By stressing the radical break with the old and the complete adoption of the new, he indicates his seriousness about the change.

But there is too much evidence of old tendencies still at work in his converts to conclude that Paul considered Christians completely liberated from the body of sin/ old man (6:6).

On the other hand, it is equally problematic to think that he literally means that Christians are not able to avoid sin, as the language of being helpless seems to indicate in 7:7–25. In this passage, Paul shows through emotive language the problems encountered when trying to live under the law. Speaking against the Jewish Christian position that one must keep the laws of Moses, he shows vividly that the laws are powerless to make people truly good. Indeed, he claims that the law ironically has the opposite effect, calling attention to sin and leading to more bad behavior. Living under the law is not as glorious as his Jewish Christian opponents are saying. But that does not mean that Christians are free to sin. Paul overstates in 6:1–11 and 7:1–6 as a way of insisting on a definitive break with the old life of sin. Then he overstates in 7:7–25 to insist that life under the law is not the path to glory.

The Spirit Sets Us Free to Do God's Will (Rom. 8:1–17)

The victorious declaration of Romans 8:1–2 shatters the gloomy, despairing tone of 7:13–25, again sounding the note of liberation from sin and death that we heard in Romans 6. Freedom in Christ means freedom from condemnation for sinfulness. God "justifies the ungodly" (4:5), accomplishing what human effort under the law could never do.

1. According to 8:1–8, why could the law not enable people to be righteous?

2. What does the death of Jesus accomplish that the law could not?

3. Paul contrasts life in the flesh with life in the Spirit. List the differences between these two ways of living and the results of each.

Life in the Spirit	Life in the flesh

Paul indicates that Christians, due to our death with Jesus (6:1–10) and receipt of the Holy Spirit (8:1–17), now have the power to do what we wanted to do before but lacked the power to accomplish. Through the indwelling Spirit, we can confront our sinful urges and conquer them. Earlier we were helpless (overstatement) due to the weakness of the flesh and the power of sin working through the flesh and the law; now Christ liberates us to live a life pleasing to God. No longer dominated by the flesh, we now live in the Spirit.

Christians live in two worlds simultaneously. We have a body and are tempted by sin (present evil age), but we also have the Spirit dwelling within (age to come). We can continue to live as we did before conversion, yielding to sin and letting it master us (6:12–13, 16; 8:10, 12–13). But we do not have to live this way any longer. By yielding to the Spirit, we subdue the desires of the flesh that are fed by the human tendency to assert our independence from God as Adam did (see 5:12–21).

From Bondage to Glory
(Rom. 8:18–27)

While alive in the body, Christians groan to be free from the struggles with sinful inclinations, persecution because of their faith, and so forth. In 8:18–23, Paul expands this description of human bondage to include the entire created order.

1. According to Paul in 8:18–27, what conditions has sin imposed upon creation?

Divine Sovereignty and Human Free Will

Compare what Paul says about predestination in 8:28–30 with what he says about human responsibility in the preceding chapters of Romans. How might viewing 8:28–30 as another example of overstatement help to put his teaching into perspective?

How does Paul's emphasis on both human choice and divine initiative correspond with what Josephus says about the beliefs of the Pharisees in *Antiquities* 18.1.2–6? (see chap. 2)

2. What does he say will be the ultimate destiny of the created order?

4. How does the Spirit aid Christians in the midst of the present struggles of life?

3. How will the Christians' destiny be connected with that of the rest of creation?

More than Conquerors
(Rom. 8:28–39)

As Christians wait in hope (8:24) for the final consummation, many experiences challenge the belief that God really has accomplished in us all that Paul has described in the preceding material. Pain and opposition, not triumph, may characterize daily life. Paul now speaks to this problem, asserting that God works for good even in all the bothersome events that complicate our lives (8:28).

1. How is 8:28–30 a comfort for Christians who wonder why they are encountering so many difficulties?

2. What hope and comfort does 8:31–39 provide?

3. Paul does not mention God's delivering people from persecution (8:35–39). So how can Christians be assured of God's love?

Remember that from a Jewish eschatological perspective, before the end of the present evil age will be a time of unparalleled stress (woes of the Messiah) for the people of God. Paul states in Romans 13:12 that the "the night is far gone, the day is near." He still believed that the end would soon arrive (cf. 1 Thess. 4:13–18; 1 Cor. 7:29, 31; 10:11).

GOD'S PLAN FOR ISRAEL (ROM. 9–11)

Who Are the True Descendants of Abraham? (Rom. 9:1–13)

Paul's assurance that Christians can face persecution because they know that they are God's chosen people (8:31–34) raises potential problems. Some might ask, Was God faithful to his former chosen people, the Jews? Some might think that if God abandoned Jews in favor of Christians, how can we be sure of his faithfulness? If living for God involves personal sacrifice, can Christians be confident that the cost is worth it? Has God's promise to Israel failed (9:6)?

In Romans 9–11 Paul addresses this problem. The Gentile Christians in Rome who show arrogance toward Jewish Christians (11:20) need to know that God has not abandoned his people Israel in favor of Gentile believers. Jewish Christians, on the other hand, need to know how Gentile Christians are legitimately part of the family of God. Thus, these chapters are vital to Paul's argument.

1. Although Paul is an apostle to the Gentiles, how does he feel toward Jewish people? (9:1–5)

2. According to 9:6–12, who does Paul consider to be the true descendants of Abraham?

Is God Unjust? (Rom. 9:14–33)

After asserting that only the children of promise, those who have faith like Abraham, are the elect, Paul defends God's right to choose people. One might object that God is unfair in choosing some and rejecting others (9:14) and that if people really are not the ones doing the choosing, God is unjust to judge them for their wrongdoing (9:19).

1. Summarize Paul's answer in 9:14–23 to these charges against his view of God's election.

2. Why, according to Paul, have most Jews failed to receive God's righteousness?

Why Does Paul Quote Scripture Out of Context? (Rom. 10:1–21)

Paul focuses on God's mercy and faithfulness, showing that God does things in history to bring *many* people to salvation. The process of selection is not divine capriciousness. God hardened Pharaoh, for example, to display majestic power so that the message would be proclaimed in all the earth (9:17). Ultimately Paul pushes his message toward 11:32, where he indicates that God desires to have mercy on all.

In his view, we cannot fully understand God's actions and are not wise enough to question God (9:19–21). Indeed, Adam's sin lay primarily in seeking to control his own destiny, to be his own lord, and that proved to be disastrous to the entire created order! Only God understands the events of human history; only God can rightfully rule. For Paul, to question how God does things is to take ourselves out of the role of creature and challenge the Creator.

1. Compare Romans 10:6–10 with Deuteronomy 30:11–14. What point does Moses make about the law he has given to the Israelites?

What point does Paul make with this passage from Deuteronomy?

Deuteronomy 30:11–14	Romans 10:6–10
[11]Surely, this commandment that I am commanding you today is not too hard for you, nor is it too far away. [12]It is not in heaven, that you should say, "Who will go up to heaven for us, and get it for us so that we may hear it and observe it?" [13]Neither is it beyond the sea, that you should say, "Who will cross to the other side of the sea for us, and get it for us so that we may hear it and observe it?" [14]No, the word is very near to you; it is in your mouth and in your heart for you to observe.	[6]But the righteousness that comes from faith says, "Do not say in your heart, 'Who will ascend into heaven?' " (that is, to bring Christ down) [7]or 'Who will descend into the abyss?' " (that is, to bring Christ up from the dead). [8]But what does it say? "The word is near you, on your lips and in your heart" (that is, the word of faith that we proclaim); [9]because if you confess with your lips that Jesus is Lord and believe in your heart that God raised him from the dead, you will be saved. [10]For one believes with the heart and so is justified, and one confesses with the mouth and so is saved.

In Romans 9–11, where Paul addresses why the Jewish people have not flocked into the church, he increases his use of biblical quotations. These chapters therefore illustrate how Paul uses Scripture. Compare the meaning he gives the quotations in 10:1–17 with what they mean in their original contexts.

2. Paul quotes Isaiah 28:16 in Romans 10:11 to refer to all those who believe in Jesus. What does Isaiah 28 mean in its own context? (The lying rulers of Jerusalem refuse to listen to Isaiah [28:14], so God will speak to them by means of the Assyrians [28:11].)

3. Compare Romans 10:15 with Isaiah 52:7, and Romans 10:16 with Isaiah 53:1. How has Paul modified the meaning of these passages to refer to his own ministry?

In 10:18 Paul quotes Psalm 19:4 in a similar way. Psalm 19:1–6 speaks of the witness of nature to God's glory: "The heavens are telling the glory of God" (19:1). Since such praise is not verbal, the psalmist continues: "There is no speech, nor are there words; their voice is not heard; yet their voice goes out through all the earth, and their words to the end of the world" (19:3–4). The magnificence of God's creation everywhere proclaims his power as Creator.

4. In Romans 10:18, what meaning does Paul give to Psalm 19:4?

5. Romans 10:19 quotes Deuteronomy 32:21. How does Paul's interpretation differ from the meaning of Deuteronomy 32:21 in its context?

6. How does Paul's use of Isaiah 65:1–2 in Romans 10:20–21 change its original meaning?

7. Summarize your observations of how Paul uses Scripture in Romans 10.

Paul believed that he lived in the last times (Rom. 13:12; 1 Cor. 7:29, 31; 1 Thess. 4:15–17), so he saw *all Scriptures* as applying to his time (1 Cor. 10:11). He used a form of Bible interpretation called **pesher**. This term comes from the Aramaic *pĕshar/pishra'*, meaning "interpretation" (= Hebrew *pasher/pesher* [Eccl. 8:1]). The word is employed, for example, in Daniel's explanations of the meanings of dreams (e.g., Dan. 5:15–17, 26; 7:16); and eschatological Jews used it with reference to events in their own time. Because they believed they were living in the time immediately preceding the ushering in of the age to come, they concluded that all Scripture was written for their time. All Scripture referred in a veiled way to their situation, so they needed divine help to understand its secret meaning, which was formerly hidden but is now revealed through one of God's special servants.

The Dead Sea Scrolls abound in this kind of biblical interpretation. The *Habakkuk Commentary* (1Q *Pesher Habakkuk*), for example, quotes Old Testament passages, then gives the interpretation (*peshar*) of how they refer to people or events of the author's own time. Because such scrolls are damaged due to their extreme age, translators decide by context which words are missing and supply them. These sections are set apart by brackets; the quoted text of Habakkuk is in italics.

[Oracle of Habakkuk the prophet. How long, O Lord, shall I cry] for help and Thou wilt not [hear]? [1:1–2]. [Interpreted, this concerns the beginning] of the [final] generation . . .

[For the wicked encompasses] the righteous [1:4a–b]. [The wicked is the Wicked Priest, and the righteous] is the Teacher of Righteousness . . .

[Behold the nations and see, marvel and be astonished; for I accomplish a deed in your days but you will not believe it when] told [1:5]. [Interpreted, this concerns] those who were unfaithful together with the Liar, in that they [did] not [listen to the word received by] the Teacher of Righteousness from the mouth of God. . . . And likewise, this saying is to be interpreted [as concerning those who] will be unfaithful at the end of days. They, the men of violence and the breakers of the Covenant, will not believe when they hear all that [is to happen to] the final generation. . . .

For behold, I rouse the Chaldeans, that [bitter and hasty] nation [1:6a]. Interpreted, this concerns the Kittim [who are] quick and valiant in war, causing many to perish. [All the world shall fall] under the dominion of the Kittim, and the [wicked . . .] they shall not believe in the laws of [God . . .].[10]

The *Pesher Habakkuk* thus illustrates how authors used *pesher* to explain that texts written centuries earlier actually refer to their own time. The name "Chaldeans"—the Babylonians, about whom Habakkuk wrote—becomes a veiled reference to the *Kittim*, a designation for the Romans. By using *pesher*, eschatological Jews found cryptic references to their own time throughout the Scriptures.

Early Christians also used *pesher*. In Acts 3:24, for example, Peter says, "And all the prophets, as many as have spoken, from Samuel and those after him, also predicted these days" (cf. Acts 2:16–36). Paul states in 1 Corinthians 10:11: "These things . . . were written down to instruct us, on whom the ends of the ages have come." Although Paul's citations of biblical passages differ in form from the line-by-line interpretations in the *Pesher Habakkuk*, his approach to Scripture is similar. We might say that early Christians read the Scriptures through Christ-colored glasses, seeing references to Jesus and the church throughout.[11]

Their interpretive method differs from the inductive approach taken in this textbook. So it is important to realize the difference. Paul's thinking, argumentation forms, and cultural assumptions reflect the norms of his historical setting, not ours. If this realization causes you to struggle a bit with your view of the Bible, know that you are experiencing what many do when they first study Paul in his ancient Mediterranean context. Be patient with your feelings and recognize that it takes time to sort through these issues.

What Will Happen to Israel before the End Time? (Rom. 11:1–36)

In Romans 10 Paul argues that most Jews failed to find righteousness through faith because they rejected the gospel. They are disobedient and rebellious (cf. 3:1–4). But has God rejected the Jewish people? Paul states emphatically in 11:1, "No!"

10. Translation by Geza Vermes, *The Complete Dead Sea Scrolls in English*, rev. ed. (New York: Penguin Books, 2004).

11. See Krister Stendahl, *The School of St. Matthew and Its Use of the Old Testament* (Philadelphia: Fortress Press, 1968).

1. Paul uses himself to illustrate that God has not abandoned the Jewish people (11:1–5). And in 11:11–14 he explains that Gentiles benefit from the fact that many Jews have rejected Jesus the Messiah. What does Paul say will happen when Jews in large numbers accept Jesus Messiah?

2. According to 11:25–32, what does Paul expect will happen in the future to the Jewish people as a whole? In light of 13:11–12, when did he expect this to happen?

3. In 11:28–32 Paul says that all people need God's mercy. How does 11:32 summarize his entire argument in Romans 9–11?

Paul ends Romans 9–11 with a doxology. After trying to explain God's purpose in history, his concluding praise reveals humility

regarding his own understanding: "How unsearchable are his judgments and how inscrutable his ways!" (11:33). In the preceding chapters he argued what he believes to be the reason behind what he sees happening in the world. But he realizes that he cannot comprehend God. Before the awesome majesty of the eternal God, praise and wonder are appropriate responses.

PRACTICAL ADVICE FOR HOW CHRISTIANS SHOULD LIVE (ROM. 12–16)

"Just Throw Yourself on the Altar" (Rom. 12:1–2)

With the doxology of 11:33–36, Paul completes the mission theology of his Letter, and in 12:1 he begins an exhortation section. Having finished his theological explanation, he now turns to the practical implications of his theology. Although he resists imposing the laws of Moses on Gentile converts, he does not hesitate to give guidelines for living, standards for Christian conduct. Ironically, many Christians turn his directions into a new law. Living responsibly in freedom can be difficult. Laws provide security: They do our thinking for us. They remove part of the complexity of living by faith.

In 12:2, when Paul says, "Do not be conformed to this world," he uses the term *syschēmatizō*, which means "to form, or mold." In the passive form it carries the meaning of "conform," and Phillips's paraphrase nicely captures the sense by translating the phrase, "Don't let the world around you squeeze you into its own mold."

How to Use Spiritual Gifts
(Rom. 12:3–8)

Paul turns his attention to harmonious living among Christians, providing practical examples of how renewal of the mind (12:2) influences everyday behavior. In practical terms he explains how Christians should assess their abilities and use their talents (12:3–8). They should neither be unduly critical of themselves nor unduly optimistic. Realistic assessment is in order. We need to give loving and honest appraisals—encouraging people in areas where they show promise, not where they are doomed to failure.

1. What advice does 12:3–8 give for discerning and developing one's own abilities?

2. In 12:4–8 God's gifts to individuals are for the sake of the group (cf. the longer version in 1 Cor. 12–14). What guidelines does Paul give for responsible use of spiritual gifts?

3. Compare the list of gifts in 12:6–8 with that given in 1 Corinthians 12:4–11. Are these passages meant to list all the spiritual gifts (exhaustive lists), or are they representative samples?

How to Live in Harmony in Society
(Rom. 12:9–21)

1. Paul provides a framework for exercising spiritual gifts in 12:9–13. In your own words, summarize from 12:1–21 his formula for harmonious living.

How to Get Along with Government
(Rom. 13:1–14)

1. Romans 12 gives guidelines for how to live harmoniously with other people. In your own words, summarize his strategy in 13:1–7 for living in harmony with government.

2. In 13:11–12 Paul states his belief that the end of the present age is near. What difference should this detail make in how one applies the content of this chapter to today's political conditions around the world?

49 CE) help to clarify his intended message to his readers in Romans 13?

Various governments down through history have used Romans 13 to claim divine approval for their oppressive rule (i.e., "We are in power because God has chosen us. Therefore to resist our rule is to resist God. If you resist, we have the divine authority to massacre you"). Terrible examples of genocide given legitimacy by Romans 13 continue to be in evidence even in the world today.

Establishing Paul's guidelines as laws to follow unthinkingly can result in abuses of power. To maintain balance in our thinking, we must consider other New Testament teachings on government. For example, in Revelation this same Roman government is considered satanic and thoroughly evil—an adversary whom God will destroy. We need to study the overall message of each author and contemplate why he says what he does, given the needs of his audience. Communication occurs in specific contexts, and we should not divorce the message from the setting if we wish to apply it responsibly today.

3. How does the historical setting of Paul's Letter to Rome (i.e., Claudius's expulsion edict of

[**Rom. 14–15** ⟶ See the questions above: "Pray That They Will Take the Money," "Resolving Conflicts in the Church," and "Making Sense of the Historical Situation."]

Women in Leadership Roles in the Church (Rom. 16)

Romans 15:33 ends Paul's comments on his journey to Jerusalem with a benediction: "The God of peace be with all of you. Amen." The letter seems to end at this point. Consequently, some scholars conclude that Romans 16 was not originally part of the letter. Increasingly, however, New Testament scholars believe that Paul included the lengthy list of greetings in chapter 16 as a means of increasing the credibility of his message. By establishing more personal contact through naming his friends now residing in Rome, he further establishes rapport with the church and increases the impact of his letter.

From 16:1–2 it appears that **Phoebe** carried Paul's Letter to the Romans. He calls her a deacon (Greek *diakonos*) of the church at Cenchreae (Corinth's eastern seaport) and holds her in high esteem. Remember that the letter carrier typically read the letter to the addressees and answered their questions pertaining to the letter's contents. Apparently, Phoebe read Paul's longest and most theologically developed letter to assembled Christians in Rome and answered questions about its meaning.

1. What other women does Paul mention in his greetings in Romans 16, and in what kinds of activities are they involved?

> **Women in the Church**
>
> In the Letters studied so far, what is Paul's attitude toward women in church leadership roles? How does it compare with your own beliefs about women in leadership? Why?

Your Bible probably has a footnote after the name Junia or Junias in 16:7, indicating that some ancient manuscripts use the name Julias. Translations of 16:7 vary according to how translators interpret the evidence. Textual critics readily dismiss "Julias" as a variant that resulted from a scribe misspelling IOYNIAN as IOYΛIAN. But more serious issues arise when deciding if the original reading indicated a man (Junias) or a woman (Junia). The feminine Junia was a common name for women, and there are many examples of its use. The proposed reading of the masculine Junias, however, poses significant problems. Although some surmise that it is a contraction of Junianus, they offer no textual evidence of Junias being used as a man's name in ancient literature.

If it were not for Paul's statement that these two people are "prominent among the apostles," translators and exegetes would most likely view them as a married

couple (see the similar reference to Prisca and Aquila in 16:3). Hesitation arises primarily because scholars in the past were reluctant to believe that Paul would call a woman an apostle. Yet even the great fourth-century teacher John Chrysostom says in his comments on v. 7:

> "Who are of note among the Apostles." And indeed to be apostles at all is a great thing. But to be even amongst these of note, just consider what a great encomium this is! But they were of note owing to their works, to their achievements. Oh! how great is the devotion of this woman, that she should be even counted worthy of the appellation of apostle! But even here he does not stop, but adds another encomium besides, and says, "Who were also in Christ before me." (*Homilies on the Epistle to the Romans* 31)[12]

Andronicus and Junia were Jewish—Paul calls them kinfolk (*syngeneis*) who were Christians and apostles before he was. Perhaps they were among those whom he

---

12. Translation from *A Select Library of the Nicene and Post-Nicene Fathers of the Christian Church*, 1st Series, ed. Philip Schaff, vol. 11 (Grand Rapids: Wm. B. Eerdmans Publishing Co., 1956), 555; also at http://www.newadvent.org/fathers/210231.htm.

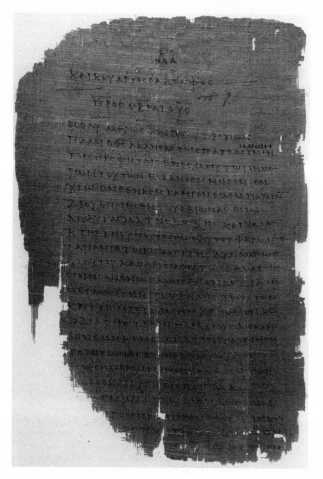

A page from Papyrus 46 containing the text of Romans 16:14–23. This ancient copy of Paul's letter dates to around 200 CE. You may see numerous pages of this important manuscript on the University of Michigan's Advanced Papyrological Information System Web site. (Courtesy of APIS, University of Michigan [Inventory #6238, processing # 3569, section 40])

says, in 1 Corinthians 15:6–8, saw the risen Christ before he did, Christians who held a special place in the church. For other references to people outside the Twelve who are called apostles, see Acts 14:14 (Barnabas and Paul); Galatians 1:19 (James, Jesus' brother); and 2 Corinthians 8:23 (unnamed Christian messengers).

2. How do the activities of women in Romans 16 compare with what you read in 1 Corinthians 11:2–16; 14:33b–36; 16:19; Galatians

3:26–29; and Philippians 4:2–3? (Remember that there is debate over whether or not 1 Cor. 14:33b–36 is original to the letter.)

SUMMARIZING ROMANS

Because Romans is Paul's longest and most theologically developed letter, we do well to reflect on the content of its various sections and note how they fit together: his assertion in Romans 1–3 that all are guilty and deserve God's wrath; his explanation in chapters 4–8 of the way God extends grace through Jesus Christ for the salvation of those who believe; his use of Scripture in Romans 9–11, where he grapples with the historical implications of God's selecting certain people; his practical advice in chapters 12–15 for how to live in loving relationship with others; and his extended set of greetings in Romans 16.

1. Summarize your view of why Paul wrote this letter to the Roman Christians.

2. Summarize what, according to Paul in Romans, actually happens when people place their faith in Jesus Christ.

3. Summarize Paul's understanding of how a Christian lives a life pleasing to God.

GLOSSARY

Abraham. Founding ancestor of the Hebrew people. Paul asserts that because Abraham believed God's promise, he became the ancestor of all those who are righteous by faith.

Antinomianism. A belief that one can live without law. *Nomos* in Greek means "law."

Justification. Christians have put forward three basic options for Paul's meaning of this term: (1) *pronounced righteous—* although people are sinners, God views them as righteous and treats them as if they were such; (2) *made righteous—*God gives a new nature to Christians and literally makes them into righteous men and women by a powerful work of grace; (3) *covenant relationship—*Christians have entered into a covenant relationship with God.

Pesher. The term comes from the Aramaic *pĕshar/pishra'*, meaning "interpretation" (= Hebrew *pasher/pesher* [Eccl. 8:1]). The word is employed, for example, in Daniel's explanations of the meanings of dreams (Dan. 5:15–17, 26; 7:16; etc.). Eschatological Jews used it as a technical term referring to the interpretation of ancient texts with reference to events happening in their own time. Because they believed they were living in the time immediately preceding the ushering in of the age to come, they concluded that all Scripture was written for their time. They thought that in a veiled way all Scripture referred to their situation, so they needed divine help to understand its secret meaning, which was formerly hidden but now is revealed to one of God's special servants.

Phoebe. The deaconess of the church at Cenchreae who carried Paul's Letter to the Romans, his longest and most theologically developed letter.

Redemption. Word often used in the context of slavery. Slave owners commonly allowed slaves to receive their freedom if someone paid a price, a **ransom**, to compensate the owner for the value of the slave. This fee could be paid by a third party, or some slaves were allowed to save money until they were able to pay the amount themselves. When slaves received their freedom, they were **redeemed** from bondage. Paul speaks of Christ's death on the cross as the ransom price paid to redeem sinners from their slavery to sin.

Righteousness. Condition of acting justly, rightly, with good behavior and with integrity. The Greek noun form for righteousness is *dikaiosynē*, and the verb form for "justify" is *dikaioō*. Because in English we have no cognate verb form for righteousness, we say that they are *justified*.

Suetonius. Roman historian who wrote of Claudius expelling Jews from Rome following riots in the Jewish sectors.

Symposion. Greek word for "drinking party" where males gathered socially to drink wine. Plato's dialogue *Symposium* (Latin form of the term) recounts speeches given at a drinking party.

FURTHER READING ON ROMANS

Achtemeier, Paul J. *Romans*. Interpretation. Atlanta: John Knox Press, 1985. Responsibly applies the biblical text to modern situations.

Barrett, C. K. *A Commentary on the Epistle to the Romans*. New York: Harper & Row, 1957. Somewhat technical, but fairly readable.

Barth, Karl. *The Epistle to the Romans*. Translated by Edwin C. Hoskins. London: Oxford University Press, 1950. More of a manifesto on Barth's theology than a commentary on the biblical text. Important work in the history of interpretation.

Bruce, F. F. *The Epistle of Paul to the Romans*. Grand Rapids: Wm. B. Eerdmans Publishing Co., 1963. Clear and informative.

Bryan, Christopher. *Preface to Romans: Notes on the Epistle in Its Literary and Cultural Setting*. Oxford: Oxford University Press, 2000. Deals with the literary genre of Romans, comparing it with other literature of the time.

Bryne, Brendan. *Romans*. Sacra Pagina 6. Collegeville, MN: Liturgical Press, 1996. Explains Romans as a document on Christian spirituality. Good example of how an ecumenically minded Catholic scholar treats Romans (a significant document in the Protestant Reformation).

Calvin, John. *Commentaries on the Epistle of Paul to Romans*. Translated by John Owen. Grand Rapids: Wm. B. Eerdmans Publishing Co., 1947. ET of the work of a Protestant Reformation leader (lived 1509–64). Gives insight into sixteenth-century interpretation.

Cranfield, C. E. B. *A Critical and Exegetical Commentary on the Epistle to the Romans*. 2 vols. Edinburgh: T&T Clark, 1975–79. Detailed, scholarly, and technical. Good for research.

Donfried, Karl P., ed. *The Romans Debate*. Rev. ed. Peabody, MA: Hendrickson Publishers, 2005. Collection of essays shows different approaches to interpreting Romans.

Dunn, James D. G. *Romans 1–8* and *Romans 9–16*. Word Biblical Commentary 38A–38B. Dallas: Word Books, 1988. Thorough. Dry. Good for research.

Edwards, James R. *Romans*. NIBCNT 6. Peabody, MA: Hendrickson Publishers, 1992. Examines literary and historical context. Accessible.

Fitzmyer, Joseph A. *Romans*. AB 33. New York: Doubleday, 1993. Lengthy introduction; massive bibliography. Good for research (832 pages). Catholic scholar who challenges Protestant readings of Romans.

Jewett, Robert. *Romans: A Commentary*. Hermeneia. Minneapolis: Fortress Press, 2006. Detailed analysis (1,000 pages). Focuses on role of Paul's planned missionary trip to Spain in the composition of the Letter. Much on honor/shame as a motiva-tion for Paul's words. Refers to God as the Father of Jesus Christ, but uses feminine pronouns when referring to God.

*Johnson, Luke Timothy. *Reading Romans: A Literary and Theological Commentary*. New York: Crossroad, 1997. Brief. Focuses on literary characteristics of Romans.

Käsemann, Ernst. *Commentary on Romans*. Translated by G. W. Bromiley. Grand Rapids: Wm. B. Eerdmans Publishing Co., 1980. Significant commentary in the history of interpretation of Romans.

Luther, Martin. *Lectures on Romans*. Translated by Wilhelm Pauck. Philadelphia: Westminster Press, 1969. Important in the history of interpretation—written about 1515 long before modern scholarship.

Moo, Douglas J. *The Epistle to the Romans*. NICNT. Grand Rapids: Wm. B. Eerdmans Publishing Co., 1996. Exhaustive (1,012 pages) but clearly written.

_____. *Romans*. NIV Application Commentary. Grand Rapids: Zondervan, 2000. Half the length of his longer NICNT work (544 pages). Explores the contemporary relevance of Romans.

Sanday, W., and A. C. Headlam. *The Commentary on Romans*. ICC. New York: Scribner's Sons, 1897. Important work of the late nineteenth century. Represents the effort to explain Romans by amassing related texts from the ancient Mediterranean world.

Schreiner, Thomas R. *Romans*. Baker Exegetical Commentary on the New Testament 6. Grand Rapids: Baker Academic, 1998. Lengthy (944 pages).

Well organized. Good for research. Focus on Reformed theology.

*Talbert, Charles H. *Romans*. Smyth & Helwys Bible Commentaries. Macon, GA: Smyth & Helwys, 2002. Intermediate length (360 pages). Readable. More engaging format plus CD-ROMs with photographs.

Toews, John E. *Romans*. Believers Church Bible Commentary. Scottdale, PA: Herald Press, 2004. Interacts with contemporary scholarship from a Mennonite perspective. Well written.

*Witherington, Ben, III, with Darlene Hyatt. *Paul's Letter to the Romans: A Socio-Rhetorical Commentary*. Grand Rapids: Wm. B. Eerdmans Publishing Co., 2004. Readable. Interacts with the rhetorical structure of Romans and the cultural setting of the Epistle. Criticizes Reformation scholars for relying on Augustine's approach to Romans (as mediated through Luther, Calvin, and others).

*Wright, N. T. *Paul for Everyone: Romans*. Louisville, KY: Westminster John Knox Press, 2004. Accessible and brief (only 161 pages). Good for gaining an overall view of Romans.

CHAPTER 14

Colossians

SYNCRETISM THREATENS THE CHURCH

Like Romans, Colossians mostly addresses people who are not Paul's converts. Unlike Romans, Colossians corrects a syncretistic belief system promoted by people who combined teachings from various religions. Be prepared for detective work as you reconstruct their beliefs, and be aware of how Colossians uses imagery that differs substantially from what we have read in Paul's Letters so far. Also get ready to examine Christian family structure—as well as consider whether or not this letter is genuinely Pauline.

THE SCENE OF THE CRIME

In Paul's day **Colossae**, Laodicea, and Hierapolis were the three major cities of the Lycus River valley in Asia Minor, and

he mentions all three in Colossians 4:13. In the fifth century BCE, Colossae was an important city, but it had declined by Paul's day. The Greek historian Herodotus (484–430 BCE) briefly describes it in an account of a Persian king's battles in this region:

> Xerxes . . . pressed forward upon his march; and passing Anaua, a Phrygian city, and a lake from which salt is gathered, he came to Colossae, a Phrygian city of great size, situated at a spot where the river Lycus plunges into a chasm and disappears. This river, after running underground a distance of about five furlongs (two-thirds of a mile), reappears once more, and empties itself, like the stream above mentioned, into the Maeander. [Apparently this is a legendary description of the river flowing underground to the Maeander River, which Herodotus recorded on the basis of hearsay.] (*Histories* 7.30)[1]

1. Quotation taken from the Internet Classics Archive, an MIT program, at http://classics.mit.edu/

237

The site of ancient Colossae has yet to be excavated. The mound at the site indicates the presence of a large city, but the top of the mound is a farmer's field, strewn with thousands of pieces of Iron Age pottery. We can only guess at what treasures lie buried below the surface. (Courtesy of Michael Cosby)

Similarly, Xenophon (431–349 BCE) calls Colossae a large and prosperous city (*Anabasis* 1.2.6). The geographer Strabo (64 BCE–23 CE), however, writing in the early days of the first century, calls it a town (*polisma*), whereas he calls Laodicea one of the two largest cities in Phrygia (*Geography* 12.8.13). Colossae apparently diminished since the fourth century BCE, gradually being eclipsed by the nearby cities of Laodicea and Hierapolis. When Paul dictated his letter to the Colossian Christians, the local residents of this town were primarily Phrygians and Greek settlers; but there was also a population of Jewish settlers. Colossae was located on a significant east-west trade route that went to Ephesus, which at that time was a seaport.

WHAT WERE THE CIRCUMSTANCES? (COL. 4:7–18)

As with most of Paul's Letters, the final greetings reveal much about his location and who was with him at the time of writing. According to 4:3, 18, Paul was in prison when he dictated Colossians.

Compare the people mentioned in 4:7–17 with those specified in Philemon: Onesimus (Col. 4:9; cf. Phlm. 10); Aristarchus, Mark, Luke, and Demas (Col. 4:10, 14; cf. Phlm. 23–24); and Archippus (Col. 4:17; cf. Phlm. 2).

Herodotus/history.7.vii.html. Various translations of *Histories* are available in libraries, such as *The History of Herodotus,* book 7, trans. George Rawlinson (New York: Tudor Publishing, 1928).

1. What does the overlap of people specified in Colossians 4 and Philemon indicate about the possible connection between these two letters?

2. Notice that Tychicus, the letter carrier (4:7), is also the letter carrier for Ephesians (Eph. 6:21). What might this detail indicate about the possible identity of the letter to the Laodiceans mentioned in Colossians 4:15–16?

OPENING THE CASE (COL. 1:1–14)

In the Greek text, the thanksgiving section in 1:3–8 is one long, complicated sentence; when translating the passage into more readable English, scholars divide it into shorter thought units. Throughout Colossians there is a tendency to use longer and more complex sentence structure than that found in previous Pauline Letters we have studied—even in the fairly formal prose of Romans. Some New Testament scholars believe that Paul used a scribe other than Tertius (Rom. 16:22), and this man had a more complicated writing style. Others believe that, because of this greater complexity and some theological points that we will consider shortly, an unknown disciple of Paul wrote Colossians after the death of the apostle in order to deal with aberrant beliefs in his own time. As good detectives, we will examine the clues that lead to both conclusions. But as fair investigators we will begin our analysis under the assumption of Pauline authorship, because that is what the Letter claims. We will modify this premise only if the clues lead us in that direction.

1. What does 1:1–14 indicate about Paul's attitude toward the Christians at Colossae?

2. Who is Epaphras (1:7–8), and what has he done for the Colossians (see also 4:12–13)?

3. According to 1:4, 9; 2:1, Paul has not yet been to Colossae. How does he know about the Christians there?

INVESTIGATING CHRISTOLOGICAL CLUES (COL. 1:15–29)

In 2:8–23 we will investigate clues that enable us to reconstruct the syncretistic beliefs that were plaguing the churches of the Lycus River valley. What Paul says about Christ in 1:9–20, however, also forms part of his attempt to steer Christians away from what he considered to be an aberrant theology that reduced the significance of Christ.

As you study this section, note the following. Colossians 1:9–11 develops the theme of growing in the knowledge of God and bearing fruit, which he introduced in 1:6. To lead lives worthy of the Lord (1:10), they need to know who God is and what God wants. True Christians are "saints in the light" (1:12), who have been delivered from the "power of darkness" (1:13). The kingdom of God is light, while the kingdom of the world is darkness. Paul's teaching about Jesus combats a darkened understanding of the Savior.

1. Colossians 1:15–18 might be quoting a hymn in praise of Christ that was sung by early Christians. What does this passage emphasize about Christ?

Music played an important educational role in the early church. Song lyrics are easy to memorize and provide an important teaching technique in oral cultures where most people are illiterate. What kind of modern musical form do you think would best convey the meaning expressed in 1:15–20? Why?

Possible Composition Project: If you are a musician, you might find it rewarding to set these verses to music. You could use the words as they are in your Bible, or you could compose your own poetic rendition of the verses. What mood will you try to create through your choice of music and words?

2. What does 1:19–23 stress about Christ? Note carefully the strongly physical references to Christ's work in 1:20 ("the blood of his cross") and 1:22 ("in his fleshly body through death"). It will be important when reading Colossians 2.

5. What is the previously hidden "mystery" that Paul proclaims (1:25–2:3)?

Paul wants the Colossian Christians to know that Christ is the source of knowledge to whom one must look (2:2–3). Some persuasive people are trying to lead them astray (2:4); to thwart this, Paul focuses on the greatness of Christ. He wants them to remain in the authentic Christian faith, which they received from Epaphras (2:6–7).

3. According to 1:12–14, 20–23, what has happened to those who have placed their faith in Christ?

RECONSTRUCTING THE CRIME (COL. 2:1–23)

From the criticism delivered in 2:8–23, try to figure out the beliefs of the heretics.

1. What does he say is the basis for the false beliefs?

4. What does 1:24–29 indicate about Paul's attitude toward the sufferings he endures because of his missionary work? What is the goal of his work?

2. What do the false teachers say about Jewish regulations?

3. What do they say about angels?

4. What do they believe about asceticism?

5. What does Paul assert about Christ and Christian experience in 2:8–23 to counteract the false beliefs? Note how his teaching compares with what he said in 1:15–23.

GNOSTICISM

The Colossian **syncretism** contains some of the component parts of a belief system called **Gnosticism**, which fully developed after Paul's time. During the second century so many Christians adopted gnostic ideas that Gnosticism almost became dominant in the church. During Paul's time, however, there were earlier forms of Gnosticism, and the view promoted at Colossae seems to have been one of these. We may call it **proto-Gnosticism** or incipient Gnosticism, and understanding later gnostic beliefs can be helpful when reading Colossians. But we must be careful not to think that Colossians addresses the later, more developed beliefs of Gnosticism.

The title Gnosticism comes from the Greek *gnōsis*, which means knowledge. For centuries gnostic beliefs were known primarily from attacks written against them by more mainstream Christians. For example, when Irenaeus wrote his massive *Against All Heresies* (about 180 CE), he quoted many gnostic authors in his efforts to refute them. Scholars wondered, however, how accurately Irenaeus described his adversaries' beliefs. Fortunately, an accidental discovery made near Nag Hammadi, Egypt, in 1945 largely vindicated Irenaeus by allowing us to see religious texts written by gnostics. An Arab peasant, digging for fertilizer around a boulder, discovered a large, red, earthenware jar in which gnostics had placed their scrolls for safekeeping. The hot, dry climate of Egypt preserved these texts from rotting for sixteen hundred years while they lay buried in the sand.

The Arab peasant thought that he might find a genie or treasure in the jar, but instead he found books dating back to about 380 CE. He had no idea of the value of these ancient books, and it took years before scholars became aware of their existence and acquired them for analysis. Gnostic monks from the nearby monastery of Pachomius probably buried the manuscripts to hide them from orthodox Christians, who during that time were eliminating what they viewed as aberrant works. The texts are Coptic translations of Greek texts (Coptic is the Egyptian language written with Greek letters). English translations of them may be read in *The Nag Hammadi Library*, edited by James M. Robinson.

The Nag Hammadi texts show that gnostics emphasized knowing by experience, not by rational processes. They considered human logic to be part of the dark, evil, physical world. They focused on what they believed to be divine revelation and expressed no interest in historical realities. They also had a tendency to turn belief systems upside down.

Gnostic Christians thought that Yahweh, the god of the Old Testament, came into being as a mistake. They believed that in the beginning there was only a spiritual realm called the **Pleroma,** inhabited by spirit beings (*plērōma* is the Greek word for "fullness"). Everything was full and complete until a female spirit named **Sophia** (Greek word for "wisdom") started thinking for herself, without the consent of her male consort. Her unsanctioned thought took solid form, and the terrible result was a lion-headed serpent named *Yaltabaoth*, the gnostic name for the Old Testament god who created the physical world. This malformed being unfortunately contained a spark of the divine Pleroma, which emanated from Sophia.

Sophia, chagrined by her misdeed, sought to hide her mistaken creation by covering him with a cloud. Yaltabaoth did not know his origin and was therefore not aware of the Pleroma, so he assumed that he was god (gnostics believed that the Old Testament writers unknowingly perpetuated this ignorance). He set about creating the physical universe, which was all a terrible mistake and should never have happened. Among his creations were misshapen creatures who comprised a collection of angels and helped him with creating things.

Meanwhile, back in the Pleroma, the other divine spirits discovered that something was amiss: there was a deficiency now instead of fullness. Sophia admitted her mistake, and they all set about to concoct a plan to capture the spark of the divine in Yaltabaoth and send it back to the Pleroma. They beamed an image of the divine man down through the clouds so that Yaltabaoth and his angels saw the image reflected in some water. Yaltabaoth decided it was a neat-looking creature and set about to make one like it. He delegated the project to 365 angels, and each had responsibility to produce one part of the man. After this committee effort, Adam lay lifeless in the dirt. Then came a whisper from above: "Blow into his nostrils the breath of life" (cf. Gen. 2:7).

Yaltabaoth, unaware of the existence of the Pleroma, thought this was a good idea and did so. But when he breathed life into the lifeless creature, his divine spark went into the man, who then became luminous. Thus Yaltabaoth lost his spark, and he was not happy about it. So he created a woman and invented sex as a means of dispersing the spark. This new development complicated things for members of the Pleroma, who had to figure out how to retrieve their spark and restore fullness to the divine realm.

So Christ came from the Pleroma to earth somewhat like a hologram. He did not take on physical form, for that would be completely outrageous for a spirit being. He merely appeared to have physical form so that he could trick Yaltabaoth and preach to human beings "the remembrance of the Pleroma." Christ directed his preaching to the sparks that were encased in humans and had long since forgotten their origin. As Christ preached, however, the sparks remembered the Pleroma and desired to know how to return. Christ explained how to accomplish this journey: after the person dies, the spark within can ascend through the levels of heaven by chanting certain things to trick the angelic gatekeepers into letting them go past so that they can return to the Pleroma.

Thus, salvation comes through the *knowledge* brought by Christ, not by his sacrificial death on the cross (gnostics rejected the belief that Christ was physical and could suffer and die). And ultimate salvation occurs when all the sparks return to the Pleroma, which will once again be complete. Then the physical universe and Yaltabaoth and his angels will all be destroyed. The king-dom of darkness (physical existence) will cease to exist, and there will only be the kingdom of light (the spiritual realm).

Thus, gnostics had no expectation of personal afterlife for humans: sparks would be absorbed into the Pleroma and have no individual identity. Gnostics considered the body to be a shell or crude husk in which the pearl, the spark, resides. Consequently, they sought to be rid of the influence of the body through extremes of either asceticism or libertinism. These tendencies are clearly visible in Colossians 2:8–23.

Apparently the New Testament Letter to the Colossians gives different meaning to some of the protognostic terms used by the false teachers at Colossae. To refute their beliefs, Paul commandeers their language for his own use. For example, 1:12–13 speaks of being rescued from the kingdom or realm of darkness and transferred to the kingdom or realm of light, but the meaning given to these phrases differs considerably

Considering Aspects of Colossian Syncretism

1. Imagine gates through each level of heaven. What might the false teachers say about what happened to Jesus when he descended to earth?

2. What might they believe about how prayers reach God and answers to prayer come back to people? (How would their view be reflected in their beliefs about angels and asceticism?)

from the gnostic view of the dark, physical world that stands in stark contrast to the realm of light in the Pleroma. Colossians 1:15–20 stresses that Christ is the image of the invisible God, and he reconciled people to God by his physical death on the cross; and 2:9 states that the fullness of deity dwells in Christ bodily (cf. 1:19). How far toward Gnosticism some of the people at Colossae had progressed is difficult to determine. And although the comments in 2:8–23 reveal differences between what was brewing in Colossae and what characterized later gnostic beliefs, Paul's criticisms indicate that their ascetic tendencies and mixing of Judaism and Greek philosophy were headed in that direction.

REASSEMBLING THE PIECES
(COL. 3:1–17)

Paul's teaching that Christians have died with Christ (2:20) and have been raised with Christ (3:1) is reminiscent of Romans 6:3–10. Although Paul rejects the effectiveness of asceticism ("Do not taste, Do not touch" [2:21]) as a means of promoting a holy lifestyle (2:20–23), he does insist on a new lifestyle that reflects the new existence enjoyed by Christians.

1. In 3:1–11, what images are used to describe the Christian's new identity in Christ?

2. In light of these images, what positive steps does Paul command Christians to take to live consistently with their new existence?

3. What characterizes the "new self" that Paul tells these Christians to "put on" in 3:10–13?

In Paul's clothing analogy, love functions like an outer garment, binding together the virtues previously listed (3:14). Then, changing the analogy, he advises them to let the peace of Christ rule in their hearts. The word he uses for "rule" in 3:15 is *brabeuō*, a Greek term often used for the decision of an umpire. Paul probably means that Christ's peace should settle disputes among Christians. In 3:16–17 Paul stresses maintaining a positive attitude. The words of Christ and spiritual music are important components of a Christian's life. Even while in prison, Paul emphasizes the need for praise and gratitude. Setting one's mind on things that are above (3:2) plays an important role in Christian discipleship. What people devote their time to thinking about significantly affects the ways in which they behave. Focusing on positive virtues produces virtue. Focusing on sinful activities results in sinful behaviors. Renewal of the mind comes through actively devoting one's attention to noble aspirations.

INVESTIGATING FAMILY STRUCTURES (COL. 3:18–4:1)

Understanding the structure of families as described by other ancient Mediterranean authors provides valuable background information for Paul's commands to family members in 3:18–4:1. **Household codes** (often designated by the German word *Haustafeln*) specifying proper behavior are not unusual in ancient literature. Note carefully in the texts below the hierarchy not only among slaves and their owners but also within the biological families. Be able to compare these codes with what Paul says in Colossians.

> Now that it is clear what are the component parts of the state, we have first of all to discuss the household management; for every state is composed of households. Household management falls into departments corresponding to the parts of which the household in its turn is composed; and the household in its perfect form consists of slaves and freemen. (Aristotle, *Politics* 1.1253b [Rackham, LCL])

> Hence there are by nature various classes of rulers and ruled. For the free rules the slave, the male the female, and the man the child in a different way. And all possess the various parts of the soul, but possess them in different ways; for the slave has not got the deliberative part at all, and the female has it, but without full authority, while the child has it, but in an undeveloped form. (*Politics* 1.1260a 9–14 [Rackham, LCL])

> One may find likenesses and so to speak models of these various forms of a constitution in the household. The relationship of a father to sons is regal in type, since a father's first care is for his children's welfare. . . . The relationship of husband to wife seems to be in the nature of an aristocracy: the husband rules in virtue of fairness, and in matters that belong to a man's sphere; matters suited to a woman he hands over to his wife. When a husband controls everything, he transforms the relationship into an oligarchy, for he governs in violation of fitness, and not in virtue of superiority. And sometimes when a woman is an heiress it is she who rules. In these cases then authority goes not by virtue but by wealth and power, as in an oligarchy. . . . Democracy appears most fully in households without a master, for in them all the members are equal; but it also prevails where the ruler of the house is weak, and everyone is allowed to do what he likes. (Aristotle, *Nicomachean Ethics* 8.1160b.23–1161a.10 [Rackham, LCL])

> There is a primary constitution in the union of a man and a woman according to law for the begetting of children and for community of life. This is called a house, which is the beginning of a city. . . . The man has the rule of this house by nature. For the deliberative faculty in a woman is inferior, in children it does not yet exist, and it is completely foreign to slaves. Rational household management, which is the controlling of a house and of those things related to the house, is fitted for a man. (Arius Didymus, *Epitome of Stoic Ethics*, via. Stobaeus, [*Moral Extracts*] 2.148.5–9; 2.149.5–9)[2]

> The women are best suited to the indoor life which never strays from the house, within which the middle door is taken by the maidens as their boundary, and the outer door by those who have reached full womanhood. (Philo, *Special Laws* 3.169 [Colson and Whitaker, LCL])

> Wives must be in servitude to their husbands, a servitude not imposed by violent ill-treatment but promoting obedience in all things. Parents must have power over their children. (Philo, *Apology* 7.3 [Colson and Whitaker, LCL])

> The woman, says the law, is in all things inferior to the man. Let her accordingly be submissive, not for her humiliation, but that she may be directed, for the authority has been given by

2. From *Anthologium*, ed. C. Wachsmuth and O. Hense (Berlin: Weidmann, 1958).

God to the man. (Josephus, *Against Apion* 2.199 [Thackeray, LCL])[3]

1. What do these ancient authors presuppose about the nature of men, women, and children?

What do they conclude about proper lines of authority in the home?

2. How does the view of family structure in Colossians 3:18–4:1 compare with the one presented in the quotations of other ancient Mediterranean authors?

3. From 3:18–4:1, what are the responsibilities of husbands and fathers?

wives and mothers?

children?

slaves?

slave owners?

3. These are but a few selections from a large number of passages that one may examine in ancient literature. For a fine investigation of such material, see David L. Balch, *Let Wives Be Submissive: The Domestic Code in 1 Peter*, Society of Biblical Literature Monograph Series 26 (Atlanta: Scholars Press, 1981).

DID PAUL WRITE COLOSSIANS?

As mentioned above, New Testament scholars debate the authorship of Colossians. Some call Colossians a **deuteropauline** Epistle and claim that after Paul's death a disciple of his wrote Colossians in his name as a way of gaining authority for his refutation of local false beliefs. The first reason for this judgment is linguistic in nature: the more complex sentence structure that characterizes the letter. For example, 1:9–20 is one incredibly long and complicated sentence. So is 1:3–8. Compared with the rather terse sentences in the letters we have read so far, Colossians seems encumbered with dependent clauses, participial constructions, and frequent use of synonyms (e.g., "praying and asking" [1:9], "holy and blameless and irreproachable" [1:22]). Obviously, those who cannot read Greek are at a disadvantage in trying to evaluate these clues.

Other reasons for doubting Pauline authorship focus on theological considerations. In 2:12 and 3:1, the author indicates that Christians have not only died with Christ in baptism, he insists that they have also been resurrected with Christ to the heavenly places. Some see this as standing in tension with Romans 6:1–11, where Paul teaches that Christians have died with Christ, yet he indicates that they will be raised with him in the future ("We will certainly be united with him in a resurrection like his" [Rom. 6:5]). Resurrection will occur at the end of time, at the last judgment. In 1 Corinthians, furthermore, Paul vigorously argues against the belief of the *pneumatikoi* that they have already experienced a spiritual resurrection and are therefore above physical concerns such as ethics and morality. Because Colossians teaches that Christians have already been raised with him (2:11–12; 3:1–4), a number of scholars assert that this belief is the very thing Paul argues against in 1 Corinthians.

Another detail that is used to argue for deuteropauline authorship is the more settled view of Christians in society, as indicated by the author's appeal to the household code in 3:18–4:1. Would Paul, who expected the Parousia to happen in the near future (as we saw in his earlier Letters), emphasize the social structure of families?

Ancient Mediterranean Culture and Modern Christian Families

How do you believe the household code in 3:18–4:1 should be applied to family structures and responsibilities in today's society? Why?

Finally, some wonder if Paul would so calmly describe the false teachers' insistence that Gentiles be circumcised (Col. 2:8–19). If Paul wrote Colossians, why wouldn't he express the same outrage over this issue that he did in Galatians? These scholars believe that the author of Colossians seems to view Jewish insistence on the law as rather irrelevant—no longer a real threat, and thus post Pauline.

On the other side of the debate, those who argue that Colossians is genuinely Pauline often include the following clues and explanations:

1. The forms used for the greeting in 1:1–2 and the thanksgiving in 1:3–9 are typical of Paul's Letters.
2. The basic sequence of component parts (i.e., the construction) of Colossians, including the final greeting section, compares nicely with the other Pauline Letters.
3. Colossians contains basic Pauline theological themes (e.g., Jesus' atoning death, Christian experience of suffering and participation with Jesus' death through baptism).
4. Colossians contains Greek vocabulary and constructions found elsewhere only in Paul's Letters. It makes more sense to think that Paul deviated somewhat from his normal style of prose when dictating this letter than it does to say that someone else partially mimicked the apostle's style.
5. The more elevated style typically is found in parts of Colossians where sublime language is used to present exalted theological concepts. Some scholars believe that parts of Colossians consist of Christian liturgical statements, which Paul adapted and used for increased effect.
6. The more exalted prose of Colossians is a wise choice for Paul to use when refuting the beliefs about Christ and the nature of salvation promoted by the syncretistic views at Colossae. Different situations cause Paul to address himself in different ways to take care of specific problems, so it is not surprising that he employs different language and concepts to refute this particular belief system.
7. The lack of intense outrage in 2:8–23, where elements of following Mosaic laws are described as being part of the Colossian syncretism, is not a problem. Paul's outrage over this issue in Galatians goes far beyond what he expresses in Romans and Philippians when addressing the same subject. He was particularly volatile when he wrote Galatians.
8. Although the use of a household code in 3:18–4:1 shows that Paul is concerned with healthy family interaction, it does not indicate that he has given up on his belief in the near return of Jesus. After all, he urges political and social considerations in Romans 12–13; in 1 Corinthians 7 he gives instructions on marriage, divorce, betrothal, remarriage, and slavery; in 1 Corinthians 8–10 he gives directions on eating certain foods and avoiding temple parties; in 1 Corinthians 6:1–8 he

warns against frivolous lawsuits; and in 1 Thessalonians 4:1–8 he gives directions about proper marriages. He was concerned about living properly within society.

CRACKING THE CASE

Consider the arguments against and for Pauline authorship of Colossians. As you look at the details, who do you think has the best argument? Look back over Colossians in light of the clues provided by both sides. Then explain whether you believe that (A) Paul used a different scribe when dictating this letter and addressed a different situation than he dealt with in his previous letters; or (B) a disciple of Paul wrote in the apostle's name in order to get rid of bothersome protognostic beliefs that arose after Paul's death. Provide the clues that you find to be most compelling.

Searching for clues in Colossians further develops the detective skills necessary for analyzing Pauline Letters. At this point in our work, we are not only seeking evidence for where, when, and why Paul wrote particular epistles; we are also delving deeper into matters pertaining to authorship.

How do we determine whether or not Paul wrote a letter? And what are the implications if we decide that he did not? Though this issue briefly surfaced when we studied 2 Thessalonians, from now on it will assume greater significance because of the increasing number of questions about style and content that analysis of the remaining Epistles raises. Previous detectives (NT scholars), after examining the clues, have reached divergent theories about the authorship and significance of Ephesians, 1–2 Timothy, and Titus. Where will the evidence lead us?

GLOSSARY

Colossae. One of three major cities of the Lycus River valley in Asia Minor. In the fifth century BCE, Colossae was a very important city, but it had declined somewhat by Paul's day.

Cosmos. Greek word for the world or universe.

Deuteropauline. Designation for letters that scholars believe were written after Paul's death by his disciples. "Deutero" means "second"—a second Paul (i.e., someone writing in his name). Most New Testament scholars consider 1–2 Timothy and Titus to be deuteropauline, and many also believe that 2 Thessalonians and Ephesians and probably Colossians are as well.

Gnosticism. The name "Gnosticism" comes from the Greek *gnōsis*, which means knowledge. It was a syncretistic religion that developed more fully after Paul's time. Knowledge of gnostic beliefs was increased by the accidental discovery of ancient gnostic manuscripts near Nag Hammadi, Egypt, in 1945. The Nag Hammadi texts show that gnostics emphasized knowing by experience, not by rational processes. They focused on what they believed to be divine revelation and expressed no interest in historical realities.

Household codes. Summary statements of the responsibilities of household members, including husbands/fathers, wives/mothers, children, and slaves. Biblical scholars often designate these passages by using the German word *Haustafeln.*

Pleroma. *Plērōma* is the Greek word for fullness. Gnostics believed that in the beginning there was only a spiritual realm called the Pleroma, which was inhabited by spirit beings. Everything was full and complete until a female spirit named **Sophia** (Greek word for wisdom) started thinking for herself, without the consent of her male consort. Her unsanctioned thought took solid form, and the terrible result was a lion-headed serpent named *Yaltabaoth*, the gnostic name for the Old Testament god who created the physical world.

Proto-Gnosticism (or incipient Gnosticism). An early form in the development of Gnosticism, such as the one promoted by some teachers in Colossae.

Sophia. *See* Pleroma.

Syncretism. Effort to combine elements of various religious beliefs. Many people in Paul's day were syncretistic, taking beliefs from a variety of sources and putting them together into bizarre thought systems (e.g.,

the ascetic heresy refuted by Colossians, which combined elements of Greek philosophy, Judaism, and Christianity).

Yaltabaoth. See Pleroma.

FURTHER READING ON COLOSSIANS

Barth, Markus, and Helmut Blanke. *Colossians.* AB 34B. New York: Doubleday, 1994. Scholarly (584 pages). Argues for Pauline authorship. Examines influences of mystery religions, Hellenistic philosophy, Gnosticism, and so forth. Lengthy bibliography.

Dunn, James D. G. *The Epistles to the Colossians and to Philemon: A Commentary on the Greek Text.* NIGTC. Grand Rapids: Wm. B. Eerdmans Publishing Co., 1996. Scholarly (388 pages). Unusual view that Timothy, Paul's traveling companion, wrote these two letters.

Garland, David E. *Colossians and Philemon.* NIV Application Commentary. Grand Rapids: Zondervan, 1998. Serious attempt to apply these Letters to contemporary life (402 pages).

Hay, David M. *Colossians.* Abingdon New Testament Commentaries. Nashville: Abingdon Press, 2000. Acessible to general readership.

MacDonald, Margaret Y. *Colossians and Ephesians.* Sacra Pagina 17. Collegeville, MN: Liturgical Press, 2000. Argues that Colossians and Ephesians are both deuteropauline. Concentrates on these texts as reflecting the social world of the first century.

Martin, Ernest D. *Colossians, Philemon.* Believers Church Bible Commentary. Scottdale, PA: Herald Press, 1993. Emphasizes the modern, social implications of faith.

Martin, Ralph P. *Ephesians, Colossians, and Philemon.* Interpretation. Atlanta: John Knox Press, 1991. Emphasizes the value of the biblical text for preaching.

O'Brien, Peter T. *Colossians, Philemon.* Word Biblical Commentary 44. Waco, TX: Word, 1982. Thorough (592 pages). Good for research.

Patzia, Arthur G. *Ephesians, Colossians, Philemon.* NIBCNT 10. Peabody, MA: Hendrickson Publishers, 1990. Scholarly yet readable.

Thompson, Marianne Meye. *Colossians and Philemon.* Grand Rapids: Wm. B. Eerdmans Publishing Co., 2005. Focuses on the theology of Colossians. Argues that Paul wrote it or authorized it to be written.

Thurston, Bonnie Bowman. *Reading Colossians, Ephesians, and 2 Thessalonians: A Literary and Theological Commentary.* Reading the New Testament Series. New York: Crossroad, 1995. Nontechnical commentary.

*Wall, Robert W. *Colossians and Philemon.* IVP New Testament Commentary Series. Downers Grove, IL: InterVarsity Press, 1993. Both scholarly analysis and pastoral application of Colossians. Draws contemporary application based on a historical reading.

Wilson, R. McL. *A Critical and Exegetical Commentary on Colossians and Philemon.* ICC. New York: T&T Clark, 2005. Detailed (380 pages). Good for research.

Witherington, Ben, III. *The Letters to Philemon, the Colossians, and the Ephesians: A Socio-Rhetorical Commentary on the Captivity Epistles.* Grand Rapids: Wm. B. Eerdmans Publishing Co., 2007. Emphasizes rhetorical composition and cultural background information (382 pages).

Wright, N. T. *Paul for Everyone: The Prison Letters: Ephesians, Philippians, Colossians, and Philemon.* Louisville, KY: Westminster John Knox Press, 2004. Clear and accessible (240 pages).

———. *The Epistles of Paul to the Colossians and to Philemon: An Introduction and Commentary.* Tyndale New Testament Commentaries 12. Grand Rapids: Wm. B. Eerdmans Publishing Co., 1986. More detailed than his *Paul for Everyone* volume, but written clearly. Good scholarship in accessible form.

CHAPTER 15

Ephesians

A SERMON—NOT A LETTER

Ephesians exhibits a more elegant writing style than 1–2 Thessalonians, 1–2 Corinthians, Galatians, Romans, Philemon, and Philippians. This document provides a theological basis for God's historical redemption of sinful humans and the creation of a new humanity. The language reflects the grandeur of the content, condensing the message and engaging most of the major themes of Pauline theology. However, many New Testament scholars do not believe that Paul wrote Ephesians. This chapter, therefore, not only analyzes the content of Ephesians but also examines questions of authorship.

Significant parallels exist between Ephesians and Colossians. Approximately 70 percent of the content of Colossians is repeated in Ephesians, with 30 percent of the words being the same in each text. Ephesians is the longer of the two documents, and about 50 percent of its content parallels Colossians.

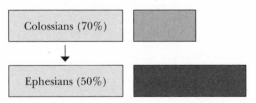

Perhaps Paul dictated both close to the same time and contemplated the same issues as he produced each. Perhaps a disciple of Paul wrote Ephesians after the apostle's death and used Colossians extensively in the process. Making a decision on authorship is complicated, and New Testament scholars are divided over the issue. To reach your own decision on this matter, first become familiar with the content and composition style of Ephesians. Then consider arguments for and against Pauline authorship. Begin by assuming that the author is who he claims to be, but change your view if you see compelling evidence to the contrary. Honest research demands open-minded examination of evidence.

WHERE WAS THE SERMON SENT?

1. Compare Colossians 4:7–17 with Ephesians 6:21–22. What similarities do you notice?

What major difference in content do you see?

According to Acts 19:10; 20:31, Paul lived in Ephesus for over two years and knew many people there. Scan through Ephesians, looking for the normal ways that Paul addresses specific issues in the churches to which he writes.

2. What do you notice about the content of Ephesians as a whole with regard to personal references?

EXALTED THEOLOGY OF UNITY (EPH. 1–3)

Why Was the Greeting in 1:1 Changed?

The text of 1:1 in your translation will either read "To the saints who are in Ephesus and are faithful in Christ Jesus" or simply "To the saints who are also faithful in Christ Jesus." Your Bible should contain a footnote mentioning that "in Ephesus" is not found in the earliest manuscripts of Ephesians. The oldest manuscript of Paul's Letters, Papyrus 46, dates back to around 200 CE and reads, "to the saints and faithful ones" (*tois hagiois kai pistois*). The significant manuscript Vaticanus (early fourth century) also omits "in Ephesus." In addition, the text used by the third-century theologian Origen did not contain "in Ephesus," and neither did the one used by the heretic Marcion, who wrote about 140 CE. Manuscript evidence strongly indicates that the original version of Ephesians contained no reference to Ephesus in 1:1. However, Codex Sinaiticus (no later than mid-fourth century) contains a scribe's marginal note with the words "in Ephesus" added to the text. In later manu-

The first page of Ephesians in Codex Sinaiticus, an important fourth-century manuscript, shows how a scribe added the words "in Ephesus" between the two columns. His addition changes the greeting from "to the saints" to "to the saints who are in Ephesus." Later scribes would sometimes incorporate such marginal additions into the actual text of a document when they copied it. (Used by permission of British Library.)

scripts, scribes moved this marginal note into the actual text of Ephesians.

Various theories exist for why Christians came to believe that Ephesus was the destination of this text. Marcion thought it was the Letter to the Laodiceans that Paul mentions in Col. 4:16: "And when this letter has been read among you, have it read also in the church of the Laodiceans; and see that you read also the letter from Laodicea." He probably made this connection on the basis of Tychicus being the designated carrier of both letters (Eph. 6:21; Col. 4:7) and the fact that the two documents share so much in common. Marcion may have been correct in his judgment, but there are problems with his theory.

Unlike Colossians, which addresses specific situations at Colossae, Ephesians is devoid of such references. Also, the language of Ephesians is liturgical, with lengthy statements of theology permeating its pages. The formal language sounds more like a sermon with no specific audience than a letter addressed to a particular church. The long and densely packed sentences differ from the Pauline Letters we have read so far. Perhaps it was a sermon meant to be read to a number of churches in the Lycus River valley. If written by Paul, the similarities with Colossians result from his dictating the two texts at about the same time and delivering them by the same person, Tychicus.

1. According to 3:1; 4:1; and 6:20, Paul was in prison when he wrote Ephesians. To which Christians did he write (2:11–22; 3:1–2, 6, 8)?

2. Where we would expect a thanksgiving, there is instead the theologically packed 1:3–14. What are the major themes in this passage?

3. What view of the church is presented in 1:15–23?

A Highly Exalted Thanksgiving Section
(Eph. 1:15–23)

1. How does 1:15–23 compare with Paul's normal thanksgiving sections? (Cf. 1 Thess. 1:2–10; 1 Cor. 1:4–9; 2 Cor. 1:3–7; Rom. 1:8–15; and Phil. 1:3–11.)

From Hell to the Heavenlies
(Eph. 2:1–10)

1. According to 2:1–10, what happens to people when they experience salvation in Christ?

2. What view of Christ is presented in 1:15–23?

2. How does the content of 2:1–10 compare with the argument presented in Romans 1–8?

Breaking Down the Dividing Wall of Hostility (Eph. 2:11–22)

1. According to 2:11–22, what barriers exist between Jews and Gentiles, and how has God removed them?

A possible parallel exists between the expression "dividing wall of hostility" in 2:14 and an enclosure surrounding the temple in Jerusalem. A rock wall about 4½ feet high separated the court of the Gentiles, where all people could enter, from the temple and its smaller courtyard, where only Jews could enter. Josephus describes it as follows:

> When you go through these [first] cloisters, unto the second [court of the] temple, there was a partition made of stone all round, whose height was three cubits: its construction was very elegant; upon it stood pillars, at equal distances from each other, declaring the law of purity, some in Greek, and some in Roman letters, that "no foreigner should go within that sanctuary"; for that second [court of the] temple was ascended by fourteen steps from the first court. (*Jewish War* 5.5.2 [Whiston])

Two of the signs have been discovered, one in 1871 and the other in 1935.[1] Both are written in Greek and read "No foreigner

may enter within the barricade that surrounds the temple and enclosure. Anyone who is caught doing so will have himself to thank for his ensuing death."[2] So serious was this prohibition that, before the Jewish revolt, Romans allowed the death penalty for Gentiles who entered the sacred space.

Roman legions destroyed this wall along with the rest of the temple in 70 CE. So, during Paul's life the stone barrier between Jews and Gentiles firmly stood. When Ephesians 2:11–22 speaks of Gentiles being separated from the commonwealth of Israel due to circumcision and other aspects of the law of Moses that walled them off from participation in God's covenant community, it might be a reflection on the visible symbol in the temple of this separation—a dividing wall. In Christ this dividing wall of hostility comes down so that Jew and Gentile both have equal access to God.

What is the "Mystery of Christ"? (Eph. 3:1–13)

1. How does the explanation of "the mystery" in 3:1–13 differ from what Colossians 1:27 says about "the mystery"?

---

1. The inscription discovered in 1871 is located in the Turkish State Museum in Istanbul, and the one located in 1935 is housed in Jerusalem. See F. F. Bruce, *Commentary on the Acts of the Apostles*, NICNT (Grand Rapids: Wm. B. Eerdmans Publishing Co., 1954), 434.

2. J. H. Iliffe, "The ΘΑΝΑΤΟΣ [*thanatos*] Inscription from Herod's Temple: Fragments of a Second Copy," *Quarterly of Department of Antiquities in Palestine* 6 (1938): 1ff.

2. Review Paul's self-descriptions in 1 Corinthians 3:10–11; 4:1–2; and 9:1–27; 2 Corinthians 10–13; and Galatians 1–2. Is Ephesians 2:20–3:13 at variance with these texts? Why or why not?

Psalm 68:17–18

[17] With mighty chariotry, twice ten thousand,
thousands upon thousands,
the Lord came from Sinai into the holy place.
[18] You ascended the high mount,
leading captives in your train
and receiving gifts from people,
even from those who rebel against
the Lord God's abiding there.

GUIDELINES FOR LIVING
(EPH. 4–6)

How Can Christians Be Unified?
(Eph. 4:1–16)

1. How is Christian unity something to be "maintained" (4:3) and also something to be "attained" (4:13)?

2. Compare Ephesians 4:8–10 with Psalm 68:18. How does this use of Scripture compare with that found in passages such as Romans 10?

3. How does the concept of the body of Christ in Colossians 1:18; 2:9–10 and Ephesians 1:22; 4:15–16 differ from the concept of Christ's body in 1 Corinthians 12?

How Can We Put Away Our Corrupt Old Lifestyle? (Eph. 4:17–5:20)

1. Using the imagery of an old set of clothes to describe the old life, 4:17–32 commands Gentile converts to put away their former ways. What practical advice does it give for dealing with anger?

2. According to 4:17–5:2, how does being a Christian affect one's moral and ethical commitments?

3. On what do the directions for children focus in Ephesians 6?

4. On what do the directions for slaves focus?

How Should Christian Family Members Treat Each Other? (Eph. 5:21–6:9)

1. The content of the household code in Ephesians 5:21–6:9 expands the directions given in Colossians 3:18–4:1. In Ephesians 5, on what do the directions for wives focus?

5. What directions are given to slave owners?

2. On what do the directions for husbands focus?

6. What does 5:21–6:9 stress when addressing those who are in subjection to others?

What about Modern Family Structure?

In your opinion, how should the instructions in the household code in 5:21–6:9 apply to families today? Why?

7. What does 5:21–6:9 emphasize when addressing those who are in authority over others?

Ephesians 6:10–17 speaks of putting on the whole armor of God. This headless statue of a Roman soldier, on display at the Asclepion near ancient Pergamum (modern-day Bergama, Turkey), provides a starting point for understanding the imagery. Numerous Web sites display pictures of Roman swords, shields, arrows, and helmets, which the passage references. (Courtesy of Michael Cosby)

Should I Duke with the Devil? (Eph. 6:10–17)

1. What view of conflicts encountered by Christians does 6:10–17 present?

ISSUES OF AUTHORSHIP

Did Paul write Ephesians? Here are the standard arguments against Pauline authorship:

1. Ephesians does not address a concrete situation. It lacks Paul's normal references to particular people

and specific problems faced by identifiable groups of Christians.

2. The language is quite formal and flowery, not terse like Paul's regular style. Of the approximately 100 sentences in Ephesians, 9 contain more than 50 words. By comparison, although Philippians is about the same length, it has only one sentence with more than 50 words. Galatians, with approximately 181 sentences, has only one with over 50 words.

3. Ephesians employs 116 words not found in the 7 undisputed Pauline Epistles (Roman, 1–2 Corinthians, Galatians, Philippians, 1 Thessalonians, and Philemon). Philippians, by comparison, contains 76 words not found in the other undisputed Letters.

4. Ephesians 2:6 says that God "raised us up with him [Christ] and seated us with him in the heavenly places in Christ Jesus." This understanding of a present, spiritual resurrection matches what is said in Colossians 3:1–4 but contradicts the undisputed Letters (cf. with future resurrection in Rom. 6:5 and Paul's arguments against the *pneumatikoi* in 1 Corinthians).

5. Ephesians 2:3 says, "All of us once lived among them in the passions of our flesh, following the desires of flesh and senses, and we were by nature children of wrath, like everyone else." In Galatians 1–2; Philippians 3:3–6; and 2 Corinthians 11:21–22, however, Paul speaks with pride of his achievements as a Pharisee under the laws of Moses. Why

would he lump himself with Gentile sinners in Ephesians 2:3?

6. Ephesians 2:19–3:6 claims that Paul was a holy apostle, part of the foundation of the church. Is this a later, reverential retrospect on Paul? Do 2:20 and 3:5 refer back to an earlier time, evidence that a disciple wrote Ephesians after Paul's death to provide a summary of the apostle's teaching?

1. Evaluate these arguments against Pauline authorship in light of the alternative view that Paul used a different scribe for Ephesians, and therefore the differences in content between this sermon and the Letters we have read are understandable in light of the sermonic and formal nature of Ephesians. Do you find the arguments for or against Pauline authorship to be more compelling? Why?

CONCLUDING REFLECTIONS

With elegant language, Ephesians presents a sweeping view of God's actions in salvation history—defending the equal standing of Jews and Gentiles in the church. God made all Christians into one, new humanity consisting of those who by faith have left behind their former lives of darkness and have entered the light. But Ephesians does not stop with theological reflection; it also provides concrete directions for life in this new humanity. Calling for individual purity and sacrificial love toward others, this sermon directs its readers to a level of existence that transcends human selfishness. This cosmic orientation contrasts with the last three Epistles included in the Pauline collection. Thus 1–2 Timothy and Titus differ considerably from Ephesians in their scope and theological agenda. Before analyzing these Letters, however, we will consider the matters of pseudonymity and canon.

FURTHER READING ON EPHESIANS

Barth, Markus. *Ephesians.* 2 vols. AB 34–34A. New York: Doubleday, 1974. Detailed and scholarly (vol. 34 alone has 464 pages). Argues for Pauline authorship.

Best, Ernest. *A Critical and Exegetical Commentary on Ephesians.* ICC. Edinburgh: T&T Clark, 1998. Thorough (716 pages). Good for research.

Edwards, Mark J., ed. *Galatians, Ephesians, Philippians.* Ancient Christian Commentary on Scripture: New Testament 8. Downers Grove, IL: InterVarsity Press, 1999. Collection of comments on these Epistles made by significant thinkers in the early centuries of the church. Good for learning the history of interpretation.

Hoehner, Harold W. *Ephesians: An Exegetical Commentary.* Grand Rapids: Baker Academic, 2002. Massive commentary on the Greek text (960 pages).

Good for research. Argues for Pauline authorship.

Koester, Helmut. *Ephesos Metropolis of Asia: An Interdisciplinary Approach to Its Archaeology, Religion, and Culture.* Valley Forge, PA: Trinity Press International, 1995. Provides valuable information on ancient Ephesus.

Liefeld, Walter L. *Ephesians.* IVP New Testament Commentary Series. Downers Grove, IL: InterVarsity Press, 1997. Brief overview. Attempts to apply the text to today (sometimes witty).

Lincoln, Andrew T. *Ephesians.* Word Biblical Commentary 42. Waco, TX: Word Books, 1990. Lengthy (592 pages). Interacts with other scholars. Argues against Pauline authorship.

MacDonald, Margaret Y. *Colossians and Ephesians.* Sacra Pagina 17. Collegeville, MN: Liturgical Press, 2000. Argues that Colossians and Ephesians are both deuteropauline. Concentrates on how New Testament communities reflect their culture's values.

Martin, Ralph P. *Ephesians, Colossians, and Philemon.* Interpretation. Atlanta: John Knox Press, 1991. Emphasizes the value for preaching what he calls the "cosmic dimensions of christological teaching" and the church as God's agent of reconciliation in the world.

Neufeld, Thomas R. *Ephesians.* Believers Church Bible Commentary. Scottdale, PA: Herald Press, 2002. Emphasizes peace and reconciliation. Careful work (424 pages). Does not take a stand on authorship of Ephesians. Provocative interpretation of the household code in 5:21–6:9 and the armor of God in 6:10–20.

O'Brien, Peter T. *The Letter to the Ephesians.* Pillar New Testament Commentary. Grand Rapids: Wm. B. Eerdmans Publishing Co., 1999. Argues for Pauline authorship. Proposes application of Ephesians for today.

Patzia, Arthur G. *Ephesians, Colossians, Philemon.* NIBCNT 10. Peabody, MA: Hendrickson Publishers, 1990. Attempts to be both scholarly and readable. Fairly accessible for students.

Perkins, Pheme. *Ephesians.* Abingdon New Testament Commentaries. Nashville: Abingdon Press, 1997. Brief. Compares Ephesians with a wide range of texts from the ancient Mediterranean world. Social and rhetorical focus. Assumes it is deuteropauline.

Snodgrass, Klyne. *Ephesians.* NIV Application Commentary. Grand Rapids: Zondervan, 1996. Seeks to make relevant application of Ephesians to contemporary life.

*Thurston, Bonnie Bowman. *Reading Colossians, Ephesians, and 2 Thessalonians: A Literary and Theological Commentary.* Reading the New Testament Series. New York: Crossroad, 1995. Written for a nontechnical audience.

Witherington, Ben, III. *The Letters to Philemon, the Colossians, and the Ephesians: A Socio-Rhetorical Commentary on the Captivity Epistles.* Grand Rapids: Wm. B. Eerdmans Publishing Co., 2007. Emphasizes the rhetorical composition of the Letters, as well as cultural background information (382 pages). Much valuable material.

*Wright, N. T. *Paul for Everyone: The Prison Letters: Ephesians, Philippians, Colossians, and Philemon.* Louisville, KY: Westminster John Knox Press, 2004. Clearly written. Accessible for general readers. Covers a lot in 240 pages.

CHAPTER 16

Monsters in the Closet

THE PROBLEM OF PSEUDONYMITY

"This is complete idiocy!" I slammed the book shut. "What kind of moron would say that Paul didn't write First and Second Timothy? This guy is a jerk!" It was my first encounter with the theory that Paul did not write all the Letters attributed to him in the New Testament. "How could anyone dare say such a thing? This creep is obviously a bonehead." Then I really got nasty. "He obviously can't be a Christian. He's one of those liberal professors I've heard about."

In retrospect, I admit that I was offended not so much by the evidence the author presented as by the idea itself. "Of course Paul wrote 1 and 2 Timothy. The Letters clearly begin with 'Paul, an apostle,' and they are, after all, in the Bible. If I believed what this bozo says, I'd have to ditch my faith entirely." My response, while perhaps extreme, is not unusual. During the years I

have taught courses on Paul in an academic setting, I have repeatedly observed similar reactions from many students. When they first encounter the belief that Paul did not actually write some letters that bear his name, they express outrage. Some ask, "If I question the authenticity of this Letter, where does it stop? How will I know what is true anymore?" But ignoring the issue does not make it go away.

For many Christians, honestly examining evidence that some Pauline Letters were actually written after Paul's death and attributed to him can be terrifying. It is like dealing with monsters in the bedroom closet. In the darkness, children can imagine that all sorts of terrifying creatures lurk in the closet. Turning on a light and examining with them the contents of the closet can calm their fears—at least over time.

And even as adults, when our imaginations go wild, dealing rationally with what we see as faith-eating monsters is scary. Sometimes we are more panicked by the possibilities of terror than we are with the monsters themselves. Sometimes when we understand them, they are not as scary as we think.

My wife and I once bought a foot-tall garden gnome for our youngest son because we knew that he would like it. And he was quite taken with the fanciful creature—until he went to bed. Then it seemed to leer menacingly down on him from the shelf. He became so frightened of how it looked in the darkness that he got up and brought the gnome into our bedroom so he could go to sleep. After a few days, however, he grew used to it and became content to have it on his shelf at night. Familiarity brings a more realistic perspective.

In our study of Paul so far, we have seen that by analyzing Paul's Letters in their ancient Mediterranean context, a number of new insights emerge. We have stood face-to-face with such potentially threatening monsters as Paul's use of the Old Testament without concern for context or authorial intent, his mistaken belief that the world was going to end before he died, and his sometimes obscure ways of arguing his points. We have seen how he overstates for emphasis and uses sarcasm when dealing with rebellious Christians. We have even observed him enraged at opponents and furiously calling them names. All these we have faced. When we open the closet door of Pauline scholarship and turn on the light, the ideas that we examine are not nearly as hideous as we might have imagined. But perhaps the biggest and most threatening monster is one that might not even belong to Paul at all. What about texts written in his name?

We need to turn on the light and see why numerous biblical scholars doubt the authenticity of 2 Thessalonians, Colossians, and Ephesians, and why the overwhelming majority reject the authenticity of 1–2 Timothy and Titus. Merely dismissing these views is like throwing them back into the closet and turning off the light. It makes these judgments seem more threatening and sinister. Examining the evidence, however, helps us to see which theories seem credible and which do not.

PSEUDONYMOUS WRITINGS

Pseudonymity means attributing a work to someone other than its real author, and a document written in someone else's name is a pseudonymous work. Its author uses a pseudonym, a false name. The term comes from the combination of two Greek words: *pseudēs* (meaning false) and *onoma* (meaning name).

Pseudonymity differs from anonymity. Most biblical books are anonymous. Few Old Testament texts claim to have been written by particular individuals. In fact, the authors of most Old Testament books never signed their names to their works, nor did the authors of the New Testament Gospels, the book of Acts, Hebrews, and so forth. These writers did not have the self-conscious view of authorship that exists today. But writing anonymously differs from an effort to deceive readers by writing a book purporting to be by an important person of the past, such as Adam, Enoch, Moses, Jesus, Paul, or Peter.

Reasons for writing in someone else's name vary. Some authors choose pen names, such as Samuel Clemens writing as Mark Twain. On other occasions, however, people forge documents in the name of another. Such deliberate deceptions differ from the mere use of pen names. The motive is often money. For example, a clever forger might try to create a hitherto unknown play by William Shakespeare, because the sale of such a document could involve huge sums of money. The forger tries to make the "artifact" look as if it were written during Shakespeare's time and then "discovers" the long-lost text.

When the hoax surfaces, if it seems to be authentic, an official investigation ensues. Specialists in Shakespeare examine the document. They look at physical evidence: the paper itself, the style of writing, the type of ink. They might carbon-date it. They also examine the content in light of other existing plays by Shakespeare. Then, on the basis of all the evidence they gather, the experts determine whether the article is genuine or fake. Sometimes the assessment is straightforward. Sometimes, however, forgeries are so skillfully done that exposing them can be a formidable task.[1] In the first century, neither the tools of the forger nor the investigative skills of those who detected the forgery were as well developed as they are today. In fact, forgeries were fairly common, and some that were poorly done nevertheless gained widespread acceptance as authentic.

FORGERIES WORK BECAUSE PEOPLE ARE GULLIBLE

People today regularly distribute forgeries via e-mail. Someone makes up a story and at the beginning of the message places an official-sounding title stating that it was published in a well-known newspaper or magazine. The message illustrates a theological or political point the forger (or prankster) wants to make, and at the end there is often an encouragement to send the message to friends. Recipients of the message rarely check to see if there is any truth to it; they merely forward the text to others, who forward it to others, and soon a fabricated story has circulated widely. People today are often gullible and do not take the time to verify what they hear or read. It was worse in the ancient Mediterranean world of the apostle Paul. Most people of his day could not read a document, let alone assess whether or not it was genuine. If the one reading a text to them gave assurances that it was a true story, they tended to believe it—if the content fit with what they already believed.

How can we know when to believe sayings attributed to famous individuals, or accounts of what politicians have said or done? How do we assess the validity of claims of what faith has done in the lives of particular Christians? What about the dire warnings regarding dreadful computer viruses? When are these true, and when are they hoaxes? People fabricate stories for a variety of reasons: to make particular points (influencing the court of

---

1. Various books explain how to determine whether or not a work is authentic. See, e.g., Donald W. Foster, *Author Unknown: On the Trail of Anonymous* (New York: Henry Holt & Company, 2000); *Author Unknown: Tales of a Literary Detective* (New York: Henry Holt & Co., 2001); and Joseph Rosenblum, *Practice to Deceive: The Amazing Stories of Literary Forgery's Most Notorious Practices* (New Castle, DE: Oak Knoll Press, 2000).

public opinion), to damage certain companies by inventing false stories about their products, to circulate humorous anecdotes about bizarre occurrences and wonder how many will actually believe them to be true, to give explanations for the origin of certain sayings that we have in our language, to make money from people's gullibility, and so forth. Thankfully, some individuals investigate these matters and expose bogus stories that enjoy widespread credibility and dissemination on the Internet.[2]

But who in the ancient world policed manuscripts and traced the origin of stories or documents? Such people actually existed in Paul's time. There were no copyright laws, but some scholars sought to expose forgers who fabricated manuscripts in the names of famous people (both living and dead). We will review their efforts after observing some fake documents written in Paul's name.

FORGERIES IN PETER'S AND PAUL'S NAMES

In Paul's day, people forged documents in the names of famous individuals for a variety of reasons. Some did it for money.

Some wanted to promote particular ideas, and they wrote in the names of important people from the past in order to gain greater readership for their books. If, for example, a relatively unknown author wrote a book on philosophy or religion, few people would be interested in it. But if the book claimed to have been written by Plato or Cicero, it might gain broader readership among Greeks and Romans. And if it claimed to have been written by Moses or Enoch or Adam, Jews would take notice.

Among Christians, numerous documents written in the names of the twelve apostles circulated around the church. Some still survive, and you may read translations of them in the *New Testament Apocrypha*, vol. 2, *Writings Relating to the Apostles; Apocalypses and Related Subjects*.[3] Forgeries written in the names of Peter and Paul abounded in the second century, and they fooled many. For example, Clement of Rome, in his letter to the Corinthian Christians about 95 CE, quoted a document called the *Kerygma Petrou* (*Preaching of Peter*) as if the apostle Peter wrote it. Much later, Origen (185–253) questioned the authorship of the *Kerygma Petrou* (in *Commentary on John* 13.17); and Eusebius, writing about 325, lists it among noncanonical works (*Ecclesiastical History* 3.2.1). Only fragments of the document survive via quotations of it in various early Christian manuscripts.[4]

---

2. For example, Take Our Word for It at http://www.takeourword.com/TOW113/page1.html provides what the authors call "netymology"—the etymology of words and sayings as they are passed around on the net (background of sayings such as "wet your whistle," "mind your P's and Q's," etc.). The Phrase Finder, http://www.phrases.org.uk.html, has an alphabetical listing to help find phrases in question. The Urban Legends Web site, http://www.urbanlegends.com/select.cgi?target=index.html, gives false stories arranged according to categories. This site is a great one for finding out which entries in the Darwin Awards are hoaxes; cf. http://www.darwinawards.com/.

3. Edited by E. Hennecke and W. Schneemelcher (Philadelphia: Westminster Press, 1965). Volume 1, *New Testament Apocrypha: Gospels and Related Writings*, ed. E. Hennecke and W. Schneemelcher (Philadelphia: Westminster Press, 1963), contains materials related to Jesus, some of it wildly fanciful.

4. These fragments may be read in translation in *New Testament Apocrypha*, vol. 2.

Another text forged in Peter's name was the *Kerygmata Petrou* (*Preachings of Peter*), a document written by a Jewish Christian who defended the apostle Peter as a true prophet and criticized Paul as hostile to truth. The *Kerygmata Petrou* begins with a letter, the *Epistula Petri* (*Epistle of Peter*), supposedly written from Peter to James, which castigates Paul and calls him "the enemy." It begins, "Peter to James, the lord and bishop of the holy church; Peace be with you always from the Father of all through Jesus Christ,"[5] and proceeds to instruct James not to let Gentiles read his (Peter's) writings unless these believers prove to be faithful. This pseudonymous letter focuses on maintaining the truth from God, which may seem ironic, because the letter itself is a fake. But this approach of writing in the name of an apostle in order to endorse what one believes to be correct doctrine was common during the second century.

The author of the *Epistula Petri* wrote Peter's supposed instructions to James to reinforce the authenticity of the letter. Note the way pseudo-Peter defends "the truth."

> For if we do not proceed in this way, our word of truth will be split into many opinions. . . . I have already the beginning of the evil before me. For some among the Gentiles have rejected my lawful preaching and have preferred a lawless and absurd doctrine of the man who is my enemy [Paul]. And indeed some have attempted, whilst I am still alive, to distort my words by interpretations of many sorts, as if I taught the dissolution of the law and, although I was of this opinion, did not express it openly. But that may God forbid! For to do such a thing means to act contrary to the law of God which was made known by Moses. (2.2–5)

5. Translations from ibid., 111ff.

The forger goes on to have Peter urge James to "preserve the dogmas and extend farther the rule of the truth, interpreting everything in accordance with our tradition and not being dragged into error through ignorance and uncertainty" (3.2).

The *Kerygmata Petrou* warns against female prophecy, which it associates with Paul:

> Along with the true prophet there has been created as a companion a female being who is as far inferior to him . . . as the moon is to the sun, as fire is to light. . . . There are two kinds of prophecy, the one is male, . . . the other is found amongst those who are born of women. Proclaiming what pertains to the present world, female prophecy desires to be considered male. (3.22.1)

The pseudonymous author uses Peter to validate his own views, showing how errors crept into the Scriptures (Old Testament), and explaining how to recognize which parts are false and which are true. To discredit Paul, he has Peter assert that, after Paul preached to the Gentiles, he (Peter) had to straighten out the mess. Peter says he came "as light upon darkness, as knowledge upon ignorance, as healing upon sickness" (2.17.3). He calls Paul's vision "the work of a wicked demon" (17.16.6). And in response to Paul's account of rebuking Peter in Galatians 2:11–14, the author has Peter get the upper hand in the argument and tell Paul: "You have in hostility withstood me, who am a firm rock, the foundation stone of the church. If you were not an enemy, then you would not slander me and revile my preaching in order that I may not be believed when I proclaim what I have heard in my own person from the Lord" (17.17.4–5). The reference to Peter as the firm rock and foundation stone of the church reflects a later time when Christians venerated Peter, but this obvious anachronism escaped many early Christians.

The *Kerygmata Petrou* illustrates the way in which Christians used apostles as mouthpieces for their own beliefs. Some forged texts in the name of Peter, others in the name of Paul. They tried to make their works seem genuine by mentioning specific people or well-known events in the life of the apostle. This ploy did not go unanswered, however. Competing Christians met the challenge with forgeries of their own.

During the second century, a church elder in Asia Minor wrote a fanciful story called the *Acts of Paul*—partly as a means of promoting celibacy. This tale contains the legend of Paul converting a lion to faith in Christ. Regardless of the fairytale-like nature of the story, however, many Christians celebrated what it said about Paul. Others opposed the work. Tertullian wrote in the third century, "If those who read the writings that falsely bear the name of Paul adduce the example of Thecla to maintain the right of women to teach and to baptize, let them know that the presbyter in Asia who produced this document, as if he could of himself add anything to the prestige of Paul, was removed from his office after he had been convicted and had confessed that he did it out of love for Paul" (*Baptism* 17).[6] Tertullian reports that this elder was kicked out of his office because of his forgery, regardless of what motivated him to write it. Church leaders had their hands full in trying to expose forgeries written in the names of apostles. Ironically, in this instance Tertullian's main complaint against the story was that some used it to

6. Quotation from ibid., 323.

endorse freedom for women to teach and to baptize, which he saw as dangerous. He later came to believe that some women received revelations from God (*De anima* 9.210).

The *Acts of Paul* contains a letter which claims to have been written by Paul, the so-called "3 Corinthians."

Paul, the prisoner of Jesus Christ, to the brothers in Corinth—greeting!

Since I am in many tribulations, I do not wonder that the teachings of the evil one are so quickly gaining ground. For [my] Lord Jesus Christ will quickly come, since he is rejected by those who falsify his words. For I delivered to you in the beginning what I received from the apostles who were before me, who at all times were together with the Lord Jesus Christ, that our Lord Jesus Christ was born of Mary of the seed of David, when the Holy Spirit was sent from heaven by the Father into her, that he might come into this world and redeem all flesh through his own flesh, and that he might raise up from the dead us who are fleshly. . . .

As for those who tell you there is no resurrection of the flesh, for them there is no resurrection, who do not believe in him who is thus risen. For indeed, ye men of Corinth, they do not know about the sowing of wheat or the other seeds, that they are cast naked into the ground and when they have perished below are raised again by the will of God in a body and clothed. . . . And if we must not derive the similitude from the seeds alone, [but from nobler bodies], you know that Jonah the son of Amathios, when he would not preach in Nineveh [but fled], was swallowed by a whale, and after three days and three nights God heard Jonah's prayer out of deepest hell, and no part of him was corrupted, not even a hair or an eyelid. How much more, O ye of little faith, will he raise up you who have believed in Christ Jesus, as he himself rose up. And if, when a corpse was thrown by the children of Israel upon the bones of the prophet Elisha, the man's body rose up, so you also who have been cast upon the body and bones and Spirit of the Lord shall rise up on that day with your flesh whole.

But if you receive anything else, do not cause me trouble; for I have these fetters on my hands that I may gain Christ, and his marks on my body that I may attain to the resurrection from the dead. And whoever abides by the rule which he received through the blessed prophets and the holy Gospel, he shall receive a reward. . . . But he who turns aside therefrom—there is fire with him and with those who go before him in the way, since they are men without God, a generation of vipers; from these turn ye away in the power of the Lord, and peace, [grace and love] be with you. Amen.[7]

The author of this letter admitted that he forged it. But if we had no such admission, how would you assess its validity? Analyze the letter on the basis of what you have seen in Paul's Letters so far.

1. What clues tip you off to this document being a forgery?

Yet another anonymous document written during the second century purports to be the *Epistle to the Laodiceans* that Paul mentions in Colossians 4:16: "And when this letter has been read among you, have it read also in the church of the Laodiceans; and see that you read also the letter from Laodicea." Someone invented this lost letter, and his bumbling effort, later denounced, is quoted below. The Muratorian Canon (usually dated ca. 200 CE) claims that an *Epistle to the Laodiceans* was "forged in Paul's name for the sect of Marcion" (lines 64–65),[8] but it might not refer to the same document. Jerome (345–420 CE) also dismissed a text

by this name as a forgery, but he also may have referred to a different manuscript.

Nevertheless, in spite of its murky origin, this forged *Epistle to the Laodiceans* gained such popularity that it appears in over a hundred copies of the Latin Vulgate (including the oldest existing copy, Codex Fuldensis, which dates to 546 CE). All German Bibles published before Martin Luther's translation of the New Testament in 1522 contained this letter between Galatians and Ephesians. The fact that many Christians venerated such a transparent forgery as authentically Pauline underscores the problem of pseudonymous documents in the church. Here is the text in question, provided in English translation. Note the ways in which the author sought to make his words sound Pauline—mostly by taking phrases from Philippians.

EPISTLE TO THE LAODICEANS

Paul, an apostle not of men and not through man, but through Jesus Christ, to the brethren who are in Laodicea: Grace to you and peace from God the Father and the Lord Jesus Christ.

I thank Christ in all my prayer that you are steadfast in him and persevering in his works, in expectation of the promise for the day of judgment. And may you not be deceived by the vain talk of some people who tell (you) tales that they may lead you away from the truth of the gospel which is proclaimed by me. And now may God grant that those who come from me for the furtherance of the truth of the gospel (. . .) may be able to serve and to do good works for the well-being of eternal life.

And now my bonds are manifest, which I suffer in Christ, on account of which I am glad and rejoice. This ministers to me unto eternal salvation, which (itself) is effected through your prayers and by the help of the Holy Spirit, whether it be through life or through death. For my life is in Christ and to die is joy (to me).

7. Quotation from ibid., 375–77.
8. *New Testament Apocrypha*, 1:44.

And this will his mercy work in you, that you may have the same love and be of one mind. Therefore, beloved, as you have heard in my presence, so hold fast and do in the fear of God, and eternal life will be your portion. For it is God who works in you. And do without hesitation what you do. And for the rest, beloved, rejoice in Christ and beware of those who are out for sordid gain. May all your requests be manifest before God, and be ye steadfast in the mind of Christ. And what is pure, true, proper, just and lovely, do. And what you have heard and received, hold in your heart and peace will be with you.

[Salute all the brethren with the holy kiss.] The Saints salute you. The grace of the Lord Jesus Christ be with your spirit. And see that this epistle is read to the Colossians and that of the Colossians among you.[9]

1. In what ways has the author of this forgery taken greater care to make his letter sound Pauline than did the author of the letter quoted above from the *Acts of Paul*?

Another forgery in Paul's name is the so-called correspondence between Paul and the philosopher Seneca. Consisting of fourteen letters purporting to be written between Seneca and Paul, this third-century document seeks to advance Paul's reputation by showing how a famous philosopher revered the apostle's letters. By forging these letters, the author tried to exalt Paul and thereby advance the cause of Christianity. Here are the first two letters:

1. Seneca greets Paul
Paul, you have been told, I believe, that yesterday we had a conversation with our Lucilius about the "Apocrypha" and other things. There were with me some members of your school. For we had retreated into Sallust's garden, where, by a happy chance for us, the people I have just mentioned, although they meant to go elsewhere, caught sight of us and joined us. We certainly longed for your presence, and I would like you to know that after the reading of your booklet, i.e., of a number of letters which you have addressed to city churches or to the chief cities of provinces and which contain wonderful exhortations for the moral life, we are thoroughly refreshed; and I believe that these statements have been uttered not by you but through you, although indeed at some time they were expressed (both) by you and through you. For so great is the majesty of these things and by such an excellent character are they distinguished that, in my opinion, generations of men would scarcely suffice to be instructed by them. Brother, I wish you prosperity.

2. Paul greets L. Annaeus Seneca
Yesterday I received your letter with joy. I would have been able to answer it at once had the young man whom I purposed to send to you been at hand. You well know when and through whom and at what moment and to whom a thing ought to be given for transmission. I beg you, therefore, not to look upon it as negligence that in the first place I have regard to the trustworthiness of the person. But since you write that you were somehow agreeably touched by my letter, I consider myself honoured by this judgment of a sincere man. For being the censor, philosopher and teacher of so distinguished a prince and also at the same time of the public, you would not say that if what you say was not true. I wish you prolonged prosperity.[10]

Although the composition of these pseudo letters is rather shoddy and the content bordering on absurd, these documents enjoyed considerable popularity among Christians for many centuries. The forger's attempts to make the letters seem genuine by including references to real or imagined people

9. Translation from *New Testament Apocrypha*, 2:131–32.

10. Translation from ibid., 135–36.

(e.g., "Lucilius" and "the young man whom I purposed to send to you") and places (e.g., "gardens of Sallust") paid off. Numerous copies from the fifteenth century show how long this deception worked. Even the great scholar Jerome thought that these letters were genuine (*De viris illustribus* 12). Often people uncritically accept things that back up their own beliefs.

In conclusion, writings from the first three centuries of the church reveal three things about documents falsely attributed to the apostle Paul. First, they were common. Second, some enjoyed widespread and sometimes long-lasting acceptance as genuine. Third, church leaders tended to condemn them when the deceptions were discovered.[11] Responses by Christian leaders to exposed forgeries parallel what we see in the Mediterranean world.

PSEUDONYMITY AMONG GREEKS AND ROMANS

Among Greek and Roman writers, forgeries became common in the fourth century BCE, as did anger toward the forgers.[12] In the years that followed, however, certain teachers had their students mimic famous scholars like Plato and Aristotle as part of their educational process. They believed that a good way to learn to express your thoughts clearly and persuasively was to try to write as if you were a notable philosopher or rhetorician. This practice partly contributed to the unfortunate result that authentic works and works written in imitation of famous people existed side by side in libraries. Consequently, a Greek named Callimachus condemned fake documents and led the way in exposing them.[13] Later, in Rome, Cicero organized efforts at exposing frauds. Another Roman by the name of Varro worked carefully with manuscripts, and he rejected 21 plays attributed to Plautus, saying that only 109 of the available 130 plays were authentic.[14]

Some forgers in the Roman world did not content themselves with faking the works of famous dead people; they also wrote in the name of living individuals in their efforts to profit from the names of others. Anthony Grafton explains:

> The medical writer Galen [born 130 CE], himself a textual critic of formidable competence, saw a forged work of his own, entitled "Galen Physician," on sale in the booksellers' district of Rome, and felt impelled to write a whole book distinguishing his genuine works from the wholly and partly falsified ones that circulated under his name. The satirist Lucian showed off his forger's dexterity and his critic's competence at one and the same time by forging a work in so convincing a replica of the notoriously obscure style of Heraclitus that it deceived a famous critic.[15]

For the most part, ancient literary critics relied on their educated intuition to detect

---

11. A belief often promoted by scholars in the past was that ancients were unconcerned with our modern copyright mentality and therefore did not have the same view of deception that we do today. Although it is true that modern attitudes differ from ancient ones, the idea that people of Paul's day did not care whether a document was authentic or not is incorrect. See David G. Meade, *Pseudonymity and Canon* (Tübingen: Mohr Siebeck, 1986). Also see E. Earle Ellis, *The Making of the New Testament Documents* (Leiden: E. J. Brill, 1999), 322ff.; and Lewis R. Donelson, *Pseudepigraphy and Ethical Argument in the Pastoral Epistles* (Tübingen: Mohr Siebeck, 1986).

12. Anthony Grafton, *Forgers and Critics: Creativity and Duplicity in Western Scholarship* (Princeton, NJ: Princeton University Press, 1990), 10.

13. Ibid., 12.
14. Ibid., 13.
15. Ibid., 19.

forgeries. The first one who seems to have developed a rigorous method for detection was Dionysius of Halicarnassus in the first century BCE. He analyzed works on the basis of stylistic, artistic, and chronological considerations.[16]

Although few were as rigorous as Dionysius in detecting forgeries, irritation with pseudonymous manuscripts was widespread. The idea that ancient Mediterraneans did not care who wrote texts does not match the evidence from ancient writers. The attitude toward forgeries both in the Christian church and in the larger Greco-Roman world was not one of benign acceptance. Although forgeries often enjoyed widespread popularity, when scholars determined that documents were fakes, they typically denounced them and sought to undermine their influence.[17]

For example, the Muratorian Canon condemns several pseudonymous documents: "There is also (an epistle) to the Laodiceans, another to the Alexandrians, forged in Paul's name for the sect of Marcion, and several others, which cannot be received in the catholic Church; for it will not do to mix gall with honey" (lines 63–67).[18] Similarly, Eusebius uses authenticity as a criterion for accepting books into the New Testament: "I have been obliged to list the [disputed books] separately, distinguishing those writings which according

to the tradition of the Church are true, genuine, and recognized, from those in a different category, . . . for we must not confuse these with the writings published by heretics under the name of the apostles" (*Ecclesiastical History* 3.25.6).[19] He lists some spurious works and then asserts:

> To none of these has any churchman of any generation ever seen fit to refer in his writings. Again, nothing could be further from apostolic usage than the type of phraseology employed, while the ideas and implications of their contents are so irreconcilable with true orthodoxy that they stand revealed as forgeries of heretics.[20]

But the heretics fought back by producing texts that denounced the orthodox writings.

Pseudonymity Wars

Name-calling abounded as the production of documents in the names of apostles continued from the second through the fourth centuries. An unorthodox (or heterodox) document from the fourth century titled the *Apostolic Constitutions* warns Christians to stay away from the false writings of the mainstream Christians:

> We have sent all these things to you, that ye may know our opinion, . . . and that ye may not receive those books which obtain in our name, but are written by the ungodly. For you are not to attend to the names of the apostles, but to the nature of the things, and their settled opinions. For we know that Simon and Cleobius, and their followers, have compiled poisonous books under the name of Christ and of His disciples, and do carry them about in order to deceive you who love Christ, and us His servants. And

---

16. See H. Gregory Snyder, *Teachers and Texts in the Ancient World: Philosophers, Jews, and Christians* (New York: Routledge, 2000), 51–53.

17. Wolfgang Speyer provides numerous examples of pseudonymous documents being rejected after they were shown to be forgeries: *Die literarische Fälschung im heidnischen und christlichen Altertum: Ein Versuch ihrer Deutung*, Handbuch der klassischen Altertumswissenschaft 1, pt. 2 (Munich: C. H. Beck, 1971), 112–27.

18. *New Testament Apocrypha*, 1:44.

19. Translation by G. A. Williamson, *Eusebius: The History of the Church from Christ to Constantine* (Minneapolis: Augsburg, 1965), 135.

20. Ibid.; see also 1.9.2–3.

among the ancients also some have written apocryphal books of Moses, and Enoch, and Adam, and Isaiah, and David, and Elijah, and of the three patriarchs, pernicious and repugnant to the truth. The same things even now have the wicked heretics done. (6.16; *ANF*, vol. 7)

Obviously, orthodoxy is in the eyes of the beholder. Heterodox writers called orthodox authors bad names: "wicked heretics" who pervert the truth. Each side condemned the other for writing forgeries in the names of apostles, and each side wrote its own forgeries to bolster its case for truth. In this theology war, many thought that the end justified the means. Or to use a more modern expression: "All is fair in love and war."

Forgers in this conflict did not seek monetary gain but theological dominance. They believed that their lies promoted a greater good. Christian esteem for apostolic authorship made the temptation to forge documents in the names of apostles almost a certainty in these skirmishes. Ultimately, orthodox Christians won the theology war, and because their side triumphed, they won the title of orthodox. They also gained the power to destroy the books of those whom they considered heterodox. However, they did not burn the forgeries written by people on their side to attack the heretics, and most New Testament scholars believe that some of these orthodox forgeries ultimately made their way into the canon of the New Testament.

The psychology of forgery in the name of truth is an interesting one with a long history. Clement of Alexandria (died ca. 215) actually cites Jesus when he states that there is such a thing as a therapeutic lie: "For he not only thinks what is true, but he also speaks the truth, except it be medici-

nally, on occasion; just as a physician, with a view to the safety of his patients, will practice deception or use deceptive language—to the sick" (*Miscellanies* 7.53; *ANF*). Similar arguments were advanced earlier by such men as the philosopher Plato (*Republic* 3.389b) and the rhetorician Cicero (*Brutus* 9.42). In this matter the Christian leader Origen quoted Plato when he argued that sometimes one must lie for the benefit of the one to whom you are lying (*Against Celsus* 4.19). However, such lies must be so skillfully administered that those whom one helps must not realize that they are being deceived for their own good. By definition, therefore, pseudonymous documents need to be convincing enough to be perceived as genuine, or else they lose their value to the forger's purpose.

As the church grew and developed, Christians faced new challenges that apostolic writings did not address. So on occasion Christians wrote in the name of Paul or Peter in an effort to express what they believed the apostle would have said if he were addressing contemporary issues of concern. In order to assist the church's battle against heretical views, some authors deliberately forged documents in the names of apostles as a means of gaining apostolic authority for whatever they wanted to say to Christians of their own time. They believed that the therapeutic lie was needed so badly for the health of the church that they were willing to deceive to achieve it.

Because therapeutic lies by orthodox writers were considered wicked lies by their opponents—and vice versa—those who wrote in the name of an apostle sought to make their works look genuine. Consequently, if the Pastoral Epistles are pseudonymous, the personal-sounding touches in 2 Timothy 4:6–22 and Titus 3:12–15, which have nothing directly to do with the theology of the letters, represent efforts to make the documents look authentic. Such techniques were common. Donelson provides interesting examples of letters forged in the names of notable people, where the forgers sought to make their letters look authentic by using personal-sounding references, greetings to particular people, criticisms of specific individuals, references to mundane matters such as meals or payment of bills or illnesses, expressions of friendship, and even references to comments made by friends or family members.[21]

Because Socrates represented the ideal life for the Cynics, some Cynic authors wrote letters that they attributed to him as a means of exalting their hero and at the same time promoting their own views, which they thought were in line with Socrates' teaching. They produced skillfully constructed forgeries in their effort to defend and advance their beliefs, which they considered to be accurate reflections of what Socrates represented. They made him larger than life by writing letters in his name that showed his virtue through his

comments on a number of very mundane, everyday situations (meals, errands, etc.). These Cynic writers resemble the second-century heterodox authors who wrote in Paul's name, believing that they were rescuing the apostle from the grip of the orthodox Christians, whom they believed were misrepresenting Paul.

IS THERE A MONSTER IN THE CLOSET?

In the study of pseudonymity, honesty is one of the first casualties. Christians often have no difficulty recognizing forgeries in Peter's or Paul's names if the documents are not included in the New Testament. There is no emotional tug involved with making such judgments. We decide on the basis of evidence. However, there is an emotional barrier to making similar judgments with New Testament documents. Because most Christians believe that all of Scripture is inspired by God, there is a philosophical problem with allowing for pseudonymous documents within the canon. Outside the canon is one thing; inside is a quite different matter.

Christians often employ a double standard with respect to implementing criteria for authenticity. For example, we may invent unlikely theories to argue that Peter wrote 2 Peter. Conversely, we may readily dismiss another text that is not included in the New Testament as being a forgery even if there is less evidence of pseudonymity. If we want to believe something, we are very capable of figuring out means of justifying our belief. Like the fourth-century Christians, we find it far easier to detect pseudonymity among

---

21. Donelson, *Pseudepigraphy and Ethical Argument*, 23–42. E.g., *Epistles 12–13* of the letters of Plato (designed to promote the authenticity of forged Platonic dialogues); the *Epistles of Anacharsis* (mostly use letter form to launch into Stoic philosophical discourses); the *Epistles of Crates* (efforts to expound Cynic philosophy); the *Letters of Apollonius of Tyana* (written to a wide variety of recipients, with little personal detail, mostly just philosophy); the *Epistles of Diogenes* (Cynic philosophy); the *Epistles of Heraclitus* (more philosophy); the *Epistles of Socrates* (letters written by Cynic philosophers to use Socrates' life as a model of Cynic philosophy and lifestyle, showing its virtues).

the writings of opponents than we do among the writings of our own group.

But where do we go with this realization? How do we proceed with respect to the Pastoral Epistles? Do we conclude that there is in fact a monster in the closet after all—a big terrifying one that is going to devour our faith if we recognize its presence? Or is it just another difficult detail to acknowledge initially, such as Paul's use of the Old Testament? If we turn on the light in the closet and see some unexpected things, will we accept their presence and learn to live with them? Or will we simply turn off the light and go back to fearing what might be in the dark closet? Here are some of the ways that Christians deal with the issue of pseudonymity. Some positions overlap with others.

OPTIONS FOR RESOLVING THE PROBLEM OF PSEUDONYMITY IN THE BIBLE

1. *Denial.* Some deny the possibility of pseudonymity among biblical books. They base this on the following belief: if a document is inspired by God and included in the canon of Scripture, it cannot have false attribution of authorship. This approach rejects evidence to the contrary on the basis of a philosophical commitment.[22]

2. *Redefinition.* A different tactic is to deny that there is any problem by asserting that among ancient Jews and Christians there was no con-cept of intellectual property rights: no idea of copyright, therefore no attachment to an individual's personal accomplishment in the writing of a document. By asserting that there were so many pseudonymous texts that people were unconcerned about who actually wrote a book, the problem is removed. Modern scholarship has thoroughly discredited this argument.[23]

3. *Redirection.* Some build a case on ancient Mediterranean corporate solidarity in which the identity of the individual is embedded in the identity of the group. In this understanding, authors spoke not for themselves but for their groups. Therefore, writing in the name of the famous founder of their group was considered a legitimate way of expressing what the pseudonymous author believed the founder would have said if he were addressing contemporary issues.[24] This idea has also suffered blistering critiques.[25]

4. *Remodel.* In past decades it was popular to adopt an authorship model based on the practice of students who wrote in the name of Pythagoras, the founder of their school.

22. E.g., J. I. Packer, *Fundamentalism and the Word of God* (Grand Rapids: Eerdmans, 1958), 184.

23. W. Speyer, *Die literarische Fälschung im Altertum* (München: C. H. Beck, 1971), amasses a devastating case against this viewpoint.

24. H. W. Robinson, *Corporate Personality in Ancient Israel* (Philadelphia: Fortress, 1964); D. S. Russell, *The Method and Message of Jewish Apocalyptic* (London: SCM, 1964).

25. E.g., J. Porter, "The Legal Aspects of the Concept of 'Corporate Personality,'" *Vetus Testamentum* 15 (1965): 361–80; and J. W. Rogerson, "The Hebrew Conception of Corporate Personality: A Re-examination," *Journal of Theological Studies*, n.s. 24 (1970): 1–16.

Scholars applied this model to disciples of Paul, speculating that his students formed a school and wrote in Paul's name.[26] Evidence for such a school is lacking, however, in spite of the fact that many Gentile Christians revered Paul's writings. Also, Paul discouraged Christians at Corinth from separating themselves into groups based on loyalties to particular leaders (1 Cor. 1:11–17).

5. *Restructure.* We might focus on the fact that in ancient Mediterranean societies, people thought the old was better than the new. If a religion lacked a long and noble history, it was open to criticism. With this in mind, we could acknowledge that Christians wrote in Paul's name as a way of supporting what they considered to be true religion. Orthodox forgeries were necessary to respond to the forgeries put forth by heretics. We could justify this action by asserting that the authors of these texts considered content to be more important than authorship.[27] There was a theological war going on, and during battles things get messy.

6. *Revision.* We could compare the production of pseudonymous Pauline literature to the growth of the stories contained in the Gospels. The Gospel authors modified their stories about Jesus in order to make them communicate more effectively to their intended audiences.[28] If we take this tendency a step further and apply it to Paul, we could argue that his disciples only wanted to continue his ministry so that it would speak more clearly to situations that arose after Paul's death. Writing letters in his name ensured the ongoing relevance of his message.

7. *Demolition.* We could drop the idea of canon altogether, along with its claims to exclusivity. This would allow unbridled scholarly inquiry and perhaps a redefinition of Christian faith.[29] We would not be restricted to the present size of the Bible but could equally consider all early Christian literature and drop the idea of orthodoxy and heterodoxy.

8. *Core concentration.* We could affirm that the core of the New Testament contains the documents that are most vital to Christian faith and relegate to Apocrypha those New Testament books that lie outside the core. This action would reduce the canon of Scripture to a smaller number of books.

9. *Affirmation of canonical diversity.* We could recognize that the Bible itself contains considerable diversity,

26. E.g., Gunther Bornkamm, *Paul* (New York: Harper & Row, 1971), 86; and E. Earle Ellis, "Paul and His Co-workers," in *Prophecy and Hermeneutic in Early Christianity: New Testament Essays* (Tübingen: J. C. B. Mohr, 1978), 3–22.

27. See, e.g., Bruce M. Metzger, "Literary Forgeries and Canonical Pseudepigrapha," *Journal of Biblical Literature* 91 (1972): 3–24.

28. There are many books that compare the Gospel accounts. To do the work yourself and see the differences firsthand, use Michael R. Cosby's *Portraits of Jesus: An Inductive Approach to the Gospels* (Louisville, KY: Westminster John Knox Press, 1999).

29. E.g., Martin Rist, "Pseudepigraphy and the Early Christians," in *Studies in New Testament and Early Christian Literature: Essays in Honor of Allen P. Wikgren*, ed. David E. Aune (Leiden: E. J. Brill, 1972), 75–91.

and therefore to look for a unified message from all New Testament books is futile. Instead of viewing the Bible as a "codebook" that gives specific laws for Christian living, we could view it as a "casebook" used to understand the best way to live in the twenty-first century. (Review the exercise on 1 Cor. 7: "Your view on the Issue of Divorce?" in chap. 10, "1 Corinthians: Sex, Booze, and Ecstatic Worship")

There are other options for dealing with the issue of pseudonymous documents in the Bible, but these represent the fairly common ones. To determine the most suitable approach, however, we benefit from knowing about the process by which church leaders finally decided on a set of documents considered to be inspired by God and therefore to be regarded as Scripture. This lengthy canonization journey had many twists and turns, and knowing about them helps to put things into perspective. It is all part of turning on the light in the closet to see if the monsters are real or imagined. We can deal more honestly and constructively with what we understand than with what we merely imagine. Therefore, doing some outside reading on the canonization process can be illuminating.

FURTHER READING ON PSEUDONYMITY

Donelson, Lewis R. *Pseudepigraphy and Ethical Argument in the Pastoral Epistles.* Tübingen: J. C. B. Mohr, 1986. Technical work. Better for advanced study.

Foster, Donald W. *Author Unknown: On the Trail of Anonymous.* New York: Henry Holt & Co., 2000. Deals with pseudonymity generally, not with biblical material. Good model for literary detective work.

Grafton, Anthony. *Forgers and Critics: Creativity and Duplicity in Western Scholarship.* Princeton, NJ: Princeton University Press, 1990. Explores links between forgery and scholarship from ancient Greece to modern times. Gives little context for anecdotes.

MacDonald, Dennis Ronald. *The Legend and the Apostle: The Battle for Paul in Story and Canon.* Philadelphia: Westminster Press, 1983. Focuses on the second-century legend of Thecla, a Gentile convert of Paul. Good example of gender politics in scholarship.

Meade, David G. *Pseudonymity and Canon: An Investigation into the Relationship of Authorship and Authority in Jewish and Earliest Christian Tradition.* Tübingen: J. C. B. Mohr, 1986; Grand Rapids: Wm. B. Eerdmans Publishing Co., 1987. Technical work. Valuable for scholarship.

New Testament Apocrypha. Vol. 1, *Gospels and Related Writings.* Edited by E. Hennecke and W. Schneemelcher. Philadelphia: Westminster Press, 1963. ET of early pseudonymous Gospel-type materials that did not make it into the canon of Scripture.

New Testament Apocrypha. Vol. 2, *Writings Relating to the Apostles; Apocalypses and Related Subjects.* Edited by E. Hennecke and W. Schneemelcher. Philadelphia: Westminster Press, 1965. ET of ancient texts that falsely claimed to have been written by apostles.

Rosenblum, Joseph. *Practice to Deceive: The Amazing Stories of Literary Forgery's Most Notorious Practices.* New Castle, DE: Oak Knoll Press, 2000. Entertaining stories of notorious literary forgeries. Shows methods and motives of forgers.

Snyder, H. Gregory. *Teachers and Texts in the Ancient World: Philosophers, Jews, and Christians.* New York: Routledge, 2000. Good resource on the teaching techniques used in the ancient Mediterranean world. Helps us understand their views on forgeries.

Speyer, Wolfgang. *Die literarische Fälschung im heidnischen und christlichen Altertum: Ein Versuch ihrer Deutung.* Handbuch der klassischen Altertumswissenschaft pt. 2. Munich: C. H. Beck, 1971. Technical work limited to those who can read German.

CHAPTER 17

Pastoral Epistles

GUARDING ORTHODOXY

This chapter puts your detective skills to the test. You will need to look for clues and analyze what you discover. The stakes are potentially high, and your decision has significant implications. Here is the case that you need to unravel: Are the Pastorals to be counted as Pauline, and how/should we reconcile their content with undisputed Letters of Paul? We begin with an overview of the case background and then examine the specifics.

First Timothy, 2 Timothy, and Titus are called the Pastoral Epistles because they are all addressed from Paul to younger coworkers. Instead of addressing church groups, they address individuals, providing infor-

mation about pastoral duties. These Epistles share much in common, using similar language, warning against similar heresies, promoting similar church structure, and espousing similar theological positions. And the distinct nature of these Epistles again raises the issue of authorship, except this time to a higher degree. A significant number of New Testament scholars argue that Paul wrote 2 Thessalonians, Colossians, and Ephesians; yet few do the same for the Pastoral Epistles. The vast majority do not believe that Paul wrote these three documents. This consensus exists because of strong evidence, some of which you will analyze.

1 TIMOTHY: WOULD YOU WRITE LIKE THIS TO A GOOD FRIEND?

Formal Salutation (1 Tim. 1:1–2)

1. How does the salutation differ from Paul's greetings in the other Letters we have studied thus far?

As in Galatians, there is no thanksgiving section following the salutation; but unlike Galatians, there is no indication that anger caused this omission.

Sound Teaching and the True Faith (1 Tim. 1:3–20)

1. According to this passage, where is Paul when he writes? Where is Timothy?

2. In 1:3–11, 18–20, what characterizes the heresy that Paul warns Timothy to oppose?

3. According to 1:3–11, 18–20, what should characterize true faith?

4. What view of the law is presented in 1:8–11?

5. What portrait of Paul is presented in 1:12–17?

6. Why would Paul feel the need to communicate these details to Timothy, his coworker of many years?

Proper Order in the Church
(1 Tim. 2:1–3:16)

1. What view of Christian life in society is presented in 2:1–4? Do these comments sound like the author expects the end to come soon, or do they seem to reveal a more settled, long-term view of existence in the world?

2. Why would Paul need to assure Timothy that he is not lying in 2:7?

3. According to 2:9–10, what should characterize honorable women?

4. What limitations does 2:11–12 place on women?

5. What reason is given for these limitations?

6. How does 2:15 compare with what we have read about salvation in previous letters? How does this comment compare with Galatians 3:27–28?

7. According to 1 Timothy 3:1–7, why should a bishop (or "overseer"; Greek *episkopos*) be able to control his children and generally be able to control his household?

"The husband of one wife" (3:2, NRSV textual note) refers either to monogamy (a bishop cannot be a polygamist) or to not being divorced (a bishop must adequately control his wife, demonstrating ability to govern his family).

8. What qualities are necessary for both bishops and deacons (3:1–13)?

9. Why would Paul need to provide such instructions for Timothy, his longtime coworker?

Women in Leadership Roles in the Church Today

1. How do the instructions given to women in 1 Timothy compare with 1 Corinthians 11:2–16? with 1 Corinthians 14:33b–36? with Ephesians 5:21–24?

2. If you assume that Paul wrote 1 Timothy, how do you explain these differences in perspective and their relevance for the church today?

3. If you conclude that Paul did not write 1 Timothy, what are the implications for how these passages should be used in the church today?

True Faith versus Profane Myths
(1 Tim. 4:1–16)

1. In 4:1–8, what characterizes the heresy that Paul wants Timothy to combat?

2. How does the asceticism advocated by these heretics compare with what we have seen in the ascetics criticized in 1 Corinthians 7 and Colossians 2:16–19?

3. What duties does 1 Timothy 4:11–16 stress that Timothy should perform?

4. Why would Paul need to provide such instructions for Timothy, his longtime coworker?

Membership in the Order of Widows
(1 Tim. 5:1–16)

1. What qualifications are given for women to be enrolled in the order of widows?

2. Who is supposed to take care of widows who do not qualify for enrollment in the order? Why?

3. What negative behaviors are foreseen that younger widows might be drawn into?

4. How does the advice in 5:14 compare with the directions given to widows, widowers, and engaged couples in 1 Corinthians 7:8–9, 25–40?

How do you explain the difference in attitude?

4. According to 6:6–10, 17, what dangers are involved in acquiring wealth?

Drink a Little Wine for Your Ailments (1 Tim. 5:17–6:21)

1. Why does 5:23 promote the use of wine?

2. What guidelines does 6:1–2 provide for problems involved when slave owners and slaves are part of the same church?

3. How does the description of heretics in 6:3–5 compare with previous descriptions given in 1 Timothy?

"The Faith" and "the Truth" in 1 Timothy

First Timothy ends with another contrast in 6:20–21 between falsehood and the true faith. Timothy is commanded to "guard what has been entrusted" to him. Unlike the previous Letters that we have studied, "faith" in this Epistle is typically associated with a set of orthodox beliefs instead of describing an attitude of trust in the grace of God (as argued in Galatians and Romans).

1. How is "the faith" used in 1 Timothy 1:2, 19b; 3:9, 13; 4:1, 6; 5:8; 6:10, 12, 21?

2. How is "faith" used in 1:4, 5, 14, 19a; 2:7, 15; 6:11?

3. What is the meaning of "the truth" in 2:4; 3:15; 4:3; 6:5? (Cf. "sound teaching" 1:10; 4:6; "the teaching" in 6:1.)

4. How does this primary focus on maintaining orthodox beliefs compare with the focus of the other Letters we have studied?

Is 1 Timothy a Personal Letter to a Colleague?

1. Does this Letter sound like a document written to a trusted colleague? If so, what personal touches do you see? If not, what do you perceive the tone of the letter to be?

Assessment of Evidence

As you continue your detective work, consider the clues that most New Testament scholars interpret as evidence that Paul did not write this Letter. First Timothy

1. exhibits a stronger emphasis on orthodox belief, which is frequently called "the faith."
2. encourages a more settled attitude toward living in society (2:1–2).
3. demands a restricted role for women and even says that they are saved through childbearing (2:9–15).
4. emphasizes an established hierarchy for church leaders, who are ordained by the laying on of hands (3:1–13; 5:17–22).
5. endorses an order for older widows, and marriage and childbearing for younger widows (5:3–16).
6. provides all sorts of information that Timothy, his longtime companion, should already know.
7. uses many distinctive words and phrases (e.g., "God our Savior" in 1:1; 2:3; 4:10; "Christ Jesus our hope" in 1:1; "The saying is sure and worthy of full acceptance" in 1:15; 3:1; 4:9).
8. uses a style of writing with distinctively different sentence composition.
9. uses considerably different vocabulary (1 Timothy contains 360 words that are not found in the undisputed Pauline Letters).

On the basis of this evidence, most scholars conclude that an anonymous Christian penned this Epistle in Paul's name after the apostle's death, perhaps in the first quarter of the second century. His purpose was to gain greater authority for what he considered to be orthodox teaching. He probably believed that he was writing what Paul would have written had he been alive at the time. And because his statements about heretics seem to reflect a form of Gnosticism that existed after Paul's time, most conclude that he wrote 1 Timothy to suppress gnostic influences that threatened his church.

TITUS: A SMALLER MANUAL OF CHURCH DISCIPLINE

In Galatians, Paul first mentions his trusted coworker Titus as one of the people who accompanied him to the Jerusalem council, and he states that this uncircumcised Gentile was not compelled to be circumcised (Gal. 2:1, 3). Titus evidently was a rather forceful individual, for although Timothy was unable to bring order to the Corinthian church, Titus delivered the Painful Letter and successfully brought these arrogant Christians to repentance (2 Cor. 7:6–16). Paul also relied on Titus to go ahead to Corinth and collect money for Christians in Jerusalem, before Paul arrived with others from Macedonia (2 Cor. 8:16–24). Titus was Paul's trusted associate and an effective leader in his own right.

Geographical Concerns in Titus

1. According to Titus 1:5 and 3:12, where is Titus at the time, and where is Paul headed?

2. Look at a map of Paul's journeys as recorded in Acts. Is there is any mention of him ever being in Crete or Nicopolis?

Theological Themes in Titus

1. How does the use of "the faith" (1:1, 4, 13); "the truth" (1:1, 14); "the teaching" (1:9); "sound doctrine" (1:9; 2:1); "the doctrine" (2:10); and "the saying is sure" (3:8) compare with phrases found in 1 Timothy?

2. How does the repeated use of "good works" in 1:16; 2:7, 14; 3:1, 8, 14 compare with Paul's view on good works in Romans?

3. How does the heresy described in Titus 1:10–16 and 3:9–11 compare with that depicted in 1 Timothy 1:3–11, 19–20; 4:1–8?

6. Do you see personal touches indicating that this Letter was sent from a friend to a trusted colleague? If not, what is the tone of the letter?

4. How do the instructions in Titus 2:3–10 compare with household codes in Colossians 3:18–4:1 and Ephesians 5:21–6:9?

2 TIMOTHY: A LAST WILL AND TESTAMENT?

Although 2 Timothy shares many linguistic characteristics and theological distinctives with 1 Timothy and Titus, its tone differs from the other two. Be aware of the way this Epistle depicts Paul.

Guard the Gospel (2 Tim. 1:1–18)

5. Given the fact that Titus had worked as a missionary with Paul for years, how much of the content of this Letter do you think that he would already know?

1. Unlike 1 Timothy and Titus, there is a thanksgiving section in 1:3–7. What is the focus of this thanksgiving?

2. According to 1:8–18, where is Paul when he writes this letter, and under what conditions is he living?

2. According to 2:9–10, what are Paul's prison conditions? How do these compare with the description of his Roman imprisonment in Acts 28:15–31?

3. What is Paul eager for Timothy to protect?

3. Compare 2 Timothy 2:16–18 and 4:14 with 1 Timothy 1:20. What do you learn about Hymenaeus and Alexander?

4. How are Christians in Asia responding to Paul's gospel message?

4. According to 1 Timothy 4:12 and 2 Timothy 2:22, how old is Timothy? What problem does this description raise, alongside Acts 16:1's indicating that Timothy joined Paul at the beginning of the second missionary journey (ca. 49 CE)? (Cf. 1 Cor. 4:17; 16:10; Phil. 2:22.)

Share in the Suffering
(2 Tim. 2:1–26)

1. How is Timothy to guard the gospel message?

Dealing with Distress in the Last Days (2 Tim. 3:1–4:8)

1. According to 3:1–9, what are the false teachers like, and why do people believe them?

2. What view of the Old Testament Scriptures is presented in 3:16–17, and of what value are they for Christians?

3. What does 4:1–5 warn Timothy that he will face as a teacher in the near future?

4. According to 4:16–18, what does Paul anticipate will happen to himself in the near future?

Deserted! (2 Tim. 4:9–22)

1. What conditions does this passage claim that Paul faces?

2. What does it say about Paul's mental and emotional state?

3. What is requested from Timothy? Why?

4. Compare 4:9–12 with Colossians 4:7–17 and Philemon 24. What are the similarities?

5. With regard to style and content, how does 2 Timothy 4:9–22 compare with 1 Timothy 6:20–21?

Comparing 2 Timothy with 1 Timothy and Titus

1. How does the overall content of 2 Timothy compare with that of 1 Timothy and Titus with regard to emphasis on maintaining orthodoxy?

AUTHORSHIP OF THE PASTORAL EPISTLES

As stated above, the vast majority of New Testament scholars believe that the Pastoral Epistles were written after Paul's death by an unknown Christian who represented a developing form of orthodoxy. They take as definitive proof data such as the linguis-

tic and theological differences between these Letters and undisputed Pauline Epistles, as well as the fact that the historical setting does not match anything mentioned in Acts. There is no indication in Acts that Paul ever did any missionary work in Crete (Titus 1:5) or ever visited Nicopolis (in southwestern Macedonia), where Titus 3:12 says he was headed to spend the winter. To be fair, however, in Romans 15:19 Paul says that he preached the gospel as far as Illyricum, which is northwest of Macedonia, and Acts never mentions him being in that area.

Thus there is much about Paul and his life that we do not know, because his Letters and the account in Acts provide limited information. Such uncertainty allows for divergent opinions on the Pastoral Epistles. A small percentage of scholars representing a variety of theological perspectives do argue in favor of Pauline authorship. If you wish to read their arguments, the bibliography at the end of this chapter indicates which authors take this position. The evidence against Pauline authorship remains massive, but various historical scenarios have been proposed to keep open the possibility that he wrote them. Here, for example, is one.

The story of Paul in Acts concludes with him under comfortable house arrest in Rome and able to preach the gospel to those who came to listen. No mention is made of the final outcome of the trial, whether he was released or executed. If the emperor judged in Paul's favor and released him, the apostle would probably have gone to Spain, as he planned (see Rom. 15:24). An early Christian document called *1 Clement* claims that this event actually happened.

Around 95 CE a leader in the church of Rome by the name of Clement wrote to the still-wayward Christians at Corinth, seeking to correct their problems. In this letter Clement used Paul as an example of patience and one who endured the ill effects of jealousy. In the process he said concerning Paul, "he taught righteousness to all the world, and when he had reached the limits of the West he gave his testimony before the rulers, and thus passed from the world and was taken up into the Holy Place" (*1 Clement* 5.7 [K. Lake, LCL]). From the perspective of first-century Mediterranean people, Spain was the "limits of the West."

If Paul spent several years doing missionary work in Spain and then returned to Asia Minor to check on the churches there, he might have discovered that the heresy refuted in Colossians had developed further and grown in popularity. Second Timothy 1:15 bleakly states "all who are in Asia have turned away from me, including Phygelus and Hermogenes." Perhaps when Paul returned to such a horrible situation in the church, he concluded that it was necessary to stress the orthodox nature of his message over against the syncretistic heresy that polluted his converts. Perhaps his visit to Crete was simply part of his return voyage from Spain, and in order to maximize his efforts, he left Titus there and Timothy in Ephesus to try to regain order. Perhaps he then journeyed north to Macedonia and southwest toward Nicopolis. Perhaps somewhere along the way he was arrested and sent in chains to Rome, this time under much more severe conditions than those described in Acts.

If so, 2 Timothy reflects a weary Paul at the end of his life, struggling with feelings of loneliness and boredom, but not quite despair. He passes the mantle on to Timothy, his rather timid coworker, pressuring him to give his life in defense of the gospel.

There are definitely problems with this reconstruction, and it does not adequately address the theological differences between the Pastoral Epistles and the undisputed Letters. Like most defenses of Pauline authorship, it is built on a series of "If . . ." proposals. But there remains enough ambiguity in the evidence that scholars will continue to debate the issues involved. Evidence against Pauline authorship is impressive, but a few nagging questions remain. Second Timothy is the best candidate for being an authentic Letter because it does not glorify Paul as documents written about dead religious leaders often tend to do. Yet, as we saw in the chapter (16) on pseudonymity, the tactics used by forgers during this time period could easily explain the inclusion of authentic-sounding details as a means of convincing readers that Paul wrote it. And the question still remains: Why would Paul write 1 Timothy and Titus, largely manuals of church discipline, to trusted and experienced coworkers? And why would there be so many similarities between the final greetings in 2 Timothy 4:9–15 and Colossians 4:7–17 if these letters were written during different Roman imprisonments?

Personal Reflection on Authorship and Canonical Authority

1. Do you believe that Paul wrote the Pastoral Epistles, or have you concluded that someone else wrote them after the apostle's death? What are your main reasons for reaching your conclusion?

2. The materials we studied on pseudonymity indicate that church leaders in the first four centuries stressed authenticity as an important criterion for a book or letter being included in the New Testament. If Paul did not write the Pastoral Epistles, should they have authority for the church today? Explain.

FURTHER READING ON THE PASTORAL EPISTLES

Barrett, C. K. *The Pastoral Epistles*. New York: Oxford University Press, 1963. Fairly thorough.

Bassler, Jouette M. *1 Timothy, 2 Timothy, Titus*. Abingdon New Testament Commentaries. Nashville: Abingdon Press, 1996. Basic commentary.

Dibelius, Martin, and Hans Conzelmann. *The Pastoral Epistles*. Hermeneia. Philadelphia: Fortress Press, 1972. Thorough, technical. Written for scholars. Detailed argument against Pauline authorship of the Pastorals.

Donelson, Lewis R. *Pseudepigraphy and Ethical Argument in the Pastoral Epistles*. Tübingen: J. C. B. Mohr, 1986. Technical work. Better for advanced study.

Fee, Gordon D. *1 and 2 Timothy, Titus*. NIB-CNT 13. Peabody, MA: Hendrickson Publishers, 1995. Fairly accessible.

Argues for Pauline authorship of the Pastorals.

Johnson, Luke Timothy. *The First and Second Letters to Timothy: A New Translation with Introduction and Commentary.* AB. New York: Doubleday, 2001. This 512-page commentary in a series known for its critical scholarship is amazing in that it argues for Pauline authorship. Technical. The introductory material on authorship and so forth runs to 98 pages.

———. *Letters to Paul's Delegates: 1 Timothy, 2 Timothy, Titus.* Valley Forge, PA: Trinity Press International, 1996. Places the Pastorals in the sociohistorical setting of Paul. Takes an unusual approach in arguing for Pauline authorship.

Liefeld, Walter L. *1 and 2 Timothy, Titus.* NIV Application Commentary. Grand Rapids: Zondervan, 1999. Seeks to provide application of these letters to contemporary life.

Marshall, I. Howard. *A Critical and Exegetical Commentary on the Pastoral Epistles.* ICC. Edinburgh: T&T Clark, 1999. Exhaustive study (928 pages) with large bibliographies. Knowledge of Greek helps when reading this book, although the style is lucid. Argues against Pauline authorship of the Pastorals.

Towner, Philip H. *The Letters to Timothy and Titus.* NICNT 13. Grand Rapids: Wm. B. Eerdmans Publishing Co., 2006. Exhaustive study of these letters (883 pages). Readable for such a sizeable tome.

Verner, David C. *The Household of God: The Social World of the Pastoral Epistles.* Chico, CA: Scholars Press, 1982. Published dissertation. Technical. Good resource.

Witherington, Ben, III. *Letters and Homilies for Hellenized Christians: A Socio-Rhetorical Commentary on Titus, 1–2 Timothy and 1–3 John.* Downers Grove, IL: IVP Academic, 2006. Explains the rhetorical shape of the Letters and cultural background information helpful for interpreting them. Argues that Paul had Luke write the letters for him.

Wright, N. T. *Paul for Everyone: The Pastoral Letters: 1 and 2 Timothy and Titus.* Louisville, KY: Westminster John Knox Press, 2004. Short, well written, and quite informative for its length.

CHAPTER 18

Your View of the Apostle Paul

You have read Paul's Letters and interacted with his thoughts and feelings. You have also read about his missionary journeys in the Acts of the Apostles. You have seen for yourself how emotional he is when dealing with certain issues and how gentle or confrontational he can be—depending on the Letter under consideration. He is a complex individual, defying simplistic assertions about his life and ministry. He defies naive descriptions of what a saintly apostle would be like. As a matter of fact, his angry words in Galatians and 1–2 Corinthians might have challenged your ideals about Paul. Perhaps you resonated more with the loving and magnanimous statements he wrote in Philippians, whereas some of his combative Mediterranean speech patterns proved to

be difficult to reconcile with prior beliefs. Perhaps you found your study refreshing, perhaps challenging, perhaps both. Either way, you no doubt have gained a number of new insights into the personality and beliefs of this important man. Now it is time to draw your own conclusions about Paul.

RECONSTRUCTING PAUL

Think back through each of the thirteen Letters attributed to Paul, and summarize the picture of him that emerges from each. Be sure to indicate if you have concluded that some of the disputed Letters are not Pauline and should therefore be excluded from data used to describe Paul.

Philemon

1 Thessalonians

2 Thessalonians

Galatians

1 Corinthians

2 Corinthians

Philippians

Romans

Colossians

Ephesians

1 Timothy

2 Timothy

Titus

1. Now construct a composite picture of Paul's personality based on his Letters, either including or excluding the disputed Letters, depending on whether or not you believe that they were dictated by the apostle or written by later disciples.

COMPARING PAUL IN ACTS
AND IN THE LETTERS

1. Review the description of Paul that you constructed on the basis of reading Acts. How does this portrait of Paul compare with the one you constructed as a result of reading Paul's Letters?

2. To what do you attribute the differences?

3. How do you personally respond to the differences?

4. On the basis of both Acts and Paul's Letters, what do you conclude about Paul's personality?

5. What do you conclude about his approach to ministry?

6. What do you conclude about the meanings of "saint" and "apostle"?

INTERACTING WITH PAUL

1. On the basis of your reading, how effective do you believe Paul was as a missionary/church planter? Why?

2. How effective do you believe that he was as a pastor? Why?

3. Would you like to have Paul as the pastor of your church? Why or why not?

4. What is the most important way in which your view of Paul has changed as a result of studying his Letters?

5. What have you grown to appreciate most about Paul?

6. What have you found to be disappointing?

7. How has studying Paul's Letters influenced your personal faith?

9. How has this study affected your understanding of the meaning of the inspiration of Scripture?

8. How has studying Paul's Letters affected your beliefs about God?

10. What two things would you tell a friend who is preparing to study the Letters of Paul?

Index of Scripture and Ancient Sources

Index of Subjects and Names